Empty meeting grounds

This book examines some of the new cultural forms and community arrangements that accompany the development of global tourism. The book focuses on matters that had not yet become salient when the author was writing his acclaimed earlier book *The Tourist* (1976). In particular, it examines the new stagings of 'primitivism' for tourists and the totemism of the postmodernite. The thesis of the book is that human kind has already arrived at the historical moment of the invention of a new kind of community, but we are not yet capable of facing the implications of our collective invention. Will it be a synthesis of the positive human dimensions of so-called 'primitive' existence and the beneficial elements of modern social systems and technologies? Or will it be the most repressive, alienated existence we have so far devised for ourselves?

The book was written in the spirit of theoretical activism: speculating about the future that is grounded in the present. However, the author has taken scrupulous care to ground his theoretical discussion in practical examples. His analysis of the Vietnam Veterans Memorial, the Statue of Liberty Restoration Project, the management of Yosemite National Park and the sale of an entire town of Chinese farmworkers is arresting and compelling. Moreover, his discussions of 'Cannibal Tours' and 'The Desire to be Postmodern' expose many of the conceits of the postmodernist discourse.

This book will be of interest to students of sociology, cultural studies and critical theory.

Dean MacCannell is Professor of Applied Behavioral Sciences and Sociology, University of California at Davis.

Empty meeting grounds
The tourist papers

Dean MacCannell

London and New York

First published in 1992
by Routledge
11 New Fetter Lane, London EC4P 4EE

Simultaneously published in the USA and Canada
by Routledge
a division of Routledge, Chapman and Hall, Inc.
29 West 35th Street, New York, NY 10001

Typeset in Baskerville by Michael Mepham, Frome, Somerset
Printed and bound in Great Britain by
Mackays of Chatham PLC, Chatham, Kent

British Library Cataloguing in Publication Data
A catalogue record for this book is available from the British
Library.

Library of Congress Cataloging in Publication Data
MacCannell, Dean.
  Empty meeting grounds: the tourist
  papers / Dean MacCannell.
  p.   cm.
  Includes bibliographical references (p.   ) and index.
  1. Cultural relativism.   2. Tourist trade—Social aspects.
  3. Postmodernism.   4. Civilization. Modern—20th
  century.   I. Title.
  GN345.5.M3   1992
  306.3–dc20   91–32508
                                                         CIP

ISBN 0–415–05692–6
     0–415–05693–4 (pbk)

Contents

Preface

About half of the following chapters have been published before. The rest were written for this book or put together from field notes. The shorter site reports on Orange County, Yosemite, the Statue of Liberty, the Vietnam Memorial, and so on, are not very much sanitized versions of my field observations, written at or near the site or on the way home. These are more autobiographical than the usual academic fare, I am afraid. The longer chapters on 'Cannibalism Today,' 'White Culture,' 'The Desire to be Postmodern,' and others attempt to theorize a new cultural subject that is emerging on the meeting ground of the ex-primitive and the postmodern. Most of the previously published material has been revised. A note at the beginning of each chapter gives the approximate date when it was first written, my reason for writing it, and the citation for any original publication.

The period during which *Empty Meeting Grounds* was written mainly coincides with my appointment to the Community Studies and Development program at the University of California at Davis. The chapters are marked by this applied, interdisciplinary context and other work I was doing at the same time, including policy studies of the effects of the industrialization of agriculture on rural and minority worker communities in California and ethnographic studies of other aspects of modern culture (for example, the re-arrangement between the sexes).

The Davis program has given me good support for my work on new social and cultural arrangements. My colleagues in Community Studies do research on ethnic migrations, the community effects of multi-national investment, problems of community identity, and other local disruptions and adaptive responses associated with the globalization of markets and culture. My colleagues are mainly admirable, trustworthy, and secure, and we have superb students.

While there are obvious benefits to be derived from working in the relative freedom and isolation of a well-organized, problem-focused program, there are also drawbacks. Foremost among these is that there is no institutional definition to interdisciplinary social research. Even if the subject is important, there are usually no clearly appropriate granting agencies, journals, or professional associations predisposed to treat it as central to their concerns. There are no national or international groups of colleagues with similar training and interests; no departments in other universities that can be counted on to have similar research programs; no logical place to turn to for advice or to send our undergraduate and graduate students to when they finish their degrees with us. These exigencies have resulted in creative adaptations when it comes to funding research, placement of students, and appropriate venues of publication. During the last fifteen years, I sent what I wrote to the four corners of the earth and to journals in no matter what discipline.

I soon discovered a bizarre effect of publishing across cultures and disciplines. Several of my discipline-based colleagues in other United States universities, seeing papers of mine on the effects of irrigation policy on community conditions, and on 'Marilyn Monroe Was Not a Man' (e.g., D. MacCannell, 1987; 1988), formed an apparently sincere belief that I was two different people. Others have approached and asked me why I 'never bothered to write anything more on tourism after *The Tourist*' (MacCannell, 1976 and 1989).

For reasons that George H. Mead would understand, having to do with the social construction of the self, I began to think that I really had done very little further work on tourism. (I stopped short of thinking that I was two different people, though there were moments when this seemed an attractive prospect.) So, when Chris Rojek approached me with the suggestion that Routledge might want to bring out a volume of my papers on tourism written since the publication of *The Tourist*, my first response was there would be insufficient material for a book-length project. After some gentle encouragement, I eventually located several hundred pages of published and unpublished manuscript – quite a bit more than can be included here.

Students of society and social relationships who are concerned about the theoretical framework of this book, as it relates to existing social theory, are invited to go directly to the 'Afterword.' The other chapters can be read in any order. This is not because there is no narrative. It is just that the narrative is not the principle of their organization. There are several redundant lines in some of the chapters to facilitate an out-of-order reading.

Acknowledgements

This book is a result of two decades of collaboration. During this period, Juliet Flower MacCannell has been my closest intellectual friend and colleague. The same twenty years is also marked at one end by the birth of our sons, Daniel in 1971 and Jason in 1974, and at the other by their entry into the university. As soon as they could read, the boys expressed an interest in literature and history as avid as any young savage could have expressed for his uncles' bows and arrows. Daniel graduated in History and Jason is a junior in Classics and Comparative Literature. For the last ten years they have carried the draft manuscript off our writing tables, bringing it back to us with incisive commentary and polite reminders that the grammar did not always conform to the standards we had taught them. There is no doubt in my mind that this is a better book because of their direct intervention, and because I knew almost the entire time I was writing it that its first readers would include my own children and that their other heroes were Orwell, Joyce and Prescott. In addition to helping me with conceptual matters, Daniel prepared the bibliography and copy-edited the entire manuscript before it went to the publishers.

Juliet made this possible. Her children, students and colleagues, who also depend on her intellectual and other gifts, can appreciate how difficult it is to separate out the influence of her thinking when it comes time to write. She is always our first collaborator, the source of our strengths, and her influence has already spread itself quietly through several literatures. Her generosity is such that everyone who has been touched by her believes she puts them first. But I know she puts me first. So I want to thank Juliet, Daniel and Jason for direct assistance with this project, but mainly for literally putting me in a position to rethink the critique of family 'tradition' and patriarchy.

In addition to Juliet, I want to thank other friends who have stayed close for five, ten, and twenty years and more, listening to the research stories retold here in some form, never hesitating to correct my errors. These would include Judith Adler at Memorial University in Newfoundland, Jim Boon at Princeton, Erik Cohen at Hebrew University in Jerusalem, Marie Lanfant at CNRS in Paris, Julia Palacios in Mexico City, Mohammed Rafique Raza at the World Bank in Nigeria, Renata Salecl at the Institute for Law in Ljubljana. My University of California friends and colleagues who never hesitated to take the time to discuss these papers with me include: Avital Ronell and Nelson Graburn at Berkeley, Benetta Jules-Rosette at San Diego, Harold Garfinkel and Teshome Gabriel at Los Angeles, Isao Fujimoto and Michael P. Smith at Davis. I have also benefited from conversations with Parminder Bachu and Beatrice Manz who study the misplacement of cultural traditions from the other side.

The idea to assemble my papers on tourism written after the publication of my earlier book, *The Tourist*, was first suggested by my editor at Routledge, Chris Rojek. Initially, I did not imagine the magnitude the task of revision and integration that the project eventually entailed. I was able to get the job done because I was aware of Rojek's excellent reputation as an editor and an accomplished scholar and published author in the area of the sociology of leisure. I knew I could count on him for the highest level of understanding and I also suspected that he would not take any nonsense. He never let me down on either score.

Many of the ideas expressed here were first tried out in my graduate seminar on Community Development at the University of California at Davis. The students who took an active role in my continuing education over the years, who served as my assistants while I was working on this project, and whose thinking may have been incorporated here without further citation, include: Joan Randall, Jerry White, Edel Kruger, Mark Campbell, Asafa Jalata, Helen Theodoropolis, Sam Manu, Fecadu Behre, Nahum Chandler, Shuo Pang, Noreen Shima, Anna-Maria White, Olayenka Otunji and Teron McGrew.

I want to thank The California Policy Seminar, the California Arts Council, the California Governor's Commission on Women, The Experiment Station of the College of Agriculture and

Environmental Sciences, University of California Energy Research
Group, Water Resources Research Group (UC), Research Center
for Conflict and Cooperation (UC), Humanities Research Institute
(UC), The Western Regional Research Council, the United States
Congress Office of Technology Assessment, the United States
Secretary of Agriculture, US Department of the Interior, and US
Bureau of Reclamation for continuous support for my applied
community research from 1976 to 1991. Several of these papers
were directly supported by grants from one or more of the agencies and organizations named above. All the others were indirectly
supported by them, at least to the extent that the funds received
helped to establish and sustain a productive environment for
students and colleagues involved in this as well as the more applied
work.

I would like to acknowledge permission from the following:
from Random House, Inc., to reproduce material from Marvin
Harris (1977) *Cannibals and Kings: The Origins of Cultures*; from
HarperCollins Publishers to reproduce an excerpt from *Introduc-
tion to the Reading of Hegel* by Alexandre Kojève, edited by Allan
Bloom, copyright (1969) Basic Books, Inc.; and from The Univer-
sity of California Press to reproduce excerpts from *Fables of
Aggression: Wyndham Lewis, The Modernist as Fascist* by Fredric
Jameson, copyright (1979) The Regents of the University of Cali-
fornia.

The chapters on 'White Culture' and ethnicity were written or
revised while I was on sabbatical leave in residence as Senior Fellow
in the Society for the Humanities at Cornell University in 1986. I
want to thank Jonathan Culler and Mary Ahl for their generous
support during this leave and for their role in maintaining the
Cornell Society as a safe place for humanistic thought.

Dean MacCannell,
Lafayette, California

Introduction

This book extends an earlier argument of mine that tourism is a primary ground for the production of new cultural forms on a global base.[1] In the name of tourism, capital and modernized peoples have been deployed to the most remote regions of the world, farther than any army was ever sent. Institutions have been established to support this deployment, not just hotels, restaurants, and transportation systems, but restorations of ancient shrines, development of local handicrafts for sale to tourists, and rituals performed for tourists. In short, tourism is not just an aggregate of merely commercial activities; it is also an ideological framing of history, nature, and tradition; a framing that has the power to reshape culture and nature to its own needs.

In the past twenty-five years, it has become evident that tourism is not fully constitutive of the new cultural arrangements that are historically associated with it. During this period, paralleling the movements of tourists, there has been a rapid growth of a reverse movement of peoples from formerly remote regions of the world into the centers of wealth and power: the current African and Asian diasporas, the flight of peasant refugees from Central American fascism, the migrations of agricultural workers, the Southeast Asian 'boat people.' The departures of these peoples from their communities of origin, and their creative adaptations to their new lives, are changing the neighborhoods of Los Angeles, London, etc., and even small towns. Every major city in the West has been transformed into a living version of the fictional compression of cultures as represented at Disney World. But the modern polyglot, composite community is not sanitized and actually de-humanized as occurs at Disneyland, where cyborgs play the part of pirates. Nor is it re-humanized as occurs at Disney World and other similar attractions where, for example, Mormon college students play the part of Tahitian 'natives.' In the real, or actual community, there are new work, family, and marriage arrangements, new hybrid cultural forms, communication networks, and revolutionary potential. The adaptations of international migrants and refugees are as much a part of emerging world culture as the resorts and 'Pizza Huts' for tourists which have recently been built on the beaches of their former countries.

There are several theoretical approaches that might be used to guide the study of cultural forms that emerge from this double movement in what I will term the 'post-tourist' or 'composite' community. These include cultural critique, deconstruction, the New Historicism, Foucauldian, Habermasian, Althusserian modes of analysis, cultural hermeneutics, Gramscian anti-hegemonic theory, post-structuralism, postmodernism, minority discourse, post-colonial theory, and subaltern studies. At times, I have been able partially, never fully, to identify with these interfoliated modes of analysis which I will hereafter refer to in aggregate as 'critical theory.' Mainly, I see their proliferation as symptomatic of an inhibition. What they appear to have in common is a desire to be free from the constraints of earlier theorizing: they claim to refuse to restrict their range of application to particular times and places, to focus on specific subject matters, or to understand themselves historically. There is a strong sense that for all their claims, they never really left home. The similarities in this regard between the tourist and the theorist have been noted.[2] Now we have theory that, like the Western tourist, can imagine roaming widely without losing its place or identity.

Critical theory, even those branches of it which want to stand outside of, even 'beyond,' history, is fully historical. It was deployed at exactly the same moment in history as the double movement of tourists to the periphery and formerly marginal peoples to the centers. In this double movement and deployment, the human 'community' has been rhetorically reduced to nothing more than a territorial entity with a unified economy, as in the 'European Community,' and perhaps a single race. This is the 'Empty Meeting Ground' of my title, and my central point is that it is not really empty. It is vibrant with people and potential and tense with repression. The human community has historically arrived at a moment where it can no longer contain everything that it does contain, at least not in the framework of older ground rules. The response, so far, on both theoretical and practical planes, has been for the community anxiously to conceive itself as empty and impossible while it awaits realization. I am concerned in this book with adumbrations of new cultural subjects that are about to appear on this meeting ground. I am especially concerned here with the barriers that have been put up against the formation of new subjects, and especially the costs of such resistance in historical terms: that is, the costs of attempting to go on with the kinds of social relationships, thinking, and curriculum we now have.

Critical theory has prepared us for the absence of the subject, for an empty meeting ground, but it does not help us to get beyond this historical moment. The corrective which I advocate here is similar to the one put forward by Anthony Giddens (1979: 9–48) in his helpful essay on 'Structuralism and the Theory of the Subject': specifically, it is to bring normative, historical, gender, class, national, and ethnic perspectives to bear on the study of cultural subjects. Critical theorists today, while focusing on some questions that originally were in the domain of sociology (for example, gender role performance and social class) have widely ignored the theory and methods sociology developed for the study of these questions, and especially the *findings* already carefully obtained by sociology. Following de Man and Derrida, critical theorists have automated analysis of undecidability; they have described the domain of the empty signifier. But they have tended to overlook the areas of human life that remain stubbornly determined. It is unquestionably true that there are some arenas in which humans are condemned to ultimate and absolute uncertainty (for instance, 'does he really love me?'). But there are other areas that are fully determined (such as 'can I afford to feed my children?'). Deconstruction gives us access to the realm of absolute possibility in theory, in the imagination, and where it exists, in life. But an allied sociology of interaction or dialogue is still necessary to gain access to the realm of contingency and determinism, and especially resistance to, and struggles against, determinism.

The starting point for each of the following chapters is a non-controversial assumption that the cultures of the world have been radically displaced and fundamentally and forever altered by the movements of peoples. I read this displacement mainly positively, which is by no means the only possible reading. Specifically, I look to the radical hybridization of cultures as a precondition for the inventiveness and creativity which will be demanded from all of us if we are to survive the epoch of the globalization of culture currently dominated by advanced capitalism. The heroes of these diasporas are not necessarily the tourists who leave on their expeditions secure in the knowledge that they will return home and that their home will be waiting for them on their return. Dialogue involving tourists is always optional. The tourist set-up is formulaic by definition. The true heroes are those who leave home not knowing where they will end up, never knowing whether their eventual end will connect meaningfully to their origins, knowing only that their future will be made of dialogue with their fellow travelers and those they meet along the way.

A central goal of the following chapters is to understand two different kinds of displaced thought corresponding to two modes of consciousness available to migrants, the homeless, refugees, tourists, and other travelers in modernity. One form of displaced self-understanding begins with a literalization of the concept of *freedom* by neo-nomads who are not ignorant of frontiers, or limits, but not bound by them either. They cross boundaries, not as invaders conquering territory, but as passersby accumulating nothing, and collecting nothing but perishables – impressions and stories. Within this variant of nomadism, there is no apotheosis of possessions or property beyond a clear understanding of basic human needs and competencies – the social, spiritual, and material resources essential to our survival as human beings. Of course, there is also a political consciousness (or unconscious) involved. The neo-nomad deeply understands that political promises that pre-suppose or support stability, stasis, the state, real estate, can never be kept. The earth, the ground, only appears to provide reference points for the sedentary. Its true character is to shift endlessly underfoot. What is called 'real' as in 'real estate' is only what has been privatized; that which is closed to the person or what closes in around the person. As opposed to nomadic freedom, the privatized and the 'real' set absolute limits on thought and behavior. For the nomad, the only reality is the imagination.[3]

But this is only one pole of de-territorialized consciousness. The other way to think travel is within prescribed paths which not only honor all territorial and property claims, but the travel itself becomes a kind of homage to territoriality. The tourist 'consumes countries' and attempts to identify not with fellow tourists but with the sedentary peoples encountered along the way. Far from abjuring all but the most essential spiritual and material resources, this other way to travel involves elaborate mobile contrivances and temporary accommodations which are designed to mock-up not merely sedentary existence but a kind of ultra-sedentary existence once the province of royalty. Every bourgeois tourist hotel promises to treat its bourgeois guests as 'royalty.' The appeal is to a particular ideal of travel in which the meals, the accommodations, the mode of conveyance, etc., should be more sumptuous, more elaborate and over-prepared than their counterparts at home. If this is accomplished with human labor rather than machines, it proves that a world standard of bourgeois comfort is universal, existing beyond the reach of technological 'labor saving' devices. There is a certain 'glory' that emanates from the effective mobilization of local peoples for the movement of enormous heaps of baggage or the installation, deep in the bush, of temporary camps with every Western comfort. The ideological aggressivity of the gesture cannot be overlooked: 'no matter where in the world we go, or how short our stay, we can have a standard of comfort and be surrounded by more things than you local people will ever have, even in your dreams.' This is an overturned nomadic consciousness in which the ultimate goal of travel is to set up sedentary housekeeping in the entire world, to displace the local peoples, or at least to subordinate them in the enterprise, to make them the 'household' staff of global capitalists. The drive here is not for freedom but for world-wide containment and control moving always toward the ideal of two economic classes ('local' vs. 'multinational'), one currency, one passport, one market, one government: i.e., global fascism.

The totemic animal of the first form of displaced consciousness would be a multi-colored bird that can learn to speak any human language without forgetting how to sing. The totem of the second form of displaced consciousness is a bird of prey, an eagle perhaps.

In short, I argue that the current dialectic between global versus local, or sedentary versus nomadic or any other dialectic that involves a contradiction between different levels of socio-cultural organization, is about to be superseded. The emerging dialectic is between two ways of being-out-of-place. One pole is a new synthetic arrangement of life which releases human creativity. The other is a new form of authority, containment of creativity, and control.

The theoretical grounding of what follows is as explicit as I can make it, but some pre-publication readers (both friendly and unfriendly) have told me it is not explicit enough for their tastes. So a brief theoretical statement may be in order:

1   The parts of critical theory that I have found most useful in this work are Third Theory (see, e.g., Jim Pines and P.Willeman, eds, *Questions of Third Cinema*, or the journal *Strategies*), Deleuze and Guattari's (1987: 351–473) 'Treatise on Nomadology,' Mikhail Bakhtin's 'dialogism,' and 'ethnosemiotics' (see Mac-Cannell and MacCannell 1982).

2   Already I am compromised because I feel very strongly that the proper place of theory is not in the notes, prefaces and asides, but is rather embedded in the story to the point that it is not possible to tell where one leaves off and the other begins.

3   I have been mindful throughout of the Heidegger-de Man-Derrida warning about the radical undecideability of anything, e.g., theory, that depends on language for its accomplishment. My 'take' on this version of the 'uncertainty principle,' as it applies to the cultural sciences, is we should heed it, but not by worrying endlessly about minute alternative possibilities (deconstruction) as its authors suggested. Rather we should simply affirm the *speculative* nature of theory as the real ground of freedom. The obverse of undecideability is possibility. Every characterization of human relationships, even those which rigorously hold themselves to be positivist or behaviorist, is a projection in the guise of 'truth' onto a future horizon of possible relationships – a 'model for' as well as a 'model of.' I can make no special claim on the truth. But I can attempt to bridge or tunnel the impossible (which I take to be 'reality') and reach for a possible truth. And I am free to decide on the direction I want to go with my theoretical tunneling.

4   The theoretical model of the form of human relationships which I have in mind is *dialogic*. Minimally, there are two interlocutors on an equal footing. I am aware (see 3 above) that this is a *theoretical* construct. That the world usually does not work this way, that our relations are often phallocentric, monological, and even though they are real they are also 'impossible.'

5   The *dialogic model* of impossible realities is related to dialectical materialism, but it is more concrete and more grounded in human interactions. It is also non-reductionist. The interlocu-

tors are not just 'subject effects' or 'fragmented subjects': e.g., male and female, owner and worker, tourist and native, town dweller and nomad. They are two subjects that have managed to preserve their integrity as *subjects*. They need not be reduced to a single consciousness in order to 'communicate.' Nor must they 'understand' each other in order to communicate. Either or both parties to the dialogue can occupy the subject position of the child: i.e., appreciate, enjoy, and learn without necessarily agreeing or understanding.

6 Within the dialogue, that which passes between the interlocutors is a *sign*. Again, this is theoretical speculation that must be set in relation to impossible reality. In reality, the object of exchange is often other than a sign. In Lévi-Strauss's infamous example, the object of exchange is *woman*: exogamous clans exchange women. Whenever the object of exchange is other than a sign, the two interlocutors are reduced to a single form of consciousness. In Lévi-Strauss's example, the substitution of a woman for a sign assures a *male* giver and a *male* receiver. Or, in the case of *commodity* exchange a *capitalist* producer and a *capitalist* consumer. If we are to retrieve our humanity from the various exchanges in which we find ourselves engaged, we must begin by examining the sign-character of that which comes between and goes between human beings. A thinking being that 'receives a woman' stops thinking. The relevant particulars have been taken care of; the structure has done his thinking for him. A thinking being that receives a *sign* must think again. A sign informs the thinking being of the existence of another mode of thought.

The 'empty meeting ground' of the title of this book also refers to the theoretical free space between interlocutors, to the realm of possibility for the future of human relationships emerging in and between the diasporas. Even if they work only as reports on Western thought and behavior that are of interest to non-Westerners, each of the following chapters is dedicated to opening dialogue.

It is also my hope that these chapters will contribute to ending the current widespread abuse of the privilege of 'understanding.' 'Understanding,' after it came to be held in ultimate regard, was enlisted as the primary stratagem for the self-preservation of institutionalized social inequality. No longer just a philosophical category, 'Verstehen' now also refers to those situations in which social superiors project a singular viewpoint upon, or demand it from, their social inferiors. This is also called 'mutual understanding' as in the ironic 'we now have a mutual understanding' sadistically uttered by the torturer who has broken the spirit of his prisoner.

The abuse of the category of 'understanding' underlying the enforced singularity of eurocentric and phallocentric perspectives draws upon deep resources going to the level of mathematics: our conception of *unity*, *singularity*, the *one*. But even here at this level, the ultimate privilege of unity and singularity cannot be preserved. There are two radically different concepts of *the one*. There is the one which stands at the head of a series $(1+1+1)$ and in effect authorizes that series.[4] And there is the Boolean irreducible $(-1 X -1 = 1)$ from which all totality is composed. The existence of two different versions of singularity is not a scandal from the theoretical perspective proposed here. At issue is what they can learn from each other; that both versions of singularity presuppose the existence of an empty set, a zero. Neither *one* is primary. Both are secondary to absence, an emptiness that precedes the *one* whichever one it happens to be. In the first chapter that follows here, there is a reading of cannibalism and capitalism in terms of the paradox of singularity. The open mouth of the cannibal is the zero, the desire, the empty set, the lack. The cannibal (or the capitalist) is *the one* that attempts to gobble up the other *one*, for gain we are told, but also to restore and literally to embody the impossible logic of singularity.

The other chapters that follow focus on the ways in which a double displacement of culture (center to periphery and vice versa) produces new subjectivity. In its earliest formation this subjectivity often appears to be stunned, suffering from the bewilderment of any refugee. Then it splits, becoming either self-aware, or it may be seduced into a position of acting against itself to preserve the prestige and privilege of forces deployed against it. (It should go without saying that older forms of exploitation involving violent force and economic terrorism have not disappeared.) When a subject is manipulated into acting against its own self-interest, it can pretend, even to itself, that it is 'disinterested' and 'neutral,' when in reality it is only neutralized; it can become a kind of simulacrum of humanity. This kind of cultural frame-up, that results in people and groups volunteering to be exploited, appears to be replacing visibly vicious forms. In the following chapters, I do not attribute this, as Marcuse did, to an innate human weakness. Rather, it reflects the strength of social engineering: powerful new techniques for the manipulation of symbols, human consciousness, and political processes for the purpose of creating democracies within which the narrowest of interests can claim to have the broadest support, by representing themselves to be the 'will of the people.'[5] An aim of *Empty Meeting Grounds* is to expose this engineering, leading in the direction of '"totalitarian" democracy,' to close critical examination as a first step toward taking it down.

Any discovery of a new cultural subject necessarily begins and ends ethnographically, with observations of real people, events, and relations. It cannot be contained in advance in philosophy, theory, or hypothesis, unless it is condemned to produce, or fail to produce, only that which the investigator already knew. *Empty Meeting Grounds* is, first and mainly, about such things as guided tours of 'cannibal' villages, the purchase of an entire town (Locke, California) for conversion to touristic purposes, the social and political beliefs of the people in the neighborhoods immediately adjacent to Disneyland, the creation of the Vietnam Memorial in Washington, DC, the restoration of national symbols, the Statue of Liberty, for example, and so on. Second, they theorize a new cultural subject. In this work, the goal of science and the struggle for creative freedom and human equality should be one and the same. Once accurate aim has been taken at the mechanisms of cultural repression, conceptual and descriptive precision serve both ethnography and the revolution equally.

In short, I see no real possibility of conflict between political effectiveness and ethnographic precision. Serious politics must be based on the best possible intelligence. And every scholarly product, even if it is something seemingly straightforward such as the project to render accurate translations of the Dead Sea Scrolls, has political use value. These are the inescapable conditions of political and scholarly life today. Everything written in the 'objective style' of 1950s social sciences or 'New Criticism,' and everything written in the opaque style of post-structural discourses, now risks being read as a kind of political cover-up, hidden complicity, and intrigue on either the right or left. Interestingly, the one path that still leads in the direction of scholarly objectivity, detachment, and neutrality is exactly the one originally thought to lead away from these classic virtues: that is, an openly autobiographical style in which the subjective position of the author, especially on political matters, is presented in a clear and straightforward fashion. At least this enables the reader to review his or her own position to make the adjustments necessary for dialogue.

So here, as best as I can state it in brief, is my politics: I am most comfortable politically on grounds that are being abandoned by the superpowers: that is, the American Bill of Rights as interpreted up to the Earl Warren Supreme Court, and Marx's labor theory of value as interpreted up to the revolution of 1917. I have not been able to accept the kinds of political 'options' that have been forced on my generation, growing up just after World War II: such things as the commonplace assertion that there is a fundamental difference between democracy and socialism, so we must choose one or the other. I could never find any more or less strong evidence for this than for the counter-assertion that capitalism and democracy are ultimately incompatible.[6] Correlatively, I have never been especially interested in the basic political opposition after 1945, that between capitalism and communism. It has always had too much of a ritual, or a game aspect, which seemed to me to be a cover for a deeper division, the site of actual violence and real wars, not 'Cold' wars; that between North and South, white and non-white, industrial and peasant, rich and poor.

The opposition between capitalism and communism would have been interesting, and might have even saved the world from a much uglier historical fate, if its strongest proponents, the USA and the USSR, had taken their own principles seriously. But the USA and the USSR destroyed their own *political* credibility long before this destruction was memorialized by tearing down the 'Berlin Wall.' The USA supported genocide against free and peaceful peasants in Guatemala, and the Soviet Union supported right-wing military dictatorships in Ethiopia and elsewhere while labeling the Chinese 'petit bourgeois imperialist puppets.' (There is no need to extend these lists. For present purposes, one crime is enough.) Both so-called 'great' powers willingly sacrificed their stated social and human principles seemingly without giving these principles a second thought. Both were guilty of building nuclear weapons and shooting billions of dollars worth of exotic equipment into space while significant numbers of their citizens suffered in miserable poverty. In short, as they pretended to be opposed to one another in the 'Cold War,' these two 'Great Powers' were mainly readying themselves for their future alliance against the poor peoples of the world.

What just happened in Eastern Europe was certainly facilitated by recent trends in the capitalist West. Beginning with the house arrest of physicists who worked on the Manhattan project, and continuing with the McCarthy hearings and the Iran-Contra affair, the trend in the democratic west, as led by the USA, has been toward fewer individual liberties, weakened guarantees of privacy, and more government decision making without democratic review and consent. Since World War II, democracy has taken the necessary steps to make itself attractive to the leaders of totalitarian regimes. Similarly, what has happened in Western Europe, Britain, and North America was guaranteed by recent trends in the Soviet Socialist bloc countries. The weakened position of the post-revolutionary international proletariat (that is, the working class in countries already socialist) struck a blow to the organization of the working class in both First and Third World countries. Soviet adventurism struck a final, perhaps mortal, blow to the solidarity of all working people to the extent that it promoted, in effect, conservative ideology in the strong imperialist countries and let reactionaries (such as Reagan and Thatcher) and their administrative clones (Bush and Major) come to power.

Neither capitalism nor communism as practiced by its super-power proponent any longer has a believable ideological base; neither provides a theory of human behavior, motivation, or relations, that any thinking person can believe. Neither system provides a true integration of thought and action at the level of concrete human affairs. They are now fully exposed as the cynical machinations of detached ruling elites whose true task is to control the lives of the majority of the people, to hold the masses in 'ready reserve' to promote the interests of a few. They no longer even take the trouble of attempting to sell their programs as based on 'universal' principles. They have reduced the people who want to support them to moronic chanting: 'USA, USA, USA, USA, USA, USA.'

Politically, what interests me now is the struggle to take back the definition of human relations, motives, and behavior at the community level. The community meeting ground for creative thought, expression, and political action is a powerful base because community can still be a *total social fact*. The power of the community as an alternative base for political action does not come from it being 'total' in the sense of autonomous, closed, and self-sufficient. Rather, it is a total matrix for every possible human relationship, thought, and act.[7] A new solidarity, emerging at the community level to the benefit of general humanity, already has assumed discernible forms. It is building a base in the social and economic planning of Euro-socialism; in the anti-war and anti-nuclear movements; in struggles for ethnic self-determination; in feminist movements and theory, especially non-Western feminism; in new social theory – structuralism, semiotics, Lacanian psychoanalysis, and neo-Marxism; in the environmental movement; and in the non-aligned Third World countries. Of course, these ways of thinking and acting are not yet self-consciously together, they are often engineered into false oppositions to one another, but they should come together rather quickly once the force deployed against them is adequately described.

NOTES

1 This point is no longer a controversial one, having been firmly established in a series of ethnographic studies of tourism and its effects. This literature is too vast to be summarized here, but see, for example E. Cohen (1979; 1982; 1989), M. Crick (1985; 1989), D. Evans-Pritchard (1989), P. Fussell (1980), N. Graburn (1976; 1983), J. Jafari (1979), B. Jules-Rossette (1984; 1989), and P. van den Berghe (1980).
2 See, for example, Georges van den Abbeele's 1980 report on 'The Tourist as Theorist' and Meaghan Morris's 1988 comment on van den Abbeele.
3 In this summary, I have closely followed the lead of Teshome Gabriel in his fine 1990 paper on 'Thoughts on Nomadic Aesthetics and the Black Independent Cinema: Traces of a Journey.' Professor Gabriel also suggests that the proper figures for the nomadic consciousness conceived in this way are 'the moon' and 'the wind.'
4 For a discussion of this version of *the one* see Juliet Flower MacCannell, 1989: 101 ff.
5 For a careful description of the process of instituting 'democracy for the few,' see Michael Parenti (1980).
6 John Urry (1981: 140–54) has registered a parallel complaint, which he carefully argues, against assertions, from both the left and the right, of a good fit between capitalism and democracy.
7 Chris Rojek (1985: 2) has noted the deep connection between the sociology of leisure and community studies:

> It [the sociology of leisure] emerged as a footnote to the narrowly focused 'plant' sociology of the First World War and the inter-war years. For the most part, it was studied as an appendix to questions

of workplace productivity and efficiency. The notable exception appears to be in the field of community studies. From the earliest days, writers like Robert Park, Ernest W. Burgess, and Helen and Robert Lynd displayed an interest in exploring life beyond the factory gates.

Part I

Ex-primitive and postmodern

Hamlet: A man may eat a fish with
   the worm that hath eat of a king,
   and eat of the fish that hath fed of
   that worm.
King: What dost thou mean by this?
Hamlet: Nothing but to show you
   how a king may go a progress
   through the guts of a beggar.
            (William Shakespeare)

Chapter 1

Cannibalism today[1]

The 'primitive/modern' opposition developed by sociology and anthropology for the study of the effects of nineteenth-century industrialization on European society, and for the study of the peoples 'discovered' during the period of European conquest and colonization, is not appropriate to the study of new cultural subjects. Tourism today occupies the gap between primitive and modern, routinely placing modernized and primitive peoples in direct, face-to-face interaction using intercultural English and other pidgins. Following is an excerpt from a brochure advertising a tour of tribal villages in Thailand:

> KAREN TRIBAL TREKKING (Opposite Suriya Theatre Kotchasarn Rd.) If you feeling a pace... We'd like to offer you take a trip to the remote and unspoiled rained forest. Visit primitive hilltribes where the breezy from high mountain which surrounding will make you feel freshly and forget all of your troubles. So follow us now.... See their culture and live among them in their timelessness.
>
> (Collected by Erik Cohen, English as in original)

It is not necessary for tourists to go to Thailand to come into direct contact with Southeast Asian tribal peoples. Highland Laotian villagers who fought as mercenaries on the side of the United States during the Vietnam War have been re-settled in apartment complexes in California and Wisconsin. Two Hmong youths, the first of their people to use writing, have taken my course on 'The Community' at the University of California. When actual contact between 'primitives' and 'moderns' occurs, there is clear evidence of economic rationality and cynical detachment on the part of the 'primitives,' and a corresponding emergence of a complex of beliefs on the part of the moderns that can be labeled 'neo-totemism.'[2]

The destruction of savagery and nature is associated with the spread of capitalism, first in the form of natural resource and labor extraction, now in the form of tourism and 'reverse' (that is, periphery-to-center) migration.[3] I have long been suspicious that advanced capitalism alone could not possibly accomplish the massive destruction of nature and the human spirit that is now occurring in its name. It must draw upon deeper ethnological resources for its savage aggressivity and its desire for total control.

THE END OF THE PRIMITIVE WORLD

Subsistence hunting and gathering can lay valid claim to having been the only common human heritage. It was certainly our most long-term collective adaptation going back over a million years, and it was the most geographically dispersed, occurring even in desert, mountain, jungle, and arctic areas that eventually proved to be ill-suited to agriculture or industrial development. Of the estimated 80 billion people who have lived on earth, fewer than 10 per cent were (and are) engaged in agricultural and industrial occupations; the rest were savages.[4] Twelve thousand years ago, the world population was 10 million people, all savages. One thousand years ago, after agriculture was established world-wide, 350 million people inhabited the earth but only 1 per cent, or 3.5 million, were still hunter-gatherers. At a conference of ethnologists and demographers in the 1960s it was estimated that the global population of true savages was fewer than 30,000 (calculated by Lee and DeVore, 1968: plate 1, no page). Even if this number has not diminished, we must add 'acting in motion pictures' and 'tour guide' to hunting and gathering as among the means by which these 30,000 souls gain a livelihood.

Enacted or staged savagery is already well established as a small but stable part of the world system of social and economic exchanges. Many formerly primitive groups earn their living by charging visitors admission to their sacred shrines, ritual performances, and displays of more or less 'ethnologized' everyday life. The commercialization of ethnological performance and display, co-developed by formerly primitive peoples and the international tourism and entertainment industries, is potentially a long-term economic adaptation. One can easily imagine a mutually beneficial deal being struck between, for example, the Masai of Kenya and MCI Incorporated, covering publicity, wage rates for contract dancers, admission fees, television and movie rights and residuals, profit sharing, and so on. If they could obtain good terms and aggressive promotion, the Masai could earn a living *acting Masai* in perpetuity. MCI already has a contract with the US Government, giving it the exclusive right to develop and market the visitors' experience in Yosemite National Park (see 'Nature Incorporated' below). If an international entertainment business can profit from thematizing and marketing 'nature,' a logical next step would be the marketing of 'savages,' the imagined inhabitants of 'unspoiled' nature.

On the surface the institutionalization of primitive-performances-for-others appears as a simple hybrid cultural form. Such performances seem to combine *modern* elements of self-interested rational planning and economic calculation with *primitive* costumes, weapons, music, ritual objects and practices that once existed beyond the reach of economic rationality. Ideally, this particular assimilation of primitive elements into the modern world would allow primitives to adapt and co-exist, to earn a living just by 'being themselves,' permitting them to avoid the kind of work in factories or as agricultural laborers that changes their lives forever. But on witnessing these displays and performances, one cannot escape a feeling of melancholia; the primitive does not really appear in these enactments of it. The 'primitivistic' performance contains the image of the primitive as a dead form. The alleged *combination* of modern and primitive elements is an abuse of the dead to promote the pretense of complexity as a cover for some rather simple-minded dealings based mainly on principles of accounting. It is a pseudo-hybrid characteristic of the ideology of 'complexity' found in postmodern groups and classes that want to think of themselves as being on the 'cutting edge' even as they no longer support, and even suppress, new and alternate ways of thinking. The image of the savage that emerges from these ex-primitive performances completes the postmodern fantasy of 'authentic alterity' which is ideologically necessary in the promotion and development of global monoculture. The 'primitivistic' performance is *our* funerary marking of the passage of savagery. In the presence of these displays, there is only one thing we can know with certainty: we have witnessed the demise of the original form of humanity.[5]

Of course, the destruction of savagery did not begin with modern capitalism. Its origins can be found among the savages themselves. Here I give some evidence that late capitalism has aligned itself against humanity with the worst human impulse; that it is an only partly sublimated form of cannibalism.[6] That capitalism has transformed itself into a *metaphoric* cannibalism should not be greeted as a positive development. I will argue that it is precisely its metaphoric character that protects it from having to admit its own gruesome excesses, empowering it in ways that the original form of cannibalism could not imagine. Metaphoric or reflexive cannibalism, driven by the same desire for absolute domination and control, now armed with high technology, need never look its victims in the face, or, even if by chance it does, it need never acknowledge what it sees.

Modernity's guilt

What was the underlying theme or consciousness of the various movements, organizations, and new ways of thinking that constituted cultural modernity as it circled the globe? Let me begin with an observation of the obvious which usually goes unsaid: the modern conscience was a guilty conscience. This was not an imagined guilt. There was a real basis for it in modern society's decadent assaults on savagery, peasantry, and on nature itself. Of course, as Freud and Alfred Hitchcock taught us, human beings refuse to live long with guilt *as such*.[7] We carry guilt around in the guise of something else, usually a manic excess of distractive activity that is easy enough to spot as symptomatic. Also, there are excuses, justifications, and accounts. The primitives had to be converted because they were different: namely, not Christian, white, or clothed. They had to be removed because they were in the way; there simply was not enough room on this planet for both primitive and industrial life. They were occupying valuable real estate. Or perhaps the savages had to be destroyed because they were evil.

Alongside such vulgar expressions, one found, and still finds, enormous mental energy being expended to theorize the savage and now the peasant in such a way as to justify their eradication. Following are two passages written in the 1950s by men who were recognized for the highest achievements in Western letters, in physics, and psychoanalysis. They both make the same point as made in the unguardedly racist accounts, but here it is shrouded in sophistication. In a little book published at the summit of his distinguished career, Dr Carl G. Jung, described on the jacket as 'the world's greatest living psychiatrist,' remarked:

> Today we live in a unitary world where distances are reckoned by hours and no longer by weeks and months. Exotic races have ceased to be peep shows in ethnological museums. They have become our neighbors, and what was yesterday the prerogative of the ethnologist is today a political, social and psychological problem....
>
> Everywhere in the West there are subversive minorities who, sheltered by our humanitarianism and our sense of justice, hold the incendiary torches ready, with nothing to stop the spread of their ideas except the critical reason of a single, fairly intelligent, mentally stable stratum of the population. One should not however overestimate the thickness of this stratum....
>
> [T]he individual in his dissociated state needs a directing and ordering principle.... A religious symbol that comprehends and visibly represents what is seeking expression in modern man could probably do this; but our conception of the Christian symbol to date has certainly not been able to do so. On the contrary, that frightful world split runs right through the domains of the 'Christian' white man, and our Christian outlook on life has proved powerless to prevent the recrudescence of an archaic social order.
>
> (Jung, 1959: 12, 74, 104)

Also at the peak of his distinguished career, the great physicist Werner Heisenberg, creator of the 'uncertainty principle' in quantum mechanics, similarly remarked:

> [M]odern science, then, penetrates in our time into other parts of the world where the cultural tradition has been very different from the European civilization. There the impact of this new activity in natural and technical science must make itself felt even more strongly than in Europe.... One should expect that in many places this new activity must appear as a decline of the older culture, as a ruthless and barbarian attitude, that upsets the sensitive balance on which all human happiness rests. Such

consequences cannot be avoided; they must be taken as one
aspect of our time.

(Heisenberg, 1958: 202)[8]

Jung and Heisenberg suggest that not merely savagery but all
non-European peoples have to be changed for their own good, to
rescue them from their anti-scientific traditions, so they can be
annexed to a world order unified by scientific and 'Christian'
principles. Heisenberg is rhetorically brilliant in his acknow-
ledgement that, in this Europeanizing process, it is the Europeans
who will be regarded as 'ruthless' and 'barbarian,' to which he
responds, in effect, 'tough,' it 'cannot be avoided,' it is an 'aspect
of our time.' It should not go unnoticed that the individuals and
groups who believe in this version of world events have sufficient
wealth and power to make their dreams come true.[9]

There is a still more ingenious method of accounting that comes
from the 'writing culture' school of anthropology: nothing actually
happened involving the so-called 'primitives' (see the highly
influential volume, Clifford and Marcus, 1986). How can anthropologists say this? By carefully demonstrating through close
textual analysis that primitives never really existed as a distinct
human type *except* as a diffuse and incidental effect of anthropological writing: 'we wrote it, so we can erase it.'

What is the underlying motive in all this work? I suspect that
the capital offense committed by the savages and the other non-
European peoples was not that they were living a life entirely
different from the Europeans who discovered them. It was that
they were living a life entirely different, and evidently *enjoying* it.
Human beings accept difference much more easily if those who
are different from themselves also appear to be unhappy. White
Americans and other Anglo-European peoples are often absolutely
intolerant of the joy of others. Evidence of great pleasure on the
part of another is as likely to be met by furious and destructive
jealousy as by a request to join in the fun. While attention has been
paid to this in the psychoanalytic literatures, it has been completely
overlooked by sociology and anthropology where it probably has
had greater impact on the subject matter. Renata Salecl (1990)
argues that this hatred of enjoyment is based on an unanalyzed
inhibition of one's own pleasure that assumes the symptomatic
form of attacks on the pleasure of others. Whatever its source

might be, in virtually every early account, the pleasure of savages is an occasion for condemnation, not admiration.

This condemnation is palpably evident in Columbus's first journal observations of the Indians he encountered in the Caribbean. So great was the admiral's desire to get to China where, he fantasized, he would meet with the 'Great Khan' and convert him to Christianity, he became enormously frustrated when, on the occasion of his second voyage, he landed in Cuba, obviously another island, not China. In what was for him a characteristic act of total denial, he threatened to cut out the tongues of anyone who would not take a solemn oath swearing that Cuba was a mainland, not an island. When, even under threat, the Indians continued to maintain that their homeland was an island, he wrote in his journal: 'And since these are bestial men who believe the whole world is an island and who do not know what the mainland is, and have neither letters or long-standing memories, and since they take pleasure only in eating and being with their women, they said this was an island' (quoted in Todorov, 1984: 21). I find it strange that no one seems to have noticed this hatred of the pleasure of others, absolute to the point of being expressed casually, without any felt need for justification. The 'pleasures' of the savages are simply listed in a litany of their despicable qualities along with their 'bestiality' and 'ignorance.' The same unconscious hostility marks the Heisenberg comment: we are going to have to upset the delicate balance of life in the non-European parts of the world, the balance '*on which all human happiness rests.*' Why? So they will be our equals in unhappiness?

The collective guilt of modernized peoples is not technically a 'Christian' type of guilt, based on 'original sin,' although Christians may eventually bear it (in a juridical sense) more heavily than non-Christians. And it is not necessarily of an Oedipal kind although it can be re-inscribed into the family romance. Specifically, I am suggesting that our guilt is not for a fall from grace, or a metaphoric murder of the father, symbolic repetitions of allegedly real events that happened in the remote past. Rather, it is for the actual murder of our forefathers, our savage ancestors, something started about seven thousand years ago and just completed. Re-inscription of this murder into the 'family romance' can be prefaced by Freud's favorite aphorism, 'The child is father of the man.' By killing off the primitives (we are all witnesses to this deed, there are literally thousands of reliably obtained first-hand accounts on our library shelves), we have killed off the childhood of humanity. The guilt for this crime is projected onto our parents in the form of blame for having tricked us into growing up, for 'killing off' our own childhood. The personal loss of innocence that figures in the Oedipus story becomes a stand-in for the collective tragic destruction. We embrace Oedipal guilt in a kind of 'plea bargain' to a lesser offense, because it involves symbolic murder, not an actual genocide. But it is actual genocide that is now operative in the formation of guilt.

This is my reading of the extended reflection on Oedipus in Lévi-Strauss's inaugural lecture on assuming the Chair of Anthropology at the Collège de France. He draws a parallel between brother–sister incest in Algonquin mythology and the Western Oedipus myth, focusing on non-standard sexual relations while excluding (without remarking on the exclusion) consideration of the Oedipal patricide (Lévi-Strauss, 1967: 34–9). He concludes, in summary, that the prohibition of incest is universal because it leads to balance and equilibrium:

> In the face of the two possibilities which might seduce the imagination – an eternal summer or a winter just as eternal, the former licentious to the point of corruption, the latter pure to the point of sterility – man must resign himself to choosing equilibrium and the periodicity of the seasonal rhythm. In the natural order, the latter fulfills the same function which is fulfilled in society by the exchange of women in marriage and the exchange of words in conversation, when these are practiced with the frank intention of communicating, that is to say, without trickery or perversity, and above all, without hidden motives.
>
> (p. 39)

It is clear that Lévi-Strauss desires nothing so much as to heal the wounds inflicted upon our savage ancestors by modern peoples. The love for the savage so clearly expressed in his work grows out of human understanding that can only have a determined base in absolute identification. Perhaps it is based on the fact that he undertook his first ethnological expeditions while fleeing for his life from the Nazis and came to terms with his own fate as he made his observations of the Indians. His partial account of Oedipus, skipping over the killing of the father, expresses his deepest desires and also provides the motive for his research program: his drive to try to reconstruct the totality of American Indian religious beliefs. This is perhaps the place where anthropology ends, having exhausted its mental energy and good will.

No matter how hard we try to forget, modern civilization was built on the graves of our savage ancestors, and repression of the pleasure they took from one another, from the animals and the earth. I suspect our collective guilt and denial of responsibility for the destruction of savagery and pleasure can be found infused in every distinctively modern cultural form.

If we are ever to end this projection of evil onto innocent others, it will be necessary to find its source, which I will argue is a still operative cannibal ego and unconscious that stupidly thinks everyone shares its fantasies.

CANNIBAL TOURS: THE MOVIE

Dennis O'Rourke's *Cannibal Tours* is the latest of his documentary films on Pacific peoples, following his *Yumi Yet* (1976), *Ileksen* (1978), *Yap ... How Did They Know We'd Like TV?* (1980), *Shark Callers of Kontu* (1982), *Couldn't Be Fairer* (1984), and *Half Life* (1986). The narrative structure of the film is unremarkable. A group of Western Europeans and North Americans, by appearance somewhat wealthier than 'average' international tourists, travel up the Sepik river in Papua New Guinea in an ultra-modern, air-conditioned luxury liner, and up tributaries in smaller motor launches, stopping at villages along the way to take photographs and buy native handicrafts. The travelogue is inter-cut with ethnographic still photographs and with 'talking head' interviews of both tourists and New Guineans who try to answer questions about the reasons for tourism and its effects on the local peoples. The background soundtrack contains occasional shortwave messages from the wider world, a Mozart string quartet, and an Iatmul flute concerto. O'Rourke (1987) says of his own film:

> 'Cannibal Tours' is two journeys. The first is that depicted – rich and bourgeois tourists on a luxury cruise up the mysterious Sepik River, in the jungles of Papua New Guinea ... the pack-aged version of a 'heart of darkness.' The second journey (the real text of the film) is a metaphysical one. It is an attempt to discover the place of 'the Other' in the popular imagination [ellipsis in the original].

The film makes it painfully evident, and the choice of the Sepik region drives the point home with precision, that this primitive 'Other' no longer exists. What remains of the primitive world are ex-primitives, recently acculturated peoples lost in the industrial world, and another kind of ex-primitive, still going under the label 'primitive,' a kind of performative 'primitive.'

During the first slow phase of the globalization of culture, colonialism, and industrialization, eventually tourism and modernization, modernity, the modern – during this phase the energy, drive, and libido for the globalization of culture came from Western European and North European cultures. But today, the older centers of modernity are demanding a return on their investments, an implosive construction of primitivism (and every other 'ism') in a postmodern pastiche that might be called 'globality.'

Postmodernity is itself a symptom of a need to suppress bad memories of Auschwitz, Hiroshima, and the other genocides on which modernity was built. Of course, it is not possible to repress the past without denying the future. Thus, the central drive of postmodernity is to stop history in its tracks, and the central drive of postmodern tourism is to discover places that seem to exist outside of history: unspoiled nature and savagery.

The opening scenes of *Cannibal Tours* neatly frame several postmodern figures. A voiceover taken from Radio Moscow world service announces a Paul Simon rock concert in Lenin Auditorium. But the film's postmodern figure *par excellence* is a self-congratulating German tourist who comes as close as anyone in the film to being its central character. He compulsively records his travel experiences on film while speaking into a hand-held tape recorder. His age is ambiguous. He might be old enough to have fought in World War II, a suspicion not allayed by his attire, which is designer re-issue of an Afrika Korps uniform. He explains to O'Rourke's camera, 'Yes I have been to Lebanon, Iran, India, Thailand, Burma, China, Japan, the Philippines, Indonesia, the Pacific Islands, Australia two times, once to New Zealand, South Africa, Rhodesia, all of South America....' He appears in the film as someone under a biblical curse to expiate the sins (or would it be the failures?) of National Socialism, and also to displace certain memories. He goes where the German army was not able to go, expressing a kind of laid-back contentment when he encounters a fascist regime: 'I liked Chile. Next year Middle America...'. Only the United States is not mentioned in his recounting of his itineraries. He asks his Iatmul guide, 'Where have you killed the people? Right here. People were killed here? (he pats the stone for emphasis) Now I need a photograph of the two of us here before the stone for the memory.'

The economics of tourist/recent ex-primitive interaction

The little reliably obtained ethnographic evidence we now have tends to confirm a central theme of *Cannibal Tours*: that the relations between tourists and recent ex-primitives are framed in a somewhat forced, stereotypical commercial exploitation model characterized by bad faith and petty suspicion on both sides. Ex-primitives often express their belief that the only difference between themselves and North Americans or Europeans is money. The German in *Cannibal Tours*, responding to what was supposed to have been a high-level question from the film-maker about commercial exchanges spoiling the New Guineans, 'agrees' that 'these people do not know the value of money,' but the workmanship 'often justifies' the prices they ask. In short, he thinks it is he, not the New Guineans, who is being exploited. He is doing them a favor by not paying the asking price – he simultaneously gives them a lesson in commercial realism and, by withholding his capital, he helps delay their entry into the modern world. He thinks their eventual modernization is inevitable, but they would benefit from a period of delay. The dominant view expressed by recent ex-primitives of white Europeans and North Americans is that they exhibit an unimaginable combination of qualities: specifically, they are rich tightwads, boorish, obsessed by consumerism, and suffering from collectomania. The Sioux Indians call white man *wasicum* or 'fat taker.' This arrangement can devolve into hatred. Laureen Waukau, a Menonimee Indian, told Stan Steiner:

> Just recently I realized that I hate whites. When the tourist buses come through and they come in here and stare at me, that's when I hate them. They call me 'Injun.' Like on television. It's a big joke to them. You a 'drunken Injun,' they say.... I hate it.

And, of course, it should not go unremarked that *intention* in these exchanges does not alter the outcomes. The tourist who calls an Indian 'Injun' means to insult, but the well-intended tourist on the same bus is no less insulting. Steiner describes an encounter between Waukau and a tourist:

One lady gently touched the young girl's wrist. 'Dear, are you a real Indian?' she asked. 'I hope you don't mind my asking. But you look so American' [both incidents are reported in Evans-Pritchard, 1989: 97].

The commercialization of the touristic encounter extends to the point of commodification not merely of the handicrafts and the photographic image, but to the person of the ex-primitive. Southwest American Indians complain that tourists have attempted to pat up their hair and arrange their clothing before photographing them, and that they receive unwanted offers from tourists to buy the jewelry or the clothing they are actually wearing.

As degenerate as these exchanges might at first appear, there is no problem here, really, at least not from the standpoint of existing social conventions. All these behaviors are recognizably boorish, so the 'problem' as represented is entirely correctable by available means: counseling ('don't use ethnic slurs'); education ('Indians were the original Americans'); etiquette ('don't be condescending in conversation,' 'don't violate another's person or privacy,' 'don't comment on how "American" they appear'); and so on. With a bit of decency and sound advice these 'problems,' including their New Guinea equivalents, would go away.

Or would they? I think not. Because I detect in all these reports on exchanges between tourists and others a certain mutual complicity, a co-production of a psuedo-conflict to obscure something deeper and more serious: namely, that the encounter between tourist and 'other' is the scene of a shared Utopian vision of profit without exploitation, logically the final goal of a kind of cannibal economics shared by ex-primitives and postmoderns alike. The desire for profit without exploitation runs so strong, like that for 'true love,' that even intellectuals can trick themselves into finding it where it does not exist; where, in my view, it can never exist.

The touristic ideal of the 'primitive' is that of a magical resource that can be used without actually possessing or diminishing it. Within tourism, the 'primitive' occupies a position not unlike that of the libido or the death drive in psychoanalysis, or the simple-minded working class of National Socialism which was supposed to have derived an ultimate kind of fulfillment in its labor for the Fatherland. Or the physicist's dream of room-temperature super-conductivity and table-top fusion. These are all post-capitalist moral fantasies based on a desire to deny the relationship between profit and exploitation. Let's pretend that we can get something for nothing. The fable is as follows: The return on the tour of headhunters and cannibals is to make the tourist a real hero of alterity.[10] It is his coming into contact with and experience of the ultra-primitive which gives him his status. But this has not cost the primitives anything. Indeed, they too, may have gained from it. Taking someone's picture doesn't cost them anything, not in any Western commercial sense, yet the picture has value. The picture has no value for the primitive, yet the tourist pays for the right to take pictures. The 'primitive' receives something for nothing, and benefits beyond this. Doesn't the fame of certain primitives, and even respect for them, actually increase when the tourist carries their pictures back to the West? It seems to be the most perfect realization so far of the capitalist economists' dream of *everyone* getting richer together.

Of course this is impossible. If a profit has been made, some bit of nature has been used up or some individuals have worked so that others might gain. It is easy enough to see how the advanced techniques of modern statecraft and stagecraft, recently merged into one, permit the destruction of nature and the alienation of work to be hidden from *view*. But how are they hidden from consciousness? The only way is by negative education, specifically the suppression of an understanding of exchange within exchange relations. In the relation between tourists and primitives, this pretense transforms the literally propertyless state of primitives into a property. Tourism has managed (and this is its special genius in the family of human institutions) to put a value on propertyless-ness itself. 'Look, there are no fences around their fields. That's worth a picture!' 'They work only for their own subsistence. That's worth reporting back to our overly commercial society at home!'

And for their part, the performative primitives, now ex-primitives, have devised a rhetoric surrounding money that perfectly complements the postmodern dream of profit without exploitation. They deny the economic importance of their economic exchanges. They will explain that they are exploited absolutely in their merely economic dealings with tourists, but also as far as they are concerned, at the level of symbolic values, these exchanges count for nothing. By the ex-primitives' own account, their economic dealings with tourists are spiritually vacuous and economically trivial, producing little more exchange than what is needed to buy trousers.[11] Their problem is not petty exploitation by tourists. Rather, it is getting money and having it. The New Guineans in *Cannibal Tours* repeat, to the point that it becomes a kind of litany, their position that money is simply 'had' and 'gotten', never earned and spent, and are quick to guard against the formation of any idea that the tourists, especially, *earned* their money. An old admitted ex-cannibal speaks to the camera about the tourists: 'These are very wealthy people. They got their money, I know not where, perhaps their parents earned it and gave it to them, perhaps their governments give it to them.' Clearly, he is thinking not in terms of earnings but *capital*. Sounding more like Donald Trump than a Western proletarian, the old warrior complains, 'I have no way of persuading them to give me money.' From an ethnological standpoint, this is not especially surprising coming from a people whose basic unit of money, their equivalent to the American dollar or the British pound, is the *tautau, nassa*, or *maij*, a string of shells, that at the time of first European contact, was estimated by Mrs Hingston Quiggin (1949: 172 ff.) to be worth the value of between two and ten months of labor. There is a deeply ironic movement of the camera in the scene in *Cannibal Tours* in which a New Guinea woman complains with bitter eloquence that 'white men got money... you have all the money.' For an instant, the camera drops down to the blanket in front of her showing what she is selling: it is *maij*, strings of shell money. She knows herself to be positioned like the Western banker, trading in currencies under unfavorable exchange conditions. The tourists think they are buying beads.

In sum, there is so much mutual complicity in the overall definition of the interaction between the postmodern tourist and the ex-primitive that the system comes close to producing the impossible economic ideal. The performing primitives claim to be exploited, but in so doing they take great care not to develop this claim to the point where their value as 'primitive' attraction is diminished. In short, they must appear as almost noble savages, authentic except for a few changes forced on them by others: they sell beads, they do not trade in currencies. They gain sympathy from the tourist based on the conditions of their relationship to the tourist. And the entire arrangement almost works. O'Rourke asks a young man on camera how it feels to have his picture taken, and points out that as he (O'Rourke) takes his picture, one of 'them' (a woman tourist) has also come up behind to take yet another picture. 'One of them is looking at you now.' The woman tourist gets her shot and awkwardly steps into O'Rourke's frame sideways to give the young man some money for letting himself be photographed. O'Rourke comments dryly, 'It's hard to make a dollar.' We can feel sympathy, but only to the point of considering the working conditions of a steel worker in a foundry, an agricultural worker in the fields of California, or even a model in Manhattan who is also paid to have her picture taken, but under conditions of somewhat greater performative demand.

Performances

The conditions of the meeting of tourists and ex-primitives are such that one predictably finds hatred, sullen silence, freezing out. Deirdre Evans-Pritchard (1989: 98) reports that sometimes this sullenness is heartfelt and at other times it may be performed as a way of humoring the tourist. Southwest American Indian males hanging out in a public place and joking around with each other, for example, have been known to adopt a frozen, silent, withdrawn stance on the approach of tourists, then they break back into a joking mode as soon as the tourist is gone, their jocularity redoubled by their mutual understanding that the tourists accepted their 'hostile Indian' act. This is only one of the ways that ex-primitives knowingly overdose tourists with unwanted pseudo-authenticity (MacCannell, 1984b).

The micro-sociology of the arrangement between tourists and ex-primitives reveals an interesting balancing mechanism. Even if the tourists bring greater wealth and worldly sophistication to the encounter, the ex-primitive brings more experience in dealing with tourists. Most tourists do not repeatedly return to a specific site; they go on to new experiences. But ex-primitives who have made a business of tourism deal with tourists on a daily basis and soon become expert on the full range of touristic appearances and behavior. I have personally been picked out of a crowded Mexican market by a vendor who called me over to look at his wares, 'Ola, professor!'

Jill Sweet (1989) reports on a Zuñi Pueblo four-part typology of tourists labeled by them as: (1) New Yorker or East Coast type, (2) Texan type, (3) Hippy type, and (4) 'Save-the-whale' type. All of these figures are beginning to appear in Indian dance routines, sometimes in the dances they do for tourists. In the Zuñi typology as reported by Sweet, 'Texas types' wear cowboy boots and drive

Cadillacs. 'Hippies' are represented as wearing tie-dyed T-shirts, attempting uninvited to join in the Indians' dances, and as incessantly asking questions about peyote and mescal, and so on. The 'save-the-whale' tourist dancer is played by an Indian wearing hiking boots, tan shorts, a T-shirt with a message, and a pair of binoculars carved out of a block of wood that he uses to study the Indians. The 'East Coast' tourist is represented as a woman played by a male Indian wearing high heels, wig, dress, mink coat, dime-store jewelry, clutch purse, and pillbox hat. As 'she' awkwardly approaches the dance ground, she stops to coo and cluck over the small Indian children along the way. In their tourist routines, the Zuñi represent all types of tourists as disappointed that they (the Zuñi) do not fit the stereotype of plains Indians who hunt buffalo and live in tepees.

The more elaborated performances that occur in the relations between tourists and ex-primitives assume what are according to Jameson (1984) characteristically postmodern dramatic forms: satire, lampooning, and burlesque. All these forms involve identification, imitation, emulation, and impersonation, to make a point. No matter how negative this point may at first seem to be, even if it might hurt a bit, it is always ultimately positive, because it suggests that relations could be improved if we pay more attention to our effects on others. Parody builds solidarity in the group that stages it and potentially raises the consciousness of an audience that is the butt of it. But to accomplish this the parodist must take risks. Intercultural burlesque is necessarily structurally similar to efforts on the part of individuals from stigmatized minority groups to emulate the appearances and behaviors of representatives of the dominant culture. So any dramatically well-constructed parody that misses its mark, even slightly, becomes self-parody, just as postmodern architecture always risks losing its ironic referentiality and simply becoming tacky junk, not a parodic 'comment' on tacky junk. It may well be insecurity in this regard that drives performers of tourist routines to cast their burlesque in such broad terms; to cause an Indian male to represent a tourist woman, and so on.

A Japanese-American student of mine recently remarked to me that some of her friends lighten their hair and wear blue contact lenses in order to look like Anglo-Americans. 'But' she added perceptively, 'they end up looking like Asian-Americans with dyed hair and blue contacts.' Something like this seems to have happened toward the end of *Cannibal Tours* in a party scene in which a heavy-set male tourist attempts to act savage for his fellow tourists. He has the necessary props. He is stripped to the waist. His face has been fucated by his New Guinea hosts. Only he can't act. His hackneyed way of making himself seem to be fierce for others is to strike a pose similar to that seen in pre–1950s publicity shots of professional boxers. It is so profoundly embarrassing that no one can even tell him that he is making an ass of himself. The New Guineans could not have done him better.

It is harrowing to suggest that these performances and aesthetic-economic exchanges may be the creative cutting edge of world culture in the making. But I think that we cannot rule out this possibility. In a very fine paper, Jim Boon (1984) has argued that parody and satire are at the base of every cultural formation. Responding to A. L. Becker's question concerning Javanese shadow theater ('"Where" he ponders, "in Western literary and dramatic traditions with their Aristotelian constraints" would we find "Jay Gatsby, Godzilla, Agamemnon, John Wayne and Charlie Chaplin" appearing in the same plot?'), Boon answers: 'I suggest we find such concoctions *everywhere* in Western performance and literary genres *except* a narrow segment of bourgeois novels.' Further suggesting that Becker has not even scratched the surface of the 'riot of types' found linked together in cultural (as opposed to Cultural) performances, Boon throws in Jesus Christ, the Easter Bunny, Mickey Mouse, and Mohammed.

> The remainder is, to say the least, impressive: miracle plays, masques, *Trauerspiele*, follies, carnivals and the literary carnival-esque, everything picaresque, burlesque or vaudevillian, *Singespiele*, gests, romances, music drama, fairy tales, comic books, major holidays (Jesus cum Santa; Christ plus the Easter Bunny), Disney, TV commercials, the history of Hollywood productions, fantastic voyages, sci-fi, travel*liars*' tales, experimental theater, anthropology conferences.
>
> (1984: 157)

Boon's comment precisely affirms the logical procedures employed in the selection of figures for a wax museum: Jesus, Snow White, a Headhunter from New Guinea, John Wayne, Aristotle. Framed in this way, the absorption of the ex-primitive into the new cultural subject is theoretically unremarkable. It simply repeats the logic of the wax museum and 'hyperreality,' which is Eco's term for the valorization of absolute fakery as the only truth. Still, there is something O'Rourke has caught in the eyes of these New Guineans, perhaps a memory that they cannot share, that suggests there remains a difference not yet accounted for.

To summarize: Overlying our common ancestors, primitive hunting and gathering peoples, we have a history of colonial exploitation and military suppression, missionary efforts to transform religious beliefs and secular values, anthropological observations and descriptions, and now the touristic encounter. This complex system of overlays is all that is left of our common heritage and it has, itself, become the scene of an oddly staged encounter between people who think of themselves as being civilized or modernized and others who are said to be 'primitive,' but this can no longer be their proper designation. The term 'primitive' is increasingly only a response to a mythic necessity to keep the idea of the primitive alive in the modern world and consciousness. And it will stay alive because there are several empires built on the necessity of the 'primitive': included among these are anthropology's official versions of itself, an increasing segment of the tourist industry, the economic base of ex-primitives who continue to play the part of primitives-for-moderns, now documentary film-making, and soon music, art, drama, and literature. Rock star David Bowie takes several Indians from the Amazon basin, carrying spears and painted for 'battle,' with him on tour.

I am arguing that at the level of economic relations, aesthetic exchange (the collecting and marketing of artifacts, and so on), and the sociology of interaction, there is no *real* difference between moderns and those who act the part of primitives in the universal drama of modernity. Modern people have more money, but the ex-primitive is quick to accept the terms of modern economics. This may be a practical response to a system imposed from without, against which it would do no good to resist. But it could also be an adaptation based on rational self-interest. The word has already leaked out that not everyone in the 'West' lives life as seen on television, that many ex-primitives and most peasants are materially better off, and have more control over their own lives than the poorest of the poor in the modernized nations. Perhaps a case for difference could be made in the area of interactional competence. Ex-primitives are often more rhetorically and dramaturgically adept than moderns, excepting communications and

media professionals. Still, up to this point, it would be tenuous and
mainly incorrect to frame the interaction as 'tourist/other' because
what we really have is a collaborative construction of postmodernity by tourists and ex-primitives who represent not absolute
differences but mere differentiations of an evolving new cultural
subject. If Jim Boon's formulation is acceptable, the new cultural
subject is probably no more or less of a pastiche than any other
culture was before it got an official grip on itself.

The psychoanalytic and the mythic

Still, one cannot visit the former scene of the primitive without
concluding that even within a fully postmodern framework, there
is a real difference that might be marked 'primitive,' but it is not
easy to describe. It does not deploy itself along axes that have
already been worked out in advance by ethnography. These
former headhunters and cannibals in *Cannibal Tours* are attractive,
have a lightly ironic attitude, and are clear-sighted and pragmatic
in their affairs. The tourists are most unattractive, emotional,
awkward, and intrusive. It is difficult to imagine a group of real
people (that is, non-actors) simply caught in the eye of the camera
appearing less attractive. This is not because of any obvious film
trick. There is no narrator to tell the viewer how to think. Everyone
on camera, the Iatmul people and tourists alike, is given ample
opportunity for expression. The film is not technically unsympathetic to the tourists. The ostensible perspective is emotionless and
empirical. The tourists do themselves in on camera. So the effect
is *really* unsympathetic. The film often feels as if O'Rourke in-
structed his subjects to do an insensitive tourist routine, and they
tried to oblige him even though they are not good actors.

That the tourists should come off second best to the Iatmul
provides a clue to the difference, but to follow up on this clue
requires yet another trip up the Sepik river. Here is the scene of
much more than *Cannibal Tours*. It is, not by accident, also the place
of perhaps the thickest historical and ethnographic encounter of
'primitive' and 'modern' on the face of the earth, suspended
between perfect historical brackets marking the first 1886 exploration of Europeans in the Schleinitz expedition, and the 1986
filming of *Cannibal Tours*. During this hundred years the headhunters and cannibals of the Sepik region were visited by
explorers, prospectors, missionaries, German colonists, labor con-

tractors, anthropologists, government district police, Rockefeller the younger, and now, tourists. The anthropologists who have visited the Sepik include John Whiting, Reo Fortune, Gregory Bateson, and of course Margaret Mead. (It has been pointed out to me that this list is much longer; that these are only the anthropologists who most successfully linked their Sepik experiences to their professional careers.)

The images that appear in *Cannibal Tours* are mainly tight shots that are geographically nonspecific. O'Rourke is careful to name the villages that hosted him in the credits at the end. But at any given point in the film, the viewer, especially one unfamiliar with the Sepik region, cannot know the precise location of the action. The only places mentioned by name on film are Kanganganuman and Anguram villages and Tchamburi lake, where the stones used in the beheading ceremonies were found. An old warrior says, 'Here in Kanganuman we....' It is remarkably strange that these lapses into specificity should also have named Anguram and Kanganuman, Gregory Bateson's headquarters while assembling his observations for writing his ethnographic classic, *Naven*, and Tchamburi lake, where Margaret Mead lived while making her observations.[12] Kanganuman was also where Bateson hosted his friends and colleagues Margaret Mead and Reo Fortune, sharing his eight-by-twelve mosquito enclosure with them while they wrote up their field notes, the scene of an anthropological romance properly-so-called, where Margaret Mead changed husbands, or as she more delicately puts it, where she fell in love with Bateson, without really knowing it, while she was still married to Fortune.[13]

There is a gravitational pull, operating at a level beyond myth and psychoanalysis, between Western ethnography and these people of the Sepik who, I am arguing, only *seem* to put the anthropological doctrine of cultural relativism to its ultimate test. The actual message of Sepik ethnography is that Eurocentric culture is based on a denial of its own violent, homoerotic, and cannibalistic impulses. Consider *Naven*, the Iatmul ceremonial celebration of cultural accomplishments. Bateson tells his readers straight away that among the Iatmul, the greatest cultural achievement is 'homicide':

> The first time a boy kills an enemy or a foreigner or some bought victim is made the occasion for the most complete *naven*, involving the greatest number of relatives and the greatest variety of

ritual incidents. Later in his life when the achievement is repeated, there will still be some *naven* performance..., but the
majority of ritual incidents will probably be omitted. Next to
actual homicide, the most honored acts are those which help
others to successful killing [.... such as] the enticing of foreigners
into the village so that others may kill them.

(1958: 6)

Ritualized murder among the Iatmul is a reciprocal form embedded in intra- and inter-group social control mechanisms to the
point that a victim's own people may arrange for a kill; for
example, by letting it be known to an enemy group that reprisals
will be light if they select the 'right' individual. But this should not
be taken to mean that only delinquents and misfits are killed. The
Iatmul people and their neighbors, it has often been noted, are
remarkably free from status distinctions, and this certainly shows
up in the range of victims, by no means limited to initiated males
but inclusive of men, women, children, pigs, and dogs. A more
recent ethnographer, William Mitchell, who took his young children into the field with him, describes a recent raid on his village:

Entering the unprotected village, the Taute men shot and killed
the first human they saw. It was a little boy. Returning victorious
to their village, the Tautes beat their signal drums in triumph
and danced through the night while the Kamnum women
wailed the death of Wuruwe's small son.

(Mitchell, 1978: 92)

And he captions a photograph of his children playing with Kam-
nun kids: 'On the sandy plaza where little Tobtai was murdered,
Ned and Elizabeth now played with their new friends' (p. 131).

The anthropologists' fascination (the sheer number of New
Guinea ethnographies is a symptom), and the tourists', with ecstatic violence, taking heads, and eating human brains, involves
displaced anal sadism which is a strong, albeit necessarily denied,
component of Western culture and consciousness. A side benefit
of New Guinea ethnography is free psychoanalysis, and not cheap
stuff either, but one that finds its authentic substrate in the Western
cogito and consciousness. For the Iatmul people of the Sepik and
their highland neighbors male homosexuality and anal sadism are
not deep secrets accessible only by psychoanalytic methods. They
are openly avowed, key features of the ritual and social order,

already well documented in ethnographic accounts of the *naven* and *nama* cults.

In *naven* celebrations, as described by Bateson, the maternal uncle dresses in women's clothing and goes about the village in search of the nephew who has done his first murder, carved his first canoe, or made some other major cultural accomplishment. The uncle's purpose is supposed to be to offer himself to the nephew for homosexual intercourse. The nephew is painfully embarrassed by this and usually manages to absent himself from the ceremony, leaving the uncle to sprawl about in the sand in a burlesque agony of sexual desire, a show that delights everyone, especially the children. Sometimes the uncle's wife will put on men's clothing and act the part of the nephew, pantomiming homosexual intercourse with her husband in the presence of the entire village. Very rarely is there actual physical contact between the *wua* (uncle) and the *laua* (nephew whose deed is being celebrated). A gesture, which Bateson calls a 'sort of sexual salute,' the possibility of which is at the heart of all *naven*, is called *mogul neggelak-ka*, which literally means 'grooving the anus.' Bateson describes his only sighting as follows:

> This gesture of the *wua* I have only seen once. This was when a *wua* dashed out into the midst of a dance and performed the gesture upon his *laua*.... The *wua* ran into the crowd, turned his back on the *laua* and rapidly lowered himself – almost fell – into a squatting position in such a way that as his legs bent under him his buttocks rubbed down the length of the *laua's* leg.
>
> (1958: 13)

Fascination for these Sepik peoples and their highland neighbors has always been a reflex of our own economic values and associated gender order. No matter whether we are for or against the homoeroticism of our own social order, in which everyone, not just women, are supposed to adore the 'great man,' New Guinea provides a certain comfort. If we oppose the arbitrary segregation of the sexes in our society and gendered hierarchies, we can tell ourselves that at least we have not gone so far as the Iatmul, Sambia, and other New Guinea peoples. If we favor our own phallic order, we can use the New Guinea materials to support our claims that the separation of the sexes and hierarchical arrangements are 'natural' or, if they are not 'natural,' they are at least 'deeply cultural' which is the new form of 'natural.' If we are for or against our system of economic exploitation, we can take certain comfort from a people who like to talk about having eaten the brains of their dead enemies. I have long suspected that this 'either/or-ism' is the unwritten social contract that establishes the conditions for the widespread acceptance of the doctrine of 'cultural relativism.' The peoples and cultural practices that are handled 'relativistically' must seem to support both sides of the deepest oppositions and ambivalencies of their observers. No ethnographic case accomplishes this at a level of intensity and detail that can compete with the New Guineans. In a celebrated remark, the father of modern phenomenology, Edmund Husserl, states: '[J]ust as a man, and even the Papuan, represents a new stage in animality in contrast to the animals, so philosophical reason represents a new stage in humanity' (quoted in Derrida, 1978: 62; and Ferry and Renaut, 1990: 102).

Approximately 100 miles south of the Middle Sepik, another group has become a famous case because they have universally enforced homosexuality for young boys until marriage, after which they are said to begin practicing normal heterosexual relations. We can read a brief account of these people in a recent *New York Times Magazine* article on homosexuality:

> Consider the Sambia of New Guinea, described by Gilbert Herdt in 'Guardians of the Flutes.' They belong to a group of cultures in which homosexual practices are actually *required* of boys for several years as rites of passage into adulthood. After adolescence, the young men abandon homosexual practices, marry women, father children and continue as heterosexuals for the rest of their lives. The lesson is threefold: first, a culture can make such a rule and get every person to conform; second, years of obligatory homosexuality apparently do not commit the average man to a lifetime of homoerotic desires. Third....
>
> (April 2, 1989: 60)

The normalizing tone of this account is remarkable in view of the subject. The 'Sambia' (it is a pseudonymous case) practice referred to, but not specified in the *Times* article, is young-boy-to-adult-male fellatio. 'Sambia' initiates are required to eat semen on a daily basis from about age seven through adolescence. The justification given for this practice is that male stature and strength, courage in war, and the ability eventually to be reproductively competent requires the ingestion of enormous quantities of semen. The more semen you eat, the bigger, stronger, more intelligent, and more masculine you will become.[14] The men, to use the economic term now fashionable, are 'investing' in the boys.[15] 'Sambia' point to the first growth of pubic and facial hair, and the first appearance of adult muscle contours as proof of the effectiveness of their initiation procedures. Herdt (1981: 3) comments:

> ritualized homosexuality becomes the center of their existence. Born from the deepest trauma of maternal separation and ritual threats, homosexual fellatio is dangerous and enticing, powerful and cruel. And from such experience is born a boy's sense of masculinity.... In short, Sambia boys undergo profound social conditioning through early, exciting homosexual experiences that continue for years. Yet they emerge as competent, exclusively heterosexual adults, not homosexuals. Contrary to Western belief, transitional homoeroticism is the royal road to Sambia manliness.

These statements can, and indeed must, be read as expressing what is meant by 'manliness' and 'competent heterosexuality' in current Anglo-European culture. We can discover, for example, that 'competent heterosexuality' means only that men marry women and have children. Modernized cultures contain well-developed internal mechanisms that effectively resist the detailed specification of behavioral rules for adult heterosexual males. The 'Sambia,' even in the context of marriage and 'normal' heterosexual relations, consider the female sex to be so polluting, that if a man should utter the word for vagina, he must spit repeatedly lest he be poisoned by his own saliva that has come into contact with the word. At about the time the boys end their homoerotic career they are subjected to the ramming of a long cane down their throats to the point of forcing (they believe) out of their anus the last bits of filthy contaminated food, and also words, given to them in their youth by their mothers.[16]

Let me suggest that the cessation of homosexual activities on the part of 'Sambia' boys does not end in heterosexual relations, at least not from their perspective. It ends with the taking of heads. The point at which they stop giving head and start taking heads ritually marks the transition when they join with the men as a man. In Herdt's accounting scheme, only the youthful fellators are engaged in homosexual activity; the adult male fellatees have 'abandoned their homosexual practices' and are simply going about the business of their offices as competent adult male heterosexuals. They also get married and father children, and initiate the young boys. Still, attention to the ethnographic record reveals that heterosexual relations remain for them frightening, dirty, and dangerous, the way that women steal their strength. Apparently also, according to Herdt's account, the kind of contamination and danger associated with heterosexual relations can be sexually exciting, working a powerful erotic attraction on certain adult males in the direction of what would be for them the exotic and the alien, namely, sex with women.

Viewing *Cannibal Tours* in the context of New Guinea ethnography one necessarily begins to wonder about what Freud gave us. It is not so much a question of psychoanalysis as mythology, a mythology of modernity that includes the primitive as a veil for our cannibal and other homoerotic desires. The primitive modality in the new cultural subject is already contained, or almost contained, in a touristic frame. Certainly O'Rourke's camera has assumed the point of view of the old paternal analyst, steady, listening, silent, pretending to be non-judgmental. Its gaze remains when the subject has run out of things to say. The tourists in O'Rourke's movie, after a pause, begin to say anything that comes into their minds; this is how O'Rourke finds the modern myth of the primitive in the touristic unconscious. When the camera is left running, the Italian girl blocks on decapitation and castration: 'It was *symbolic*. For survival but also *symbolic*. It was *symbolic* when they cut off the heads of the white explorers. Not with malice, but a part of a *symbolic* tradition.'

The ex-primitives, for their part, maintain much more expressive control. When the camera is left running, they often comment, 'that is the end of my story,' or 'that's all I have to say,' gladly telling about taking heads and eating brains, but stopping short of revealing the secret of *Naven*. But their rhetorical brilliance does not nevertheless permit them completely to escape the touristic or postmodern frame around their consciousness. Within this frame, it is the ex-primitives who have internalized and who rigorously apply the doctrine of cultural relativism. They maintain that there is *no* difference between themselves and Europeans, with the single exception that the Europeans have money and they don't. An old warrior states, 'If I had money I would be on the boat with the tourists,' and later relates his past, making an ultimate statement of the principle of relativism. 'We would cut off the heads, remove the skin and then eat. The Germans came, but white men are no different.'

Language

All that remains is the question of language. Within the touristic frame, there is a characteristic deformation of language. This deformation might originally have resulted from non-competency ('the breezy from high mountains which surrounding...') but now it has grammaticality and intentionality of its own. Deirdre Evans-Pritchard describes an interchange between an Indian artist, and a tourist who unfortunately mistakes him for someone with less than full competence in English:

> A lady was examining the balls on a squash blossom necklace. She turned to Cippy Crazyhorse and in the slow, over-emphasized fashion for someone who does not understand English, she asked 'Are these hollow?' Cippy promptly replied 'Hello' and warmly shook her hand. Again the lady asked, 'Are these hollow?' pronouncing the words even more theatrically this time. Cippy cheerily responded with another 'Hello.' This went on a few more times, by which time everyone around was laughing, until eventually the lady herself saw the joke.
>
> (Evans-Pritchard, 1989: 95–6)

Jacques Lacan (1977: 113) once remarked, 'beyond what we call the "word" what the psychoanalytic experience discovers in the unconscious is the whole structure of language.' I prefer to take this as a methodological, not theoretical, statement to mean that we can arrive at the unconscious without necessarily naming it as our destination if we are sufficiently attentive to language. Of course, 'primitives,' or 'unlettered' peoples cannot be moved by the *letter*, but only by the *sound* of the word: 'hollow' equals 'hello.' Attention to the structure of tourist language suggests the possibility of building a case for real differences in primitive vs. modern modalities and to find a way out of the singularity of the postmodern touristic frame. Tourist language, pidgin English, or, in pidgin, 'Tok Pisin,' has reached its point of greatest perfection on the Sepik.

Tok Pisin, Tourist English, Tourist German, or, viewed from the other perspective, what some of my respondents call 'Tarzan

English,' like all other languages, are built out of transvaluing mechanisms. This is so they can draw on their own internal resources for meaning, which is only another way of saying that they can function as languages. In the early stages of its development, the transvaluing exchange of tourist language may be between language and language, or even language and some extra-linguistic material. A woman tourist repeatedly asks a New Guinean to smile and gets no result. Finally, in frustration, she asks, 'can you smile like this?' and pushes up the corners of her own mouth with her fingers. Cippy Crazyhorse would have obliged her, saying in effect, 'sure I can smile like that,' by manually pushing up the corners of his own mouth.

The two master tropes on which all languages depend for internal self-sufficiency are metaphor and metonymy. The transvaluing mechanism is blatant in metaphor: 'my love *is like* a red, red rose.' Metonymy depends on concrete association and a violation of the boundaries that Western science has erected around 'cause and effect' relations. A metonymic transvaluation has occurred, for example, when we think something is poisonous because it tastes bitter. Metaphor contains much more potential power to transvalue across originally disconnected and separate matters. A 'shining' example rests on a metonymic association of glittering, glistening, diaphanous, golden, perhaps crystalline exemplarity. But effectively to 'make an example' of someone requires false identification with a victim, necessarily a metaphoric reach and suppression of one's own humanity.

Gregory Bateson provided a model that is potentially helpful here: the double-bind theory of schizophrenia (Bateson *et al.*, 1956). I would like to think that 'the hand that strikes the blow can heal the wound,' that Bateson's later work on language and madness was also a product of his earlier New Guinea experience, at least in part. According to Bateson, well-formed language is so because its users have achieved a synthesis, balance, and harmony between metaphoric and metonymic mechanisms of transvaluation, to the point that both are found in any given utterance. Deformed languages develop increasing specialization, dependence and separation of the two master tropes, eventually prizing one over the other as the only 'proper' medium of exchange. The talk of schizophrenics is rigorously tropo-logical, that is, too metaphoric, for example, as when a patient refuses to state anything directly, coding every message in elaborate allusions and allegories. Or it may be defensive in a metonymic direction, admitting no allusion, as when an unguarded remark like 'there were about a thousand people in the elevator' causes a schizophrenic to hallucinate a compact cube of gore.

This kind of imbalance is well documented at the level of the 'speaking subject.' What I want to suggest here is that we begin to attend to something like the same phenomenon at the level of *language*. This move potentially leads to real analysis of Fredric Jameson's (1984) assertion that 'postmodern society is schizophrenic', which is airy in the way he presented it but also intuitively correct. Tourist language is deformed by an odd internal specialization and separation. There is a basis in the language that is used in tourist settings for designating a primitive modality deployed along the metonymic axis and a modern modality along the metaphoric. At least there is a strong statistical tendency in all the examples that I have collected for tourists to speak metaphorically and primitives to speak metonymically. If this is supported by further investigation, we would have a case of a discourse that is itself, in its totality, perfectly normal, built out of two complementary schizoid subvariants. This is a theoretical model for a structural mechanism for producing a normal speech community within which all discourse is schizophrenic, a postmodern speech community.

The raging metaphoricity of the language of the tourists marks virtually every one of their utterances. In rejecting a large mask, a woman in *Cannibal Tours* cannot bring herself to say 'I think it's ugly.' She cannot even say, 'it would not look good in my house.' Instead, she says, 'It would not go in a house *such as* mine, in Chicago.' Each metaphoric move to disconnect and to separate (her husband might take note – at some level she evidently desires to exchange her own house for one like it in Chicago) builds up an absent authority, or standard, a power that controls every decision, a power that has no name except, perhaps, 'Chicago.' Another Papuan mask is said to be 'like Modigliani.' Even direct experience is assimilated only as metaphor: a couple walks briskly down a path, 'This is *definitely* jungle.' A German man gazes across the Sepik, 'It reminds me of the Zambezie.' This same man understands himself, only as metaphor, 'For me *as tourist* it is very impressive.' The Italian family tries to come to terms with what they perceive to be the happiness of the Papuans, 'They don't seem sad. No. The experts assure us they are satisfied.'

The ex-primitives in *Cannibal Tours*, for their part, appear unable to get a metaphor past their lips in either direction. Their way of assimilating the German colonist was to eat his brains. It is noteworthy in this regard that Americans also eat their former enemies, the Germans, but only metaphorically, of course: as frankfurters, and hamburgers.[17] When the old ex-cannibal told O'Rourke's camera about the loss of his 'sacred symbols', he was not speaking of traditional values, beliefs, or ideals that are fading from thought. What he had in mind were some carved wooden objects that had been stolen from the spirit house and destroyed by the German missionaries or sent to European museums. New Guinea languages are possessive and imperative, even when command and presence are not called for. One of the most frequently occurring words in Tok Pisin is 'bilong.' The Tok Pisin name for a dildo-like penis sheath, an instrument that teleotypically stands for standing in, that is, for absence, is 'skin bilong kok.' The term itself takes the form of a miniature moral harangue about the importance of presence, association, connection: this is a dildo but don't forget, skin belong cock.

Metaphor always involves suppression: a veiling of the obvious through which the outlines of the obvious can be seen. The tourist's historical dependence on metaphor necessarily produces something like an unconscious. The cannibalism, violence and homoeroticism of the primitives are openly avowed and principled. The New Guineans experience their myths as myths, while the tourists experience their myths as symptoms and hysteria. It should not go unnoticed that this is the exact opposite of the difference conventionally attributed to 'primitive' vs. 'modern.' An old man tells the story of the reaction to the arrival of the first ships carrying German colonists. This is a fascinating moment in O'Rourke's film because it marks the moment when the ex-primitive makes his move to the other side, to the side of the postmodern. He uncharacteristically mobilizes a strong *metaphor*, 'the tourists are like death,' which he deftly proceeds to explicate, situate historically, and render concrete. In listening to this story, neatly packaged as it is with its own interpretation, we must not forget that *death* for an old Iatmul warrior is close and real. The tour boat as the death star would be a fitting end to a tragic narrative. He tells the camera with a smile that his grandparents ran down to the river to look at the ship, shouting, 'Our dead ancestors have arrived! Our dead have come back! They have gone

someplace and gotten new faces and skin, and now they are back!'
And he continues, the sly grin never leaving his face, 'Now when
we see the tourists, we say the dead have returned. That is what
we say. We don't seriously believe they are our dead ancestors –
but we say it.' He might also believe it. It is possible to frame his
point with some theoretical precision: that the Western tourists are
indeed the embodiment of the spirit of dead cannibals.

One does not find among the tourists any similar lightness of
sensibility, and detachment from what might be taken as their
deepest insights. The woman in *Cannibal Tours* who is perhaps an
'art historian' from New York explains that after the 'disappearance' of Governor Rockefeller's son in New Guinea, 'I became an
exponent of primitive *art*.' The word 'art' as it escapes her lips
inscribes itself heavily on the film. At this embarrassing moment,
in searching for another place to look, the viewer's gaze may fall
upon her eyebrows which seem to have been penciled onto her
forehead with an almost brutal force. Again, there is the same
contrast with the New Guinea face-painting scenes where the
touch is always light.

Here is the only difference between primitive and modern, as
well as I can make it out from the materials at hand. The modern-
day tourists are incapable of a conscious detachment from their
values, a detachment that is the most evident feature of the New
Guinean images and discourse. As the tourists cannibalize the
primitive, they repress and deny the myth of modernity, so it
necessarily expresses itself always as an out-of-control force leading
to a kind of violence that has no ritual outlet. An Italian family
states, 'We must enter their villages as the missionaries did. We
must make them desire our values, our convictions, to teach them
something, to do things for themselves, to teach them to desire our
point of view, to make them want to wear our kind of clothes.' The
language of the Iatmul people is filled with concrete images of
violence: 'one of our spears went down the barrel of his gun... it
wouldn't fire, so we captured him and took his head.' The language of the tourists is filled with repressed violence: 'we must
make them want to wear our kind of clothes.' The 'art historian'
never confronts her own denial and suppression of the 'primitive'
on the Sepik and in her own soul. Instead, she states somewhat
shrilly as she buys artifacts, 'I for one think it is too bad if they
deviate [from their traditions] and work for tourism as such.' The

potential for evil and cruelty lurking unsaid in this statement is far greater than anything openly expressed by the old warriors.

THE CANNIBAL AND THE NEW CULTURAL SUBJECT

The figure of the cannibal in modernity

In the beginning, there was a type of error called parapraxis. When his Indian hosts said 'Cariba,' Columbus heard 'cannibal.' The error was no mere phonetic confusion of the sort that always occurs when people who do not share a common language try to converse. Columbus's hearing of 'cannibal' was guaranteed by his desire for success in his search for China – the teleotype of groundless desires. The Indians were trying to warn him about the Cariba, fierce inhabitants of neighboring islands, eaters of human flesh. Convincing himself that these must be the guardians of the outer boundaries of the Empire of the Great Khan, Columbus could only hear 'Khan-ibal.' It made sense to Columbus that those responsible for the first line of defense of the empire would have a reputation for hideous behavior. According to Todorov (1984: 30), who recounts this story, the Indians were well aware of Columbus's enormous mistake and tried to set him straight. In subsequent dialogue, Columbus would hear 'cane-bal,' or dog people, which he interpreted as a simple-minded effort on the part of the Indians to cover up the truth after they had divulged too much, willfully blinding himself to something that he knew perfectly well: that these people were not speaking a Romance language. His (mis)interpretation served to increase his certainty that he was on the threshold of his 'discovery.' Thus the word for 'cannibal' is overdetermined by a layering of error. It names the human practice of eating human flesh, and it also bears the mark of an initial refusal on the part of Europeans to learn from savages or even to acknowledge what they already know if it gets in the way of conquest.

Not quite one hundred years after Columbus's discovery, Michel Eyquem de Montaigne wrote an exemplary short text, 'Of Cannibals,' which secures the ethical and methodological ground of modern anthropology, better perhaps than anything written before or since. Montaigne based his comments on cannibals on the first-hand observation of a servant, a man whose objectivity was guaranteed by his simplicity: 'This man I had was a simple crude fellow – a character fit to bear true witness; for clever people observe more things and more curiously, but they interpret them; and to lend weight and conviction to their interpretation, they cannot help altering history a little' (Montaigne, 1943: 76). From his servant's eyewitness account, Montaigne would deduce that cannibalism is an act of courage, passion, and ultimate respect for the highest human qualities. The enemy is eaten for reasons of hatred, revenge, and desire to possess his strength and bravery. Assisted, perhaps, by the memory of his family's recent escape from the Inquisition, Montaigne's grasp of the ethnographic dialectic was instantaneous and certain. He discovered in the descriptions of the most reprehensible act of savages the basis for his critique of Europeans who had taught themselves to torture and kill dispassionately. 'I think there is more barbarity in eating a man alive than in eating him dead' (p. 85). Keeping a close eye on the victim, while never forgetting that they are cannibals too, Montaigne reports:

> there is not one in a whole century who does not choose to die rather than relax a single bit, by word or look, from the grandeur of an invincible courage; you do not see one who does not choose to be killed and eaten rather than so much as ask not to be.... These prisoners are so far from giving in, in spite of all that is done to them, that on the contrary, during the two or three months they are kept, they wear a gay expression; they urge their captors to hurry and put them to the test; they defy them, insult them, reproach them with their cowardice and the number of battles lost to their men. I have a song composed by a prisoner which contains this challenge, that they should all come boldly and gather to dine off him, for they will be eating at the same time their own fathers and grandfathers, who have served to feed and nourish his body. 'These muscles,' he says, 'this flesh and these veins are your own, poor fools that you are. You do not recognize that the substance of your ancestors' limbs is still contained in them? Savor them well; you will find in them the taste of your own flesh.'... Those that paint these people dying, and who show the execution, portray the prisoner spitting in the face of his slayers and making faces at them. Indeed, to the last gasp they never stop braving and defying them by word and look. Truly here are real savages by our standards;

for either they must be thoroughly so, or we must be; there is an amazing difference between their character and ours.

(pp. 86, 89)

Montaigne admires the cannibals for a concrete, as opposed to transcendent, humanism, for never giving up their honor, and for bestowing upon their enemies, in death, an ultimate compliment.

In his 1912–13 essays on *Totem and Taboo* (1950) Freud would ascribe to cannibalism even greater significance: civilization itself owes its existence to an original act of cannibalism. According to Freud, the incest taboo, religion, and morality appeared in the first place as a reaction against a terrible crime committed collectively, as ways of spreading the guilt and attempting to make certain that the original crime would never recur. He arrives at his double reconstruction of human pre-history and the collective unconscious via an attempt to account for the near universality of certain features of totemism: clan exogamy and the prohibition against eating the flesh of the totemic animal *except* under certain precisely defined ritual circumstances, the totem feast. Freud finds the clue to the riddles of totemism in Darwin's observations of behavior in animal groups in which the alpha male succeeds in intimidating and driving away all younger males, his own offspring, thereby securing for himself exclusive sexual access to the females, the mothers and sisters. Freud reasoned that if this arrangement is found among other mammals, there is no reason to believe that it was not also a characteristic of life among our humanoid ancestors, establishing the ground for the original collective crime that he reconstructs in the following terms:

One day the brothers who had been driven out came together, killed and devoured their father and so made an end to the patriarchal horde. United, they had the courage to do and succeed in doing what would have been impossible for them individually. (Some cultural advance, perhaps, command over some new weapon, had given them a sense of superior strength.) Cannibal savages that they were, it goes without saying that they devoured their victim as well as killing him. The violent primal father had doubtless been the feared and envied model of each one of the company of brothers: and in the act of devouring him they accomplished their identification with him, and each one of them acquired a portion of his strength. The totem meal, which is perhaps mankind's earliest festival, would thus be a repetition and commemoration of this memorable and criminal deed, which was the beginning of so many things – of social organization, of moral restrictions and of religion.

(Freud, 1950: 141–2)

Freud has given this story in the form of a myth, beginning with 'once upon a time' and ending with 'that is the origin of....' The perverse logic of myth requires that its language be made unbelievable in order to encode, protect, and preserve the deepest truths. And Freud's text is heavily marked by mythic unbelievability. But this should not obscure the range of phenomena neatly accounted for by his simple formulation: the seemingly contradictory theme of the son's hatred and admiration for the father; the denial of sexual access to the mothers and sisters as expiation for the guilt for having killed the father. The incest taboo is a collective agreement that no one should benefit from the original collective crime. And in addition to its strong explanatory powers, Freud's projection has the second advantage of having been proffered as a projection.

Ethnography would eventually bring scientists and cannibals face to face. After World War I, the ethnographic atlas had been filled in with sufficient detail that anthropological contact with cannibals (or 'recent ex-cannibals' as it is usually stated for the record) became purposeful and routine. Far from avoiding cannibals, anthropologists have been powerfully attracted to them, jealously guarding access gained, and begging for access denied. Papua New Guinea and its neighboring islands, home to head-hunters and cannibals, would eventually become the jewel of twentieth-century ethnography.[18] The scientific phase of contact with cannibals did not much diminish tendencies to fantasize about them. They remain the site of an unnamed desire. Compare Margaret Mead's plea to be allowed to leave the American Indian reservation where she was doing research to her excitement a year later after she was allowed to change her field study area to New Guinea. Following are excerpts from a letter she wrote to Ruth Benedict from the Omaha Reservation, July 21, 1930:

This is a very discouraging job ethnologically speaking. You find a man whose father or uncle had a vision. You go see him four times, driving eight or ten miles with an interpreter. The first time he isn't home, the second time he's drunk, the next time his wife's sick, and the fourth time, on the advice of the interpreter, you start the interview with a $5 bill, for which he offers thanks to Wakanda, prays Wakanda to give *him* a long life, and proceeds to lie steadily for four hours.... They are rich, know very little and fear death if they tell. And anyway, it's not worth getting. The head man of the Marble (Pebble) Society is a Carlisle *graduate* .... [T]hey aren't poor enough to be tempted by anything less than $25 or so, and then there is no check on their telling the truth.... Don't think I am a thankless wretch please. And scold me if you think I still deserve it and am overestimating the difficulties. It costs $100 here to join Peyote. Do you think it is worth doing? It seems dull. We've seen the peyote death ritual. I feel as if I had no sense of values left.

(*Letters from the Field*, 1977: 96–8)

And a letter to William Fielding Ogburn written soon after her arrival in Kenakatem, New Guinea, September 1932:

In the mind of the most suburban Rabaulite and in the mind of the wildest bush native, the Sepik stands for mosquitoes, crocodiles, cannibals and floating corpses – and I can assure you we have seen them all. We are not on the Sepik itself – that is Bateson's stamping ground – but on a tributary eighty-seven miles from the mouth of the Sepik which runs east into the Mandang area.... [T]he mosquitoes deserve their reputation; as for the rest, the crocodiles do eat people quite often, they make drawing water from the river at night a dangerous matter, they provide the art motif and a great model crocodile actually swallows the initiates, and most important of all, one can cook with crocodile eggs. 'Making corn fritters with crocodile eggs among the cannibals.' They were all cannibals until about four years ago; boys of twelve have eaten human flesh and they show merely a mischievous and merry glee in describing their previous diet but the idea of eating rats fills them with shuddering nausea. And we've had one corpse float by, a newborn infant; they are always throwing away infants here....

(ibid.: 130–2)

Part of Mead's motive for representing cannibals as slapstick comic characters may be based on a need to control her own fear, or to reassure her research committee at Columbia University that she was indeed capable of holding up under the physical and emotional demands of New Guinea fieldwork. To some degree, we can know that the lightness of tone is forced, especially in the comment on 'throwing away infants here.' When Mead wrote these lines, she had recently been told by her doctor (in error as it happened) that she would never be able to conceive and carry a child, news which she did not receive happily. Indeed she left her first husband when she heard it.[19] Even, or especially, if the giddy tone is partial cover for a personal tragedy, we must continue to wonder about the figure of the cannibal as a site for fantasy.

Cannibalism and 'community'

Cannibalism and the various responses to it, emotional and analytical, can be approached as prototypical of complex human solidarities. What is the value placed on other human beings across lines of social difference in and between human groups, differences that are thought by the people involved to be more absolute than any human difference need be? Every sociology that qualified as such attempted to provide a general answer to this question, the ultimate basis for the composite human group, the 'community,' the social 'tie,' or 'bond,' and its difference from other communities and groups. There is broad agreement in existing sociologies that social solidarity is bi-modal, having two forms that roughly correspond to the distinction primitive vs. modern.[20] It is a necessary component of the belief system of modern cultures, that cannibal practices are found only at or near the primitive/folk/Gemeinschaft/mechanical end of the continuum. Cannibalism is a kind of practical or applied science of social solidarity that antedates formal theoretical models. It provides a variety of concrete performative declarations concerning the value of the other.[21] A close examination of cannibalism as a site for modern fantasy also reveals a deep division in the modern/organic/Gesellschaft/ urban solidarity, which is suppressed or masked by the organic models.

Modern reflections on cannibalism can be assigned to two modalities, roughly the *symbolic* and the *economic*, which correspond to two types of modern solidarity or the ways modern peoples understand the ultimate grounds for human relationships. Montaigne wanted to inscribe cannibalism in the symbolic register. He tried to find, not so much in the act itself but in the behavior surrounding it, the basis for honor and courage. According to his way of accounting for it, in the dealings between cannibals and their victims, the other is a source of *knowledge*. Even the deepest hatreds and the most abject fears are overridden by care and concern about what the other *thinks*: the victim becomes dead proof that a human being is capable of maintaining dignity, pride, honor, and courage in the face of no matter what tortures, until the last breath. While it would be easy to demonstrate that Montaigne overstated the case for cannibalistic bravery in the face of certain death, it remains clear that he has named a real phenomenon that has not altogether disappeared even in modernity. It is said that when his executioners came to remove him from the cabin where he was being held, the revolutionary Che Guevara turned to his fellow prisoner, a journalist, and remarked, 'Why don't you come along and see how a man dies?'

Cannibalism and capitalist accumulation

The second mode of valuing the other, absolutely antithetical to the first, but fully integral to modern cannibal fantasy, is the other imagined to be a hoarder of wealth, ultimately as a repository of nutrients. According to this mode of accounting, which for reasons soon to become evident must always keep its motives secret even to itself, *death* is a way of improving the standard of living, the only way that does not require work. Each death is an occasion for the redistribution of material wealth, food, space, surviving mates, prestige, recognition, and everything that is valued, increasing the shares to the living. Mourning is the way the living give thanks to the dead for having turned over their share.

The capitalist fascination is for a particular cannibal fantasy with its own distinctive mythic contours. It is not Montaigne's cannibal with an unbreakable resolve to maintain honor. Rather, it is cannibalism as a crude but effective method of producing capital gain through legalized murder, plunder, and/or inheritance, and compounding the gains by eating the dead. In 1977, the distinguished anthropologist Marvin Harris published a book entitled *Cannibals and Kings: The Origins of Cultures*. His thesis, carefully argued and widely discussed, was that non-Indo-European peoples who, unassisted, made the transition to empire, gained their military and economic advantage from a dietary protein supplement of human flesh. Harris comments:

> As recently as fifty or a hundred years ago, small-scale sacrifice of prisoners of war and the redistribution of their flesh were

common practices in hundreds of pre-state societies scattered across Africa south of the Sahara, Southeast Asia, Malaysia, Indonesia, and Oceania. I have reason to believe, however, that the eating of human flesh was never an important aspect of the redistributive feasts in the cultures that immediately preceded the rise of states in Mesopotamia, Egypt, India, China, or Europe.

(Harris, 1978: 169)

I am not concerned with the correctness of this thesis on the role of cannibalism in the building of autochthonous African, Asian and Native American empires. Apparently there are questions that might be answered by specialists in ethno-history and comparative ethnicity. Although these inquiries are important in other ways, what interests me here does not depend on their outcome. What is interesting to the student of current socio-cultural arrangements, what I am calling the new cultural subject, is the depth of Harris's commitment not merely to an economic mode of accounting for human origins and the origin of empire, but to a particular economic mode that separates profit from work, that is, to capitalism, or rather to a mythification of capitalism as existing, in a sense, before human culture.

This commitment is evident in Harris's description of Aztec cannibalism. The Aztecs were the builders of the mightiest non-Indo-Greco-European empire. Therefore, according to Harris's thesis, they would also be, *ipso facto*, the greatest cannibals of all time. He reports on the dedication of the great pyramid of Tenochtitlan as recounted to Cortez by the Indians, an event that took place five years before the landing of Columbus: 'four lines of prisoners stretching for two miles each were sacrificed by a team of executioners who worked night and day for four days' (p. 158). Harris is faced with scant descriptions of Aztec cannibalism in the eyewitness record. He provides an explanation: the witnesses were distracted by the spectacle of sacrifice. He writes: 'conventional descriptions of the Aztec ritual of sacrifice end with the victim's body tumbling down the pyramid. Blinded by the image of a still-beating heart held aloft in the hands of the priest, one can easily forget to ask what happened to the body when it came to rest at the bottom of the steps' (p. 161). Following is Harris's mythified account of Aztec cannibal sacrifice:

[E]ach prisoner had an owner –*probably* the officer in charge of the soldiers who actually made the capture. When the prisoner was brought back to Tenochtitlan, he was housed in the owner's compound. *We know little about* how long he was kept there or how he was treated, but *one can guess* that he was fed enough tortillas to keep him from losing weight. *It even seems likely* that a powerful military commander would have kept several dozen prisoners on hand, fattening them up in preparation for special feast days or important family events such as births, deaths, or marriages. When the time for sacrifice approached, the prisoners *may have been* tortured for the instruction and amusement of the owner's family and neighbors. On the day of the sacrifice, the owner and his soldiers *no doubt* escorted the prisoner to the foot of the pyramid to watch the proceedings in the company of other dignitaries whose prisoners were being sacrificed on the same day. After the heart was removed, the body was not tumbled down the steps so much as pushed down by attendants, since the steps were not steep enough to keep the body moving all the way from top to bottom without getting stuck. The old men, whom De Sahagun refers to as Quaquacuiltin, claimed the body and took it back to the owner's compound, where they cut it up and prepared the limbs for cooking – the favorite recipe being a stew flavored with peppers and tomatoes [no citation or evidence given].... *There is some question* concerning the fate of the trunk with its organs and the head with its brains. Eventually the skull ended up on display on one of the racks described by Andres Tapia and Bernal Diaz. But since most cannibals relish brains, *we can assume that* these were removed – perhaps by the priests or spectators – before the skulls ended up on exhibit. Similarly, *although according to Diaz* the trunk was tossed to the carnivorous mammals, birds and snakes kept in the royal zoo, *I suspect that* the zoo keepers – Tapia says there were large numbers of them – first removed most of the flesh. I have been pursuing the fate of the victim's body in order to establish the point that Aztec cannibalism was not a perfunctory tasting of ceremonial tidbits.

(pp. 163–4, emphasis supplied)

What could cause a scientist to go on such a sustained flight of fantasy? It could not have been a desire to sensationalize his material to increase book sales. His entire anthropological training rigorously guards against sensationalism. It could not have been a desire to fudge his data to strengthen his case for having 'discovered' the hithertofore unknown extent of Aztec cannibalism. His own internal qualifiers (emphasized in the quote) belie any serious interest he might have in representing his account as some kind of proof. We can be certain of only one thing: Harris's quasi-real account of Aztec cannibal sacrifice is a projection of his sense of humanity, a desire to deepen the ethnographic record beyond the level of mere fact, to use ethnography and history as the point of departure for the discovery of 'universal' economic values. The empire-building cannibal is the totemic ancestor of modern-day (tribal) capitalism.

In the end, Harris's account is more useful than not in helping us to understand the new cultural subject. By linking cannibalism to capitalism, he opens the possibility for further analysis of the mythic base of current socio-economic arrangements.[22] This is a crucial move. Modern peoples incessantly tell themselves that they have no tribal ghosts controlling their behavior; that there are no mythic antecedents or implications to their economic activities. We are taught, and indeed we are supposed to believe, so there is a moral element here as well, that modern capitalism is a phenomenon *sui generis*. Modern decision making is based on a rational calculation of self-interest, guided by accurate accounting, devoid of passion, and so on. Modern economic institutions are aligned with science and free of historical coloration. The *imagination*, which might otherwise 'run wild,' has been restricted to specific functions and departments: in 'research and development,' among the 'creatives' in advertising, or locked in the 'suggestion box.' There is a strong normative requirement operating everywhere in the modern world that when one hears the word 'incorporation,' and 'corporate headquarters,' we are not supposed to think about cannibals and headhunters, at least not concretely. We are supposed to think metaphorically about business procedures, organizational matters, decision-making processes, policy implementation, and so forth. We are not supposed to question the origins of practical expertise in the handling of anal sadism. Harris has peeled back the metaphoric insulation around the modern political economy, a necessary first step in close critical examination of it as a cultural subject.

CANNIBAL POLITICAL ECONOMY TODAY

There are at least three current political-economic modes that can be classified as *neo-cannnibalism*; that is, as based upon and/or giving rise to, a consciousness and world view that is not easily distinguishable from classic cannibalism. These are found mainly on the 'political right', but they are not restricted to self-consciously right-wing political thought and action.

1 Ego-ecology

This is a particular response, that of cannibal/capital-ist incorporative solidarities, to the requirement that human groups enter into a more balanced relationship with nature; a response to demand for sustainable agricultural, mining, fishing, and forestry practices, for example. It can be characterized as a frightened-aggressive reaction to the ecological insight that humankind, the plants and animals, the water we drink and air we breathe, now primitive, peasant, and modern, are a single interdependent totality. According to cannibal/capital-ist logic, if we are all *one*, in order to survive as ego, it is necessary to incorporate *everything*, to leave nothing outside the self. Cannibal narcissism is concrete to the point of going beyond narcissism. It is not merely that everything is a mirror image of the self; everything, including other human beings, *is* the self. When such an all-inclusive being is thrown into the biosphere the only rule that governs its behavior is 'eat everything or risk being eaten.' This is the reason why 'kinder, gentler' capitalism and growing ecological awareness has been accompanied by increasingly vicious exploitation; the reason why we just witnessed the destruction of the original form of humanity, or its incorporation as a side show; and why we are now witnessing an aggressive attack on peasantry and nature at exactly the moment of heightened ecological insight concerning interdependence.

2 Putative heterosexuality

This designates the current practice, by no means universal but still pronounced in diverse groups and classes, of 'going through the motions' of heterosexual relations without any strong sense of the value of such relations: getting married for no particular reason except that others do it, 'because you have to,' and so on.

The absence of specificity in the arrangement between the sexes, and a corresponding tendency toward ritual avoidance of cross-sex relations outside of those specified by formal marriage contracts, is a strong theme of both contemporary and classic cannibal societies. All that is required in both kinds of society is that heterosexual relations should not be *conflictual*. The ideal is for 'relaxed,' 'cordial' relations marked by an absence of 'strain.' It is argued by those involved in these set-ups that a kind of minimal heterosexuality is necessary to free the men to organize themselves for the common defense and the common good, while at the same time insuring biological reproduction. Thus, at the highest levels of contemporary society little metaphoric cannibal CEOs speak, with only a touch of self-irony, of 'survival' in the corporate 'jungle,' of 'cut-throat competition' and 'picking each other's brains,' of corporate 'raiding' and 'headhunting,' of the 'men's club.' They may even fantasize about 'making a killing.' But these superficial references to classic cannibalism only reflect a failure of the modern imagination to come up with rhetoric of its own to mask male narcissism. There are also economic issues.

The particular type of 'balance' that is promoted by late or decadent capitalism is not solely dependent on an unavowed death cult; profiting from the death of another. Individual loss of wealth through its ever wider distribution can also be avoided by restricting the number of births. Theoretically, any method of birth control could contribute to this end, and every one has been tried, even institutionalized, including sexual abstinence, infanticide, contraception, and abortion. But it is the most certain form of contraception, *homosexuality*, with its more than metaphoric oral-anal common ground with cannibalism, that emerges as central in capitalist mythology, the subject matter of constant collective fascination. There is a near-perfect cultural basis for this fascination. Within the framework of capitalism, prestige, hierarchy, and power are based on external, visible accumulation. Male homosexual prestige, hierarchy, and power are a precise inversion of the capitalist mode: surplus and accumulation are radically internalized. The fit between the cannibalistic type of capitalism and the anal-sadistic type of homosexuality is so tight as to suggest that one is the sublimated form of the other.

The mythic/psychoanalytic framing of homosexuality does not necessarily have a great deal to do with *actual* homosexual practices or relationships. Culturally, it is a question of ideological express-

ions of homophobia (even by homosexuals) and its opposite; that
is, the promotion (even by heterosexuals) of homosexuality as a
superior form of sexual expression: for example, Greek revivalism
at the beginning of the industrial revolution; the idea that physical
unification of same-sexed partners is more satisfying than any
heterosexual 'mating' could ever be; or the notion that heterosexual relations are just 'breeding,' an essentially animal act, whereas
homosexuality is on a more spiritual, or philosophical plane.
Freud commented on homosexuals, 'They are men and women
who are often, though not always, irreproachably fashioned in
other respects, of high intellectual and ethical development, the
victims of only this one fatal deviation. Through the mouths of
their scientific spokesmen they represent themselves as a special
variety of the human species.... Of course they are not, as they also
like to assert, an '*elite*' of mankind...' (1966: 304–5). Against Freud,
I assume that it is possible to be a practicing homosexual without
necessarily believing oneself to be superior to heterosexuals in the
relevant particulars, just as it is possible for heterosexuals to exhibit
tolerance toward homosexual claims to be superior. This liberal
attitude is evident, for example, in Evelyn Fox Keller's (1985:
21–32) recounting of Plato's claims that sexual attraction between
two adult males is the highest form of love, and his further
suggestion that he owed his scientific creativity to a kind of sexual
discipline that he practiced, specifically his amorous involvement
with young boys that he stopped short of consummating, throwing
himself instead into his philosophical speculations.

The normalization of the ideology of homosexual superiority;
the prestige accorded to its adherents; the denigration of heterosexual pleasure, a denigration engaged in by homosexuals and
heterosexuals alike; the highly stereotypical way in which the fear
of homosexuality manifests itself and is represented; the *de facto*
establishment of the single-parent family as the social norm; the
aggressive experimentation with medical technologies that detach
reproduction from parenting; the promotion of arbitrary beauty
standards as the only basis for heterosexual attraction; all these
attitudes and actions are well developed among modernized peoples for whom capitalism is established as the only economic mode.
The sexual contract under cannibal-capitalism is a grudging
acceptance of heterosexual relations as a matter of reproductive
necessity. But heterosexuality is also widely regarded as potentially

disruptive of the kinds of solidarities that are necessary to advanced, late, or decadent capitalism.

Families and stable adult couples, including homosexual arrangements that resemble the heterosexual set-up (namely, long-term stable couples as opposed to the 'Tea-Room Trade' model), are 'dysfunctional' within the framework of corporate capitalism. It is not that sexually paired couples are likely to spend their time together plotting the overthrow of the symbolic order. It is a simple matter that couples and family members have a demonstrated capacity to entertain each other almost endlessly using only their bodies, facial expressions, gift for language, and the simplest of technologies. The preclusion of heterosexuality as a *social* form, as something other than a residual biological act, within late capitalism is overdetermined in the sense that it has more than one cause: (1) heterosexual relations threaten decadent capitalism because they potentially increase population size, reducing per-capita wealth, and (2) heterosexual arrangements, and any others modeled on them, disrupt the individual's attachment to 'higher' orders of organization: for example, the gang, the state, the corporation.[23] A man who can be entirely satisfied by the love and companionship of a woman is lost to the state. One reason the discrimination against women goes beyond anyone's ability to account for it is that they are being punished for their support of heterosexuality. Modernized men do not support heterosexuality, at least not rhetorically; and an emerging criterion for a certain kind of visible success, 'star' status, for professional women, is a public declaration of homo- or bi-sexuality, or at least a denial of interest in heterosexual relations and their associated cultural baggage, the family, the 'mommy track.'

Putative heterosexuality is not an avowed sub-theme of Marvin Harris's book on cannibals, but it is certainly manifest throughout. Every five or ten pages, we can read comments suggesting, either openly or in effect, that 'heterosexual relations' are the source of all human problems and the probable cause of cannibalism. For example:

> My aim is to show the relationship between material and spiritual well-being and the cost/benefits of various systems for increasing production and controlling population growth [p. xii].

Since heterosexual activity is a genetically mandated relationship upon which the survival of our species depends, it is no easy task to thin out the human 'crop' [p. 6].

Each advantage of permanent village life has a corresponding disadvantage. Do people crave company? Yes, but they also get on each other's nerves.... One must whisper to secure privacy – with walls of thatch there are no closed doors. The village is filled with irritating gossip about men who are impotent or ejaculate too quickly, and about women's behavior during coitus and the size, color, and odor of their genitalia [p. 16, no citation given].

Infanticide runs a complex gamut from outright murder to mere neglect. Infants may be strangled, drowned, bashed against a rock, or exposed to the elements. More commonly, an infant is killed by neglect [p. 22, etc. passim].

These quotations do not necessarily suggest an unconscious acceptance of the ideology of homosexual superiority, but they clearly indicate deep antipathy to heterosexual pleasures and especially to the methods heterosexuals have used to limit the number of births resulting from their sexual activity. As I have already suggested, this antipathy is by no means limited to Harris's text. Any attack on heterosexual modes of birth control, linked in the mode of the double bind to a simultaneous demand for a restriction of the number of births, fully supports the singular ideal of living off of capitalist accumulation, of not spreading the wealth and not inventing new ways of gaining a livelihood. Not surprisingly, so too is the official position of the party of decadent capitalism, the US Republican Party, which likes to dwell endlessly on the surgical details of abortion while holding that heterosexual reproduction should not be rewarded with welfare assistance, but should rather be punished with poverty; which mythifies a content-free ideal of *the traditional family* while fighting to hold the minimum wage to below poverty levels.

3 The doctrine of historylessness

Classic cannibals believed they had assimilated the courage and strength of their enemies, and through eating them, the powers of all of his own ancestors that they (the enemies) ate. The cannibal is the literal 'end of history,' the original 'post-historical' subject.

A certain measure of anxiety marks the recent declaration of the 'end of history' by Francis Fukuyama, deputy director of the US State Department policy planning staff in response to the disintegration of political regimes in Eastern Europe. The fascination that socialism holds for the officials of capitalist regimes, their fixation on the plight of their socialist enemies, precisely parallels cannibal conflict with its theme of triumphal incorporation, of ingesting the entire being of the enemy. Fukuyama writes:

> The triumph of the West, of the Western *idea*, is evident first of all in the total exhaustion of viable systematic alternatives to Western liberalism.... [T]his phenomenon extends beyond high politics and can be seen also in the ineluctable spread of consumerist Western culture in such diverse contexts as the peasants' markets and color television sets now omnipresent throughout China, the cooperative restaurants and clothing stores opened in the past year in Moscow, the Beethoven piped into Japanese department stores, and the rock music enjoyed in Prague, Rangoon, and Tehran alike. What we may be witnessing is not just the end of the Cold War, or the passing of a particular period of postwar history, but the end of history as such: that is, the endpoint of mankind's ideological evolution.
>
> (*National Interest*, summer, 1989: 3–4)

That this is a cannibalistic celebration of the incorporation of the enemy is immediately evident when one examines the original source of the 'end of history' idea. It does not come from the heart of liberal political or capitalist economic theory. It comes direct from Hegel and Marx. In Marxist doctrine, the name of the end of history is 'communism'; the end of history occurs after a successful socialist revolution wipes out the reason for class antagonism. The cannibal feast is evident in the *New York Times* editorial comments on the Fukuyama article: for example, when they repeat Fukuyama's phrase, 'The *Wall Street Journal* school of deterministic materialism'; or in the remark that 'Hegel... has become something of a fashion in Washington.' Fukuyama and the *Times* are attempting to swallow the enemy's doctrine whole, not bit by bit, as occurred, for example, when Reagan and Thatcher enjoyed referring to their political success at the polls as 'Revolutions.'

Interestingly, the politically conservative idea of the 'end of history' as a kind of appropriated Marxism, or right-wing

Marxism, is not new, and in fact it has a history. Whenever there is action on the left, whenever the left threatens to steal the 'head'lines in the capitalist West, as is occurring at present in the Soviet Union and Eastern Europe, a conservative ideologue steps forward and declares the end of history. The last time this happened was the student-worker rebellions in the United States and Western Europe in 1968, and the spokesperson was Allan Bloom, in his introduction to the English translation of Kojève's lectures on Hegel. Trusting perhaps more to the 'State' than anyone would today, Bloom summarizes:

> If thought is historical, it is only at the end of history that this fact can be known; there can only be knowledge if at some point history stops.... [T]he enunciation of the universal, rational principles of the rights of man in the French Revolution marked the beginning of the end of history. Thereafter, these are the only acceptable viable principles of the *state*. The dignity of man has been recognized, and all men are understood to participate in it; all that remains to do is, at most, to realize the *state* grounded on these principles all over the world; no antithesis can undermine this synthesis, which contains within itself all valid possibilities.... [P]ost-historical man with none of the classic tasks of history to perform, living in a universal homogeneous *state*.... is free,... has no work,... has no worlds to conquer, *states* to found, gods to revere, or truths to discover.
>
> (Bloom, 1969: x–xi, emphasis supplied)

Bloom is only trying to make certain that we do not miss the subtle handling of the 'end of history' idea as appropriated by the political right via Kojeve's 1938–39 lectures:

> The disappearance of Man at the end of history, therefore, is not a cosmic catastrophe: the natural world remains what it has been from all eternity. And therefore it is not a biological catastrophe either: Man remains alive as animal in *harmony* with Nature or given Being. What disappears is Man properly so-called – that is, Action negating the given, and Error, or in general, the Subject *opposed* to the Object. In point of fact, the end of human Time or History – that is, the definitive annihilation of Man properly so-called or of the free and historical individual – means quite simply the cessation of Action in the

full sense of the term. Practically, this means the disappearance of wars and bloody revolutions.

(Kojève, 1969: 158–9)

In the 1930s Kojève suggested that history would end in the United States, the first truly 'classless' society. (Note that for a 'Marxist of the right' classlessness does not imply that there are no *economic* classes, only that there is no longer widespread belief in the traditional privileges of aristocracy. So long as the poor think of themselves as the same kind of human beings as the rich, the society is technically 'classless' according to this view.) Later, in 1959, Kojeve would have occasion to update his view of the end of history, suggesting that history does not end in America but rather with the 'Japanization' of every other country:

From the authentically historical point of view, the two world wars with their retinue of large and small revolutions had only the effect of bringing the backward civilizations of the peripheral provinces into line with the most advanced (real or virtual) European historical positions. If the sovietization of Russia and the communization of China are anything more than or different from the democratization of imperial Germany (by way of Hitlerism) or the accession of Togoland to independence, nay the self-determination of the Papuans, it is only because the Sino-Soviet actualization of Robespierrian Bonapartism obliges post-Napoleonic Europe to speed the pre-revolutionary past. Already, moreover, this process of elimination is more advanced in the North American extensions of Europe than in Europe itself. One can even say from a certain point of view, the United States has already attained the final stage of Marxist 'communism,' seeing that, practically, all the members of a 'classless society' can from now on appropriate for themselves everything that seems good to them, without thereby working any more than their heart dictates. Now several voyages of comparison made (between 1948 and 1958) to the United States and the USSR gave me the impression that if the Americans give the impression of rich Sino-Soviets, it is because the Russians and the Chinese are only Americans who are still poor but are rapidly proceeding to get richer. I was led to conclude from this that the 'American way of life' was the type of life specific to the post-historical period.... It was following a recent voyage to Japan (1959) that I had a radical change of opinion on this point. There I was able to observe a Society that is one of a kind, because it alone has for almost three centuries experienced life at the 'end of history'.... 'Post-historical' Japanese civilization undertook ways diametrically opposed to the American way. No doubt, there were no longer in Japan any Religion, Morals, or Politics in the 'European' or 'Historical, sense of these words.... [I]n spite of persistent economic and political inequalities, all Japanese without exception are currently in a position to live according to totally *formalized* values – that is, values completely empty of all 'human' content in the 'historical' sense.... This seems to allow one to believe that the recently begun interaction between Japan and the Western World will finally lead not to a rebarbarization of the Japanese but to a 'Japanization' of the Westerners including the Russians.

(Kojève, 1969: 160–3)[24]

In short, according to Kojève, although he would never put it quite so simply, Japan is as far West as as one can go and still find fascism. Kojève precisely traces the genealogy of senile capitalism both forward and backward to the cannibal, designating the 'self-determination of Papuans' as marking the moment before the end of history. It is evident this cannibalistic capitalism, or 'Marxism of the right,' is worthy of attention as having enjoyed some success in transforming its vision of the world into political programs and public policies. In the summer of 1989, Fukuyama and his group in the US Department of State were working on the problem of how to make life interesting again, now that 'we have eaten the last cannibal,' precluding any future need for courage, imagination, and idealism.[25] Fukuyama comments:

[At the end of history] the struggle for recognition, the willingness to risk one's life for a purely abstract goal, the worldwide ideological struggle that called forth daring, courage, imagination, idealism, will be replaced by economic calculation, the endless solving of technical problems, environmental concerns, and the satisfaction of sophisticated consumer demands. In the post-historical period, there will be neither art nor philosophy, just the perpetual caretaking of the museum of human history. I can feel in myself, and see in others around me, a powerful nostalgia for a time when history existed.

(p. 18)

The 'intellectuals' of the right increasingly see it as their task to find ways of keeping the masses entertained or at least distracted now that there is no history for them to do. And, increasingly, they are looking to the entertainment value of drugs and crime as a way of putting excitement back into 'post-historical' existence. The *New York Times* summarizes: 'Mr Fukuyama's proclamation has produced a certain anticipatory fear that the West, having won, will fritter away its victory, seeking excitement and satisfaction in an ever more obsessive pursuit of wealth and sensation. In the post-historical epoch there will still be drugs and crime' (August 27, 1989: E5). They forgot to mention political spectacle or the 'news,' touristic travel, including cannibal tours, and wars staged as media spectacles.

At this point, it is necessary to remark to my colleagues in 'critical theory' who think they are working for a just cause, that it would be best not to continue to use the term 'the other': the political 'other,' the savage 'other,' and so on. The term 'other' itself is fully implicated in the same constellation of cannibal/capital-ist values that I am trying to describe. The use of the term 'other' (small 'o') promotes the self, ego, the first person singular, by pretending to do the opposite; that is, by bringing up 'the other.' The unmarked, undifferentiated 'other' is nothing other than the self-interested expression of ego masked with sociability: the 'discourse of the other' is the way a cannibal ego manufactures an aura of involvement with the world outside itself while neutralizing it. Cannibalism in the political-economic register is the production of social totalities by the literal *incorporation* of otherness.[26] It deals with human difference in the most direct way, not merely by doing away with it, but by taking it in completely, metabolizing it, transforming it into shit, and eliminating it. The metabolized 'other' supplies the energy for auto-eroticism, narcissism, economic conservatism, egoism, and absolute group unity or fascism, now all arranged under a positive sign and referred to by Fukuyama as 'a truly universal consumer culture that has become both the symbol and an underpinning of the universal homogenous state' (p. 10).

Cannibalism is a 'total social fact' that extends the range of application of Mauss's formulation one hopes 'beyond his wildest dreams.' In addition to having specific 'economic,' 'juridical,' 'aesthetic,' 'religious,' and other components as conceived by Mauss for 'total' social phenomena, cannibalism has medical and ecological aspects, and an element of disordered orality and anal sadism. In short, here is a total social fact that operates at the nexus of the 'primitive' and the 'modern' simultaneously in empirical social relations and in the unconscious. The routinization of the cannibal feast has produced a clear border region for homophobics and vegetarians who wish to be involved while at the same time manifesting some distance or detachment. Rousseau tried to warn us about this, as he tried to warn us about so many other things, with his figure of the great mouth of the 'sovereign' that devours everything.

It is characteristic of 'cannibal solidarity' that it is based on mutual complicity, on getting everyone involved in an economy of guilt. In Freud's (1950: 134) account, the food at the sacrificial meal (or totemic meal) was shared with the gods, but also communally, as a 'confirmation of fellowship and mutual social obligation.' The original terrible deed transforms into its opposite, the altruistic social bond. Consumers in capitalist societies today know that they do not need what they buy, but they also know that the entire system on which their, and their brother's, livelihood depends requires that they continue to consume what they do not need. What would have happened at Freud's primal picnic if one of the brothers had refused to partake, had, even if unsuccessfully, tried to talk the others out of it? What will happen today if some of us fight against the genocidal attack on peasants begun immediately after the successful annihilation of primitives?[27] Cannibal solidarity is designed against this contingency running deeper than anyone's conscious politics. It operates across the spectrum from the religious to the scientific; from 'This is my blood – drink it, this is my body – eat it,' to surgical organ transplants. Conscious opposition to cannibal solidarities does not automatically prevent unconscious supportive alignments with them.

Of course, all such alignments will manifest themselves symptomatically. For example, Nancy Chodorow, a humanist and scientist with strong sociological and psychoanalytic competencies, and a person of unimpeachable goodwill; in short, one who would seem to be incapable of it, nevertheless writes cannibal theory. For example, 'People inevitably incorporate one another; our sociality is built into our psychic structure and there is no easy separation of individual and society or possibility of the individual apart from society' (1989: 149). Judgment of such lapses must be tempered by an understanding that cannibalism today *is* a total phenomenon; that there is no publicly recognized alternative to the 'inevitable incorporation.' Cannibal incorporation is the original site of all exploitation. The corporations promote this 'inevitable incorporation' with an aggressiveness that can only be labeled 'savage.' For example, consider the following news item, entitled 'Genetically Engineered Calves Born,' from the *San Francisco Chronicle* (June 8, 1990):

> In producing the genetically engineered calves, which look no different from ordinary calves, scientists in the United States have now completed their goal of inserting foreign genes into the chromosomes of every important food animal.... Researchers expect the genes... to speed growth and make the cattle leaner. The four calves are a first step in understanding how direct genetic manipulation of the chromosomes of cattle will affect meat and milk.... US farm specialists say the technology holds vast promise for altering production practices and changing the structure of the $35 billion beef industry and the $20 billion dairy industry. For instance, cattle companies could sell to McDonald's beef animals specifically designed to produce more meat for hamburgers.
>
> (p. A–18)

Even though from a bio-technological standpoint a bamboo gene could have served as well, from the standpoint of cultural determinism it had to be a human gene: 'The team's first transformed calf was born March 17, 1989. The animal, now a husky 15-month-old bull, contains a human gene in its chromosomes' (ibid.). If everything goes according to the quoted scenarios of the bio-technologists, agricultural economists, and international food-marketing companies, 'billions' of humans will be served human genetic material in their Big Macs. Again, it is the normalizing tone of the news account, the strong sense that there is nothing unusual happening here, which is symptomatic of the pervasive cannibal unconscious.

NOTES

1 Earlier versions of the section of this chapter that treats Dennis O'Rourke's film *Cannibal Tours* appeared in *Anthropos*, 1988, and in *Visual Anthropology* (1990, vol. 6, n. 2: 14–24). The paper was also given as a Plenary Address to the International Conference on Culture and Communication, held at Carleton University on the occasion of the

opening of the new Canadian Museum of Civilization in Ottowa, April 5, 1989, and at the National Meetings of the American Folklore Society in October, 1990. The author wishes to thank Deirdre Evans-Pritchard for calling O'Rourke's film to his attention and the conference organizers for support.

2 See Mark Campbell (1989) for an interesting ethnographic description of intensive Hmong hunting and gathering practices in the San Joaquin Valley of California, and the criticism of these practices made by white sportsmen who pride themselves in using more 'natural' lures, baits, traps, tracking methods, and so on.

3 I pretend to no technical expertise when it comes to the economic structures of late capitalism. My understanding is limited to what I have been able to gain from reading Immanuel Wallerstein (1974), Alejandro Portes (e.g., 1977), Ernst Mandel (1978), and others. My interest is in contributing to the description of cultural forms associated with the global extension of advanced capitalism, the way human life is lived in its compass.

4 While I am aware of the very negative meaning this term can have, as in the phrase 'savage attack', I would like some leeway to use it in the French sense of 'wild,' as in 'wild flowers,' and in the popular sense of 'wild party,' without prejudice, meaning only undomesticated, or not tame. Montaigne wrote ('Of Cannibals,' 1943: 77):

> Those people are wild, just as we call wild the fruits that Nature has produced by herself and in her normal course; whereas really it is those that we have changed artificially and led astray from the common order, that we should rather call wild.

Understood in this way, I think 'savage' comes closer than 'primitive' to communicating a proper sense of the original form of humanity. Of course I am aware that some savages were 'savages' savages' or cannibals. There is a tendency today for cannibals to be seen as the 'model' savage even though this is far from being statistically true.

5 There may still be a small number of real savages left. They would be found among those who took flashlights, carbines, chainsaws, kerosene, matches, and a few other portable amenities and retreated further into the forest or set up a defensible position on their reservations. They would not be found among those who dress in 'authentic' costumes and demonstrate the use of bows and arrows for tourists.

6 For a similar argument from a Native American perspective, see Jack Forbes (1979).

7 The critical link between Freud and Hitchcock was made in a recent book by Slavoj Zizek (1988).

8 I am grateful to Juliet Flower MacCannell for having brought this important passage to my attention. Interestingly, in a text that otherwise treats rather arcane matters having to do with the philosophical implications of recent discoveries in quantum mechanics, it is this little aside that catches the eye of distinguished Yale professor F.S.C. Northrop, who repeats it in his own words at the beginning of his introduction to the Harper edition of the Heisenberg book:

[Heisenberg's theory] rests on philosophical as well as physical assumptions. When comprehended, these philosophical assumptions generate a personal and social mentality and behavior quite different from, and at points incompatible with, the family, caste and tribally centered mentality and values of the native Asian, Middle Eastern or African people.

(Heisenberg, 1958: 2)

9 Just as I was making final changes on this manuscript to send it to press, my country mounted an intense and sustained air attack on Iraq. Attempting to find words to support this military action, to give good reason for it, a syndicated news columnist describes it as

the studied punishment of an Arab nation whose crime is transgressing values enunciated most clearly by the United States, the symbol of Western political values and of cultural modernity. Iraq's fate in the fighting will demonstrate redundantly, that militarism is not an alternative to political modernization. In the modern age, military proficiency is increasingly a function of scientific, cultural and commercial modernity.

(Will, 1991: 10B)

10 This structure has been carefully described for the literary case by van den Abbeele (1984: 43–52). He comments, for example:

The voyage is an articulation of positions, a play of spaces, whose *sense* depends on the privileging of a single position (ideally the traveler's home).... Closure is attained by the coincidence of the point of departure with the point of arrival, thereby redefined as the point of return. On the other hand, the voyage can have value only if the points of departure and return are not rigorously coincidental.... The voyage of discovery, for instance, is justified if it succeeds in reaping the epistemological profit of an increased knowledge of the world.

(p. 43)

11 Few accounts of cannibals neglect to remark that they need exchange to buy pants. Montaigne ends his essay 'On Cannibals' with the words, 'All this is not too bad. But wait. They don't wear trousers' (p. 92). It should not come as any surprise that covering the penis is the first requirement for absorbtion in a new cultural arrangement in which hierarchy based on material wealth, with males at the top, is taken to be the 'natural' order. Any re-appearance of the penis in this context would reveal the ludicrous basis for the rather vast claims made on behalf of males. Primitive men can afford to expose themselves because so long as they live in a primitive condition, they have nothing to loose: men and women, the young and old, the rulers and the ruled all live in virtually the same material circumstances. But as soon as differences in material well-being become socially significant, the men begin to cover their 'privates': the wealthier, the more covered. The young man

in *Cannibal Tours* says simply that he needs money to buy the 'things I like,' and the woman says she needs it to send her children to school. But the powerful old men and the tourists always give the purchase of 'trousers' as the reason these almost ex-primitives need money.

12 A recent *San Francisco Examiner* (April 29, 1990: T–11) travel section description of a visit up the Sepik contains a report on an authentic postmodern attraction in Tambunum village:

> 'Margaret Mead lived here,' an old man in the village tells me. 'We have another anthropologist now. That is his house.' Jan adds that the present anthropologist has gone to Wewak, because 'Once a month he has to call his mother in New York to convince her that he hasn't been eaten by cannibals.'

13 Amply described by Mead (1972) and interpreted by James Boon (1985).

14 On the relationship between eating semen and such intelligence factors as ability to learn foreign languages, see Schieffelin, 1976: 124.

15 They also 'invest' in women. Initiated males marry girls who have not yet reached full maturity and assist them in growing their breasts, pubic hair, and so on, by feeding them semen. Herdt also collected this account of the meaning of vaginal intercourse with a barren woman as a failed investment:

> The womb [of a *kwoliku* or barren woman] – that's all – it is dry and closed. We [men] question – that semen – where does it go in the *kwoliku?* [Great laughter] Where does it go? The lovers fornicate for nothing.... A man who has no other *woman* [emphasis], he does it for nothing, to relax his penis, that's all. We wonder... does the semen go to the *tingu* of the *kwoliku?* She has no *kwalai'u-ketu* [emphasis].
> (Herdt, 1981: 194; ellipses, brackets and stress as in original)

16 See the reference to ramming out 'bad talk' in Herdt, 1981: 224. 'Bad talk' is the mother's nagging reprimands and insults that stultify and 'block his growth'.

17 Marshall Sahlins (1976: 166–79) has provided an alternate, more normative, 'vegetarian' solution to the problem of the cannibalistic drive in contemporary culture. He refuses to use the term 'frankfurter.' For him, they are only 'hot dogs.'

18 For a helpful analysis of the New Guinea and other Pacific materials that understands ethnography to be a constitutive part of the new cultural subject but does not resort to the kinds of evasions that sometimes mar the other 'Writing Culture' accounts by anthropologists, see James A. Boon, 1985 and 1990.

19 As told by her daughter, Mary Catherine Bateson, in her (1984) autobiographical memoir of her famous mother and father (p. 14). When Margaret herself wrote her own autobiography she would recall the dead baby in the river in quite different terms:

> Most difficult of all for me to bear was the Mundugumor attitude

toward children. Women wanted sons and men wanted daughters, and babies of the wrong sex were tossed into the river, still alive, wrapped in a bark sheath. I reacted so strongly against the set of the culture that it was here that I decided that I would have a child no matter how many miscarriages it meant.

(Mead, 1972: 238)

20 See the discussion of Durkheim's mechanical vs. organic solidarity, Tonnies's gemeinschaft and gesellschaft, and Redfield's folk-urban continuum in the 'Theoretical Afterword'.
21 Teresa Porzecanski (1989) argues that in American Indian cannibalism, the primary value of the other was medicinal.
22 It should be repeated here that for Harris, this linkage is necessarily only metaphoric. He repeatedly asserts that the ancestors of Indo-European peoples did not practice cannibalism. He prefaces his section entitled 'The Lamb of Mercy' with these words:

The availability of domesticated animal species played an important role in the prohibition of cannibalism and the development of religions of love and mercy in the states and empires of the old world. Christianity, it may yet turn out, was more the gift of the lamb in the manger than the child who was born in it.

(Harris, 1978: 166)

23 The idea that capitalism is the economic form of repressed or sublimated male homosexuality recently received ethnographic support in D.K. Feil's (1987) excellent comparative ethno-historical study. Feil argues that in avowedly homosexual New Guinea communities, surplus and accumulation of material wealth is never honored. They conceive of surplus and accumulation (of semen and manliness) as a secret, male-to-male, fully internalized matter that can never be revealed to the entire community. Ritual homosexuality declines, however, as pig husbandry is introduced and economic surplus and accumulation properly so-called replaces the 'spermatic economy.' Homosexual practices continue but not as an official part of the ritual order, as required in male initiation ceremonies, for example.
24 Interestingly, Fukuyama, who is openly dependent on Kojève for his ideas, asks his readers to 'see' the note quoted above, then provides the following odd gloss on it:

I use the example of Japan with some caution, since Kojève late in his life came to believe that Japan, with its culture based on purely formal arts, proved that the universal homogenous state was not victorious and that history had perhaps not ended.

(Fukuyama, 1989: 10)

My reading of Kojève is that he suggests the opposite: namely, that history ended first in Japan, and the Japanese, as the oldest 'post-historical' society, will eventually come to be recognized as the model for the rest of the world. Perhaps Fukuyama deflects understanding of Kojève at this point motivated by a nice sense of modesty surrounding his own ethnic identification with the original 'historyless' culture.

25 I am indebted for this phrase to Slavoj Zizek (1990: 89–110), who argues that the 'eating of the last cannibal' is the precondition for the establishment of the rule of law and the grounds for the 'split subject' of the law, the fact that it has a 'neutral, solemn, pacifying, and sublime' side, and also an oppressive, nasty (he calls it 'mean' and 'obscene') side. Zizek relates: 'In response to the question of explorers researching cannibalism, the native answers: "No, there aren't any more cannibals in our region. Yesterday we ate the last one"' (p. 97).

26 Alternatives to cannibal solidarity are found in dialogic and exchange models: in Bakhtin's 'dialogism,' Mauss's *The Gift*, Saussure's semiotic, Goffman's interaction theory, and Lacan's 'symbolic register.'

27 For a strong account by one such fighter who lived to write her first-hand description of the current military genocide against the Guatemalan Indians, see Manz (1988).

Chapter 2

Orange County, Yugoslavia[1]

> Think of how much of the Hegelian dialectic might be summed up, as an overall title, in the idealist Coleridge's favorite proverb, 'extremes meet.'
>
> (Kenneth Burke)

AUTOBIOGRAPHICAL COMMENT: WHY I DID NOT VISIT DISNEYLAND

When I was 18 or 19 and in my early 20s, I drove past Disneyland many times, cruising the freeways of Orange County in southern California, but I never stopped.[2] I knew that this was the pilgrimage center of fundamentalist capitalism, Mickey Mecca, and that terminally ill children often expressed their desire to visit Disneyland before they died, as their 'last wish.' At age 19, this seemed to me reason enough not to go. But there were still more personal reasons for my resistance. At that time, I was active in mountaineering – I passed Disneyland most often on my way to meet other climbers in the southern Sierra. From my moving vantage point on the freeway, all I could see of the park was the huge plaster model of the Matterhorn sticking up above the fences. Each time I saw the fake mountain, I thought of the four climbers who perished in the Whymper party when their rope broke on their return from the first successful ascent of the real Matterhorn in 1865. Disneyland became associated in my mind with death. Disney's Matterhorn itself reminded me of the grotesquely distorted plaster 'death masks' I had seen in museums. It made no sense to me, at the time, that someone would want to make a death mask of nature.

Disneyland is also the palace of little hyper-real celluloid animal deities, not dead, and not alive either. Mickey Mouse and his friends are an evident reprise of American Indian mythology. But in Disneyland, the animals appear as a virtual inversion of the mythic Indian figures. At Disneyland they are innocent, stupid, and entertaining, not willful, crafty, and instructive. The thematic outlines are the same for the Indian spirit quest and the touristic visit to Disneyland: both involve a sacred journey to a distant objective to obtain a few precious words from a protective animal spirit. But the libido, energy, and wealth are flowing in the opposite direction at Disneyland, not into the youth as a special kind of power, but from the youth into the park as a special kind of place. As a quasi-religious center, Disneyland bears too strong a resemblance to other similar places before it: it was built on a violent denial or suppression of the religious beliefs of the people who had previously occupied the same site.

In 1960, in my sophomore version of dialectical materialism, I 'read' Disneyland both as a suppression, and as a false excuse for the failure of the surrounding society. If the freeways of southern California are jammed up, the monorail at Disneyland moves with perfect precision. If the people in the neighboring communities are condemned to live in their own waste, 'Main Street USA' at Disneyland is pristine. If society has become violent, in Disneyland there is peace. If society has become too commercialized and materialistic, at Disneyland one can get by on discount 'Disney dollars.' If California seems to have no center or reason, Disneyland at least beckons as a center, real place, or destination. In other words, Disneyland's reason for existence is to 'prove' that capitalist social reality is some kind of weird accident that should not be associated with actual political and economic relations: the heart of the system is pure and good.

In 1981 I spent five months in Orange County making ethnographic field observations. I visited Disneyland once, especially to see the 'Music Fountain' at the Disneyland Hotel, because it was the attraction my respondents in nearby communities, the 'locals,' often mentioned as the one they enjoyed the most.

WHY I VISITED ORANGE COUNTY

Coleridge's favorite aphorism, 'extremes meet,' at first appears as a liberal way of obscuring distinctions and foreclosing arguments. Extremes may eventually meet and even merge, but only in the

realm of myth, and then only under conditions where consciousness of contradiction in thought and life is totally repressed.
Nowhere in America, I think, is everyday life more mythical, the
contradictions more extreme or more repressed, than in Orange
County, California. In the 1950s, before Disneyland was built,
Orange County, just south of the city of Los Angeles, was rural and
suburban. Today, it is densely populated with almost 3 million
souls. It is also ethnically diverse, with communities composed
almost entirely of Vietnamese refugees in Garden Grove, Mexican
American communities in Anaheim, thousands of Cambodian
refugees living on Minnie Street in Santa Ana, and so on. But it is
not the 'demographic reality' of Orange County which interests.
Nor is it anymore even Disneyland. It is the mythic side of Orange
County, south of freeways, the blond side – John Wayne Airport,
the Irvine Company, Newport Center, Fluor Corporation, and the
matrix of 'up-scale' housing developments in which these corporate structures are embedded.

   This is the side of Orange County responsible for its *Zeitgeist*, its
self-appointment as the geographic capital of conservative ideology in America today. The people of south Orange County openly
express their political conservatism. They freely state their hostility
to 'big government' and are proud to explain that this was the first
place to be known as 'Reagan Country.' State Senator John
Schmitz, who represents this area, was elected to public office after
disclosing his membership in the ultra-conservative John Birch
Society. Savvy political analysts suggest he was elected, not in spite
of, but *because* he confessed to being a Bircher. On this side of the
freeways, the communities are mainly white; the 1980 US census
gives the population of the city of Irvine as 62,134 inclusive of 916
'black' individuals.

   The social and historical origins of Orange County conservatism are clear enough. The last mass migration of white people into
southern California was from the Bible Belt in the 1930s, dust bowl
migrants from Arkansas, Missouri, and Oklahoma. They arrived
poor but became, if not wealthy in every case, at least middle class
and better off than the Mexican Americans with whom they share
the region. Theirs is not a Philadelphia, Mainline, or New York,
Wall Street-type conservatism based on clear class divisions and
the preservation of traditional privilege. It is a petit bourgeois
conservatism based on trivial distinctions, hair color, automobile
'detailing,' whether or not one's children can afford cocaine (as

opposed to 'déclassé' marijuana), or a few thousand dollars' difference in the average price of the same model home in adjacent tracts.

There are visible contradictions on the surface of this life, most of them silly or a little bit sad. In suburban neighborhoods, otherwise strongly anti-romantic in design practice, one finds the street names 'Goldenglow,' and 'Hon.' The latter is not named for a Laotian general, but is thought to be a slang contraction of 'Honey,' a term of endearment. 'Pro-family' Senator Schmitz, who is author of legislation limiting sex education in the schools, has a 'honey' living here. In 1982, Schmitz had both a family and a mistress living in two adjacent Orange County housing tracts. We learn of this when the mistress, who was described in the newspapers as 'a longtime Republican Party volunteer,' was arrested for having mutilated the genitals of one of the senator's illegitimate sons (*Sacramento Bee*, July 21, 1982: A3).

The arrangement that Schmitz had is ethnologically unremarkable. It would be commonplace in Africa, for example. But this is certainly not the way in which the Schmitz family would want to understand itself. The fundamental feature of the Orange County ethos is the difference and distance between public self-understanding and the barely repressed underlying passions. What is socially important in Orange County is not actual values, but the public expression of inflated values. Bumper stickers on silver and black BMW and Honda sedans proclaim 'God Loves Me,' and 'My Other Car is a Mercedes Benz.' Orange County is also a place where some 'spec-built' houses are made twice normal size, on the plan of English country houses, and named by their developers before they are sold, 'Claredon Hall,' and so on. The people who live in these over-sized tract homes sometimes imagine themselves to be *Gentry*, which is the name of *The Magazine of Orange County People* (published by Gentry, Inc., Costa Mesa, CA). A newspaper survey (*Orange County Register*, April 16, 1985) reports that the main cause of mental depression in Orange County is 'money worries,' and the way respondents generally relieve 'deep depression' is by going shopping.

These are mere surface contradictions, the sorts of things that could happen in any community in a hurry; matters that time, an election, or a little cosmetic surgery can heal. There are other contradictions in the mental life of Orange County that are not susceptible to an easy fix.

There is no clear line where the earth meets the sky in Orange County. The soil is sandy loam, excellent drainage for growing citrus. There are places where one can run one's fingers through the dirt without resistance. And the same could almost be said of the sky. Super-saturated with automobile emissions, it is brown and heavy, more substantial than the San Gabriel mountains which it can hide even on a cloudless day. This local absence of a distinction (earth/sky), fundamental to consciousness in other communities, in American Indian communities, for example, is the first indication of the way the Orange County mind defends itself against the requirement of clear thinking. This mind survives contradiction by rejecting fundamental distinctions, accepting only minute and particulate matters. The Orange County mind identifies itself with the dirty indistinction of its earth and sky and shields itself with shining surfaces. It is dirty on the inside, while assiduously maintaining sparkling exteriors. Once thought has moved itself to inhabit the framework of Orange County consciousness, every sign is drained of meaning and is only self-referential. Thus, the revelation that Senator Schmitz had two families at the same time, seven children in one and two in the other, a wife and a 'mistress' living in separate households a few miles apart, provided no scandal.[3] Nor was there any scandal as a result of the revelation that the 'mistress' was not a fully competent mother. Schmitz had only to make public re-affirmation of his conservative views and the evident passion leading up to the affair was buried. In fact, he was able to seize the disclosures as an opportunity to make anti-abortion speeches and to affirm his credentials as a 'good family man.' Schmitz represents Orange County in both literal and metaphoric senses.

In this system of expression, auto-referentiality is all that counts. We are to accept everyone's public self-accounting at 'face value,' never subjecting the circumstances of life to alternative re-interpretation. Owning a Porsche is supposed to mean that the owner is affluent, not insecure. The question 'Why?' is taboo. Passions that bind and separate one person from another exist as they do in all human communities, but in Orange County they disappear in a literal and metaphoric smog.

Automobiles, invested with as much symbolic and libidinous importance here as anywhere else on earth, brilliant in every other way, are typically colorless. More than this, they are intentionally colored colorless. By overwhelming preference, they are metallic grays with just enough of a true color added to produce a mysterious hint of some possible color. They are pure shining essences reflecting commitment to the appearance of cleanliness and precision but without any statement or mood. A true red or blue, anything that might lend itself to political or other interpretation is avoided. This valorization of vagueness when it comes to basic values extends itself to the total arrangement of the housing tracts. The streets meander in overlapping spirals and ellipses. The total design is purposefully centerless; that is, without absolute internal distinction.

This is not merely a local aberration: Orange County is also being held up as a model for the future development of Western Civilization; even more, 'a kind of hypersuburbia,' Orange County is, as a southern California businessman put it, 'a demonstration city for the world' (Zalaznick, 'The Double Life of Orange County,' *Fortune*, October, 1968: 139). This suggests we might learn something about the future, and perhaps gain some control of the future, by studying what is distinctive about Orange County values and the form of their expression, especially in politics where they are providing models that go beyond the county line.

Orange County is ur-form of 'community' organized around conservative, anti-government, anti-socialist values: a monument to individualism, private initiative, and 'freedom.' This is not to say that everyone who lives there subscribes to these values. Only about 70 per cent voted for Reagan, for example. But the organization of the communities is the most perfect expression of conservative values, even for those residents who would disagree, as those who disagree, especially, would affirm.[4] In the precise form of its local expression, this is a guilty ideology at best. We can quickly learn from the revenue balance sheets that 75 per cent of the wealth of the area comes directly from 'big government' in the form of contracts to industry and support to the El Toro Marine Corps Air Station.[5] The same contradiction appears in the appeal of a Costa Mesa tax consultant which approvingly quotes former President Ronald Reagan: 'Are you entitled to the fruits of your own labor, or does the government have some presumptive right to spend and spend and spend?' Then, in the same appeal, separated from the President's words by only one period (.), the consultants claim that they can show you how to extract wealth from the poor: 'You legally avoid taxes.... Uncle Sam will buy an apartment for you, stock it with tenants, pay 75 per cent of their rent, give you $100,000 in legitimate tax deductions over a five-year period, guarantee you rehabilitation loans and eliminate 99 per cent of the risk' (*Gentry*, Holiday edition, 1984: 11). Apparently, in the smog of the Orange County consciousness, it is okay for an avuncular government to 'spend and spend and spend' for evil purposes, that is, to set you up as a slum lord. The psychology is obvious: once the original contradiction is repressed, its ill effects are also hidden, or even transformed into beneficial results. The advertisement ends on an up-beat: we will tell you how to exit the shelter and 'turn a problem into a huge profit.' The conservative ideological attack on 'big government' is a simple displacement, a pre-emptive strike against the government as a way to avoid having to credit government for schemes and accomplishments they want to call their own.

In Orange County ideology, the existence of another class, somewhere on the other side of the freeways, a tenant class that you can 'stock' your apartments with, is always assumed. There is never a direct confrontation with significant human differences or positive principles, especially those that might be widely shared, for example, a commitment to social equality. There cannot be. The idea of equality necessarily produces an anxious vacillation in the Orange County mind as any serious concern for equality might expose their pseudo-solidarity with exploited classes with whom they pretend to unite against 'big government.' Instead, there is an attack on socially progressive methods. The way social workers, social scientists, and socialists want to achieve their version of 'equality,' according to Orange County myth, is by suppression of individual expression, privacy, private initiative, by making humankind 'un-free.' This is a crude psychological appeal to Americans who have proved themselves highly susceptible to precisely these kinds of manipulations that are attributed to 'socialists': namely, a willingness to give up individualism in a desperate drive toward standardization of thought, behavior, and aesthetic display. In short, they find in their alienation from their own passions, from the greed and lust that they cannot acknowledge even to themselves, in their own self-imposed lack of freedom at the level of appearances, exactly what they think they should fear most, not from themselves but from 'Socialism.'

This contradiction and the false consciousness which covers it up manifests itself at every level of thought, behavior, and organization in Orange County. The city of Irvine, a place now grown to more than 150,000 souls trapped behind the corporate curtain, was centrally planned in every detail, including precisely controlled social class composition. An official Irvine Chamber of Commerce information bulletin mailed in reply to a query from a prospective migrant to the area reads, in part, as follows:

If you are looking for a great place to live – Southern California style [try] Irvine, Calif. Uniformly designed homes in Irvine, Calif., are controlled by the strictly enforced rules of the planned community. In this cluster of quiet villages the scent of the Pacific freshens the air above homes all painted in earth tones.... Life is zoned by master plan around the university campus, industrial parks, living and recreation areas, green belts and small shopping centers. Residents may observe the five-member City Council in action from their homes, all wired for cable TV. Neighborhood committees make sure that dwellings are painted in bland colors and that lawns are trimmed. Even the citizenry is fairly homogeneous: surveys show that 56 per cent of all families have annual [1982] incomes of $40,000 or more, 73 per cent own their own homes and most household heads are college graduates. Some may find the uniformity overpowering, but to most it is a small price to pay. The schools are rated superb. Crime, though a problem, is not rising as fast as the population. Urban fears are no part of life in Irvine. Says language teacher Susan Salessi: 'I feel very safe. I don't have to drive long miles to work, to the beach, to enjoy all the cultural activities I could want. Here I have everything.'
(Sent to the author in an informational packet on Irvine Chamber of Commerce letterhead)

Irvine, built from scratch on a former ranch, is a perfected Levitt Town type of community jointly owned by the Taubman-Allen Irvine Company, Mobil Oil Corporation, Donald A. Bren, Henry Ford II, and several others. The land within the community was arranged, in advance, according to formula: 1.5 per cent for a new university, 40 per cent for housing stratified by class, 30 per cent for agriculture, 5 per cent for industry, and 25 cent for park and wild land. 'Problems' experienced by natural communities were planned out. There is no housing for the poor. The effect of industry on residential property values has been controlled. If there happened to be appropriate housing available near the university, students might remain in Irvine for longer than they are in school, potentially giving the place a shabby, leftist character. So the area immediately surrounding the Irvine campus is purposefully kept free of all development. The entire urban space is organized according to the concerns of corporate planners, an 'ideal' or literally ideological community with the 'social problems' of natural communities solved in advance.

This set of ideals extends itself to the level of individual households and family life in the form of total subservience to corporate central control. The homes, clean and comfortable with 'many luxury touches,' come in four or five models per tract which repeat themselves along the landscaped streets according to formula: ABCD, ABCD, ABCD, etc. While these homes are technically 'privately owned,' because their ownership is in the hands of individuals, not corporations, freedoms traditionally associated with private home ownership no longer exist. One finds, for example, restrictive rules binding home owners vis-à-vis such matters as the species of shrubbery which can be planted in the yard, the types of dogs they can own, as well as the already mentioned color restrictions on house exteriors. There is a general rule operative throughout the area, rigorously upheld by covenant and collective agreement, 'earth (that is, dirt) tones throughout,' an only partially repressed color bar, based on the prevailing folk theory that bright or primary colors are associated with 'colored' people and other minorities known for unrestrained expression. The Chamber of Commerce document mentions that every house is wired for cable television. It does not go on to state that no house may display an external television antenna. Recreational vehicles and small boats cannot be parked visibly on driveways or in the streets in front of the home (they must be stored in special lots), cars cannot be left with their bonnets open, even on private drives (all automotive repair must take place in closed garages), and so on.

While nominally espousing 'privacy,' 'private property,' and 'private enterprise' as primary values, false consciousness reveals itself at the level of architectural detail. One notes immediately that the most elaborated, over-scale, and over-decorated part of these homes is not the 'back region': dens, children's bedrooms, or other truly private spaces. It is the entry hall. Every procedure has been employed to make these entrances the most impressive part of the house: hand-carved, double-doors 5 meters tall; Italian tile floors; fountains and full-sized palm trees just inside; 'cathedral' ceilings with crystal chandeliers hanging from gold ropes, and so forth. The entire ensemble is designed to impress the paper boy or cosmetic sales person and others who visit infrequently and do not penetrate the children's cramped quarters in the back. In short, the house is designed to impress strangers. In architectural reality, which is one of the 'realest' forms of reality, public opinion is again valued highly, and that which is private is repressed.

The rules constraining home owners in Irvine read much like those which occupants of military base housing must sign before moving in, and for good reason. The corporate executives who are the 'owners' of these homes must operate in a rigid framework of control extending from small details of life (length of facial hair and front lawn) to its total organization; for example, periodic interstate and international transfer required to maintain one's place on the 'corporate ladder.' In addition to the requirement of moves by corporate transfer, families also face disruption by divorce and other voluntary intra-regional moves driven by desire to live in a marginally 'better' place. And even if none of this happens in one's own family, it is a dominating concern in any network of friends. One can visit homes in Irvine where the family expresses pride that they have lived for several years with thick sheets of clear plastic spread over the carpets, cleverly increasing the resale value of the house, they believe. No urban-based Eastern Europeans subjected themselves to more restriction at the level of everyday life. It might be argued that Orange County 'un-freedom,' extending into one's own home and beliefs, cannot be compared to socialist central control, because in Orange County, it is fully accepted and desired by everyone as contributing to the common good and is not, therefore, totalitarian in character. This is precisely the argument that loyal party members in East Germany or Yugoslavia gave for their regimes before the people expressed themselves differently on the same matter.

Nowhere in the world can one find an airport recording ('the white zone is for loading and unloading only') that speaks with greater authority than the one at the John Wayne Airport. And if, in mid-week, one should happen to leave the airport on foot and try to find a motel room nearby, there is nothing for less than $150.00 per night for a single with brown plastic furniture. When confronted on this point, the motel staff will quickly agree that no individual person should ever have to pay such high rates, but they argue that no individual ever actually pays his or her own bills.

Everyone is on a company account. That is why the rates can be so high. Sometimes the person staying overnight on a company account ultimately works for the same conglomerate of corporations which own the motel. One recognizes the pattern immediately: it is socialism, a kind of international corporate socialism which has the same base and affects as the other kinds: central control and total economic dependence leading to mental incompetence; corruption; unearned privilege for the 'party loyal'; blind acceptance of all prevailing values.

Orange County was not my first experience with totalitarianism. In the 1960s I visited Yugoslavia and saw immediately that any romantic ideals I might have held concerning socialism were clearly wrong. The roads of Yugoslavia were also filled with Mercedes-Benz and BMW sedans of party officials. I was detained often by the police on small pretexts. Once I was with ten or fifteen people arrested at dusk in a remote rural area for riding in the back of a truck licensed to transport commercial goods, not humans. The confusion attracted a large group of peasants who had been working in the fields nearby. They gathered around. I saw an opportunity and seized it. The corrupt police were now surrounded by socialist peasants, even tougher appearing than the police themselves. It was a populist issue. Why shouldn't the people ride free so long as the truck was empty? So I purposefully escalated the conflict, raised my voice, snatched my passport back, and insisted that everyone be set free. The peasants joined in and began yelling and growling and brandishing their crude tools. It worked, I thought, and was elated until I realized that the peasants had joined in on the side of the police: socialist false consciousness.

In Zagreb as in Irvine it was also difficult to find a room. The one 'tourist' hotel was too expensive. But there were black market rooms to be had for pennies. Someone would lead the way through labyrinthine alleys, looking furtively about, perhaps for the police. The path would lead eventually to a couch or spare bed in a worker's apartment and perhaps a light supper of hard bread, tomatoes, oil and sweet basil. Extremes meet: there is corporate socialism in Orange County and free enterprise in Yugoslavia.

For the average-person-in-general today the difference between capitalist and socialist modes of production is not a real one. It is felt mainly as the dominant form of ideological expression, a pure abstraction which is lived as a myth. If you live in Orange County you must be certain that under socialism you would be 'un-free'; if you live under socialism you must be certain the capitalists exploit the working classes and use force to maintain their historical advantage. But in Orange County you learn to live without freedom while pretending otherwise, and in Yugoslavia you learn to be a capitalist.

One might ask how thinking subjects can live with this much contradiction. In the case of Orange County, the people seemed to be sustained by a crude sensuality, perhaps also derived from their Bible Belt heritage, an equation of sex, dirt, and power. I observed two sun-tanned women, a mother and daughter with matched, platinum-tipped hair and nails, wearing designer tennis outfits, driving a new Mercedes convertible, the one with the largest engine. They were the perfect embodiment of Orange County bourgeois respectability, but their personalized license plate revealed the aggressive crudeness that seems as basic to Orange County life as the contradiction itself. The plate read 'WAY 2 GO' and beneath, on the custom frame, 'Anything Else Sucks.' The same psychology has been raised to a science of display in the 'model' homes which are shown to prospective buyers. These homes are over-decorated with wallpaper and furniture and purposeful 'lived in' touches. Among the latter, one notes a pair of men's pants, with belt in loops, draped over the back of a chair in every second room. These are not just model homes, they are also places where we are supposed to think that men come to remove their pants. Perhaps the license plate is right. It gives the standard answer to the question of how to live a contradiction: have a dirty mind.

NOTES

1 This chapter is based on transcriptions of tapes made of a lecture I have given since 1982 in my introductory course, 'The Community.' This material has not been previously published.

2 There is excellent literature by theorists and others who did take the trouble to visit Disneyland. Refer, for example, to Marin (1984), Eco (1986), Jameson (1984), Baudrillard (1988), Gottdiener (1982), Boorstin.

3 'Conservative politician involved in sex scandal' is a virtual myth-theme or 'tale type' in modern culture which is reason enough to attend to the details of any given example. The language used in this particular disclosure is instructive. Given the facts of the relationships that occurred here (Schmitz's son and daughter-in-law by his 'wife' explained that they were 'god-parents' to the 'illegitimate' children of

the 'mistress'), I would have preferred to use the more sociologically accurate phrase 'wife and wife' in this sentence. The English language is very nicely set up to cover for male bigamists in a way that it cannot cover for female bigamists, this being only one of its built-in gender inequalities.

4   One hesitates to base a sociology on the 'group mind' concept, especially in America where there is substantial disagreement on 'basic' values. But we are dealing here with communities in which the homeowners' associations have passed binding covenants requiring every home to have beige curtains in the windows, or at least beige drape liners so that the sides of the curtains exposed to the street are uniform in color, not merely intra- but also inter-household. As a regulatory norm, the 'beige drape liner' covenant has a kind of auto-referentiality that can only signify uniformity of thinking. It differs from other community regulations, the common agreement not to operate power mowers before 10: 00 am on Sundays, for example. Every individual can have a different good reason for not wishing to hear a power mower – it disrupts worship, it hurts the head after a night out drinking, and so on. But the only possible reason for requiring everyone to have beige drapes is so that everyone will have beige drapes.

5   I am indebted here and elsewhere to a fine paper by Alain J.-J. Cohen (1978).

Chapter 3

Postmodern community planning
Notes on the homeless and other nomads[1]

> Now we see what remains of a house where cannibalism was
> practiced. Only the posts remain.
>
> > (A German tourist speaking into
> > his own tape recorder in Dennis
> > O'Rourke's film, *Cannibal Tours*)

Every human community once had a specific character, identity,
a manner of existence in which its residents also partook, accepting
as their own its problems and virtues. According to the record
carefully assembled for us by sociology, rural sociology, and
anthropology, each type of community – primitive, rural agricultural, urban industrial, suburban – was a crucible in which formed
a human type and a distinctive social conscience. There were thus
alienated suburbanites, industrial masses, agrarian 'plain folk,'
rebellious frontiersmen, liberal urbanites, and others, each a
human response to the social contract: under what conditions and
agreements does one live in this particular community?

Variations in the form of human communities reflected not
merely economic differences but also differences in the most
deeply held non-economic values and needs, shaping the relations
between families, men and women, children, locals and strangers,
believers and infidels, the fortunate and the abject. The measured
pace of life in farming communities, for example, was thought to
be an expression of the intimate connection between work in the
fields, regular seasonal changes, the constant need for food, and a
quasi-necessary naive teleological philosophy. If one plants a tomato seed, a *tomato* plant grows from it. Given his circumstance, a
farmer would find it difficult not to believe that all human relationships are pre-programmed to grow and develop according to
a grand design; a simple coming into being of what was there in

the first place. The frenzied pace of life in industrial towns, characterized by sudden and unpredictable stops and starts, reflected the linkage of human work to machines and the fickle demands of distant markets. Here, too, ideology springs from the contingencies of daily life. Industrial peoples faced the uncertainty in their lives with a fierce belief in human agency. How could a steel-worker not believe that he is capable of bending nature to his own will?[2]

THE POSTMODERN COMMUNITY AS A SOCIAL TYPE

Culture criticism has provided a list, sometimes internally contradictory, of the characteristic features of 'postmodernity.' This list includes narcissism, emphasis on the *simulacrum*, historical rupture, valorization of surfaces, the death of the critical subject, and the recycling of styles and genres in a postmodern 'pastiche.' There is some evidence in architecture, political rhetoric, commercialized aesthetics (for example, advertising, the music industry, clothing styles, and so on) that these forms are established in communities in Orange County, California, and elsewhere. As these cultural forms come to dominate certain communities, we should ask what sorts of social contracts are found there too; what sort of humanity will this type of community produce?

From the perspective of empirical science, such questions are premature. Self-conscious postmodernism did not exist before the end of the Vietnam War. At this moment, the oldest native postmodernite is about twenty. Still, there are compelling reasons for attempting a preliminary assessment. First, even though the postmodern community type is far from dominant in the world today, even in the wealthiest areas, it is the type which is now receiving the greatest promotion. John Seymour, recently appointed US Senator from California, commented on assuming office, 'Orange County epitomizes the California dream of creating a better life and passing it on to future generations. [He said his goal as Senator is] to keep the dream alive and spread that opportunity to every Californian' (*Contra Costa Times*, Friday, January 4, 1991: 12A). Second, there is some early evidence that the postmodern community is not a community at all, at least not in any sociological sense of the term. In its purest expression, as occurs in Orange County, for example, the 'communities' have little in common with what are called communities elsewhere. The entire community has been built on the model of a corporate headquarters with the added twist that here the 'employees' pay to occupy their work stations: neat little homes, luxurious, sanitized, scheduled, and controlled as only corporate office space used to be. If indeed, the postmodern ideal is to get every thought and action onto a balance sheet, to extend commercial values into every space and human relationship, the central problem of postmodernity will be to create ersatz 'communities' to manufacture and even to sell a 'sense' of community, leaving no free grounds for the formation of relations outside the corporation. The complexity of this feat of social engineering – that is, the construction of a believable symbol of community where no community exists – should not be underestimated, nor should the drive to accomplish this feat be underestimated.

THE SYMBOL OF COMMUNITY

Although the empirical incidence of postmodern community forms do not count for much *statistically*, they are capable of reproducing themselves *symbolically* in economically overdeveloped regions. A disjunction often occurs between statistical and symbolic significance, and produces a certain amount of methodological embarrassment in the sociological sciences. It is just this embarrassment that we must overcome if we are ever to be able to conduct a dialogue as equals (and hopefully betters) with those who are responsible for the creation and promotion of pathological social forms.

There is a precedent. In 1941, admitting to a felt need to dispel some of the mumbo-jumbo surrounding the use of the word 'symbolic,' Kenneth Burke proposed a new equation of symbolic and statistical. In a move that seems strangely antiquated today, he was interested in claiming some of the prestige of 'the statistical' for studies of symbolic action. Burke based his argument on the following parallels between statistical and symbolic: (1) Both the statistic and the symbol are ultimately grounded in experience or observation. Each has one foot in the realm of the real and the other in the realm of interpretation or ideas. (2) Both the statistic and the symbol are ways of dealing with the question of 'representation' or 'representativeness'; both deal with the determination of what is 'characteristic.' One speaks of a 'representative' sample in statistics, and in a novel of a character who is

'symbolically representative.' (3) Both statistical and symbolic analysis address the question of community on a methodological level
by problematizing association, relationship, and correlation. On
the symbolic side, Burke comments: 'the work of every writer
contains a set of implicit equations.... "associational clusters."'...
You may, by examining his work, find 'what goes with what' in
these clusters – what kinds of acts and images and personalities
and situations go with his notions of heroism, villainy, consolation,
despair, etc. (Burke, 1941 and 1957: 18.) (4) Finally, in both the
statistical and the symbolic *association*, there resides a strong sense
of the possibility of a search for *causes*. At least there is a drive to
rule out certain possible causes, but not others, in statistical regression models. And in symbolic analysis, one eventually attempts to
discover motives for actions, intentions, or the causes of community formation and deformation and historical change.

In the fifty years since Burke wrote his defense of the symbolic
in statistical terms, there has been a great deal of advance in both
statistical and symbolic studies. These advances confirm Burke's
equation at the descriptive level but they also reveal deep division
between the two approaches. On the plane of similarities, we now
know that all statistical measures of association, correlation coeffi-
cients, and regression models are also metaphors and metonymies.
They name and specify contamination effects, accidental or spuri-
ous connections, and the transfer of qualities between x and y: 'my
love is like a red, red rose'; 'how do I love thee, let me count the
ways.' At this level, symbol and statistic are precisely equivalent
giving rise to the concrete similarities that Burke discovered. Any
figure, whether it is symbolic or statistical, that is taken as representative, is synecdochic. Both its elocutionary and statistical force
are functions of the precision with which it cuts a part from the
whole and makes the part stand for the whole. All of this is
fundamental to the formation of any possible human community.
Of course there is a certain amount of anxiety, math, and other
types as well, that might attach itself to this amputation – for
example, to the potentially gruesome democratic image of 'a show
of hands,' which latently reminds us of the sacrifice sometimes
necessary to secure democracy.

So much for the grounds of similarity. On another level, when
symbolic and statistical methods are found in use in the community, when they attempt to inhabit the space of real human
action, each approaches the question of 'form' from completely

different angles. Statistical significance rests on the determination of *frequencies* of the occurrence of a characteristic or quality. Frequency rests on number, and number on the assumption of *individuation*. One cannot speak of the 'statistical significance' of the relationship between x and y unless x and y are conceived to be bounded and separate series. Statistics is not equipped to specify the direct relationship between x and y, if any should exist, only the co-relation. The probable incidence of x occurring by chance is compared to the probable incidence of y occurring by chance. When x and y vary together and certain conditions are met that make it possible to assert that the observed incidence of x and y occurring by chance is fewer than five times in 100, or one time in 100, their co-variation is said to be 'statistically significant.' In short, anything that may or may not have happened *between* x and y is specifically suppressed from statistical analysis which rigorously restricts itself to a precise specification of the *effects* of what happened.

Symbolic analysis of community that operates on the form of human action is the *direct* study of relationships; of that which comes between and goes between subjects; of the ways one subject makes itself known to another as occurs on a concrete level in talk, glances, gifts, stories, everything that is exchanged. Symbolic significance occurs when there is an opening, even a violation of consciousness, a transfer of qualities, and/or resistance to the transfer. The effects of symbolically significant community relationships are the establishment of 'impossible' equivalencies, or a splitting of the 'indivisible,' anything that undermines belief in ultimate separation and unified self-sufficiency of individual human subjects. Symbolic significance is not driven by an original quantifiability, enumeration, and frequency of occurrence. Thus, it is possible for something to be symbolically significant without it being statistically significant – for example, the postmodern 'community' – but never vice versa. Every statistical correlation contains, often hides, a symbolically significant relationship, even if it is a relationship that is long dead. Symbols are not well bounded, not subject to enumeration, and even if they could be counted, their frequencies would have no bearing on their significance. On the other hand, every number *is* a symbol. Some are more symbolically significant than others. This is even, or especially, so for those who would want to believe in the separation and self-sufficiency of the ego, such as the 'number one' that we are supposed to 'look out for.' The H-bomb is a significant symbol of our epoch. The precise number of H-bombs makes no difference in assessing their symbolic significance. Do we have more or fewer than our enemies? Are they all accounted for? Is one missing? Are there enough to blow up the entire Earth? Even, or especially, if no one knows the answers to these questions, the H-bomb remains a significant symbol of our epoch, of the death drive, and of a scientific desire to occupy the place of the sun in modern mythologies.

The social sciences occupy the gap between statistical and symbolic significance. The condition of their existence is to struggle endlessly with the question of the possibility of a convergence of the symbolic and statistical orders on more than a superficial level.

THE POSTMODERN SOLUTION

I have suggested that the postmodern 'community' is really some other kind of social formation under the stolen label of *community*. This raises a series of interesting questions about how the statistical and symbolic convergence works in this case. How is a 'sense' of the postmodern 'community' engineered? The actual procedures resemble the Jungian general theory of the self and the social symbol. According to Jung, the ultimate basis for the social 'relation' is the shared archetypal symbol, a 'primordial image,' or form which gives shape to consciousness. The *individual* dispositions and attitudes are not archetypal, but the *social* common ground is – inborn, pre-formed, and pre-conscious. He calls it the 'collective unconscious.' Jung modestly compares his studies to Aristotle's and Kant's, and congratulates himself as follows: 'If I have any share in these discoveries, it consists in my having shown that archetypes are *not* disseminated only by tradition, language, and migration, but *they can re-arise spontaneously, at any time, at any place, and without any outside influence*' (Jung, 1959: 13, emphasis supplied). The Jungian symbol meets the statistical requirement of original individuation and separation in that it is located in each individual consciousness. At the same time, it is the ground of the most powerful correlation because it is universal. The correlation is not dependent on any *communication* that might have taken place between subjects – that is, on any symbolic apparatus that may have fallen into the hands of the people. It is a repetition of qualities that arise out of the self, *independent* of the relationship of the self to others. In short, this is the perfect model of an integrative mechanism for a 'community' that is, at once, absolutely unified *and* which does not require any *interaction* between members for its unity. Its unity 'goes without saying,' ensured by the shared archetypal symbol.

The archetypal 'community' stands in a position of theoretical opposition to the concept of a socio-semiotic symbolic *tie, link,* or *connection.* From an interactional standpoint, it is a step backwards into a past that never existed. Subjects that make a shared 'inborn' quality the basis of their common existence can relate to one another as they might to their own image in a mirror. Technically, it is a narcissistic solidarity which need not, indeed cannot, go beyond a mutual monitoring of appearances. The postmodern community is not technically a Jungian archetype; he did not name it among the universal symbols. It is doubly removed from both theory and reality; like a planner's dream of an archetype. It comes into existence *as if* it is founded on a universal unifying symbol. It is the 'grass-roots' basis for totalitarian democracy. Within the postmodern community the commonality and universality of values is simply assumed. There is no real need for discussion, identification of unmet needs, or other negotiation of the form of communal relations. Indeed, all such language-based activity is a needles surplus, a 'waste of time and energy,' and probably subversive. The postmodern community is deeply satisfying to those who would want to live beyond the reach of any corrective or other specification of their behaviors that another person might provide (excepting, of course, gentle reminders concerning 'appearances'). The postmodern subject need never distinguish between love of its own image and love of another. This narcissistic or 'yuppie love' obviates the need for social relations; or perhaps the destruction of social relations is the empirical ground for the spread of narcissistic self-sufficiency when it comes to the emotions. In his discussion of the self, Jung consistently refers to those others to whom the self is related as 'the environment.'

By individuating the 'symbol,' by subordinating symbolic to statistical significance, the postmodern community reproduces itself without internal resistance. The denial of the difference or gap between statistical and symbolic significance is what empowers 'postmodernism' to be the cultural cutting edge of global capitalism. It is a kind of oversimplification that responds to deep problematics of end-of-the-millennium culture. The postmodern community, as anti-symbol, or Jungian symbol, is a kind of glitzy warehouse for souls. It binds people together by destroying all ties between them. It claims to put them in touch with their 'innermost' feelings, but does not allow them to talk to their dead ancestors.

Postmodern 'communities' are realized mythic form. If there was a fifth Jungian archetype, 'Community,' alongside of 'Mother,' 'Rebirth,' 'Spirit,' and 'Trickster,' the actual postmodern community would be its closest manifestation, as these others are said to manifest themselves in fairy tales and patient narratives. The first indication of their mythic status can be found in political narrative: 'Orange County is, or ought to be, a universal model for community everywhere.' The official bumper sticker of the city of Irvine reads, 'Another Day in Paradise.' Ethnologically, their quasi-sacred aspect is manifest in the ritual concern for cleanliness that is lavished upon them by their residents and shamanistic zoning code enforcers. Alternatively, under conditions under which it is too late or too expensive to clean up the community front, dirt and disorder can be mythified, as occurs in Berkeley, California. It is not locally taken to be 'real' dirt, it is more like 'movie set' dirt, 'gritty reality,' or a white fantasy of ghetto existence.

The archetypal postmodern community is composed of the physical and mental spoils of the tourist crusades: 'nouvelle cuisine' and ethnic restaurants, adequate 'space' for recreational drug marketing and use, and recycled, nostalgic elements including reconstructions of old homes, districts, and offices, and fairs featuring traditional handicrafts. Everywhere in the archetypal postmodern community, there is an emphasis on 'folk arts,' 'natural,' or 'natural-seeming' materials, woods, fabrics, and fibers, and 'earth-tone' beige and cream colors for homes, businesses, and other large architectural elements. These are connected by public landscaping for which there is a claim that it has a 'natural look,' even where the grass is uniformly green and evenly trimmed.

THE SOCIAL CHARACTERISTICS OF POSTMODERN COMMUNITIES

Even if the postmodern community is not technically a community, and even if they are designed against the contingency that human relationships might form in them, they are beginning to exhibit some emergent pseudo-social features. These are *narcissism*,[3] *the embedding of tradition*, and *putative classlessness*. (1) *Narcissism*: The social manifestation of the narcissistic drive in the postmodern community is a collective striving for self-sufficiency when it comes to 'otherness': an incorporation and domestication of other peoples and traditions to the point that they disappear. (2) *The embedding of tradition*: Postmodern places are designed around a totemic exaltation of *the past* not as history. This is no longer merely a matter of political rhetoric in which there is a nostalgia for the past and tradition, as for example when conservative candidates claim they 'stand for' or they will help us 'return to' the virtues of traditional community and family life. There are now new suburban places which are made on the model of the 'traditional' small town, and rural and urban re-development projects, once called 'gentrification,' in which shabby areas are not so much restored as they are transformed into ideal images of what they might have been. (3) Finally, within the postmodern community one finds *the pretense of classlessness* and a corresponding trivialization of political differences.

The way postmoderns are attempting to overcome otherness bears an interesting relationship to previous programs. They are not demanding that everyone, no matter how different we might otherwise be, live under the stern gaze of a single god. Postmodernists only go so far as to suggest that collective life cannot be other than a frenzied pastiche, and that everyone should develop a capacity to enjoy playing a bit part on a single world stage. What do we have to give up after all? Only our negativity. Wouldn't a life lived beyond old moral distinctions, as between truth and lie, simply replace fiction, or make fiction real? Couldn't such a life be truly creative and free of stress and conflict?

Perhaps not everyone can follow the tourist and learn to live happily ever after in postmodernity. Postmodern cultural forms always appear to be exploding and drifting apart, as our universe is said to be drifting apart. But even this nuclear figure can be transformed into a 'positive resource,' providing a necessary sense of danger and excitement; after all the swamps have been drained, the remaining forests turned into parks, and the dark 'others,' once thought to be dangerous, turned into productive members of the new community, after everyone has come together under the 'United Colors of Benetton.' The strongest possible critiques of the postmodern community can be turned into positive resources for its continued development. Suppose, for example, someone were to suggest that as it incorporates everything, everything becomes disconnected in the postmodern community; that it never provides more than a uniform plastic existence without center or direction. A positive postmodernist could answer that it is possible to discern within postmodernity the outlines of a revolutionary new morality; the first truly universal morality; a morality completely unlike the old morality that was based on opposition between groups ('we are good – they are bad'), the one that led to wars, racial hatred, class antagonisms. Specifically, as the postmodern consciousness gains confidence, it begins to face moral failings of the past: discrimination against gays and lesbians, people of color, injustices of class, the destruction of nature, and so on. Is it not the case that the ovens at Dachau, the Kennedy assassination site, Verdun, the Berlin Wall, and Ground Zero at Hiroshima are now tourist attractions? Doesn't the horror and disgust that is called forth by these attractions, along with the admiration for the positive ones, for the Statue of Liberty or Yosemite, provide moral stability to the expanding awareness of postmodern peoples? Isn't the postmodern community itself, its neighborhoods and attractions, functionally equivalent to the sacred texts that underlie traditional societies? No. We are far from having read what is 'written' in the postmodern community. So far, all we have read, even in criticism, is its hype, its 'jacket notes.'

THE POSTMODERN SYMBOLIC 'COMMUNITY' AND ITS CRITIQUE

There is obviously a temptation to interpret aspects of postmodernity as bearing traditional and therefore sacred values, and being capable of giving form to a new morality. Empirically, they do bear traditional values. That is the precise point to the theory behind their design. A classical anthropological training could lead to an interpretation of the postmodern as a reprise of tradition, based on the tremendous energy and imagination devoted to the reconstruction of 'traditional markets,' 'Renaissance Pleasure Faires,' 'Dickens Christmas Festivals,' and the like. But it is still more accurate to read these forms *not* as bearing traditional values, but as specifically designed to *appear to bear traditional values*, which is a different matter. The postmodern evokes the prestige of 'tradition' as its method of destroying tradition and other social arrangements. The postmodern conscience must accomplish its work without the benefit of any meaningful distinction that one might attempt to continue to make between the sacred and the profane, truth and lie, good and evil. Postmodern communities mock up, or make a mocking reference to the 'sacred,' to 'tradition,' 'morality,' the 'good life.' The cynically nostalgic reprise of traditional forms is most evident in the Thatcher-Reagan monumentalization of 'traditional morality' as an absolute value just as it disappears from public life.

THE SPATIAL ESTABLISHMENT OF POSTMODERN SYMBOLIC 'COMMUNITY'

There was already a critical anticipation of a new community mythology expressing itself in and through urban spatial arrangements in the writings of Henri Lefebvre. According to Lefebvre, the burden for the reproduction of the relations of production has been shifted from social *class* to social *space* (see, for example, Lefebvre, 1976). The perpetuation of the capitalist mode of production is no longer primarily a matter of social relations, work activities, and ideologies associated with membership in specific classes. Rather it is specialization of function in the built environment. The dialectic has shifted from the class struggle to the opposition between *center* and *periphery* and perhaps beyond. For example,

> capitalism and the state in general need the 'town' as *centre* (centre of decision-making, wealth, information, of the organization of space). But at the same time, they cause the 'town,' as the historically constituted political centre, to fragment and disappear. Centrality collapses into the space which it has generated, i.e., into the existing relations of production and their reproduction.
>
> (1976: 17)

The thesis that the tension between center and periphery is an extension of an earlier conflict between classes provides a base for neo-Marxist explanation of diverse phenomena, most notably Third World underdevelopment.[4] But where does the postmodern community fit into the 'collapse of centrality into the space of its own creation'? If we continue to try to make the kinds of observations of urban settings that Lefebvre was making in the early 1970s, it becomes evident that new concepts are needed to address spatial arrangements under senile capitalism: for instance, 'postmodern,' 'truth effects,' 'manufactured tradition,' 'staged morality.' Also 'repression' with a double connotation, political and psychoanalytic.

In the 1960s and 1970s, urban centers had become the stage on which there was a visibly bounded, well-marked region for every social class that had emerged in the industrial world, and also the stage for conflict: Levittown, Jonestown, Harlem, The Main Line, Watts, People's Park. As Lefebvre suggested, during the modern phase of 'community development' the relations of production became dramatically evident components of social space. The postmodern community is the next 'logical development.' The postmodern community attenuates and partially resolves the center/periphery conflict, which is already an attenuation and partial resolution of class conflict. Postmodern cultural forms accomplish this attenuation mainly via repression.

For Lefebvre and some other Marxists, the category of 'repression' can only refer to an aspect of the state apparatus of authoritarian control. Within classical Marxism, there is a sweet tenderness toward a human capacity for enlightenment; a dogmatic belief that humans are automatically able to see through what is merely ideological to know where they stand in the real relations of production even without the benefits of a demythologizing education; that working people, who are the ultimate source of all wealth, will eventually realize that they have been exploited and engage in revolutionary struggle based on a rational calculation of self-interest; and that the state, so long as it is under the control of the privileged classes, stands ready to repress all revolutionary action through threat, force, violence, and state terrorism if necessary. Thus, for Lefebvre, there can be no *ideological* repression. He writes, 'ideologies act by persuasion, complementing the state's repressive apparatus.' On this point alone, I think it is important to disagree with Lefebvre's analysis. Perhaps ideologies at the earliest stage of their development, ideologies that are still framed entirely in words, must advance by persuading. But ideologies that are manifest in the physical layout of entire communities enjoy the luxury of seeming already to have succeeded at total persuasion. Ideologies that inhabit objects and signs no longer require discourse for their perpetuation; they continue to exist by virtue of a *pretense of agreement*, a silence, a repression.

If there has been a 'collapse of the center into a space of its own making,' this can only be seen as the construction of postmodern communities on the former sites of potential historical conflicts. The postmodern community neutralizes the conflict that might have emerged from center/periphery dialectics. It does so first by transforming 'center' and 'periphery' to a touristic 'modern/traditional' opposition. Then the postmodern community contains this pseudo-opposition in architectural, landscape, and leisure practice, which I am here calling a neo-totemic reprise of 'tradition' as lived ideology.[5] It is important, while disagreeing with Lefebvre's analysis of the role of ideology, to recall that this disagreement is based fully on his analysis of social space. Nothing much has changed except the focus of study and the implications for action. That is, I should not want to disagree with Lefebvre on the matter of the spatially defined community as the site of perpetuation of the relations of production, even in the postmodern community. I am only going so far as to suggest that these kinds of communities have achieved a certain 'consciousness-for-itself,' an understanding paralleling the Marxist critique that might be made of them, that social life cannot be reduced to economic relations. The postmodern community is, of course, a virtually pure expression of economic values, but these are raised to the level of 'community.'[6] We are supposed to think that human relationships still exist in them. The defensive move of capitalism is a constant shifting of the 'base' to 'superstructure' to the point that there is no longer any real distinction to be made between the two, between myth and ideology on the one hand and concrete social relations on the other. This is not to say that there are no longer any fundamental social relationships. It only means that it is not possible to change basic structure by operating on it by revolutionary and other direct means, assuming that the 'correct' ideology will fall in place once basic structural arrangements have been straightened out. Fundamental change now requires a total attack on structure and on myth and ideology.

THE POSTMODERN COMMUNITY AS AN EXPRESSION OF CAPITALIST ENVY

In its role as a component of the defensive bulwarks of capitalism – that is, as proof of capitalism's ability to continue to deliver 'the good life' – the postmodern community represents itself *not* as what it is: the site of particular economic values and place of residence of a spoiled social class. It represents itself as having no real class base, *not* as being fully absorbed in the reproduction of the relations of production. It represents itself as 'universal value,' as a generalized norm to which *everyone* is supposed to conform. And not grudgingly either; they should *want* to conform. Wouldn't everyone, if they had a choice, want to live in one of the better neighborhoods of California's Orange County or Berkeley? In the context of a cannibalistic desire to possess *everything*, it is not especially bizarre for capitalists to want what only socialists can have, universal brotherhood in a life free of material want and social contradiction. The postmodern community is the realization of the capitalist fantasy of the socialist goal of a classless society. In Berkeley, one hears frequent reference to the community by its residents as 'the People's Republic of Berkeley.' Postmodernization can be read as the real aftermath of an imagined bourgeois revolution; a premature move to an 'administrative phase' during which the victors attempt to institutionalize their values. There was no real need to redistribute the wealth. All that was necessary was the creation of new communities in which there is no place for the working classes, even in their former neighborhoods. The pretense that the working classes have somehow been 'absorbed,' transcended, or superseded is built on their exclusion. This is a desperate or amateurish kind of repression on the face of it. Anyone who enters a postmodern community can immediately see the strain, and the artificiality of its 'classlessness.'

MODERNIZATION VS. POSTMODERNIZATION

The methods used in the planning and development of postmodern communities differ from older models of development and constitute a revolutionary change in the technical manipulation of human lives. Older development models made no effort to disguise their aim of annihilating 'otherness,' admitting that their goal was to make over traditional or 'backward' peoples so they would resemble the industrial proletariat of the developed countries. They were candidly clear that the advancement of an 'underdeveloped' group required hard work and the copying of cultural practices of groups already in the mainstream. Of course, this was not a very effective approach to 'development' and 'modernization' because it admitted its real goals and was, therefore, in the manner in which it was set up, a virtual invitation to resistance. Developers and planners in the 1950s and 1960s are to be excused a certain measure of naivety in this regard because they were operating at a time when it was widely assumed that rural peoples of Africa, Asia, and Latin America *would really be better off* if they lived a life more like that of a Detroit assembly line worker. Some Vietnamese disagreed.

Postmodernization eliminates the obvious grounds of resistance to planned development because it can represent itself as being based on a principle opposite to that of assimilation. Traditional peoples, including ex-primitives, especially those who have adopted tourism as their way of getting a living, now have the option of basing their economic advancement on making a show of their distinctive qualities, their cultural uniqueness. One finds the same tendencies in postmodern or 'issue' politics which claim to transcend class interests and the old parties which orchestrated class conflict. In their struggles, not for *equality* but for 'acceptance,' leaders of ethnic, gay, and gender movements stress the *difference* between their group and the oppressive majority: 'Black *is* beautiful,' 'It's *great* to be an Italian American.' Apparently, at some point in the postmodernization process, it becomes necessary not merely to *be* an African American, or Asian American, or American Indian, or gay, it becomes necessary to start *acting* like one. This is explicit in the name of the gay rights group, ACTUP, and in anti-essentialist theory which assumes that human differences are not real; they are arbitrarily legislated and/or enacted.

Getting an act together to play a part in the 'universal' drama of postmodernity is complicated and may be beyond the competency or desire of many groups. Not every traditional group will exhibit the same cleverness as the Amish of Lancaster County, Pennsylvania, who have set up life-size, realistic Fiberglas replicas of themselves and their horse-drawn carts for tourists to photograph. Not every postmodern public figure would want to commission a famous artist to make life-size lawn sculptures of tourists taking pictures and have them installed on his front lawn.[7] In short, not everyone is interested in living a life in which they must be always conscious of themselves as a cultural entity in the eyes of others. Some other peoples, as the examples above suggest, are quick to adapt to the exigencies of postmodern existence, either as a matter of economic necessity or because they enjoy role playing or both. Thus we can find in the postmodern community some individuals who actually like Early American and other traditional décor, as well as peasant garb and the 'authentic' costumes of 'workers' (cowboys, soldiers, mill hands, and others), 'naturalness' in food, cosmetics, and manners, and a concern for the preservation of the past and nature. In short, what is new about the postmodern community and consciousness is not so much the practices and behaviors it promotes. In the new agricultural community, for example, one finds a re-birth of some very old practices – composting, limited use of pesticides and herbicides, and so on – coupled with a critical attack on high-energy agriculture, the introduction of harmful chemicals into food, the supermarket system, exploitation of farm labor, and so forth. What is new about the postmodern community is seizure of manufactured 'tradition' as a new kind of 'natural resource' for development. In short, an 'organic farmer' is not, in and of himself, by virtue of being 'organic,' postmodern any more than an authentic primitive is 'primitive.' What *is* postmodern is the new California labeling law which specifies that 20 per cent of produce labeled and sold as 'organic' can be grown industrially, using chemical pesticides, herbicides, and petroleum-based fertilizer. In short, the postmodern is the raising of the 'organic,' 'tradition,' 'morality,' and so on as an ultimate kind of value and a hiding of that which is not organic, traditional, or moral behind those 'values.'

A community becomes postmodern, then, when it develops consciousness of itself as a model and learns to profit from its image. The result of community self-consciousness is a whole new series of concerns, not all of them in and of themselves deleterious: community attractiveness, quality of community life, the impact of the community on the surrounding environment. It is no longer possible to think of community development as a matter of increasing population and dollars. 'Development' is now conceived as the production of a consistent, clean, and positive image of the community in the wider world. Older notions of 'economic self-interest' are now almost entirely a matter of maintaining 'folksy' aesthetics – such as a restored, traditional 'main street,' or *Sunset* magazine style landscaping – in order to preserve the resale value of the homes.

It was once relatively simple for an individual to navigate a life course guided by identification with one pole or the other of conventional oppositions: men/women, rich/poor, gay/straight, socialist/capitalist, modern/traditional, and so forth. It is these oppositions which have collapsed into the space of the new community where they continue to exist not as life-shaping absolutes but as amoral alternatives, mere differences. It was the tourists who first transcended these differences, who first treated social and natural phenomena equally, who visited capitalist *and* socialist countries on the same trip, who demanded to see modern *and* ancient sights. The homosexual community of San Francisco became one of its attractions along with Chinatown, the aging Hippie enclave in Haight-Ashbury, and the Golden Gate Bridge. In the postmodern community, black and white, square and deviant, the aging and the young, and radical and conservative, exist side by side, but not in their original unreflected cultural condition. Nor are they necessarily united by a common liberal tolerance for real differences, because in a structural existential sense, they are not really different. Rather, they function as a kind of massive cultural experiment, coexisting in the mode of being-themselves-for-others.

'NOUVELLE RACISM' OR 'RACISM LITE'

The postmodern community is also the site of the putative exclusion of racial factors in neighborhood and workforce composition. Segments of minority populations are admitted even into the richest areas of the postmodern community on condition that they can carry off an appearance of agreement with its values. But this is not to say that racism no longer shapes the experience of nonwhites who are 'accepted' into postmodern communities. Racism continues to exist even for those nonwhites who are admitted to the elite neighborhoods and corridors of power. But it is a new, or postmodern, kind of racism. From the perspective of the bourgeois blacks and other minorities who live and work in them, the postmodern community is panoptic. The minority individual begins to feel that the reputation of the entire ethnicity is riding on every detail of his or her behavior, diction, attire, condition of the lawn, appearance of the car and the living room, comportment of the children, the dog, and so on. The home, the marriage, the job performance, cease to be a home, and so forth, and are transformed into a showcase for conformity: not mere conformity, but a kind of ultra-conformity which always has to go beyond that which it emulates.

Of course, the desire here is to be worthy of being thought of as a leader or even an equal, but this is unattainable by these means within the postmodern setup. The formula for 'nouvelle racism' is a first derivation from the pretense of classlessness. Now that some of the Joneses are black, the white members of the postmodern community declare that there is no reason to keep up with them. The entire competitive arrangement of class-based social relations is now said to have been 'materialistic' or even 'capitalistic.' The reason for buying a Mercedes Benz could never be because the black family next door bought one. The 'proper' reasons for buying a Mercedes are exactly those given in the Mercedes ads: 'engineering excellence,' 'resale value,' and so forth. Even the few friendship ties struggling for existence in the postmodern community are no longer based on vulgar class considerations, occupational status, and material wealth as they once were. They are now based on 'lifestyle,' or what one chooses to do with one's leisure time.

A postmodern minority may thus find itself to be in the community but not necessarily of it. Its presence is conditional on its transparency. This comes out in small details of inter-'personal' interaction that go unnoticed by one party while they produce deep shame in the other. For example, a black professional learns to accept that her white neighbors consistently call her by the name of the other black woman on the block. This is not merely a matter of hurt pride. Exclusion from social functions and networks, especially the kind of exclusion that is operational when the excluded is physically present, eventually produces serious disadvantages when it comes to the associations and contacts necessary to exploit opportunity or to ride out adversity. No matter how isolated the individual or fictionalized community life becomes, real relationships remain crucial to any advantage a human being may enjoy.

THE MIRROR OF FUNCTIONALISM

In his classic *Division of Labor in Society*, Durkheim (1893 and 1984) taught us that modern (as opposed to primitive) communities are held together by mutual dependence based on functional specialization. No individual, group, or class is self-sufficient; each contributes something unique to the totality; each is dependent on the others for something crucial. This would seem to explain the awesome power of modern solidarities to subsume, supplant, and transcend all others, to make a place within modernity for every human type. As Lefebvre reminded us, there was a place in the modern community for everyone, no matter what their relation to production, no matter how strange or down on their luck. Eventually, Talcott Parsons and others would see in Durkheim's formulation the outline for a moral justification for the unequal distribution of wealth under capitalism. If every group or individual is functionally related to the whole – that is, has a role in capitalism – the cramped and inelegant place of the workers must reflect the relative insignificance of their contribution. They work only for themselves, after all, while a high capitalist builds companies, develops entire regions, puts others to work. A rational society would reserve its highest rewards for those individuals and classes that make the more crucial contributions to the whole. This is precisely the opposite of the moral implications of Marx's analysis of the relationship between work and reward under capitalism, and is, in fact, the most sophisticated moral justification so far devised for unequal reward in the relations of capitalist production.

But this moralism becomes unsustainable in the postmodern epoch. It is already evident that senile capitalism reserved at least some of its highest rewards for those who are successfully involved in the promotion of rock music groups, export of toxic waste to Third World countries, windfall oil profits from international belligerency, marketing illegal drugs, looting the savings and loan industry and/or the public treasury, and so on.[8] One doubts that even Talcott Parsons would be able to discover the contribution of these highly rewarded activities to the functional integration, stability, and the long-term political-economic development of late capitalism. This is perhaps the ultimate reason why within the postmodern community there can no longer be any serious discussion of flawed character, social stain, or stigma. Now that the discussion of any major delict will involve some of the highest-status members of the community, the terms of the discussion are re-cast into liberal 'developmental disabilities,' 'structural disadvantage,' 'special' people, and the like. The tough rhetoric formerly devised to account for the abject people who once lived in the industrial ghetto can no longer be used because it would now apply with greater accuracy to community leaders or at least to their sons.

As I have already suggested, the postmodern response to this dilemma is to pretend that there are no real classes, that we are living in the classless aftermath of a successful bourgeois revolution. To the extent that class differences force themselves on awareness, postmodern propaganda relentlessly promotes the idea of moral uniformity across the classes, and that class is only one among several consequential differences including gender and ethnicity, and by no means necessarily the most important of these differences. This is accomplished by every possible means, by blunting moral rhetoric as it applies to the lower classes, and by aggressively promoting the idea that the highest circles of government and industry are run by 'gangs' not unlike urban neighborhoods. The state and the most powerful media have succeeded in producing a widespread belief that virtually everyone who lives in urban ethnic neighborhoods is lucratively involved in a massive, unstoppable, internationally articulated illicit drug trade, not unlike the global corporation. Within this drug trade at the street level, there is an almost messianic drive to build a positive cult around drug use, the articulate user earnestly justifying his or her activities as contributing to the development of the only place in American society where rich and poor, black and white come together as true equals. Karl Marx may have had the right idea when he said that 'Religion is the opiate of the masses' for early industrial capitalism. But in senile capitalism, opium is the opiate of the masses.

A more effective gloss on postmodernity could not be devised; no matter how corrupt the leadership and the wealthy, the poor are pre-judged to be just as corrupt. There can be no capital investment in social programs, first because the recipients are undeserving and would only abuse the facilities (turn the public housing project into 'crack houses,' for example), and second because such projects are not needed because the poor are really rich. Until the successful overthrow of the postmodern, there will not be another home built for a lower working-class family anywhere in the Western world.

Certainly by now my direction should be clear enough: that the 'homeless' are something more than an accidental statistical correlate of postmodernity; they are materially and symbolically essential. There is no 'place' at the 'bottom' of a society that must pretend to itself that it is 'classless' in order to avoid confronting its own moral failings. Those who will not even try to conform to the generalized bourgeois norm have been banished. This is not considered to be a class issue; it is conceived more as an 'attitude problem.' After all, there are few requirements for fitting into the postmodern community: tacit acceptance of its values, average personal hygiene, a tennis outfit or a jogging suit, and a private place to sleep. In short, homelessness is the one and only thing that is guaranteed in the postmodern community.

There is still some unfinished business with Durkheim. The postmodern fictionalization of social relations as the pseudo-basis for antisocial forms that masquerade as social life simply could not occur in a universe that works according to the principles laid down by Durkheim and Parsons, or even by Marx to the extent that he believed the 'superstructure' to be in a supporting role. Let me suggest, against Durkheim, and especially against the functionalists, that functional specialization cannot have any direct bearing on a 'social totality' or any other quasi-communal social form. Specialization, or as we now say, 'differentiation,' is not a total social fact. Marcel Mauss's *The Gift* (1925 and 1967) is actually a devastating critique of Durkheim which is not read as such because of the polite language he used in referring to his uncle's work.

In the simplest model of social complexity, we say that A and C are not related directly but they are part of the 'totality' by virtue of their connection to a third party, usually 'god.' To the extent that B is not a god, and is functionally specialized, that is, to the extent that B is competent to compartmentalize and keep the A: B relationship separate from the B:C relationship, A has no relationship to C, even indirectly. The only circumstance under which A would influence C would be if there was a certain amount of leakage across B's role sectors; in other words, if there was a breakdown in B's capacity for functional specialization. A surgeon's (B) relationship to his wife (A) is not supposed to affect his relationship to his patient (C), or vice versa. The wife and the patient should not be related systemically (that is, 'a change in one produces a determinate change in the other') as a matter of principle. When the behavior of the wife can be shown to influence the fate of the patient in the hands of the surgeon, the principle of functional specialization weakens in direct proportion to the strengthening of the social 'totality.' In concrete social situations governed by the principles of specialization and 'functional integration' there is a double effacement of both 'self' and 'society.' The functionally specialized and integrated community is technically composed of the absence of human relationships where they might be. Such communities can be said to 'function' only to the extent that human relationships are denied or suppressed.

It is common to note that the problem with functionalism is its transcendent conception of society: 'society rewards.' But the academic social sciences, while they have provided an intelligent critique, have been stumped when it comes to an alternate conception. The wait is over. Postmodernism provides a model of the 'post-functional.' 'Society' is not transcendent. It is immanent. Under the transcendent conception people will not behave morally except for pay, for the promise of a better life, either here and now, at the end of the month, after the diploma, or after death. The amoralism of postmodernity only ratifies the way functionalism and modernism really work. Functional or modern 'morality' was designed to be corrupted; that it is really immoral to suggest that one should be paid to 'do the right thing.' So it is possible to go back and re-conceive the modern, industrial community, Durkheim's community, filled with every imaginable human type, *none of which* ever really had a 'place' in the 'totality.' What they had were a few human relationships, some good, others not so good, and often a functionalist *dream* of making a difference beyond their few relationships. This is mainly a bad dream in which 'place' or 'roots' or 'fame' are substituted for the missing link that might connect the person to the social totality except that such linkages don't exist outside of social theory and bourgeois fiction. Postmodernity comes into existence because modernity never operated according to its own rules as given by its most sophisticated observers. And we *are* somewhat stuck here because there is nothing to go back to. An honest rendering of modernity only gives us rust-bucket postmodernity. Is it possible to conceive, as an alternative, a human relationship that does not appeal to a transcendent order, within which morality is its own reward?

There are two directions for thought and planning at this point. One approach would be to continue to search for language to describe a possible community relationship that corresponds to the Jungian version of the symbol. It is not mechanical, not organic, certainly not dialectic, and only statistical in an aggregative sense, but still somehow a 'relationship.' I will mainly abandon this task here. There are numerous others who aggressively pursue it. The second approach involves a refusal to think that individuals, classes, and communities are just fragments of a former totality sharing space in an expanding universe. After the dramatic moral failures of both Marxist and capitalist regimes, perhaps we can minimally assert that no class has any more *right* to the space it occupies than any other class. Minimally, each person, group, class, or segment is potentially a model for the others, not necessarily a model that is copied or emulated, but one that can help to shape knowledge and existence even by negative example. We can all still help one another out in this way, learn from one another.

The most difficult challenge standing in the path of this direction of thinking would be coming to an understanding that some human relationships are not a matter of choice but are *specified* in a new way. They are not specified functionally and/or dialectically as between workers and management. The functional type of relation is precisely the type that need not lead to any new understanding. It is simply given as a dead relation. What I am trying to describe is a still live relationship that is attempting to escape into history but has not yet succeeded in doing so. I will try to show below that it is possible to approach the relationship between the homeless and the postmodern as this kind of urgently necessary, unstable mutual modeling relationship that might provide an opening into history.

Statistically, the homeless have been around longer than post-modernity. Before the emergence of the postmodern as a social type, though, the homeless were called 'drifters,' 'bums,' 'tramps,' and 'winos,' never 'homeless.' Now that these kinds of people are beginning to have a certain symbolic significance as 'homeless,' when one utters the word, the point is that one is supposed to be able to congratulate oneself for having a home. But without a simultaneous hygienic suppression of any capacity for dialectic thought, this word 'homeless' is potentially dangerous in use in the postmodern community, the community that invented it. It brings up a series of potentially embarrassing questions: If you have a home, who owns it? You? The landlord? The bank? Are there written and/or unwritten rules which restrict the kinds of things you can do in or with your home? Can you knock down the wall of your apartment to make the room bigger, or pound a nail in the wall to hang a picture? Can you paint the exterior of your house barn-red? And what about your relationship to those with whom you share your home? Would you be enthusiastically willing to give up your 'home' in exchange for a divorce or, in the case of minors, emancipation? These questions and their answers tend to

reveal that the postmodern community, like every other, is ultimately 'authentic' in the sense of actually being the grounds for a
deeply held set of shared values. It has achieved a kind of capitalist
purity within which the only differences between its members are
material. Everyone in the postmodern community, the rich and the
homeless, share the same social fate on a *spiritual* level. Beyond the
difference in the amount of wealth they control, what is the
difference between the latch-key only child of working professionals and the men and women who gather at the campfire in the
park every evening, to share their stories of the day and whatever
food or booze they have been able to cadge? What is the difference
between the single man sleeping on the subway grate and the
recently divorced woman who would rather spend the night
almost anywhere but in her empty condo?

Quoting from Georges Dumézil, in their 'Treatise on Nomadology,' Deleuze and Guattari (1987: 351–423) describe the kind of
relationship that holds between the postmodernite and homeless:
'at once antithetical and complementary, necessary to one another
and consequently without hostility, lacking a mythology of conflict;
a specification on one level automatically calls forth a homologous
specification on another. The two together exhaust the field of the
function' (ibid. : 351–2). This is a kind of awkward definition
of a mechanical-organic-dialectical-functional relationship, but it
might help us pull through an awkward moment. In applying it
to the homeless and the postmodernite, can it really be said,
'without hostility'? There has been violence. But mainly the postmodernite and the homeless do not know how they should actually
relate. One suspects that there is a deep recognition on both sides
that they belong to reciprocal moieties. As happens in other
situations of this kind, their formal communications are marked
with touching respect. I noted a neatly lettered official sign in a
park: 'The sprinkler system is controlled by a random timer.'
Talmadge Wright and Anita Vermund (1990), in their study with
the homeless, found that their dealings with officials were made
easier, and their self-respect increased, when they supplied them
with business cards giving their name, title ('Representative of the
Homeless Advocacy Group') and the telephone number of a
store-front organization where they could be 'reached.'

The homeless have been expelled from the interior of the
postmodern community and projected to a new kind of 'outside'
that is also a postmodern production. They are the expulsed

subjectivity of a social form which, by rejecting even one human being, loses all rightful claim to have a conscience or feelings. Wherever there is a fixation on surface appearances, a rigorous thematization of surfaces, there is also a deep repression, a denial of feeling. The homeless are the soul of postmodernity if it can be said to have a true soul. They move around in public space, their carts filled with worthless 'belongings,' a parody of the other postmodern figure, the yuppie tourist. They are actually carrying heavy ideological responsibilities within the postmodern setup. In the postmodern community (I will not apologize for insisting that I now have the right to say this) 'as a whole,' they represent *lack*. It is precisely this crucial *lack*, this particular lack of a 'home,' which is generic to postmodernity. It is suffered in varying degrees by every postmodernite, but it can never be admitted, not by the others. Only the actually 'homeless' can tell the truth. What can we learn from the homeless, from a close examination of the soul of postmodernity? Just that everyone in a postmodern community is 'excluded but present.' Everyone lives their relation to production trading in their human relationships and eventually their spirit for some material possessions, an 'immense accumulation of commodities' in the case of the yuppie, an overflowing shopping cart full of broken and discarded objects in the case of the homeless. The unsatisfied yuppie, the invisible black bourgeois, and especially the homeless, is each an answer to the question of how, and under what conditions and agreements one lives in the postmodern community.

There is a final sense in which there can be no comparison between the homeless and the tourist, especially not on economic grounds. Their movements are only superficially similar. Here is the place where tourists might learn something about themselves from the homeless if they would but take the trouble to observe them closely and follow their movements. Both the homeless and the tourist can be said to constitute a territory by their movements following known pathways between points.[9] But the tourist weaves together all the various attractions and sanitized public fixtures world-wide. His movements are a binding together of the high points of his culture. The movements themselves are merely necessary to the reconstruction of culture. The tourist believes in the circularity of the tour, that he can go home again. The homeless person knows better. The movements of the homeless have nothing to do with the official definition of social spaces.

Their movements and passages are the grounds for their very existence. If there is a stop along the way to watch television in a store window, to piss in the privacy of a stairwell, to sleep next to the hot lights of a billboard, it is because these places have been forgotten, at least temporarily, by the official marking and policing apparatus. They are temporal interstices in the postmodern produced by the presence of the homeless. The tourist identifies with the property owner and accedes to the demands of the gatekeeper, scheduler, and so on. The tourist follows the officially marked path, while for the homeless, the marked path, the road, the sidewalk, the trail, is only one way of going from place to place, and not necessarily the best way or the way that offers the least resistance. The homeless may even feel the need to stay off the road for purposes of movement, or to use the road for something other than passage. They may harvest the road for aluminum cans, for example. The homeless have no proper use for the proper boundary, the separations and hierarchies encoded in spatial arrangements. There are no internally imposed limits or boundaries around their space. And for this reason, the homeless know that they could never effectively hide their feelings at the interior of a personal or private 'subjectivity.' They must hide out in the open, fully exposed.

Compare their plight in this regard to the problem experienced by the postmodern conscience which must wage a constant fight to appear to have a subjective interior, a certain subjective intensity, perhaps a history of its own of which it can be proud. The postmodern consciousness can no more prove itself than the homeless can hide themselves. In its very drive to represent itself as community in the symbolic sense, in its make-over that refers to 'tradition,' even after it has its colors done, it all the more perfectly becomes nameless and placeless. As the postmodern mind becomes disconnected from everything that it pretends to value, it engages in frenzied thematization. Everything is thematized: restaurants have themes, neighborhoods have themes, streets are named after trees in alphabetical series (Aspen, Beech, Cypress, Dogwood, and suchlike), everything. The homeless, cutting across this same thematized surface, know that everything remains problematic, nothing is really thematized, not even a 'theme park.' The only ultimate resource the postmodern community will ever be able to draw upon as proof of its unique subjectivity, its 'safe' and 'clean' interior, is the filthy homeless drifter, and the only way it will ever be able to lay claim to having a distinctive consciousness, interesting, contradictory, and worthy of respect, is if it takes the homeless back in, all of them.

NOTES

1   This chapter was originally published in *The Annals of Tourism Research* under the title 'The Tourist and the New Community' (MacCannell, 1977b), revised September 1990.

2   Here and elsewhere, I am indebted to the early rural sociological writings of Josiah Galpin (1924), from whom the figures of the farmer and the steelworker have been adapted.

3   My treatment of narcissism has been negative because I see it as the most antisocial form of self-consciousness. For an argument *for* narcissism, see Leo Bersani (1990), who suggests that the strongest human sentiments can be felt only for those few others who are exactly like oneself, and that any social arrangement not based on narcissism is necessarily feeble. For an incisive critique of Bersani, see Teresa Brennan (1990).

4   See, for example, Sassen-Koob's 1983 study of *The Mobility of Labor and Capital*, Michael Timberlake (1987), or Alain de Janvry (1975).

5   The term 'neo-totemic' was coined by Juliet Flower MacCannell in her *Regime of the Brother* (1991).

6   Of course, there is also substantial propaganda stating that economic activity *is* all there is to human life, and apparently this effectively absorbs the energy of the socially feeble-minded, taking considerable pressure off the postmodern community in its capacity as a repressive form.

7   The house referred to here is located on the 'star map tour' of Beverly Hills, and the life-sized, sculpted tourist figures, somewhat but not broadly parodic, are set up in such a way as to appear to be taking pictures of the house. Apparently it is initially unnerving to the tourists who come to take pictures of the house to find themselves lining up alongside of images of themselves engaged in the same act. But this has not deterred sociologists and anthropologists from flocking to the site.

8   I have purposefully conflated, as the culture seems to be conflating, activities and rewards that would have been socially approved and socially disapproved before postmodernity. In the postmodern community, any moral differences that may still exist between professions are less important than the level of monetary success one achieves in no matter what 'profession.'

9   Conceptually, I continue to be indebted here to Deleuze and Guattari's (1987) discussion of the nomad. In the manner of their existence in their relationship to 'the city,' the tourist and the homeless stand on either side of Deleuze and Guattari's 'nomad.' The tourist is more aligned to the official structure than the nomad, and the homeless less.

Chapter 4

Nature Incorporated[1]

Nature in Yosemite seems almost to have achieved intentionality or 'self-consciousness.' The walls of the valley are vertical, the floor is flat, the entry is dramatically indicated. It is not just a place of exquisite beauty; it is a natural place which by virtue of its highly bounded form makes an insulting reference to the built environment *avant la lettre*. Coventry Cathedral, accidentally improved by the Nazi attempt to destroy it, now open to the sky, aspires to insert itself into nature and become a *yosemite*. There are lesser *yosemites* everywhere in capitalist culture – from the 'canyons' of Manhattan to the gift box that has had its top torn off in eager anticipation. None of these express themselves with the power and intensity of the original. *Social* lines are arbitrary, and the design practice that follows them promotes status and other shallow distinctions. By contrast, in Yosemite the oppositions in *nature*, the line that separates the rock from the sky, for example, do not serve to separate one human being from another. The edge of Mirror Lake, where the water touches wildwoods and boulders, traces itself directly on the soul as a sensual contrast of rough and smooth, of male and female principles, of every gentle touch of opposites which unite humankind and makes life sweet. Psychoanalyst Jacques Lacan has remarked that a mountain reflected in a lake is the perfect image of a consciousness without ego.

My childhood impression of Yosemite was affected by a great deal of camping in parks 'designed' by my paternal grandfather, Earle Edgerly MacCannell, who was Washington State Parks architect during the Depression. He made the Indian Museum at Vantage, at the confluence of the Snake and Columbia rivers, and several other large projects, but mainly my grandfather's parks consisted of a dirt road, unisex latrine, a central well with a hand pump, a sign, and sometimes fireplaces. I do not recall ever having seen a ranger in a Washington State park in the 1950s.

My family enjoyed our week in Yosemite, the farthest away from home I had ever been, but we maintained suspicious distance from the Curry Company facilities. A park with a gift shop, cafeteria, and laundry suggested some kind of corruption. The 'Presidential' Ahwahnee Lodge, arrogantly named for the Indians whose humble lodges it displaced, was something simply to be feared like the evil cartoon castles of Dr Frankenstein or Snow White's step-mother. I attended the nature interpretation campfire where the ranger explained the tradition of the Firefall. Everyone maintained silence, as requested, waiting to hear the shout from the valley floor, 'Let the fire fall,' and we witnessed the burning embers (an 'entire tree' the ranger said) shoveled off Glacier Point, cascading into the valley. It was amusing, but I couldn't figure out what it had to do with anything 'natural.'

The great parks, even great urban parks, Golden Gate in San Francisco or Central in New York, but especially the National Parks, are symptomatic of guilt which accompanies the impulse to destroy nature. We destroy on an unprecedented scale, then in response to our wrongs, we create parks which re-stage the nature/society opposition now entirely framed by society. The great parks are not nature in any original sense. They are marked-off, interpreted, museumized nature. The park is supposed to be a reminder of what nature would be like if nature still existed. As a celebration of nature, the park is the 'good deed' of industrial civilization. It also quietly affirms the power of industrial civilization to stage, situate, limit, and control nature. By restricting 'authentic' or 'historic' nature to parks, we assert our right to destroy everything that is not protected by the Park Act. This contradiction is buried in human consciousness under the ideology of re-creational nature, the notion that the individual is supposed to forget the sense of limits which society imposes on us, and on nature, as we enter these parks. We are admitted to these parks on the moral condition that we enter only with our essential humanity. We are not supposed to bring our *social* needs, desires, statuses, and so on with us, nor to demand from the park that it satisfy these desires. This is, after all, the reason the park was established in the first place; out of guilt that we had already gone far enough in forcing nature to satisfy our social needs, perhaps too far.

None of this applies to Yosemite Valley. We want to project upon Yosemite a certain narcissism. It did not bother to wait for an Act of Congress or Presidential decree. It seems to have marked *itself* off from its surroundings. It is so beautiful that it just might be immune to the ravages of civilization. It challenges the worst in us, the part that wants to compete with nature and eventually to win. If great cities have parks, then this greatest of parks must have its city. The Curry Company concessions have been purchased by MCA Incorporated, an entertainment conglomerate. Yosemite City is a capitalist ideal, a 'company town.' El Capitan looks down upon 2.6 million paying customers annually, their arrivals now scheduled by Ticketron. There are hydro-electric power and sewage disposal plants, a Federal court, jail, hospital, clinic, and dentist offices, a morgue, dog pound, and kennel, stables, ice-skating rink, shopping mall, golf course, tennis courts, swimming pools, snack bars, art galleries, photo studios, cafeterias and restaurants, beauty parlor, barber shop, a US Post Office, commercial bank, supermarket, churches, paved parking for more than 2,000 cars, shuttle buses, several bars (some with big-screen televisions), a mountaineering school, cross-country and down-hill skiing facilities, an Indian Cultural Center and, of course, the National Park Service.[2] Social values are raised to 'ideals' in Yosemite City. The entire range of social statuses has been reconstructed in the accommodations, from the 'homeless' sleeping on the ground ($4/night) to presidents and kings sleeping at the Ahwahnee ($187/night) with its rule of 'jacket and tie' in the dining hall. Yosemite City is even developing a moral sense: rock-climbing on El Capitan and hang-gliding are acceptable, but parachute jumping off Glacier Point and snowmobiles are specifically prohibited. There used to be a horse-race track but it has been decommissioned. Conventions and other large group meetings are permitted during the off-peak season only. The Firefall is gone because it created traffic jams. Yosemite City is not just any city but one that promotes specific values: monopoly capitalism, material comforts, status distinctions, and especially the right to be entertained. The Curry Company and MCA are successfully transforming Yosemite into a 'Nature Theme Park.'

It is tempting to look upon Yosemite as the final battleground of 'nature' versus 'society': two of the worthiest adversaries head-to-head; the most beautiful natural place on earth against an entire postmodern city owned by a major corporation, attempting to take the place over from within. But this is a pseudo-battle. Its outcome is rigged. It is not nature vs. society, but 'framed' nature vs. corporate society. Society already won. The 'battle' is only another entertainment. Unless, of course, we decide to change society.

NOTES

1 This chapter was originally written as a contribution to a 'Place Debate on Yosemite' and published under the same title in the journal *Places* (MacCannell, 1990b).
2 Soon after this paper was first published in the spring of 1990, all the facilities and services in Yosemite were sold as a block to Matsushita Electric Industrial Company of Japan. This might have raised the same issue that is central to 'The Locke Case,' having to do with the limits (or lack thereof) of what can be bought and sold as a commodity in the international market. But it did not. The matter was subject to brief public debate in a subcommittee hearing of the US House of Representatives. The main outcome of the discussion so far has been a suggestion that the franchise fee to whomever owns the park facilities be raised to an undisclosed figure higher than the less than 1 per cent of gross revenue the US Government had been collecting from Curry Company and MCA International.

Part II

Majority discourse

It was the whiteness of the whale that above all things appalled me.... Though in many natural objects, whiteness refiningly enhances beauty, as if imparting some special virtue of its own, as in marbles, japonicas, and pearls; and though various nations have in some way recognised a certain royal pre-eminence in this hue; even the barbaric, grand old kings of Pegu placing the title 'Lord of the White Elephants' above all their other magniloquent ascriptions of dominion; and the modern kings of Siam unfurling the same snow-white quadruped in the royal standard; and the Hanoverian flag bearing the one figure of a snow-white charger; and the great Austrian Empire, Caesarian heir to overlording Rome, having for the imperial color the same imperial hue; and though this pre-eminence in it applies to the human race itself, giving the white man ideal mastership over every dusky tribe; and though besides all this, whiteness has been made significant of gladness, for among the Romans a white stone marked a joyful day; and though in other mortal sympathies and symbolisings, this same hue is made the emblem of many touching, noble things – the innocence of brides, the benignity of age; though among the Red men of America the giving of the white belt of wampum was the deepest pledge of honor;... yet for all these accumulated associations, with whatever is sweet and honorable and sublime, there yet lurks an elusive something in the innermost idea of this hue, which strikes more of a panic to the soul than that redness which affrights in blood.

(Herman Melville, 'The Whiteness of the Whale,' ch. 41 of *Moby Dick*)

Chapter 5

White Culture[1]

Ethnosemiotic research[2] involves repositioning social scientific activity in such a way as to privilege boundary situations and settings of culture contact over emic descriptions of 'pure' or undisturbed cultural facts. However, this simple re-framing of cultural studies has potentially radical implications for the future of intercultural understanding.[3] Perhaps the most disturbing of these implications, the one with the greatest potential institutional impact, is the implicit disavowal of conventional ethnographic expertise as the final arbiter of inter-group relations. In focusing on real relations between real groups, denial, refusals and failures of understanding are more important in the historical formation of relationships and identities than are scientific neutrality and descriptive precision in accounting for one group to another.[4] The introduction of 'expertise' into this setting is virtually guaranteed to be politically motivated and misleading. What is needed to improve our understanding of inter-group relationships is not an increase in 'truth seeking' in ethnographic accounts, but better analysis of the kind of error that is generic to inter-group relations.

This chapter is a first attempt to describe an error that is buried in the structure of touristic and other forms of white–nonwhite discourse, an error that sets the limits of that discourse. The data and evidence used here include both characterizations of whites by nonwhites and vice versa, and attempts to communicate which are specifically marked as being *between ethnic groups*. There is some insensitivity, frustration, and impoliteness in this material, on all sides. The ethnosemiotic question is this: In their interactions with others, how can groups in power manage to convey the impression that they are less ethnic than those over whom they exercise their power; in other words, how can they foster the impression that their own traits and qualities are merely correct, while the corresponding qualities of others are 'ethnic'? Similarly, and perhaps more important, how is consensus achieved on this matter, a consensus which extends to include both the groups in power and the ethnic peoples out of power? This consensus structures our institutions so that, for example, in tourism we have ethnic cuisine but no white cuisine; in the university we have ethnic studies programs, but no white studies programs. This structural imbalance is fundamental, operating on grammar and rhetoric as well as in social and economic relations.

GRAMMAR AND HIERARCHY

The grammatical elements most intimately implicated in the dialogic form are the personal pronouns and pointers, 'I' and 'you,' 'this' and 'that,' all of which depend upon the immediate situation of their utterance for their meaning. The reality to which *I* and *you* refer is solely a reality of discourse. *I* and *you* have no linguistic existence except, in Benveniste's helpful phrase, in the 'situation of "address."' The grammatical relationship between the personal pronouns, *I*, *you*, is one of impartial, non-hierarchical equivalency. Any given individual can occupy the position *I* or *you*. But what about *he* and *she*? There is, of course, an evident gender qualification here which has already become somewhat controversial, and there is something more. Within the framework of grammar, *I*, *you*, *he*, and *she* are treated as equivalent members of the class 'personal pronoun.' There would appear to be no advantage or disadvantage of any sort accruing to someone in the grammatical position of *she* rather than *you*, for example. In fact, one might go so far as to suggest that the intentional structure of categorization is to secure the impression of classificatory equality on the intersubjective or grammatical level. Accordingly, one would predict that a common grammar would *institute* a kind of original 'equality before the word' even among ethnically different interlocutors in any actual interaction setting. It is deep belief in the ultimate neutrality of grammar that causes us to resist, as a form of affectation or silliness, the recent usage shift of mainly male feminists who substitute *she*, *her*, and *hers*, for *he*, *him*, and *his*, either routinely or at random when the grammar but not the situation calls for the masculine form. The pronominal equivalency of *he* and *she* is evidently false as shown by the contradiction implicit in the selection of the masculine form over the feminine under conditions in which empirical gender is unknown or unknowable, as in the sentence, 'A scientist is expected to keep his test tubes clean.'

But what if the logic of grammatical classification is fundamentally flawed at a level that does not signal itself so obviously as it does in the putative grammatical equivalency of 'he' and 'she'? Here it is helpful to make use of Benveniste's (1971: 217–22) critique of pronominal equivalency, extend it somewhat, and explore its implications for situations of inter-ethnic interaction. According to Benveniste, '*I* signifies "the person who is uttering the present instance of the discourse containing *I*." This instance is unique by definition and has validity only in its uniqueness' (p.18). '*I*' does not refer to a class of objects or to a clear or fuzzy mental image. Its referent is entirely contextually bounded. Each utterance of *I* establishes or sets up a unique being who is both the referrer and that which is referred to. Within the 'situation of address,' *you* is symmetrically related to *I* as the one who is spoken to in the discourse containing the *you*. *I* and *you* are grammatically equivalent, forced into a relationship of equivalency by the practical exigencies surrounding the determination of their value in the actual situation of interaction. The parties to an inter-ethnic interaction, if they occupy the positions *I* and *you*, are *grammatically equal*, independent of any social inequality which may exist between them.

But none of this applies to *I* and *he*. Benveniste goes so far as to suggest that the proposed equivalency of *I*, *you*, and *he* as personal pronouns, as first, second and third 'persons,' 'simply destroys the notion of "person."' Person can be attributed only to *I* and *you*, but not to *he*. The referent to *he* need not be present in the immediate situation of face-to-face interaction. Indeed, standards of politeness in middle-class Anglo-American conversation prohibit reference to someone who is present as 'he.' The primary referent of *I* and *you* is the immediate situation of discourse, and it is only in and through the immediate situation that one can arrive at a correct pronominal determination. *He* operates on a completely different linguistic plane. *He* is not restricted to the here and now, but is free to range through the there and then. Moreover, this is an absolute freedom which begins just beyond the boundaries of discourse and extends to the beginning and end of time and space. 'In the beginning, He [not you or I] created the heavens and the earth.'

The grammatical *he* is enormously more powerful than *I* or *you*. It *seems* that through the use of *I* a speaker projects a sense of his or her own irreducible subjective identity. What is actually happening is that the *I* permits a speaker to appropriate for his or her own use all the resources of language. But this appropriation has great cost. The apparent power of the speaking subject is based on the existence within language of empty signifiers, terms which have no referent outside of their use in specific instances of discourse. The power of the speaking subject is based upon terms that have no referent, meaning, or value outside of the immediate situation, that are connected to the rest of language only by agreement with the verb. The speaking subject, on some level, has always known this, and experienced guilt associated with the knowledge that it can seem to have a self, an identity, without doing anything except connecting itself to language through discourse in the position of a speaker or hearer, an *I* or *you*. The speaking subject covers this guilt by projecting *being* onto the third person, the *he*, and subjecting itself to the judgment of the third person (For discussion, see J. MacCannell, 1986: 64–6). The power of the third 'person' derives from an entirely different source; that is, by reference not to the 'immediate' situation but to the 'objective situation.' Again, 'The scientist is expected to keep *his* test tubes clean.' *He* exists in a relationship of substitutability with all other possible *he*'s given the objective constitution of the world or universe outside the immediate, subjectively apprehended situation. In short, unlike *I* and *you*, *he* participates in and is constituted by all the powers of language to characterize, convey images, to model relationships, to establish itself as logic, and so on.

The grammatical secret of power in discourse is for the speaking subject to move into the position of *he* without seeming to leave the position of *I* or *you*. This move is anticipated in advance, facilitated, and covered up by the alleged grammatical equivalency of the personal pronouns. In the following sections on inter-ethnic interactions, whites appear to have mastered several interactional forms which permit them to operate as interactants while also seeming to be detached from the situation, to be both an *I* or a *you* and a *he* at the same time; to operate within the situation and as its external judge.[5] It is the third person vs. the Third World.

ETHNICITY AND RHETORIC

What can be said with precision about those aspects of personal identity that are marked 'ethnic'? These are certainly real and consequential in interactions of the sort to be examined here. In the social science literature, the term 'ethnicity' occupies the space between biological and genetic conceptions of race, and anthropological theories of culture. Ethnicity has never been subject to rigorous definition, and has evolved rather as a residual category capable of framing any number of observations ranging from assertions about character, to mental competency, physical beauty, susceptibility to disease, and so forth. Observations of ethnic 'traits' are ethnological not by virtue of the method of their collection, but only by virtue of their being attributed to a people which has somehow obtained a reputation for being an ethnic group. This designation itself is often far from innocent (for a discussion, see Forbes, 1979; MacCannell, 1984b and 1986b).

Until more precise definitions are available, I propose that we restrict the use of the term 'ethnicity' to refer only to those traits and characteristics which communicate 'ethnicity' to other groups, which serve to persuade others that the group in question has a legitimate claim for a distinctive ethnic identity. Similarly, it could be used to refer to traits and characteristics that are attributed to others as 'ethnic': '*I* am ———; *you* are ———; *he* is ———' ('black,' Chicano,' 'white,' and so on). This definition is closer to existing technical usage than it first appears. The main difference is that it brings to consciousness a principle underlying all previous ethnological research: ethnicity is a form of rhetoric.

In emphasizing the rhetorical component of ethnicity, it is necessary to distance oneself from the most rhetorical of rhetorical stances, namely that rhetoric is 'mere' rhetoric. Rhetorical functions lie very close to the member and class identity of all socially organized and communicating animals. Our biological constitution itself may be grounded in rhetoric. Nowhere is this principle more eloquently stated than in Charles Darwin's (1874 and 1956: 106–7) discussion of the interaction of snakes and pigs. Darwin observed:

> He who has merely shaken the rattle of a dead snake, can form no just idea of the sound produced by the living animal.... [The sound] of the rattlesnake is louder and shriller than the puff adder.... I conclude from the threatening gestures made at the

same time by many snakes, that their hissing – the rattling of the rattlesnake and of the Trignocephalus [an Indian snake that beats its tail against dry grass], – the grating of the scales of the Echis, – and the dilation of the hood of the cobra, – all subserve the same end, namely, to make them appear terrible to their enemies.

Darwin is suggesting that, for a venomous snake, it is insufficient simply to *be* venomous; it is also necessary, by whatever means are readily available, to *act* terrible – to persuade and convince enemy and prey alike. By making this distinction between *being* and *doing*, Darwin was able to make sense of several observations of snake behavior and physical form which were, until then, meaningless. (1) Pigs, which can kill snakes and be killed by them, might be warned away from a dangerous encounter by the sound of the rattle. (2) Small prey become fascinated or paralyzed by the same sound, perhaps resigned to an inevitable fate. (3) In Darwin's own words:

> [I]f we suppose that the end of the tail of some ancient American species was enlarged, and was covered by a single large scale, this could hardly have been cast off at the successive moults. In this case it would have been permanently retained, and at each period of growth, as the snake grew larger, a new scale, larger than the last would have formed above it, and would have likewise been retained. The foundation for the development of the rattle would thus have been laid; and it would have been habitually used, if the species, like to many others, vibrated its tail whenever it was irritated. That the rattle has since been specifically developed to serve as an efficient sound-producing instrument, there can hardly be a doubt.

When sounds, vocalizations, gestures, and so forth are used to move or convince an audience, we are technically dealing with *rhetoric*, the art of persuasion. The snake does not rattle at random, but in specific response to signs given off by other animals. The rattler has developed its power to persuade to a high degree, and has changed its entire physical character and mannerisms in the process. In other words, its biological constitution is an adaptation to the exigencies of cross-species communication. The rhetorical interdependence of all beings is nicely illustrated by Darwin's example of the snake–pig interactions. The snake is also the biblical figure of rhetoric and occupies a prominent place in inter-group communications intended to dramatize identity, resolve, and boundary definition as in the slogans 'White man speaks with forked tongue,' 'Don't tread on me,' and so on. Communication mediated by 'figures of speech' is not restricted to human relations. The snake handled its relations with pigs by stating, in effect, 'I am a snake.'

Darwin's model is intuitively more applicable to ethnosemiotic studies of inter-ethnic interaction than to animal communication. Something like rhetorical processes can be shown to operate in inter-specific communications in the animal world, but they are even more developed and characteristic for inter-ethnic communications in the human world. In this regard, it is interesting to note that a residual totemic system survives even in and among modern societies in which human groups draw primarily upon animal name designations in their negative classification of ethnic others as 'frogs,' 'pigs,' 'dogs,' 'apes,' and so forth. On the intra-human level, rhetoric is complex and formalized, involving the use of figured language to persuade via eloquence and style. Figures of speech, or rhetorical tropes, include metaphor, metonymy, synecdoche, catechresis, allegory, and metalepsis. One could say that Darwin's snake is making a metaleptic substitution of a hiss for a bite. But this would certainly be over-interpretation. Among humans, however, it is necessary to utilize the full conceptual framework of semiotics to explicate matters of *style* in communication patterns between groups. The new ethnosemiotic studies, cited above, have made matters of style their central concern, as in tourist art style, or black and white styles in conflict.

In inter-ethnic communication, one finds highly developed use of figured language, and other self-conscious expressive forms. In his influential 1980 Black Hills speech, American Indian Movement leader Russell Means began by saying how much he hated trying to communicate with white European peoples. He commented that his was a vital, oral tradition based on human closeness and the requirement that each individual be the bearer of fundamental truths. He understood that white people had removed themselves from the immediate situation of inter-ethnic face-to-face interaction, and suggested that this made them unable to speak and hear the truth, summing up, 'the only way to communicate with the white world is through the dead dry leaves of a book' (1980). Apparently the use of rhetorical figures, especially metaphor, is not among whatever other distinctions Means wanted to make between written and oral language. Fifteen years earlier, 'Black Power' leader Stokely Carmichael (1966) claimed that not just language but also collective action was intended as persuasive communication:

> For too many years, Black Americans marched and had their heads broken and got shot. They were saying to the country, 'Look, you guys are supposed to be nice guys... why don't you give us what we ask, why don't you straighten yourselves out?'... We cannot be expected any longer to march and have our heads broken in order to say to the whites: come on, you're nice guys. For you are not nice guys. We have found you out.

On the intra-human level, rhetoric is more than the use of figured expression in order to persuade. It is also a trick that works much like a magical illusion to produce the impression that some language is figured, that it is intended to persuade, and is therefore a cover for something that is in itself insubstantial, weak, or false, while other language is non-rhetorical or free of devices. As first Nietzsche and later Paul de Man pointed out, this is a false pretense. For whatever else it may do, language is also condemned to be composed of rhetorical figures and tropes. One can only pretend to speak without them. In Nietzsche's words:

> No such thing as an unrhetorical, 'natural' language exists that could be used as a point of reference: language is itself the result of purely rhetorical tricks and devices.... Language is rhetoric, for it only intends to convey a *doxa* (opinion), not an *episteme* (truth).... Tropes are not something that can be added or subtracted from language at will; they are its truest nature.
>
> (Quoted in de Man, 1974: 35)

We should not, however, take this to mean that the truth value of everything expressed in language is ultimately undecidable. Language may be entirely rhetorical in its essence; that is, free of all bias because it is pure bias. But language cannot survive for long outside of the social relation at the point of intersection of rhetoric and grammar. And grammar *is* biased in specific ways that can be transferred to the social relation. Dominant groups will always want to occupy the grammatical power position; that is, assume the external, objective, and judgmental role of the *he*, to become The Man, by articulating the pretense that their use of language is simply real (in other words, non-rhetorical, or non-persuasive). It may not be possible to get out of language. But it should be possible to win back some grammatical high ground for all the people, not just for those who currently dominate.

Tropes vary, of course, in the degree to which they are marked as such. It follows from this that the most rhetorical stance, the most effective form of persuasion, is that which claims to be free of rhetoric, to be non-persuasive, or 'merely grammatical.' Now it is possible to bring together the two fields of battle for human equality: the field of social relations and the field of grammar. Some will want to continue to wage this war at the level of demands for ameliorative social change. Others will want to 'deconstruct' inequality itself, which strikes me as being little more than the most sophisticated way yet devised for taking power away from newly emergent groups as soon as they get it. For my taste, the only interesting campaign would be one to win back the territory of the *he* for all people, not just for the currently dominant few. I would like to have the opportunity to look directly in the face of a different kind of ultimate subject, the third person of the Third World.

WHITE CULTURE

> White: that colour produced by reflection, transmission, or emission of all kinds of light in the proportion in which they exist in the complete visible spectrum, without sensible absorption, being thus fully luminous and devoid of any distinctive hue.
>
> (*Oxford English Dictionary*)

It should be evident enough that by 'white culture' I am not referring to this or that enclave of mainline WASPs or Afrikaners. 'White Culture,' as used here, is the structural (that is, social, linguistic, and unconscious) pre-condition for the existence of 'ethnic' groups. White Culture is an enormous totalization which, within current social arrangements, corresponds to the *being* of the third 'person' on the plane of language, and to 'white light' in physics. It arrogates to itself the exclusive right to totalize and represent all other hues 'in the proportion in which they exist in the visible spectrum.' As a cultural totality, 'whiteness' is founded on a few simple principles: the principle of depersonalization of all human relationships and the idealization of objective judgment and duty. One wonders how a culture founded on a non-dialectical relation of language and the unconscious could have survived for so long. To say that White Culture is impersonal is not the same thing as saying that it does not function like a subject or subjectivity. It is a subjectivity. But it is the kind that is cold, the kind that laughs at feelings while demanding that all surplus libido, energy, and capital be handed over to it. (For a comment on Kant's contribution to our understanding of this form of subjectivity, see Juliet Flower MacCannell, 1986, p. 127 and especially 139 ff.) White Culture begins with the pretense that it, above all, does not express itself rhetorically. Rather, the form of its expression is always represented as only incidental to the 'truth.' And its totalizing power radiates from this pretense which is maintained by interpreting all ethnic expression as 'representative,' and therefore *merely* rhetorical.

Both Stokely Carmichael and Russell Means sensed this arrangement and were greatly frustrated by it. Means cautions:

> Beware of coming to believe the white world now offers solutions to the problems it confronts us with. Beware, too, of allowing the words of native people to be twisted to the advantage of our enemies. Europe invented the practice of turning words around on themselves.
>
> (p. 25)

And Carmichael:

> When the Lowndes County Freedom Organization chose the black panther as its symbol, it was christened by the [white] press, 'the Black Panther Party' – but the Alabama Democratic Party, whose symbol is a rooster, has never been called the White Cock Party. No one ever talked about 'white power' because power in this country *is* white.

The transparency the White Culture claims for itself is also the basis for many of the observations Kochman makes in his (1984) GURT, 84 paper on 'The Politics of Politeness: Social Warrants in Mainstream American Public Etiquette.'

These and other criticisms of the Mainstream, the 'Establishment,' tend to attack a specific local irritation, the ground rules for handling a dispute, a bureaucratic procedure, a specific policy, evidence of 'institutional racism,' and so on. By now it should be evident, on both logical and historical grounds, that as important as this work has been for shoring up the self-respect of 'minorities,' it will never add up to structural change because it is entirely framed by the assumption of the dominance of White Culture.

The main defensive work of White Culture is the universalization of the concept of 'exchange values.' Once all of the groups on the face of the Earth are drawn into a single network of 'civilized' associations based on monetary or some other system of equivalencies, the transcribability of all languages and the translatability of any language into any other language, the division of the entire surface of the Earth into nation states, themselves subdivided into real-estate holdings with known owners, boundaries, and values, when the 'worth' of every human being can be calculated and compared to every other, and when this precisely calculated property, wealth, and poverty is bound together with roads and telecommunications; once all this has been accomplished, the White Cultural totalization will be complete. Within the White Culture, 'ethnicity' is the only form which indigenous groups can assume in order to be a part of the totality. This is already a pronounced and evident feature of those parts of the world in which tourism figures heavily in the economy.

White lies and white truth

The culturally unmarked term of a binary opposition – such as *male* as opposed to female, *white* as opposed to nonwhite, or *modern* as opposed to primitive – always occupies the grammatical position of *him*, never *I* or *you*, and always operates *as if* not dependent on rhetoric to maintain its position. That is, it aligns rhetoric with non-truth, and maintains itself as essentially restrained, neutral, transparent, beige, or recently, in the field of sexual relations, 'vanilla.' All the while, it projects on the other category an array of specific qualities and characteristics: emotional, spontaneous, uncontrolled, attractive, exciting, colorful, wild. This system, which operates in and between all our social institutions, is supported by a myriad of expressive procedures ranging from legal language to everyday usage. Three principal tactics are employed to preserve the apparent neutrality of White Culture, while marking cultural others as biased or self-interested; that is, personal or personalistic as opposed to impersonal, general, or universal. First, white rhetoricians focus attention on the *manner* in which others express themselves on the social or natural order, often characterizing the expressions of others as 'rhetoric,' or 'mere rhetoric.' This tactic effectively undermines the truth value of any critical comment or interpretation of social arrangements that originates outside of White Cultural consciousness. Second, White Culture suppresses from its own discourse any sustained or penetrating analyses of its own social arrangements, organization, class and status systems, policy discussions, and so forth. Understanding of these matters is kept at the banal level of official charts of organization, economic modeling, and reports written in a language that is required to be flat, thoughtless, and boring. Any *attitudes* on the white order, which are expressed from within, can, and usually do, take the form of pure signifiers, raised eyebrows, knowing looks, a smile followed by silence, such phrases as, 'he's a good man,' 'he's effective,' 'someone has got to do what's got to be done,' and so on.[6] Third, disrespect for ethnic others is publicly expressed only indirectly, so that when the system is working perfectly, as most usually it is, there is never any visible evidence of the general circulation of prejudicial sentiment.

The power of this paradigm can be illustrated by turning it against the privilege it was designed to protect; that is, by applying it to an example of white rhetoric which, once it is attended to as such, can be found infused in virtually every usage in our society. The following example was supplied by a dependable source, William F. Buckley, Jr. In a column, Buckley comes to the defense of twelve Dartmouth students who, 'after weeks of frustration over an exhibitionistic protest against apartheid,' organized themselves one night to raid and destroy the shantytown the protesters had built on the campus green. The interesting phrase here, from the standpoint of characterizing the manner of expression of the anti-apartheid protesters, is 'after weeks of frustration.' This is more complex than a simple deformation of language such as calling fascist Contras 'Freedom Fighters.' By using this phrase, Buckley suggests that the perpetrators of a violent act were actually using restraint, while the non-violent protesters were unrestrained, or 'exhibitionistic.' Buckley continues, '[the raid] was done without anybody's being threatened, let alone hurt, never mind the caterwauling of two girls sleeping in the shanties, who chose under no provocation to act hysterically.' In the current framework, the sentence needs little analysis. The night raid to knock down the shanties is characterized as unexceptional behavior, as 'no threat' to the girls sleeping in the structures that were destroyed. 'Caterwauling' is interesting. Its proper use is to describe the sounds made by a female cat to attract males. Buckley's literal meaning provides a more powerful metaphor and is rhetorically more important than the surface figures, his 'style,' with which he decorates his prose. The use of the term 'caterwauling' suggests that the female protesters were oversexed and taunting, bringing upon themselves uncontrolled aggressive male responses, 'after weeks of frustration.'

Attenuation and indirection in the negative characterization of others is accomplished by producing a system of equivalencies at the literal level so, for this purpose, he need never use a metaphor or figured language that is marked as such. For example, he need never come right out and say that the white women students who embraced the cause of black South Africans are 'like cats in heat.' But the *Oxford English Dictionary* gives us no alternative definition of the word he chose, 'caterwauling,' on which to build another interpretation. Nor would he ever say that 'Indians are like dogs.' But he does explain the current situation at Dartmouth in these terms:

> What is going on at Dartmouth is a kind of solipsistic crystallization of ideological interest groups whose cause militant, a few years ago, was the elimination of the Indian, which for generations was Dartmouth College's symbol, implying ethnic prejudice against Indians only to the extent that Yale graduates could be accused of a contempt for bulldogs.

The essential equivalence of the dog and Indian 'mascots' is so basic to Buckley's white consciousness that it need not be expressed metaphorically: that is, 'Indians are like dogs.' Indeed, such equivalency should not be expressed metaphorically since, in metaphor, there is always some shock or surprise resulting from the realization of non-equivalency. My love isn't really like a red, red rose. To say it is is a 'little white lie.' An Indian *is* like a dog, though. Indians live off of scraps on the margins of white society; they are faithful companions (Fido and Tonto); they are sometimes unpredictable and vicious. This is a white 'truth' and as such should never be expressed in language that is marked as metaphorical. In the framework of White Culture, the 'truth' should never be expressed in such a way that it might be apprehended as mere metaphor.

To summarize procedures, it may be possible to begin to undo the white pretense of transparency with a kind of reading that, after Bateson, Deleuze and Guattari, can be called 'schizophrenic.' Specifically, what I am recommending here is that we read white literal pronouncements metaphorically and metaphorical pronouncements literally. There is more at stake here than catching Buckley's 'bad faith,' something we knew was there all along. Ethnic formations themselves are a function of parallel processes. In other words, inequality, or the perpetual striving for equality, was built in to the original White Culture-ethnicity setup.

Subjugation: grammatical and socio-economic

A phase in the development of the White Culture totalization which is now virtually complete might be called the pre-tourist, pre-colonial, pre-ethnic, initial contact situation. There are standardized forms for this initial contact – at least from the standpoint of White Culture – so much so, in fact, that one of the anthropoid apes (the orangutan) was originally mistakenly classified as a sub-group of *Homo sapiens*. There is a great deal of rhetorical commentary (masked as 'history') surrounding initial contact, most of it intended to justify the impending subordination of the newly contacted group. Examples would include accounts of raids, massacres, fabulous naivety (for example, the 'sale' of Manhattan), headhunting, cannibalism, human sacrifice, and so on. We are now beginning to see some carefully considered anthropological accounts of the transition from the rhetorically charged moment of initial contact into the period of 'ethnicity,' and the specific ways in which the original characterization of the group shapes its 'ethnicity.'

Renato Rosaldo (1978: 240) has studied a group that resists incorporation within the political administration of a nation state, the Philippine Ilongots. He discovered his own ethnographic observations to be at variance with the characterization of Ilongots by Philippine officials, who call the Ilongots 'wild Indians' and 'bandits.' Rosaldo's opening question is, 'What happens to language?' What happens to language when the state and its agents confront peoples who remain beyond conventional social role and class positions – beyond the state's jurisdiction? What happens when those who are 'civilized' and 'controlled' attempt to incorporate peoples who are perceived as 'wild' and 'savage'? Rosaldo

terms the deformation of language that occurs under these conditions 'the rhetoric of control,' and provides several examples.
Citing a nineteenth-century Dominican friar's report on the Ilongots, Rosaldo comments:

> In his eyewitness report the friar said that Ilongot 'gardens were
> miserable, filled with undergrowth and untended.' Yet my
> observations led to the very opposite conclusion.... He advanced
> a further argument: the 'houses corresponded perfectly with
> the gardens.' They were 'silent, unkept, miserable.' He went on
> to characterize the people as 'impertinent' and 'filthy' and
> attributed their character to the 'moral atmosphere in which
> they were raised.' Through a series of correspondences, moving
> from garden to house to people, the Dominican friar piled
> evidence on top of evidence (actually rather messily) to demon-
> strate that Ilongots lived in a condition of moral disorder and
> evil. Thereby he justified his enterprise introducing a lawful
> order that consisted of his religion and civilization.
>
> (1978: 246–7)

The Ilongots, for their part, strengthen the hands of those who
would control them by the direct manner in which they express
themselves to whites. They kill whites and take their heads as
trophies. Rosaldo comments: '[T]heir reputation was considerably
blackened after they murdered an anthropologist, William Jones.
They, as a member of the constabulary put it, were "rated the worst
of our wild non-Christians"' (p. 249). And

> [In 1959] a member of the Philippine constabulary murdered
> an Ilongot father and son and Ilongots in turn retaliated by
> beheading forty-four Christians, creating panic in the towns
> and valleys and receiving headline coverage in the Manila
> press.... One local mayor urged the bombing and extermination
> of the Ilongot people, saying 'the only good Ilongots are dead
> Ilongots.'

Freud taught that decapitation is metaphoric castration. This is
perhaps not the only case in which the metaphor is ultimately more
meaningful or fateful than the underlying 'reality' of which it is
supposed to be a mere reflection. It is also operative in the rhetoric
of the mayor in which he equates vitality with evil in his framing
of Ilongot ethnicity. Only Rosaldo, it seems, persists in his drive
for accuracy in descriptions of Ilongot behavior:

Since the Ilongots were 'uncivilized,' and since their lack of civilization threatened town and roadway, they became categorized as butchers. This elaboration was built on a grain of truth. Ilongots did in fact raid and take heads. However, to be strictly accurate, they did not rob.

(p. 245)

Rosaldo appears to be blind to his own most important insight: namely, that ethnic characterizations are more a reflection of the conditions of contact with White Culture than they are based on ethnographic truth. The only role ethnography has ever been able to play in this larger drama is the undoing of stereotypes. Rosaldo does not consider that all stereotypical characterizations are 'built on a grain of truth.' Human behavior is such that a factual base can be found for any rhetorical elaboration of human character one would wish to make. As one moves up in hierarchies of control, eventually arriving at the top of Western bureaucracy and the other command centers of White Culture, one finds increasingly self-interested exploitation of this principle, by definition. The social construction of 'ethnicity' in white narrative is the ultimate base for the power to control others, and the way this power perpetuates itself.

The only real conflict that occurs in the process of incorporating the diverse peoples of the world in the framework of White Culture is over the value and meaning of land and money. All other arrangements – class position, territorial rights, the arrangement between the sexes, equality, and so on – are determined in advance once the ethnic group accepts white definitions of land and money. Specifically, land and money are ultimate values; control of the land by the state and/or private parties has precedence over any collective territorial rights based on traditional use such as swidden agriculture; and a person's worth can be measured in money. Although these notions are taken for granted within the framework of White Culture and its control mechanisms – modern economic science, for example – they are not universally accepted as valid.

The sharpest conflicts occur over attempts to universalize these principles, for example, when a representative of White Culture discovers that a 'savage' group has little or no interest in money, when it is discovered that money is not universally transvalued as a medium of exchange (See Parsons, 1975, for an excellent analysis of money). As long as the people who are about to be incorporated in the framework of White Culture, as an 'ethnic' group, understand the value of money and are willing to use it, there is an effective medium through which the process of their subjugation can operate in the only effective way; that is, in terms that are acceptable to them. It is relatively easy to prevent them from accumulating money in any appreciable quantity. The trick is to get them to agree that money is important. Rosaldo makes the same point: 'My investigations indicate that civilized society is most likely to infer the social character of indigenous peoples from those acts which *impede commerce*' (p. 240). When the savage is disdainful of money and/or unwilling to sell his land, the 'civilized' become utterly frustrated and begin to define their own actions as 'pacification,' the 'maintenance of security,' and so on. In 1967, I asked a Defense Intelligence Agency operative, who was then in charge of covert activities for a region of Laos, why he was putting bombs in bags of food destined for some mountain tribes. His immediate reply was, 'because they are sitting on some valuable real estate.'

Interestingly, peoples not yet incorporated into the framework of White Culture, who are attempting to resist it, may judge one another in terms of their dependence on money, admiring most those who can do without it. Lee Drummond (1977: 81) reports:

> On a trip I made to one of the most remote Carib households on the river, I was accompanied by an elderly Arawak man.... The Carib family, he pointed out, lives two days by dugout from his own Arawak village, where the last shop on the river is located. They travel down river every month or so, depending on when they have a supply of smoked bush meat, fish poison, or logs to trade with the shop owner for provisions. My informant described the situation in the Creole English of the river: 'The coffee finish, the sugar finish, the Kero [kerosene] finish, and still they remain at home. When the matches about finish, then they does leave. That is the real Carib way. If it was Arawak now, the coffee finish and he again back at the shop.'

George Marcus (1980: 58–9) found a document which provides a rare glimpse into this matter from the point of view of the people who are being incorporated. Following are portions of the 150-year-old narrative retelling the story of the humiliation of a Tonga chief and his wife at the hands of a colonial governor who had invited the Tonga royalty to be his 'house guests':

The first thing that he and his wife had to do when they arrived at the governor's house, where they went to reside, was to sweep out a large courtyard, and clean down a great pair of stairs. In vain they endeavored to explain, that in their own country they were chiefs, and, being accustomed to be waited on, were quite unused to such employments. Their expostulations were taken no notice of, and work they must. At first their life was so uncomfortable, that they wished to die; no one seemed to protect them; all the houses were shut against them; if they saw anybody eating, they were not invited to partake. Nothing was to be got without money, of which they could not comprehend the value, nor how this same money was to be obtained in any quantity. If they asked for it, nobody would give them any, unless they worked for it; and then it was so small in quantity, that they could not get with it one-tenth of what they wanted.... Thus, he said, even being a chief did not prevent him from being used ill, for, when he told them he was a chief, they gave him to understand, that *money* made man a chief.... He expressed his astonishment at the perseverance with which white people worked from morning till night, to get money; nor could he conceive how they were able to endure so much labor.... He still thought it a foolish thing that people should place a value on money, when they either could not or would not apply it to any useful (physical) purpose. If, said he, 'it were made of iron, and could be converted into knives, axes, and chisels, there would be some sense in placing a value on it; but as it is, I see none.... If provisions (i.e., yams, pork, or gnatoo] were the principal property of a man, and it ought to be, as being the most useful and the most necessary, he could not store it up, for it would spoil, and so he would be obliged either to exchange it away for something else useful, or share it out to his neighbors, and inferior chiefs and dependents for another.' He concluded by saying, 'I understand now very well what it is that makes the Papalangis so selfish – it is this money.'

While negative ethnic stereotyping is guarded against in European and American public life, and seems to be on the decline, it recurs more or less automatically, even in public settings, whenever an 'ethnic' group stands as a barrier to the unfettered economic pursuits of whites. 'Ethnicity' was invented in the first place for use on such occasions. The following was gleaned from a 1981 article (D. Campbell) in the Real Estate section of the *Los Angeles Times*. The Cahuilla Indians apparently own much of the land in and around Palm Springs, which they lease rather than sell to the whites who build condominiums and resorts on it. The article characterizes the situation as a 'crazy quilt division of land ownership, here – half Indian controlled, half free.' The rhetorical charge of the word 'free' should not go unnoticed. Again, it seems to have slipped directly from the white unconscious. The article goes on to report that: (1) the property values in the area have inflated to the point that the 'average five bedroom home sells for $603,000'; and (2) every ten or twenty years, half the property owners must renegotiate their leases with the Cahuilla. The rhetorical characterizations of the Indians flow logically from these structural conditions. In the same article we read:

> Off-stage, in the wings, the fewer-than–200 stoic-faced members of the Agua Caliente band of the Cahuilla tribe watch with satisfaction and count their money for they are the dominant, united voice as to where the popular watering spot for the wealthy goes next.

> The Agua Caliente are clearly in the catbird seat. And no one in memory ever quite 'fell into it' the way the rag-tail forty Indians did who made up the entire band in 1876 when President Ulysses S. Grant signed over to them 'San Bernardino Township... Section 14.'

> Establishment of the reservation was of absolutely no interest to the tribe... living in almost complete isolation from any large group of civilized humans, and even from other tribes – very primitive.

The article goes on to estimate huge wealth for the Indians and to document Indian history of alleged irresponsibility in the handling of money. And it concludes with the white myth of the oil-rich Indian

> who would go in and lay down several thousand dollars in cash for a new LaSalle and then he would drive in it until it ran out of gas. He was used to horses. When the car stopped he presumed it was dead. So he would go back and buy another one. He ended up on welfare.

The aim of this standardized bit of white rhetoric is to put the

ethnic group in a double-bind relative to money. They are supposed to be in the money economy, but not to have any surplus
money of their own. Moreover, there is no reason to honor debts
to them, because they would not know what to do with the money
if they received it.

Association and antithesis in rhetoric and ethnicity

Darwin gives two main principles which determine the meaning
of an expression: *association*, or identification; and *opposition*, or
antithesis. An example of an associational determination of
meaning is the kneading response of an adult cat when stroked
and pleased. This is the same action used by the cat as an infant to
stimulate production of its mother's milk – presumably resulting
in pleasurable gratification. Association and antithesis are also
basic terms in the analysis of rhetoric and ethnic interactions. The
kneading of the cat is a clear case of a cat making a metaphor. The
cat eloquently expresses that 'being stroked in this way is like
sucking on a tit.' Ethnic expression is also organized around
identification and assimilation (association) on the one hand, and
resistance, opposition, and antithesis on the other.

Most of Darwin's examples of antithesis in the expression of
emotions are drawn from the behavior of dogs in their relationships with humans. He notes that when a dog is about to attack an
enemy, he holds his tail rigid, raises his upper lip exposing his
canines, presses his ears close and backwards to the head, and
emits a savage growl. Darwin (1956: 51) elaborates:

> Let us now suppose that the dog suddenly discovers that the
> man he is approaching is not a stranger, but his master; and let
> it be observed how completely and instantaneously his whole
> bearing is reversed. Instead of walking upright, the body sinks
> downward or even crouches, and is thrown into flexuous move-
> ments; his tail, instead of being held stiff and upright, is lowered
> and wagged from side to side; his hair instantly becomes
> smooth; his ears are depressed and drawn backwards, but not
> closely to the head, and his lips hang loosely.... Not one of the
> above movements, so clearly expressive of affection, are of the
> least direct service to the animal. They are explicable, as far as
> I can see, solely from being in complete opposition or antithesis
> to the attitudes and movements which, from intelligible causes,

are assumed when a dog intends to fight, and which consequently are expressive of anger.

In ethnic studies we have come to think of *association* vs. *opposition* as two completely different ways in which a subordinate group can relate to a dominant group. Edwin Almirol (1979: 368) has described the process of association and assimilation among the Otome:

> [A]n Otome, in order to assume political leadership, must assume a Mestizo role; he must be seen around Mestizos, he must have connections with other leaders (mostly Mestizo), he must leave the *milpa* and acquire a nonagricultural occupation. He is expected to cultivate obvious visual attributes such as wearing Western-style clothes, refusing to speak Otome in the presence of Mestizos [etc.].... In other words, an Otome who aspires to a political office aspires to a Mestizo identity. He begins to act increasingly like a Mestizo.

To this can be added many other examples: the eye-rounding operations of the wives of Vietnamese Generals Thieu and Ky, the decline in women's undergarment sales in Japan after Marilyn Monroe claimed not to wear any, and so forth. It is perhaps worth noting in this regard, that in the human as in the animal world, emulation and passing are often accomplished with such finesse that the resulting 'copy' is better than the original. Of course, no matter how perfectly conceived, the entire associative effort can fail miserably, and inevitably does, when the socially superior group shifts its grounds, as occurred prior to the following conversation that was reported to me by one of its parties. Two French university students heatedly engaged an African exchange student in a restaurant in the south of France. The African had proudly proclaimed that his people were fully converted to Christianity, whereupon the French replied with disgust that only proved their continued susceptibility to mumbo-jumbo. The African reacted with genuine shock, 'You don't believe in Jesus Christ our Lord? I thought only Barbarians did not believe in God.' And the French students answered, laughing uproariously, 'Wrong, it is only the barbarians who *do* believe in God.' The incident is isolated, of course, but it nicely illustrates the logical flaw in equating assimilation with equality.

On opposition, or antithesis as the way of relating subordinate to dominant groups, Michael Hechter (1975) comments:

> To the extent that social stratification... is based on observable cultural differences, there exists the probability that the disadvantaged group will, in time, reactively assert its own culture as equal or superior to that of the relatively advantaged core [p. 10].

> Since increased contact between core and periphery does not tend to narrow the economic gaps between the groups, national development will best be served by strengthening the political power of the peripheral groups so that it may change the distribution of resources of its greater advantage. Ultimately this power must be based on political organization. One of the foundations on which such organization might rest is, of course, cultural similarity, or the perception of a distinctive *ethnic identity* in the peripheral group [p. 34, Hechter's emphasis].

One of the problems with the literature on *opposition* as an interaction strategy, is that it places too much emphasis on positive romantic images of the exploited sub-groups. In the literature there is little evidence of understanding of the power to profane that comes from being an 'underdog' or an outcast. Yet this kind of understanding operates in many of the oppositional interactions between subordinate and dominant groups. One of Dan Rose's respondents in his (1977: 140) ethnography of Philadelphia blacks, knew full well both his rhetorical power and his negative power derived from his sub-proletarian position: 'He waved his arm and asked, "See all this space?" His motion took in the southern half of the city – where blacks and other ethnics live. "I'm fucking all this space."'

There are two possible models for ethnic conflict and assimilation. The one I am proposing here is that the real relationship of ethnic groups to White Culture is determined by a logical flaw in the grammatical classification of 'persons.' Another approach which is followed by some social theorists and leaders of ethnic solidarity movements involves a modified game-theoretical model in which ethnic–white interactions are only two among many possible combinations. The standard political-theoretical position is that White Culture is the culture of just one group among many, not the only model that exists for cultural consciousness, and that whites occupy superior social positions only because they have been historically lucky, or mean, or that they started the game with more chips. The problem with all such models is they underestimate the power of the White Cultural totalization operating outside of the immediate situation of face-to-face interaction and on an ideological level. The failure to provide an adequate model of the source of white power, beyond its administrative power, its buying power, and its fire power, comes out most clearly in conflictual relations involving two or more non-white ethnic groups. These interactions assume the form of a fantasy of a fair fight with whites, one in which the other ethnicity stands in the place of the whites in a dream of a true *I/you* relationship, moreover, one which guarantees the victory of a nonwhite. But these dreams quickly turn into slapstick.

Many years ago, before there was any Black Power or American Indian movements, a black singing group, the Mills Brothers, turned their creative thoughts to the site of a famous white defeat, and composed and sang this song about the Indian and some tourists, 'Across the Alley from the Alamo':

Across the alley from the Alamo
Lived a Pinto pony and a Navajo
Who sang a sort of Indian 'hy dee ho'
To the people passing by

They used to make frijoles and corn, you know
For the people passing by.

The lyrics and the up-beat, jivey tune suggest a kind of friendly, half-hearted, harmless pushing and shoving between two low-status minorities, the urban-based black musicians and the fictional Indian 'across the alley from the Alamo.' Lee Drummond (1977: 85) reports a pattern of interaction between the Carib and Arawak when they get together, which might be characterized in similar terms:

Birthdays, weddings, baptismal celebrations, and even a simple abundance of manioc provide opportunities for intertribal socializing, which invariably takes the form of a 'spree,' as it is known in Creole dialect.... I was told by several informants that a decade or two ago, when feelings between Arawak and Carib were reportedly stronger than today, sprees at which both parties were present invariably involved some fighting along tribal lines. The institution of the fist fight assumes a benign form among Guyanese AmerIndians. The combatants do not come to grips until both have drunk enough to be well past the ability of doing one another serious harm. The fight, rather than being a form of aggravated conflict, is simply the terminal phase of the spree, ending perhaps in the departure of one party and a lapse into unconsciousness of the other.

Drummond may be overplaying the unseriousness of these affairs. The secret to any slapstick is the constant possibility and avoidance of potentially life-threatening mishaps. What appears on the surface to be silly, comedic behavior only partly conceals a death wish. Drummond also reports that, when Creoles fight, 'rum and machete (called a "cutlass") make a lethal combination that results in the mutilation or occasional murder of one of the antagonists.' And the Mills Brothers song, already cited, does not ultimately conceal their wish for the sacrificial death, in the form of an erasure, of the Indian here standing in the place of the whites in the framework of black–nonblack interactions:

The pinto spent his time swishin' flies
and the Navajo watched the lazy skies
And very very rarely did they rest their eyes
On the people passing by.

One day they went a walkin'
Out on the railroad track
They were swishin' not a-lookin'
Toot Toot, they never came back.

The ultimate futility of nonwhite inter-ethnic conflict provides the best available evidence of the effectiveness of White Culture to produce the impression that it is simply the most successful player in the inter-ethnic power game, not the only one allowed to play.

I want to suggest that assimilation vs. opposition are not two distinctly different or opposing forms of interaction between subordinate and dominant groups in a 'society.' Rather they are merely two different ways of expressing the same grammatically determined relationship of an 'ethnic' group to white culture, of *you* and *I* to *him*. From this perspective, the notion of society itself is a hypostatic entity, or a limp ideological construct of White Culture which functions to perpetuate the illusion that there is some entity other than itself (namely, 'society') which supersedes and contains white–ethnic interactions in a framework of potential equality. Of course, if there is no higher order cultural frame than White Culture, if White Culture is not merely a social and economic but also a flawed grammatical construct that sets the limit on all thought about human relations, there can be no prospect for human equality, at least not until a full disclosure of these arrangements is put into the widest possible circulation.

NOTES

1 This chapter was originally given as a paper under the same title at the Georgetown University *Roundtable on Languages and Linguistics*, March 12, 1986. An earlier version of it was published in French under the title 'Tourisme et identité culturelle,' D. MacCannell, 1986. This is the first time it has appeared in print in English.

2 Ethnosemiotics is the study of signifying practices of ethnic groups including folk taxonomies, folk-lore, -literature, and -music, myth, ritual, and ceremony, as discursive forms occurring *between* groups, intentionally and unintentionally relating groups to one another in multi-group systems. See Greimas and Courtès, 1979; MacCannell, 1979; MacCannell and MacCannell, 1982. Ethnosemiotic research has revealed that inter-group communication defines the group as much as vice versa.

3 In an earlier (1979) article, I summarized the program for ethnosemiotic studies as follows: (1) research on the production of culture as interpretation motivated by social differences; (2) turning existing anthropological insight derived from the study of remote groups back onto our own social life; and (3) continued discovery of new perspectives of 'Third' and 'Fourth World' peoples which have developed alongside, often in opposition to, the official anthropological version (p. 151).

4 Recent examples of studies of inter-ethnic interaction include research on the role of 'culture brokers' in anthropology, Nelson Graburn's (e.g., 1982) studies of the deformation of folk traditions under pressures of tourism, Bennetta Jules-Rosette's explicitly ethnosemiotic studies of African tourist art (1984) and 'Ethiopian Jokes' (1986), Jim Boon's (1977 and 1979) literate accounts of the romanticization of anthropological subject matter, Lee Drummond's (1977) description of the contribution of inter-ethnic bar-room brawling to the formation of Carib 'ethnicity,' and Thomas Kochman's important (1981) study of ethnic interactions in the United States, *Black and White Styles in Conflict*. When a group's name appearing in the *Ethnographic Atlas* is actually a pejorative term from a neighboring language, it is obvious that the group's identity has been shaped by interaction and communication processes. Less obvious examples include situations in which the need to maintain distance takes the practical form of food taboos which 'incidentally' reduce inter-group commerce.

5 The perspective presented in this chapter may help to clear up an

apparent paradox in ethnosemiotic studies of white–nonwhite interaction: specifically, the reason nonwhites cannot translate the interactional advantage they often have in face-to-face interaction into more generalized forms of power. Kochman, for example (1981 and 1984), convincingly makes the case that in black/white interactions, blacks enjoy several cultural advantages, including emphasis on and practice at repartee, higher tolerance for disagreement, and so on, and they often win arguments face-to-face. So why do they not move into positions of authority in business and government, at least those positions which emphasize verbal skills? Alternatively, how does white culture preserve its historical privilege against the flow of outcomes of day-to-day interaction?

6   I first heard of this interesting phrase used by a white professor leaving a meeting at which an academic (ethnic studies) program was disestablished. One month after this paper was read at GURT 86 in Washington, DC, President Reagan attempted to justify his air attack on Libya using the following phrase: 'Today we have done what we had to do.'

Chapter 6

The Liberty restoration project[1]

Sometime in 1984, I was called without warning by a journalist from New England and asked about the restoration of the Statue of Liberty. The work had just begun. Pictures were circulating in the press at that time of metal skin eaten through by acid rain and airborne chemicals. I was not involved in the project to restore Liberty, but the reporter assumed that I would have a well-formed opinion on it. I am afraid I disappointed him:

> 'They shouldn't do it.'
> 'What?'
> 'Restore the Statue. It's wrong for America.'
> 'What should they do?'

I thought for a moment and could not come up with an answer, so I just repeated my reaction. 'Let time wear at her, like a mountain or a Greek temple.'

'Why?' Again, I could not answer. The call prompted in me a powerful feeling of the impropriety of the restoration project, so when I hung up I began to make these notes.

I certainly did not wish the statue ill. I recalled a friend, a Jewish refugee from the Nazi terror, describing her feelings as a little girl on entering the New York harbor and seeing her new country and the statue for the first time. She was overcome with enormous relief that she had escaped horror and had a chance for a new life's beginning. How could I oppose the restoration without also wanting these memories to fade, something I certainly did not want. The incident reminded me that no matter how analytical one's turn of mind, love of liberty is always deeply irrational and completely personal. Before I could discover the reasons for my antipathy toward the restoration project, I had first to ask myself, Why do *I* love liberty?

Liberty originates between peoples and cultures as an agreement, a relation and dialogue between equals. In our US case, we undertook a major collaboration with the French to determine the eventual form of our 'Liberty.' The word still slips easily into French, as in *'liberté, egalité, fraternité.'* The statue stands in a series of crucial gifts from the French that began with the Founding Fathers' reading of the *philosophies* and includes Lafayette's blood on the field at Brandywine, Admiral de Grasse's defeat of the British naval evacuation force at Chesapeake Bay, and General de Rochambeau's victory at Yorktown. There is little emphasis on Yorktown in American schoolchildren's history books, perhaps because the British surrendered to the French there, not to George Washington, as American children are taught to believe. France was first officially to welcome America as an equal into the order of free and independent nations.

Americans predictably love and hate the French, who taught them about freedom, who first accepted the premise of their freedom, who fought alongside them to secure their freedom, who did not steal their freedom from them at Yorktown, and who gave them the statue of Liberty, the symbol of their freedom. There is much still to be learned from the early French example and, of course, much resistence to that lesson.

Because there remains a strong French accent on 'lee-bear-tay,' I can, if I wish, still go against my inborn American pragmatism. If I feel free to follow my heart instead of the voice of authority, I tell myself at least the French are with me. In short, I love 'Liberty' irrationally, the way I love structuralism and Saussure's *sémiologie*, and Lévi-Strauss's and Barthes' *Mythologies*, Durkheim's sociology, Rousseau's *Confessions* and *Second Discourse*, Marx's *18th Brumaire*, and the most improbable, honest, and bloody revolution in human history. But my irrational attraction is already forced to work against a repression: in our schools and at the university we are taught that all this French stuff is wrong, especially the revolution.

Liberty is the most ideological of all concepts. A normal human being has to believe in *freedom* in order to commit atrocities; a person must believe in the cause of freedom in order to be duped by authority and turned into a mental slave or a part of the propaganda machine, a supporter of 'freedom fighters.' Only one who thought he was acting in the cause of freedom could use a

B–52 to carpet bomb other human beings, breaking everyone in his path to fist-sized chunks, literally shredding the eardrums of survivors for miles from the blasts.

Under 'Liberty' in *The New Columbia Encyclopedia* (1975 edn: 1,574) it is said that 'Liberties are acquired through the joining together of like-minded individuals to gain special privileges for themselves.' The entry does not go on to say the obvious, 'at the expense of the liberty of others.' Well-trained, or schooled, thinking about 'liberty' necessarily takes the form of suppression of the obvious. Oklahomans have a gift for the opposite kind of thought; that is, unruly or 'careless' thought which makes the obvious obvious:

> OKLAHOMA CITY (UPI) – A bill that would make women equal partners in marriage was defeated Thursday in the Oklahoma House ...
>
> Rep. Freddye Williams said her bill, which was defeated 37–56, would have repealed a section of law that makes the husband the head of the household. She said that under her proposal women would be equal partners in a marriage.
>
> 'This is an idea whose time has come,' she said.
>
> Opponents, led by Rep. Frank Harbin, said the measure was in opposition to the scriptures.... Rep. Stephen Sill said marriage was 'ordained by God.' He discounted claims that women are discriminated against.
>
> 'Discrimination is the very fulcrum of liberty,' he said. 'Every time you discriminate, you make a choice.'
>
> (*Sacramento Bee*, Feb. 24, 1984: A3)

The establishment of 'liberty' as an ideal is also the establishment of constraint as socially approved practice. Recent feminist theory enlightens us as to the reason why the figure of a woman, covered with a veil and hollow at the center, should have been chosen to do the dirty work of representing 'liberty.'[2] Liberty would have to be double-wrapped, first to cover up its origin in determinism and unfreedom, then to cover up the cover-up. The touristic act of getting inside Liberty only establishes the ground of the dialectic of the first veil: she is like the Virgin Mary, the mother is the antithesis of the whore; she is like a 'libertine' who takes on all comers.

Nothing less than an enormous maternal figure could accomplish the ideological work of spreading the pretense of freedom and equality among the 'huddled masses' who have just arrived to take their place at the bottom of the most hierarchical society the world has ever known. There is no equality in America, of course, except we are all equal in her eyes, as her children.

It is no accident that some of the saddest moments in the life of the nation took place on Ellis Island, directly at the foot of Liberty, and that this sadness is repressed to the point that it must be officially remembered as joy. Until the Theodore Roosevelt reforms of 1901, immigrants were forced to exchange their life's-savings for a dollar or two, families were divided and some members sent back to Europe alone, and immigration service agents issued landing cards in exchange for sex, often demanded from the children of an arriving family. A Lebanese woman who made a contribution to the restoration project sent this note along with her donation:

> When we got to Ellis Island, after months of struggle and red tape, my mother was literally dragged back on the ship.... My uncle, who was sponsoring us did not get the cablegram in time to meet us. [After two years in France, the mother tried again and made it.] I must tell you here that the men who dragged my mother back to the ship all wore derbies. For months and months when I saw a man with a derby on, I would go to the other side of the street.... I am glad they went out of style.
>
> (Bundeson, 1986: 26)

How is it possible to experience, even to hear about, such things and not become bitter? There are good grounds here for hating Liberty rather than loving her while projecting the hatred onto the derby hats of official thugs. One's relationship to Liberty can never be completely intellectual.

Having gone through these reasons why I should not love her, and recognizing that I still do, I conclude that I love her for her looks. To me, she has a beautiful face which contradicts absolutely what has evolved as the American standard of feminine beauty. Liberty could never be Miss America. First, she is *big*, not merely the tallest woman, but at the time of her creation, the tallest structure ever erected. Even when her scale is taken into account, she has enormous breasts which would certainly be judged as 'vulgar' in the swim-suit competition. Her eyes are too large and wide-set. Her nose is much too strong – narrower at the tip than at the bridge. And her mouth, in spite of having arguably the most

sensuous lower lip in the history of facial representation, is judgmental.

By contrast, the Miss Americas that I have been told I am
supposed to love for their looks have mythic faces: the purity they
achieve is in a perfect equation of stupidity and cuteness, captured
in a precious instant precisely between girlhood and womanhood.
As she walks up the runway with her bouquet of long-stemmed
roses, trembling lips, and tears of joy, Miss America always wears
the expression of one who is being 'deflowered.' Not Liberty. To
look Liberty directly in the eye necessarily raises questions about
the equation of freedom, feminine sexuality, and strength of
character. There is nothing weak about her face, and nothing
masculine. Emma Lazarus called her a 'mighty woman.' She does
not hide her strength by playing 'daddy's little girl,' nor does she
hide what is feminine about her strength by pretending to be a
man.

Liberty is mainly intolerable as a figure in current American
cultural schemata, even in the movements for gender and ethnic
equality. There were persistent reports, always denied, that when
she was hidden from view by the scaffolding during the restoration
process, the workmen enjoyed urinating on her (see, for example,
The Sacramento Bee, May 9, 1986: A16). Still, there *she* is, a big
woman somehow concerned with our freedom, and engendering
male agression and ritualistic evasions at every turn. We are not
free to think that she possesses sexuality, that there is a hint of
sexual tension in her face. We are not free to discuss the indelicate
matter of the way she is dressed, how much more this light gown,
held with a single clasp, promises to reveal to sight and touch than
even the smallest metallic bikini. We are not free to imagine that
she is leading the way to bed. We are supposed to think that she
is just standing in the harbor, even though it is clear from her
posture (she is pushing off from the ball of her almost bare right
foot) that she is hurrying forward. Can we end the evasion? Of
course, she will produce monumental anxiety in anyone who is
expected to satisfy her. Perhaps we can continue to pretend that
we are all her children, saved once again by the incest taboo.[3]

Or perhaps we can rob her of her strength by showing her up
as decrepit, as in need of 'restoration.'

There is, or should be, a dignity to aging. And it was this dignity
that was denied by the restoration project. It made the statue too
much like Americans who are fearful of getting old, who believe

they derive their status from 'looking young.' At first I thought this was the reason I was reflexively against the restoration. She should be permitted to grow old naturally. Perhaps she really could continue to watch over us until the *Planet of the Apes: II*. I admit to being embarrassed when someone tells me they think they need a face- or body-lift, or when they put on a mini-skirt at age forty-five. But this cannot be the whole reason for my opposition to the restoration. If someone I loved really wanted a mini or a face-lift, I would go along with it.

A restoration means that something important is gone forever. Even when the greatest care is exercised, as it certainly was in the case of the statue, technically there is no such thing as 'restoration.'[4] A restoration is really the production of a new object which stands in a dialectical relation to the original. Already before the statue was set in place, someone had altered Eiffel's design specifications, offsetting her head and her upraised arm by almost 2 feet, clumsily fitting the assembly together with inelegant bricolage that would eventually buckle under pressure. The restoration team very honestly describes the impossibility of achieving a convergence between philosophy and practice:

> Whatever the reason for the displacement, from a structural standpoint the modification of Eiffel's original design was incorrect. The connection of the right arm to the pylon was eccentric, too flexible, and overstressed. There was a lack of continuity in the joints. This allowed twisting and excessive movement. Previous repairs had compounded rather than solved the problem. The design team was confronted with the decision to repair or replace the shoulder framing. It proved to be one of the most difficult... dilemmas of the project, pitting restorationists against preservationists, French against Americans, engineers against engineers. We recommended returning the framing to the structurally and visually more elegant Eiffel design. Cliver wanted to keep the original bracing and any subsequent reinforcement, even if inadequate, as a historical record.... When the engineers finally resolved their differences and produced designs of equal structural soundness for both solutions, the Park Service insisted that the shoulder be repaired rather than replaced.
>
> (Hayden and Despont, 1986: 77)

Even before the last restoration, the flame in the torch had been remodeled several times, indicating not a small amount of anxiety about what constitutes the proper source of illumination: should it come from without, or from within. The French sculptor, Bartholdi, called for the dialogic solution – an external light focused on the flame. But the Americans opted for a positivistic approach. During the installation of the statue, the US Army Corps of Engineers cut holes in the flame and mounted lights inside. Bartholdi did not complain about the changed source of illumination, but he did remark that it gave off less light than a 'glow worm.' So larger holes were cut and fitted with colored glass. In 1916, Gutzon Borglum, sculptor of Mount Rushmore, cut 250 holes in the flame and filled them in with amber glass. This modification resulted in water leakage from the torch down the inner arm that accelerated the deterioration of the entire statue. During the 1984–6 restoration, a new flame was built, resembling Bartholdi's original in aesthetic shape and structural design, and illuminated from without as Bartholdi wanted. The restorers claim to have returned to the original, but close examination reveals that they have also added an extra plume to the flame, to make it flamier perhaps. The rhetoric of restoration is always in bad faith. What has been happening to the statue, behind the protection of the rhetoric of restoration, has been a guilty appropriation of an intercultural French–American object, surreptitiously being made into an American object.[5] It was the US Parks Department that decided that the flame should be more phallic, and the American modifications made to the arm at the time of installation should be retained in the 'restoration.'

Even if the restoration materials were selected to reproduce the original precisely, even if the restoration team had chosen to replace the corroded interior braces with 'puddling iron' using Eiffel's formula instead of using stainless steel 316L and ferallium, even if the restoration had been driven by fanatical concern for 'authenticity,' the result would not have been the return of the original, but an even more magnificent supplement to the original. The restoration of the statue put something in the past and constitutes an ending. Of course, all this is happening just beneath consciousness. It may be too late to negotiate what was lost in the restoration of the statue of Liberty, to keep what we might have kept by letting it fall apart, etching its trace indelibly into history and nature. If the restoration was an American appropriation of an originally intercultural object, the greatest good that might result would be if it compels us to ask, 'Is an authentic purely *American* liberty possible?' And we would have to speak the answer: Certainly not.

The original intercultural statue tried to embrace all Americans. On her base, which *was* made in America, are inscriptions which tell the story of the American Indian migrations across the ice floes, and the prejudice suffered by the Japanese migrants during World War II. But she was herself of European origin, and it is the *European* immigrant who is most identified with her. It was the son of European immigrants, Lee Iacocca, who led the movement to restore her. For the Europeans, she represented a new beginning, free from the constraints of unwanted tradition, freedom to follow only those traditions which they wanted to preserve. In addition to the famous line, 'Give me your tired,/Your poor, your huddled masses,' Emma Lazarus has the statue say, 'Keep, ancient lands, your storied pomp.' The America watched over by Liberty was a kind of do-it-yourself, make-over European culture, youthful, belligerent, and a little hedonistic, built on a Puritan foundation. The result is not unlike what happens when a teen-aged child goes for the first time to a clothing store, or to a restaurant, alone. America is the end of European civilization, in the sense of its culmination, what it was leading up to all along, and the possibility of a new beginning. Every social form invented in Europe – individualism, Protestantism, capitalism, democracy – was brought here for the fair test in the clean laboratory of a society which could pretend to be without history, class, religion, or race. The Liberty restoration marks the end of European immigration as the energizing force in the building of a European America.

The Statue of Liberty is by no means a universal symbol, at least not yet. The dialectics of inclusion always imply an exclusion. It produces a sense that there is a proper kind of immigrant to America, even a proper kind of European immigrant. The restoration project irreparably damaged any continuing efforts to universalize Liberty.

Consider the restoration from the perspective of the new non-European immigrant from Latin America or Asia. To these new Americans, it means the end of nation-building by inclusion of new immigrant groups. The restoration of the statue enshrines European immigration, and marks it as something of the past and different from what is happening today. Is there any evidence of work which will assure that the principle of American liberty has not been inextricably and exclusively bound to European America and put in the past also? For the majority of poor Asian and Latin American immigrants of today, the welfare offices of Fresno and Los Angeles and the labor camps of the California Central Valley are arguably equivalent to Ellis Island. But where are the institutions designed simultaneously to serve the new immigrants, and as building blocks of American society: the current equivalent of the late-nineteenth-century New York City public school system, the Homestead Act, or the labor unions, for example? When I asked a Chicano friend of mine what he thought of the Bill of Rights, he replied: 'I know all about the Bill of Rights as it applies to minorities. We have the right to remain silent. We have the right to have a lawyer present during our questioning...' The current willful shoddiness of the enforcement of immigration laws as they apply to Latino and Asian populations stands in sharp contrast to the heavy-handed enforcement in dealing with Europeans. The result of the current lax policy will be to taint non-European migrants, and their progeny, with the stigma of probable illegality, assuring marginality even for those who have entered following proper procedures.

A mighty woman, standing with a torch in a harbor, cannot serve as the symbol of the arrival of a person who was sneaked into the country in the false bottom of a truck. As it always has for African slaves, it will eventually come to stand for the *difference* between the current arrival of Asians and Latinos, and the earlier arrival of 'true' Americans. The only possible way to signify continuity between the old European and the new immigrations would be to enshrine the Statue of Liberty as a *ruin*. The ruin would symbolize a double appropriation of the original Liberty by nature and by non-European immigrants.[6] In the place of the restoration, the statue should have been reinforced, pinned together, made safe for schoolchildren and others to go inside her, to touch her aging skin. Her natural decay would evoke sympathetic concern for the liberty of all Americans, without any perceptible breaks between epochs and peoples.

As Liberty fades away, one would hope that a new monument could be built, as great as Liberty, and as meaningful to the new immigrants as Liberty was to the Europeans. It could not be a restoration, copy, or replica; and after feminism, it could not be an allegorical woman. In fact, it will take brilliance. After Hiroshima, Vietnam, and Iraq, after the annexation of Texas and

California, after the siege of Chapultapec, Grenada, the Bay of Pigs, Panama, and Congressional support for the 'Nicaraguan Freedom Fighters,' what could possibly serve as a symbol of the human connection of the United States to the peoples of Asia, the Middle East, and Latin America? Perhaps an African American, a Chinese American, or an American Indian genius will give us a second symbol of 'Liberty' properly so-called, one that works for all Americans and the future as well as for European-Americans and the past.[7]

NOTES

1 This chapter was published in Spanish as 'La "Libertad" nunca podria ser Miss Norteamerica,' in *Relaciones*, 49, Montevideo, Uruguay, June, 1988. The people of Uruguay had just managed to extract themselves from a vicious fascist regime without calling too much world attention to the process. I was helping several librarians and academics to restore their sociology and semiotics collections, two fields specifically banned by the former government. *Relaciones* had just been established for the rapid diffusion of the kind of thinking that was suppressed under the dictatorship. The editors asked me for a personal reflection on the meaning of 'freedom' for one of their early issues. I wish to thank Teresa Porzencanski for encouragement in undertaking this project and help in translating it for its original publication. This is its first English publication.

2 I am indebted here to a very helpful unpublished paper by Michael Cowan, 'Competing for Liberty: The Political Culture of "National" Celebrations.'

3 The strangest scheme that I have come across to neutralize Liberty's power as a free feminine figure is a joint Spanish-American enterprise to find her a worthy mate and marry her off. The following item appeared under the heading 'Colossal Match' in the 'What's Next' section of *USA Weekend Magazine*, June 29, 1990: 24.

> Miss Liberty and Columbus to tie the knot. Here comes the bride, all 111 feet, 1 inch of her. In Las Vegas on Valentine's Day, 1992, the Statue of Liberty will 'wed' the Christopher Columbus Monument of Barcelona Spain.... Already, US cities are contributing to Liberty's trousseau. The trans-Atlantic nuptials, to commemorate the 500th anniversary of Columbus's voyage to America, are the brainchild of the Spanish artist Antoni Miralda, who sees the wedding as a 'way to extend communication' between cultures. Liberty already has a three foot diameter engagement ring from New Yorkers and a gargantuan gown and petticoat from Spanish artists. Philadelphia provided a $193,000 cape shaped like the Liberty Bell. The couple will marry in abstentia, of course. But the garments and gifts will go to the Las Vegas [marriage] chapel.

4 For a fascinating first-hand technical account of the restoration project, see Hayden and Despont, 1986.
5 Suggested by Jason MacCannell.
6 This point was also made by Timothy Murray in his (1987) article on the spectacle of the unveiling of the restored Liberty. Murray comments, 'The four day birthday party was calculated to transmit a maternal image of a politically unified America regardless of the deep divisions of race, gender, and class, better signified by the statue's corrosion than by Lady Liberty's debut' (p. 111).
7 There is an abundance of talent for such a project. See, for example, American Indian architect Douglas Cardinal's brilliant Museum of Civilizations in Ottawa, Canada, Maya Lin's Civil Rights memorial, or her Vietnam memorial which is described in a later chapter.

Chapter 7

Reconstructed ethnicity[1]

Tourism and cultural identity in Third World communities

In a speech to his people, American Indian Movement leader Russell Means (1980: 25) stated:

> No European can ever teach a Lakota to be a Lakota, a Hopi to be a Hopi. A master's degree in 'Indian Studies'... cannot make a person into a human being or provide knowledge into traditional ways. It can only make you a mental European, an outsider.

Means is attempting to build a 'correct' image of Indian peoples in opposition to forces of assimilation into the Western mainstream, to gain widespread acceptance of that image as a model for actual behavior. In this chapter, the term 'constructed ethnicity' is used to refer to efforts such as Means's, and to the various ethnic identities which emerged by way of opposition and assimilation to White Culture during the colonial phase of Western history and in the new 'internal colonies.'

Constructed ethnicity is only a conceptual springboard to a more complex phenomenon. The global diffusion of White Culture, internal colonization, and the institutions of modern mass tourism are producing new and more highly deterministic ethnic forms than those produced during the first colonial phase. The focus is on a type of ethnicity-for-tourism in which exotic cultures figure as key attractions: where the tourists go to see folk costumes in daily use, shop for folk handicrafts in authentic bazaars, stay on the alert for a typical form of nose, lips, breast, and so on, learn some local norms for comportment, and perhaps learn some of the language. There are, of course, many other types of tourism and even other ways that tourists relate to 'local color' (mainly in service encounters), but these are less likely to produce specifically ethnic effects, so the focus here is on those occasions in which the tourists attend primarily to ethnicity. The concern here is not with the often bizarre results of the tourists' efforts to 'go native.' Rather, it is with the natives' efforts to satisfy the touristic demand, or to go-native-for-tourists.

The tourists' approach to ethnicity differs methodologically from earlier military, scientific-ethnological, religious, and political-colonial approaches. Specifically, tourism promotes the restoration, preservation, and fictional re-creation of ethnic attributes. In other words, tourism operates in much the same way as, and can superficially resemble, the behavior of leaders of ethnic separatist movements, only the energy comes from without, not from within. 'Reconstructed ethnicity' here refers to the kinds of touristic and political/ethnic identities that have emerged in response to pressures from White Culture and tourism.

A BRIEF INTELLECTUAL HISTORY OF ETHNICITY

'Ethnic' was originally a term referring to all groups not Jewish. By the time of Columbus, it had been narrowed somewhat to mean all groups neither Jewish nor Christian. Ethnicity did not then refer to any specific characteristic of heathens and infidels – it only suggested a structural opposition of us/them – and it held the Western culture to be the specific measure or standard for all other groups. Even before the term became a part of the technical vocabulary of ethnology (which was about the time of Darwin and Marx), it was known that some so-called 'ethnic' groups were as determined as whites to maintain the us/them opposition – but the whites were the 'them.'

As I have already suggested, in actual use, 'ethnicity' occupies the conceptual space between bio-genetic ideas of race and socio-genetic ideas of culture. The accounts of nineteenth- and early twentieth-century travelers and missionaries constitute the most thoroughgoing effort thus far to fill this space with observations of physical traits, genetic constitution, social behavior, and moral character. Here is an account of the Iranians from about seventy-five years ago:

> The Persian [is] easy-going, and always ready to make things as pleasant as possible for everyone else. Unlike most Asiatics, he is well disposed to the foreigner, extremely hospitable, and

fairly honest in his dealings. Persians of pure blood have a quick apprehension, a ready wit and a persuasive manner. They are fluent in oratory and have more sense of beauty than the Turks.... On the other hand, it must be admitted that the Persian is a great liar.... Their culture, industry, readiness of address, and subtlety – in a word, the combination of their good and bad qualities – have earned for the Persians the reputation of making first-rate diplomatists, negotiators, and brokers.

(Hutchinson *et al.* nd: 236)

One of the things that is interesting about this and similar accounts is their easy authoritarian tone: they leave little room for questions and doubt, at least not in the way they are expressed. The authors have unhesitatingly attributed oratorical powers, appreciation of beauty, and so forth, to purity of blood.

In the twentieth century, academic anthropology opposed itself to the excesses of 'pre-scientific' accounts of ethnicity by making a radical separation of questions of race from questions of culture. By the 1950s anthropological statements about race had been purged of all behavioral commentary and most observations of physical traits. Race, it was argued, is population and its geographical dispersion, the distribution within the population of blood groups, and inherited susceptibility to certain diseases. In 1958, William Boyd (1960: 17–18) wrote:

One of the features that impresses the common man and the scientist alike are the differences in customs, languages, skin color, and physique between human beings from different parts of the earth.... Long ago people began, on the basis of such differences, to classify into races.... Originally people tended to confuse cultural traits, which are simply learned differences, with physical differences which are inherited and are not much influenced by environment. Thus the layman and early students of man attempted to classify mankind into races, for example, on the basis of language, and one heard of the Latin races, the Germanic races, and the Slavic races, the Greek race, and even the Anglo-Saxon race. It is true that in some cases language is a guide to racial origins, as in the case of the French Canadians of Quebec or the Pennsylvania 'Dutch' of the United States, but languages can be, and are, forgotten by their original speakers and/or acquired by people of unrelated stocks, as the American melting pot shows us every day, so that the differences in the world's languages, fascinating and useful as they are to the linguist, are very shaky foundatians for racial classification. Later skin color was utilized.... But it is too broad and vague a classification to be of much scientific value.

Thus, for Boyd there is no clear division between ethnic groups (as, apparently, there is between 'the scientist' and 'common man.') Boyd might have stressed even more than he did the mutability of physical traits. There are readily available skin lighteners and darkeners, hair curlers and straighteners, hair dyes, breast implants and breast reduction operations, tinted contact lenses, mechanical penis enlargers, permanent skull deformations from head bindings, eye rounding operations, 'nose jobs,' and much more. In Los Angeles, a man who faces the apparently daunting prospect of appearing in public with a woman taller than himself can go to a special studio and have himself stretched to a guaranteed minimum gain of two inches in stature lasting up to eight hours. Students of anthropology are assured that they are being trained to go around such dodges for purposes of scientific classification of races. But this seems to miss the important question of why people do such things in the first place. Why does virtually every human being on the face of the Earth approach his or her own phenotypic characteristics as a plastic medium of expression reflecting currents of opinion? The answer proposed here is that these modifications of physical traits constitute a metalanguage for communication across important structural divisions such as exist, for example, between the sexes and other groups which command a primary sort of identification. They are a language for communicating in settings in which there can be no presumption of mutual openness to conversation.

This definition, which emphasizes the communicational aspect of ethnic characteristics, is different from approaches suggested by a recent phase of analysis of ethnicity and related phenomena as put forward by socio-biologists. By its own account, socio-biology, in its first iteration, was committed to putting genetics and behavior back together again. There was a great deal of promise claimed for this program. For example, Edward Wilson (1975: 4) wrote that socio-biology is the 'systematic study of the biological base of all human behavior.' But socio-biology did not produce anything resembling revisions of the earlier characterizations of Iranians and others, while placing them on a more scientific footing. Wilson's comment notwithstanding, one after another, the leading socio-biologists lined up to say that ethnic differences are precisely the kinds of behaviors that socio-biology is not about. Van den Berghe (1979) restricted his analysis of family systems to what he terms 'cultural universals' or 'species-wide uniformities.' Barash (1979: 5) suggested that one stops being overwhelmed by superficial ethnic differences and studies what 'remains the same about people underneath their customs and habits.' Their founding claims notwithstanding, socio-biologists left the field of 'ethnicity' open to the tourists and leaders of ethnic solidarity movements to do with what they wished.

One cannot help remarking in passing that socio-biologists may have backed away from ethnic differences too quickly. On the surface there is an interesting alignment of concerns between leaders of ethnic solidarity movements and socio-biologists: both speak freely of life and death, survival, struggle, adaptation, and the like. On a more basic level, it is intuitively evident that ethnic differences in food production, sexual and other health practices, behavior, attitude, and so on, overlap and interact with the immune systems in concrete and complex ways that would provide a fertile field for socio-biological research. Of course, apparently, according to Thomas A. Sebeok (1980) and others (for example, Blacking, 1977), students entering this field will discover early on that physicians and biologists know even less about the immune systems than sociologists know about society.

STRUCTURE, RHETORIC AND ETHNICITY

Even if there is unfinished work in socio-biological studies of ethnicity, here I will shift to a semiotics of ethnic differentiation. As a minimal kind of working definition, assume that an ethnic group is a sub-system of a larger social order composed of two or more interacting ethnic sub-systems. Further, assume that all ethnic traits which appear to be 'intrinsic' are the product of a kind of natural selection of strategies for communicating with the other group or groups in the larger system. They are eventually framed as emic qualities in order to make them more effective communicational strategies, a reason for one group to be stubborn in its dealings with another, as in such statements as 'This is our sacred way,' or the white bureaucrat's classic passive-aggressive 'I don't make the rules, I just enforce them,' which is *his* sacred way. There is ample evidence that language itself becomes regular only in opposition to other languages. In other words, assume that ethnicity is an aspect of an extended vocabulary used by groups to communicate their differences and similarities with other groups, but primarily their differences. Of course, as in all areas of social life, for the thing to work it is necessary for everyone to be taken in by their own fabrications.

These are the assumptions implicit in an ethnosemiotic or dialogic model for the social construction of ethnicity, for constructed ethnicity. Further assumptions (about which more later) are necessary for reconstructed ethnicity. This definition of constructed ethnicity is not necessarily in alignment with academic theories of race and ethnicity, but it is fully congruent with statements made by some leaders of movements for ethnic self-determination. In the mid-1960s, for example, at the peak of the unpleasantries between blacks and whites in the United States, Stokely Carmichael, then head of the Student Nonviolent Coordinating Committee (SNCC), insisted that rhetorical changes are necessary preconditions to political and economic change, and change in ethnic identity and self-esteem. Note the use of such phrases as 'tone of voice,' 'speaking for,' 'speaking to,' and so on, in the following quote for the opening sections of an important policy statement widely circulated by SNCC in 1966:

> One of the tragedies in the struggle against racism is that up to now there has been no national organization which could speak to the growing militancy of young black people in the urban ghetto. There has only been a civil rights movement, whose tone of voice was adapted to an audience of liberal whites. It served as a sort of buffer zone between them and angry young blacks.... An organization which claims to speak for the needs of a community – as does the Student Nonviolent Coordinating Committee – must speak in the tone of that community, not as somebody else's buffer zone. This is the significance of Black Power as a slogan. For once, black people are going to use the words they want to use – not just the words whites want to hear.
>
> (Carmichael, 1966)

By the late 1970s, the main architects of ethnic opposition to the white majority in America were no longer black; they were Indian. Still, one finds an overriding concern for rhetorical forms, manners of speaking, and the way things get said. Here are the opening lines of the Russell Means speech (quoted above) to the Black Hills International Survival Gathering in the summer of 1980 on the Pine Ridge Reservation in South Dakota:

> The only possible opening for a statement of this kind is that I detest writing. The process epitomizes the European concept of 'legitimate' thinking; what is written has an importance that is denied the spoken. My culture, the Lakota culture, has an oral tradition, so I ordinarily reject writing. It is one of the white world's ways of destroying the culture of non-European peoples.... I will allow this [writing] because it seems that the only way to communicate with the white world is through the dead, dry leaves of a book. I don't really care if my words reach whites or not. They have already demonstrated through their history that they cannot hear, cannot see; they can only read.... You notice that I use the term American Indian rather than Native American or Native indigenous people or Amerindian when referring to my people. There has been some controversy about such terms... Primarily it seems that American Indian is being rejected as European in origin – which is true. But all the above terms are European in origin; the only non-European way is to speak of Lakota – or, more precisely, of Oglala, Brule, etc.
>
> (Means, 1980)

The statements made by Carmichael and Means, when read from within the ethnicity, translate into a new stress on the blackness of blacks or the Indianness of Indians, and intensification of a particular set of ethnic forms which are selected as 'correct' for purposes of dialogue with other groups, especially dominant groups. Often the process emphasizes a new inter-ethnic realism where formerly negative self-images are neutralized or made positive.

In so far as Carmichael, Means, and others are giving voice to an efficacious form of collective self-reflexivity which selects, modifies, and enhances certain ways of dressing, believing, talking, marrying, and so on, one can speak of a literal construction of ethnicity. From an ethnosemiotic standpoint, constructed ethnicity is a redundancy: all ethnic traditions are constructed according to this or paralleling (ethno)methodologies.

THE SECOND PHASE OF ASSYMETRICAL INTERGROUP RELATIONS – INTERNAL AND EXTERNAL COLONIES

The chapter on White Culture deals with 'Wild Indians,' 'Bandits,' and other ethnics beyond the frontier. Here it is only necessary to recall that this pre-colonial or initial contact phase in the evolution of assymetrical intergroup relations has now almost passed. There are excellent anthropological studies of the continuing specific ethnic effects of this earlier contact, including, for example, James Boon's work on Bali (e.g., see Boon 1977, 1984, 1985 or 1990), Renato Rosaldo's (1978) study of Ilongots, and Rolena Adorno's (1981) work on the lasting effects of the initial contact between the Spanish and the great Indian civilizations of the Americas.

Once all, or almost all, the groups on the face of the earth are drawn into a single network of associations based on the monetary and other systems of equivalencies (that is, the translatability of any language into any other language), the stage is set for an explosion of group-level interactions requiring greatly expanded production of 'ethnicity' and a metalanguage for the global dialogue, an arbiter or referee which I have named 'White Culture.' White culture stages ethnic interaction as a two-dimensional process. The two dimensions are structural superiority–inferiority and rhetorical association and antithesis. Structural superiority–inferiority refers to evident differences in wealth and power between groups, wherein one group occupies the residential and occupational higher ground and controls the wealth, decision making, and information at the supra-community level. Rhetorical association and antithesis is quasi-independent of structural status so that, for example, it is possible to admire Chinese cuisine even while regarding China as an inferior enemy, or to mock white males even while acknowledging their superior power. These suggest four basic forms of relationship between groups in the production of ethnicity as framed by White Culture.

First, a structurally inferior group can attempt to associate itself rhetorically with a superior group; second, the inferior group can define itself as the antithesis of the superior group or it can define the superior group as the antithesis of itself; third, a superior group can attempt to associate with and copy the ways of an inferior group; and fourth, a superior group can define itself as the antithesis of an inferior group. All these possibilities can be shown to exist in real situations, each producing different ethnic results. Of course, the model could be made much more complex without changing its basic terms by considering interactions between three or more groups and/or by looking at both ends of a relationship simultaneously. On this last point, for example, when both the superior and the inferior group relate by way of the form of antithesis, one has a working consensus about the definition of the situation and perhaps a war. When a superior group opposes an inferior while the inferior seeks to emulate or to associate with the superior, one has what is sometimes called the 'status quo' or a 'pre-revolutionary' situation. The following comments are restricted to the basic four interactions.

First, a structurally inferior group attempts to associate itself with the values, imagery, and so forth, of a superior group: this is a common pattern, perhaps the most common. The typical arrangement is an exploited minority attempting to adapt itself to the needs and requirements of a larger, containing system. Louise Lamphere (1976), Michael Hechter (1975), Joe Jorgenson (1971), and others have begun to refer to groups in this situation as 'internal colonies.' Frank Young (1971) calls them 'reactive subsystems.' In an earlier paper (MacCannell, 1977a), I have suggested that they are examples of 'negative solidarity.' Frederik Barth (1969), Pierre van den Berghe (1970), and Edwin Almirol (1979) have nicely documented adaptations of ethnic groups along these lines. Specifically, they have shown that upward political and/or economic mobility is associated with assuming the ethnic characteristics of the larger containing system.

Two points should be noted. First, emulation of social superiors is often accomplished with such finesse that the resulting ethnic behavior of 'converts' is more coherent and convincing – that is, 'better' than the original – to the point that the superior group is eventually composed, at least in part, of idealized copies of itself. Second, there is a tendency in much of the literature on ethnicity and ethnic change to assume that this is the only arrangement that can exist between inferior and superior groups. This is a serious error and a barrier to understanding several other modes of the social production of ethnicity. Social superiors from Marie Antoinette to the middle-class hippies of the 1960s have made it a point to dress like, and even clumsily to emulate the behaviors of, the people oppressed by their class. Of course, any effort on the part of a social inferior to 'pass' can also fail miserably, and inevitably does when social superiors shift their grounds.

Second, an inferior group defines itself in opposition to or the antithesis of the values of a dominant group. This is the pattern which most interests Michael Hechter (1975: 10 ff.) in his theory of ethnic change. Hechter's work on internal colonies is especially valuable as a theoretical description of this particular mechanism for the production of ethnic effects. He specifically argues that 'disadvantaged' groups will eventually come to emphasize their distinctive ethnic attributes to gain advantage in their dealings with the dominant culture. Something like this strategy and result evidently operates in the materials discussed above from the American Indian and Black Power movements.

Third, a superior group associates itself with an inferior group (see the comment on Marie Antoinette, above). This is, in effect, the final ratification of the results of a white cultural totalization. Culturally dominant individuals often costume themselves as workers, peasants, cowboys, even as Third World 'revolutionary' types. Upper-middle-class households often valorize 'naturalness' and simplicity in their decor, cuisine, and so on. When this occurs, there is no more powerful line of evidence that the reconstructed ethnic forms from which this imagery is being borrowed have been fully incorporated and neutralized.

Fourth, a superior group defines itself in opposition to an inferior group. This is an infamous, ugly pattern marked by openly discriminatory decisions and everyday life conversations laced with gratuitous ethnic slurs and characterizations, such as those found in Malinowski's diaries and Hemingway's correspondence. A great deal of attention has recently been focused on the ways this kind of behavior affects the slurred group. From an ethnosemiotic perspective, it would better be examined as an aspect of the ethnicity of the speaker. Midwestern farmers in the United States, who probably have fewer significant contacts with Jews than any other minority (for example, with blacks or even Chicanos), still use the term 'Jew' as a generalized negative adjective: such as 'the jew tractor broke,' or 'the jew horse ran away.' This somewhat bizarre usage, where it is found among midwestern males, should be regarded as a part of *their* ethnicity. Dominant group antithesis has been carried to extremes in Germany and South Africa.

It might be noted that dominant groups in modern society are aware that it has become unfashionable and even dangerous to define themselves in this way, especially in public, and they have

begun to police their own language and behaviors without necessarily changing the underlying sentiments that produced the
behaviors in the first place.

RECONSTRUCTED ETHNICITY

Reconstructed ethnicity is the maintenance and preservation of
ethnic forms for the persuasion or entertainment not of specific
others as occurs with constructed ethnicity, but of a 'generalized
other' within a white cultural frame. There is no specific message
such as 'Indians are more interested than whites in the spoken
word as a personal bond.' Rather, there is just a diffuse marking
of ethnic difference, as in 'these feathers are supposed to signify
"Indianness" or "Indianicity."' Reconstructed ethnicity is fully
dependent on the earlier stages in the construction of ethnicity.
But it represents an end point in dialogue, a final freezing of ethnic
imagery which is artificial and deterministic, even, or especially,
when it is based on a drive for authenticity. The new reconstructed
ethnic forms are appearing as the more or less automatic result of
all the groups in the world entering a global network of commercial transactions. Under these conditions, ethnicities can begin to
use former colorful ways both as commodities to be bought and
sold, and as rhetorical weaponry in their dealings with one another. Suddenly, it is not just ethnicity any more; it is understood
as rhetoric, as symbolic expression with a purpose or an exchange
value in a larger system. This is the basis for a distinctive form of
modern alienation, a kind of loss of soul, which Goffman (1959:
25) first described in his studies of face-to-face interaction:

> As performers [and here we might say, 'as performers of our
> ethnicity,' DMacC] we are merchants of morality. Our day is
> given over to intimate contact with the goods we display and our
> minds are filled with intimate understandings of them; but it
> may well be that the more attention we give to these goods, then
> the more distance we feel from them and from those who are
> believing enough to buy them. To use a different imagery, the
> very obligation and profitability of appearing always in a steady
> moral light, of being a socialized character, forces one to be the
> sort of person who is practiced in the ways of the stage.

CONCLUSION

Here and in the other chapters in this section, I have tried to document some of the effects of transforming all of life into rhetorical figures and tropes. These effects are the more or less automatic result of efforts to maintain a giant, or global, socio-economic system, a 'New World Order,' in which there is a necessary pretense that all the sub-groups and communities are actually phased together in some kind of relational equilibrium. There is a real division between White and Nonwhite Culture which, I have been arguing, is not so much a matter of color as it is two different modalities in relating to values. In the white cultural framework one finds aggressive attempts to universalize *exchange value* to the exclusion of all other values: formulas for the translation of speech into writing, of time into money, of labor into a commodity, language into language, land into property, property into money. Within 'nonwhite' culture the emphasis is on *use value*: on the stewardship of the land to protect its capacity to provide; on the home as a place to live, not to sell; on words that are not just meaningful, but also convey a bond and a trust; on work that is satisfying in itself, not just for its monetary reward; on friendship; and so forth.

The pretense that we can have one world system requires a suppression of the incommensurability of exchange and use values on all levels. The form of this suppression is now discernible as a highly fictionalized white ethos of 'unity' or 'unification' which promotes the idea that all human differences shade imperceptibly one into another; that it may be difficult for a black executive to live in the white world, but not impossible; that working-class minorities can be 'mainstreamed,' and so on. It should be immediately evident that this ethos springs from the same ground as the idea that distinctive ethnicity must be artificially preserved in tourist attractions. Without artificial demarcation and preservation efforts, how would anyone know where the black proletariat leaves off and the brown *petit bourgeoisie* begins?

By now, almost every individual on Earth has been informed that he or she is related to every other individual in 'The New World Order.' The message is usually accompanied by a sinking feeling that all of our actual relationships, even with former intimates, are falling apart. A secondary effect of the alleged globalization of relations is the production of an enormous desire for, and corresponding commodification of, *authenticity*. Like the desire for *freedom*, the desire for authenticity becomes a weak point of entry for political and psychoanalytic repression which have now merged into a single force. Within the frame of White Culture, freedom and authenticity are fully mythologized. Expressions of desire for them, and quests for them, are now the shortest possible routes to unfreedom and inauthenticity.

Rather than appearing as a choice between living a life that is for sale versus some other kind of life, we are encouraged to think that we are suspended, or caught, between two systems of value. In this position of suspense, which Goffman (above) suggested is exactly that of a commodity, and which Lévi-Strauss suggested, in an infamous aside, is exactly that of a woman, neither system of value, neither exchange value or use value, is real, or even symbolic. They are imaginary, so that (1) structural inequality of wealth is imagined to be an open model – that is, those at the top can fall, and those at the bottom can realistically aspire to reach the top; and (2) white/nonwhite relations are imagined to be closed, a concentric framing of ethnicity in which the outer circle, the ultimate frame, is white Anglo-European. Of course, this white outer circle that imagines it can contain all human differences could never see itself as 'white.' Rather, it imagines itself to be neutral, transparent, universal, and principled as the rightful 'container' of that which is 'nonwhite,' 'colored,' 'slanted,' or otherwise marked by specificity. According to the white cultural totalization, none of these specific bits of 'nonwhiteness' could ever provide a universal framework for all of humanity. They must learn to fit themselves into the white totality, either as a part of its apparatus, or as cultural entities in the eyes of others. The success of white culture is measured by the degree to which custom and tradition are quantifiable, marked off, bounded, marketable: to the extent that Amish, Black, Chicano, Dervish, Eskimo, Guyanan, are all frozen in their otherness, now exploitable under both a negative and a positive sign, as labor and as attraction. They can never *be* the body, they can only be incorporated, contained, 'assimilated,' taken into the body, eaten up. The unassimilable becomes the expendable; it is expelled, expulsed, excreted, or extruded as abject waste. Ethnic tourism is the mirror image of racism. Psychoanalytically, that which is contained in the body, that which is 'nonwhite,' is unclean.

None of this need be consciously understood for the system of ethnic relations as it is now evolving on a global base to work. Indeed, conscious understanding of it at any level could cause it to falter. From the nonwhite perspective, all that is required for 'modernization' and 'development' is a lightly ironical attitude, born of a willingness to relate to an administrative structure that is run by white males who can never admit to themselves that they occupy their positions of power because they are white and male. They imagine themselves to be *really* powerful and otherwise colorless, odorless, tasteless, sexless, at least in their official capacities – that is, the guarantors of a 'universal' order which corresponds to the grammatical third person, the *he* that pretends to be the 'it' (or the id), that over which there is no control, as in the phrase 'It is written,' or 'It is customary.' The administrative structure of white cultural arrangements has been set up as a 'universal subject' exerting force on all thought and behavior. Again, from a nonwhite perspective, all that is necessary for 'development' and 'modernization' is to work quietly, never pointing out the obviously mythical nature of white bureaucratic consciousness.

If a revolution were to succeed in dislodging white males from positions of power, no change will necessarily have taken place so long as authority itself continues to be represented as 'white' or 'transparent,' and 'colorful' ethnic groups are represented as 'something to see.' Within the white cultural totalization, a military general, though black, can be white, and a Prime Minister or a Supreme Court Justice, though a woman, can be a man, but only a man in the sense that white bureaucrats are men.

NOTE

1 This chapter was originally prepared as a paper for the seminar on Ethnic Tourism presented by the Committee on Comparative Studies in Ethnicity and Nationalism in the School of International Studies, University of Washington, May 28, 1981. It was published under the same title in the *Annals of Tourism Research* (MacCannell, 1984b). I want to thank Pierre van den Berghe for helpful suggestions, and the Comparative Cultures Program at the University of California, Irvine, for hosting me on sabbatical while I was writing the paper.

Chapter 8

The Locke case[1]

Although it has been illegal to buy and sell human beings in the United States for over a hundred years, there is apparently nothing in the law to prohibit an individual or business from buying an entire human community, as happened to Locke, California, in 1977.

Any such purchase should raise ethical questions about the limits (or lack thereof) of what may be defined as a 'commodity' under capitalism. Should a community be a commodity? This question is further complicated in the purchase of Locke for three reasons. First, Locke is the home of the last survivors of a distinctive group – the Chinese farm laborers who were among the earliest of the non-Anglo-European peoples to provide the labor for the large farms of California's Central Valley. Second, the buyer of the town of Locke was Asian City Development, Inc., a 'foreign' investor, ironically in this case a closely held Hong Kong-based corporation. Third, the new owner of the town plans to convert it into a major tourist attraction, connecting it to the already popular restored tourist section of 'Old Sacramento' by narrow-gauge railway, with plans for a temple, a giant Buddha, World's Fair type pavilions representing six Asian countries, a country club, yacht basin, 'high end' condominiums, and a floating restaurant.[2]

Locke was originally a 'company town' built in 1915 by Chinese businessmen and farm workers on the corner of a large ranch owned and operated by the family of a Sacramento investor, George Locke. On the basis of a verbal agreement, the Chinese were allowed to build and own the structures in the town while the Locke family retained the deed to the land under the buildings. The deal effectively short-circuited the Alien Land Law of 1913, which made it illegal for Chinese to buy or sell land in the United

States. Locke immediately became a small center of Chinese commerce and culture, operating outside the framework of California municipal codes, effectively governed by the Chee Kung Tong, and inhabited mainly by immigrants from the Chungshan district of China. The first structures that were built included homes, a restaurant, boarding house, dry-goods store, hardware store, and two gambling establishments. A few of the early Chinese residents of Locke were economically well off, but most were poor agricultural laborers who traveled widely in the region in search of work, returning to Locke as a 'home base' where they could re-establish ties with friends from their district in mainland China, speak their own language, plant small gardens, and so on. In addition to receiving money from ground rents and leases, the Locke family was assured a ready supply of labor to pick and prune the trees on their adjacent (or incorporating) 1,000-acre farm.[3]

This original arrangement contained the seeds of the controversy over Locke which erupted after the 1977 sale of the town: the creation of an 'authentic' Chinese tourist attraction in the Sacramento Valley, a place often referred to as 'the only intact rural Chinatown in the US,' a town that could be bought and sold as a single unit, a town inhabited by politically powerless and poor old people, yet one that might be developed for tourism.

It was argued by Tor Tai Ng, the Hong Kong businessman who is the primary investor in Asian City Development, Inc., that by converting Locke into a tourist attraction, he would 'promote Chinese culture' and advance the cause of better ethnic relations in American society. Several hundred thousand annual visitors to Locke would perhaps come to appreciate that the town's original inhabitants had laid the first railroad tracks, dug the first irrigation and flood control levees, and then provided the stoop labor for the first huge ranches which became economically viable only after these same Chinese had built the infrastructure. And they had done all this for under one dollar per day in wages.[4] By making a 'living monument' of Locke alongside other planned tourist attractions, Ng would preserve a significant and neglected piece of ethnic history. He argued that one should think of a reconstructed Locke as having been 'saved' and as an educational institution where mainstream Americans could come to learn of the important contribution of Chinese farm laborers to the early economic development of California. He also thought it should provide a new source of pride in heritage for the younger generation of

Chinese-American visitors who may be losing contact with their roots in America.

These same 'positive' motives are evident in an alternative plan for Locke created by the California State Department of Parks and Recreation. This plan would involve moving the entire town to a 15-acre park nearby, rebuilding it, bringing its structures up to California code, and moving the elderly inhabitants back in. The Parks Department would then manage the town as a 'living historic preservation.' This alternative has been touted as a way to rescue Locke from the over-commercialized private-sector plan.[5]

Different as they may be from a public- vs. private-sector standpoint, both the Asian City Inc. and the California State Parks plans are largely equivalent from the perspective of the people of Locke. A 30-year-old woman who grew up in Locke, the child of farm workers, comments:

> It's a very precious town.... God-awful precious. It's a place of peace, and whenever I go away for any length of time, I always come back to Locke.... [N]obody cared about us before when we were just little kids playing. When we were just a little ghetto town. Now all of a sudden everybody wants to cash in on us. You are in a little bottle and here is the rest of the world, you know, and everybody wants to break it. If people want to make money, that's fine and well. Just give us a fair chance. Because the old folks, this is their place until they die, their place of peace.[6]

Ethnic tourism is not unique to Locke. The customs and traditions of cannibals, American Indians, even Pennsylvania Amish 'Plain Folk,' have been developed as tourist attractions. The main lesson tourism researchers have learned from this type of development is that ethnic tourism follows existing structural pathways. Regions with egalitarian social systems develop diversified, multi-functional, and non-exclusive tourist complexes. Areas with a history of serious exploitation of one group by another develop 'plantation style' or exclusive resort-type tourism, which squeezes the local people out of every role except the menial positions they have always occupied. The problems Locke now faces began with the structure of agriculture in California's Central Valley and are now only amplified by development for tourism. Either public- or private-sector tourism development in Locke would continue the pattern of exploitation of the Chinese farm workers. The exploitation began with the expropriation for a dollar a day of their labor, crucial to the development of the valley. Now that they are too old and feeble to work the fields, the pattern of exploitation is continued by expropriating the details of their everyday lives, just the look of them as they shuffle down the street, marketed as an 'experience' for tourists.

Ethnic reconstructions for tourists inject new complexities into the relationship of social and economic values. While the attention of tourists may provide some intangible 'payoffs' in the form of flattery, it is difficult to find concrete benefits in this type of ethnic tourism for the people of Locke whose life (and I suspect also their death – 'a way of life that no longer exists') is the attraction. The economic structure of ethnic tourism in Locke and elsewhere is such that most of the money does not change hands at the site. Most tourist money is spent on luggage, cameras, film, and especially film processing, special clothing, air-plane tickets, and tour-bus rides, before and after the actual visit. Even though the ethnic attraction may be the entire reason for making the trip, while in Locke itself, tourists often spend nothing at all. Sometimes they make whimsical purchases of souvenirs, or buy a beer or an ice-cream cone, or make a dollar donation to a local restoration project.

Also, the kinds of changes that are necessary to develop a community for ethnic tourism rarely improve the lives of its members as sometimes occurs in development for other forms of tourism. Note, for comparison, that when historical shrines are the attraction, as in Philadelphia, they can be enjoyed by locals and tourists alike and augment the resources of the community's education system in a meaningful way. But if, as a local representative of an allegedly colorful minority, you are the attraction, it is hard to figure out how you might come to benefit from the role or learn anything 'ethnic' from yourself. Or, for another comparison, when a still-useful old piece of machinery or large building is the attraction, as in the case of San Francisco's cable cars or Fisherman's Wharf, again, these things can be used by tourists and locals alike for necessary transportation, entertainment, and so on. But if, as a local representative of an 'ethnic attraction,' it is your very own house and garden that the tourists come to see, they can only be a source of inconvenience and potential embarrassment. In sum, ethnic tourism is especially vulnerable to a form of social disorder. Touristified ethnic groups are often weakened by a history of exploitation, as occurred in Locke, limited in resources and power, and they have no big buildings, machines, monuments, or natural wonders to deflect the tourists' attention away from the intimate details of their daily lives.

Modern mass tourism is based on two seemingly contradictory tendencies: the international homogenization of the culture of the tourists and the artificial preservation of local ethnic groups and attractions so that they can be consumed as tourist experiences. Both liberals and developers believe that ethnic groups should be playing a part in this larger system, while the people themselves are understandably bewildered by the sudden interest. Tourism has the capacity to make dizzying leaps over existing political, cultural, and social class boundaries, enmeshing a great diversity of local groups, communities, artifacts, and natural attractions in its expansion. What is evolving is not Marshall McLuhan's Utopian vision of a 'global village' where high technology permits a return of simple, friendly, and close social relations. Increasingly, the 'village' resembles an empty meeting ground: a place where people live and tourists visit, a place that has been decorated to look like an ideal town of some sort, but no one is related to anyone else. Tourists are not global villagers, nor are they destroying the villages of the world as some critics of tourism have claimed. Fortunately, most of the villages of the world, in Africa, Asia, the Middle East, Latin America, and even the 'depressed' areas of the developed world, remain untouched by tourism. What one witnesses, in villages that are transformed for tourists, is a reification of the simple social virtues, or the ideal of 'village life,' into 'something to see.' The village is not destroyed, but the primary function of the village shifts from being the base of human relationships to a detail in the recreational experiences of a tourist from out of town. Ironically, the tourist is often seeking to experience a place where human relationships still seem to exist. This process not only affects real communities such as Locke, but is sufficiently advanced that it is producing pseudo-communities for touristic attention: for example, 'Tahitian Village' in Hawaii, or 'African Village' in Georgia.

Ethnic attractions always stress the importance of emerging self-consciousness and self-determination of the ethnic 'minority,' the need to correct the historical record in so far as it undervalues the contribution of the 'minority,' and it reminds the visitors of past discrimination against the 'minority.'[7] It is worth recalling that this kind of understanding was once the product of humane scholarship and a liberal arts education. Interestingly, the expansion of tourism corresponds almost perfectly to the decline of the humanities in higher education in the United States and elsewhere. We should ask what can happen to the quality of our understanding of other peoples, other places, or other times, when it is based on touristic visits to places like 'Main Street USA' or 'Locke' and not on historical or ethnographic research. On the one hand, the experience may be more tangible and real-seeming. But it also rests on a social relationship between tourists and locals which is fleeting and superficial and subject to a great deal of self-interested manipulation by both parties. In some areas, such as the Right Bank of Paris, tourists are looked down upon as boorish slobs. In other areas tourists are envied or hated for their wealth and worldliness. In either case, the relationship between the tourists and the local people is temporary and unequal. Any social relationship which is transitory, superficial, and unequal is a primary breeding ground for deceit, exploitation, mistrust, dishonesty, and stereotype formation. The opposite is a long-term relationship involving many reciprocal rights and obligations that is based on mutual trust and respect, or even hatred. In short, no matter what the content of the message about 'ethnicity' may be, the structural framework of ethnic tourism can only support transient, exploitative, and stereotypical relationships of tourists and 'ethnics.'

When the 'ethnic' Chinese of Locke first became enmeshed in the global monetary system, they were discriminated against on the basis of skin color, not paid a fair market price for their labor, not allowed to bring their families (including their wives) from China, not educated, and labeled as inferior. Now we are asked to believe that they will fare better under tourism. At first glance, it would seem they might. Perhaps they will not receive any economic benefits from tourism, but at least they will receive recognition for their past perseverance and dignity: they worked hard on the bottom rung of the occupational ladder, they did not attain material success in the eyes of the larger society, but they maintained self-respect nevertheless. On this basis, one might make a case that plans for converting the people of Locke into a tourist attraction indicates that the world has changed in a progressive direction; that whereas they were once despised for being ethnically different and allowing themselves to be exploited, they are now accepted as moral if not economic equals.

But it is also possible that this is a pseudo-change. Perhaps what really happens in ethnic tourist contexts is only that the rhetoric of ethnic relations changes to create the impression of progress while older forms of repression and exploitation are perpetuated beneath the surface. This is how the psuedo-change works. When an ethnic group begins to sell itself, or is forced to sell itself, or, as occurred in the Locke case, is sold as an ethnic attraction, it ceases to evolve naturally. The group members begin to think of themselves not as a people but as *representatives* of an authentic way of life. Suddenly, any change in lifestyle is no mere question of practical utility but a weighty matter which has economic and political implications for the entire group. Consider, for example, the planning question of whether or not the future of Locke should include an authentic Chinese laundry among its main street attractions. Some have argued that there should be no laundry because its presence would tend to reinforce an unwanted, negative stereotype of the early Chinese experience in America. Others argue that a laundry is an essential service and a non-Chinese laundry would both disrupt the authentic character of the town and take revenues away from Chinese business.

Any touristic definition of an ethnic group or community puts it in a cultural double bind. A typical response to this double bind is for the group to 'museumize' itself, or otherwise become a frozen image of itself. The group becomes a thing and, Durkheim's methodological dictum notwithstanding, that is exactly what people are not. A still vital community is a system of practices, values, and ideas that can shift and transform over time and fit together with other communities in a larger society, first in one way, then in others. A society, if it is to evolve and adapt, is dependent on the capacity of its sub-communities to align themselves continuously in new ways. In a society with no frontiers, this process is the only means of social renewal, the only way a society can create internal frontiers and draw upon its own creative potential. If, on the other hand, the various sub-communities of society are transformed into tourist attractions and relate to one another only by way of commercially enforced stereotypical self-images, they cease to develop in themselves and only contribute to the development of white culture. Groups and communities in today's world must be able to undertake self criticism and to change in any way they wish until they begin to restrict the similar rights of others. The touristic requirement that a group internalize an 'authentic' ethnic identity, even if the promoted image is widely held to be a positive one, is no less a constraint than the earlier form of negative ethnic stereotyping. Conforming to the requirements of being a living tourist attraction becomes a total problem affecting every detail of life. Status as an attraction affects the job you have, the way you are supposed to behave off the job, the kind of authentic clothes you wear, the way you wear your hair, and so on. Everything becomes a serious matter for discussion, authentification, clearance. Any deviation from the touristic cultural ideal can be read as a political gesture that produces conflict not between groups but within the group.

In other words, it appears that tourism has helped in getting beyond the phase of ethnic relations where minorities are kept in place with light salaries, heavy prison terms, and redneck cruelty. But one may have come full circle. In so far as White Culture extends its acceptance conditional upon the sub-community restricting itself to an 'authentic' image of itself, one is only doing with admiration what was done earlier with dogs, guns, and bureaucratic and economic terrorism. As the rhetoric of hostility toward minorities is replaced with a rhetoric of appreciation, the circle of their potential exploiters is dramatically expanded. Now with a clear conscience, even the Chinese can exploit the Chinese or 'promote Chinese culture.'

NOTES

1 This chapter was prepared with support of a small grant from the California Arts Council and was first published (D. MacCannell, 1982) as part of a study guide for the film *American Chinatown*, made by Todd Carroll for the Locke Project of the Chinese Historical Society of America. My involvement in the Locke case was in 1978 as an unpaid consultant, representing the people of Locke in their dealings with Asian City, Inc. and the California Department of Parks and Recreation on matters having to do with the development of tourism. My effort was part of a larger initiative undertaken by the University of California Community Development and Asian Studies faculty, on behalf of the people of Locke. For more detailed analyses that treat ethnological and historical issues related to Locke, see the work of my colleagues Peter Leung (1984) and George Kagiwada (1982). Locke continues successfully to resist development by Asian City, Inc. and the Parks Department.

2 Here and elsewhere in this chapter, I am indebted to a helpful 'Report on Locke' by George Kagiwada (1982).

3 For a history of the founding of Locke, see Lortie (1979), Chu (1970), or Thompson (1957). These and other works are reviewed and summarized in Kagiwada, 1982.

4 See Leung (1984) for a discussion of wage rates and physical deformations caused by hard work.

5 There have been other plans for Locke. In 1985, Dorothy O'Malia, a Sacramento astrologer, offered Asian City $2 million for Locke. Her plan included shops, restaurants, bed-and-breakfast inns, a performing arts theater, a marina, and a 36-hole golf course. She was more interested in the 'Victorian' quality of the community than its ethnic Chinese aspect, but she did offer to build a 'convalescent home for Locke's elderly Chinese population' and to remodel a Chinese recreational center. The 'emphasis of the remodeling will be a Chinese flavor,' she said (quoted in *The Business Journal of Greater Sacramento*, week of August 19, 1985: 1 and 14). I am indebted to Peter Leung for bringing this to my attention.

6 Excerpted from Gillenkirk and Motlow's (1987) oral history of Locke as quoted in the *Sacramento Bee Magazine*, November 15, 1987: 19. Actually, it is not quite correct to suggest that the people of Locke regard both Asian City and Parks Department plans as equivalent. Resident Tommy King clearly distinguishes them:

> I don't know much about what is happening to the town. All we hear is rumors. The guy [Ng Tor Tai] never hold[s] a meeting to say, all right, this is what's happening.... Ideally, I want the state to take over the town. The state's the only one that's not going to make money. Everybody else comes in here is going to make money, right? If they're going to put money in, if they're going to buy it, you've got to expect them to make their normal profit. But the state is different. They don't need to make money. They just want to improve it and let the citizen enjoy it. Once you develop the town, then Locke don't mean anything.
>
> (1987: 18)

7 It should be obvious that the term 'minority' belongs in quotes in this context because the kind of community transformations for tourism described here never occur unless the minority is actually a local majority, as in the case of Locke.

Part III

Postmodernization and its discontents

Continued energy waste implies continued US dependence on imported oil, to the detriment of the Third World, Europe and Japan. We pay for the oil by running down domestic stocks of commodities, which is inflationary; by exporting weapons, which is inflationary, destabilizing, and immoral; and by exporting wheat and soybeans, which inverts Midwestern real-estate markets, makes us mine groundwater unsustainably in Kansas, and increases our food prices. Exported American wheat diverts Soviet investment from agriculture into military activities, making us increase our own inflationary military budget, which we have to raise anyhow to defend the sea-lanes to bring in the oil and to defend the Israelis from the arms we sold to the Arabs. Pressures increase for energy- and water-intensive agribusiness, creating yet another spiral by impairing free natural life-support systems and so requiring costly, energy-intensive technical fixes (such as desalination and artificial fertilizers) that increase the stress on remaining natural systems while starving social investments. Poverty and inequality, worsened by the excessive substitution of inanimate energy for people, increase alienation and crime. Priorities in crime control and health care are stalled by the heavy capital demands of the energy sector, which itself contributes to the unemployment and illness at home at which these social investments were aimed. The drift toward a garrison state at home, and failure to address rational development goals abroad, encourages international distrust and domestic dissent, both entailing further suspicion and repression.

(Amory Lovins, testimony before two committees of the US Senate, December 9, 1979, full transcript reprinted in Nash, 1979: 15–34)

Chapter 9

The desire to be postmodern[1]

> Among Aryan peoples, the earliest ties of the individual to a
> super-individual order of life seem to be rooted in a very general
> instinct or concept of the normative, the decent, the Ought in
> general.
>
> (Georg Simmel, 1950: 99)

REPORT FROM CALIFORNIA

California already has a kind of postmodern consciousness-for-
itself as the focal point of world culture, the economic miracle and
jewel of the Pacific Rim.[2] Virtually the entire postmodern literature which emphasizes the *simulacrum*, historical rupture,
valorization of surfaces, and the death of the subject attempted to
qualify itself as California ethnography: Baudrillard's *America*
(1988) begins and ends in California; Umberto Eco starts his
Travels in Hyperreality (1986) with a trip down Highway 101; Louis
Marin discovered 'dystopia' at Disneyland. Certainly the paradig-
matic piece, Jameson's 'Postmodernism, or the Cultural Logic of
Late Capitalism,' is centered in California. Jameson developed his
critical framework on two campuses of the University of California
(San Diego and Santa Cruz), and the essay would disappear if the
California examples were removed from it: its mini-reviews of
Hollywood movies and personalities, Marilyn and Brando; the
weak poem by a little-known San Francisco writer; the comments
on Disneyland; the extended critical evaluation of the Bonaventure hotel in Los Angeles; and so on.

The primary signifier of postmodernism is lack of depth in its
art, architecture, and social relations. Jameson refers to this as a
'depthlessness that is not merely metaphorical' (1984: 58). This

feels like California; like communication via bumper stickers; like black velvet paintings that 'work' only if the pigment touches just the tips of the nap of the velvet, only the surface of the surface; like Steve Jobs, California-based inventor of the Apple Computer, who, when he was fired from the corporation he founded, designed the 'NExt' computer, beginning not with design specifications but with several months of intensive work on the name and logo.[3] Umberto Eco found seven copies of Leonardo's 'Last Supper' between San Francisco and Los Angeles, and he was incensed to learn that each of them claimed to be superior to the original located near his home:

> At Santa Cruz the Last Supper is... the sole attraction in a kind of chapel erected by a committee of citizens with the twofold aim of spiritual uplift and celebration of the glories of art.... Then you step out into the sunshine of the Pacific beach, nature dazzles you, Coca-Cola invites you, the freeway awaits you with its five lanes, on the car radio Olivia Newton-John is singing 'Please, Mister, Please'; but you have been touched by the thrill of artistic greatness, you have had the most stirring spiritual emotion of your life and seen the most artistic work of art in the world. It is far away, in Milan...; you may never get there but the voice has warned you that the original fresco is by now ruined, almost invisible, unable to give you the emotion you have received from the three-dimensional wax, which is more real, and there is more of it.
>
> (Eco, 1986: 17–18; note that this was written before the decision to 'colorize' the original 'Last Supper' using Japanese technology.)

Overvaluation of the reproduction is aggressively promoted throughout the postmodern world in the 'Small Town USA' exhibits, no longer found only at Disneyland, where the picket fences are whiter, and the grass (nourished by timed sprinkler systems) *is* greener than in any of the originals. Real alligators sleep motionless in the mud of California zoos while the latex alligators at Disneyland mount ferocious attacks on the tourist-carrying boats. Again, the fakes do a better job; they live up to our sense of what an alligator ought to be. All of this is made possible only by developing surface details to the point that copies appear to exceed the level of realism of their originals. Not entirely satisfied with the bronze statue of the cowboy actor that now guards the John Wayne

Airport in Orange County, its caretakers sent it to a firm in Texas to be colorized. It now conforms precisely to Orange County aesthetics (see Chapter 3 above), coated with pastel metallic colors. These processes, when they appear in a touristic frame, seem innocent enough. But there is reason for concern. In what follows, I will treat this well-documented characteristic of tourist settings as a symptom, my attention having been recalled to it by the fact that it repeats in its structure Nazi aesthetics wherein historical and peasant motifs were 'recycled' and made 'better.' Even the grandest design, the 'Thousand Year Reich', was supposed to be a high-tech Holy Roman Empire, an improved copy.

SOFT PATH FASCISM[4]

Beginning with the 'paper clip conspiracy' and the McCarthy era, powerful institutional forces have effectively suppressed the kind of thinking I want to recommend here.[5] The House Un-American Activities Committee blacklisted Pete Seeger, Woody Guthrie, and the other Lincoln Battalion volunteers who fought on the side of the partisans in the Spanish Civil War on the grounds that they were 'premature anti-fascists.'[6] The obvious point is that good US citizens are not supposed to engage fascism critically unless their nation is officially at war with a fascist state, and even under this rare condition, the terms of the critical engagement should be circumspect. The strongest taboo prohibits their thinking about what life would be like in a successful fascist state, one that was able to cover up its brutal beginnings and export its terrorism beyond its own borders.

If one is to think further on this, one should not continue to focus exclusively on the evils of National Socialism, as Theweleit (1987), Koonz (1987), and others have done so effectively. It is important to recall that state-sponsored terrorism and official racist policies were not ends in themselves, but only means to an end; specifically, the establishment of a 'New World order,' a United States of Europe with its capital in Berlin: one parliament, one passport, one currency. It is time that we stop deferring the question that is on everyone's mind: Would a kind of soft-core fascism, one that was not too anti-Semitic, not too anti-democratic, not too violent, be acceptable if it was necessary to maintain 'our nation's' competitive position in global capitalism?[7]

Historical evidence suggests that European adherents to fas-

cism in the 1930s experienced it as a valorization of supreme
central authority, a hypertrophy of rationality, and a freely
granted gift of individual subjectivity to the state, experienced as
a kind of melancholic happiness or falling upward. Euro-fascism
was evidently an enormously attractive doctrine among persons
who needed a simplified logic of social existence, especially among
those who were trapped in a caricature of the Western philosophical tradition: that is, those who believe that the Enlightenment
opposition of individual freedom and social determinism is a deep
inconsistency eventually threatening Western civilization from
within. National Socialism provided a way out of this 'contradiction' by subsuming all individual feelings and beliefs within a
singular, in this case nationalist, framework, promising to eliminate any tension between the determinism of the state and
individual desires.

Was the destruction of strong fascism also the founding of soft
fascism, which no longer needs to use physical force to achieve its
goals? Certainly the defeat of strong fascism did not rid the world
of the most effective instrument of institutional terror: the 'Black
List.' Once there is a full convergence of the libidinal and the actual
economy; once everyone is hooked up to the artificial breasts of
state bureaucracy and the ubiquitous Corporation, all that is
needed for total control is the threat of withdrawal of the livelihood
from anyone who would think themselves in opposition. And the
functionaries responsible for maintaining this system need never
see themselves as having silenced criticism; having denied a voice
to those who are admitted to the system only on the warrant of
their physical labor; as conspiring against the formation of new
thought; or blocking the self-determination of minorities. All these
functionaries need to be is hard-nosed administrators with the
ability to defund programs, to 'just say No.' Of course, if they are
really to enjoy this line of work, they have to be fascists.

If the hard path to fascism could be ripped up, if it could be
turned into a garden with monuments, if we could make a museum
at Auschwitz, what would be left of a successful fascism, if communism, the deadly enemy of hard fascism, could be defeated? We
would witness not the end of class, but the end of class antagonism.
There would be an almost complete absorption of labor unions
into the corporations so that everyone would genuinely think of
themselves as working for the good of the company and the
general good. Education and propaganda would conflate into a

singular unity, which would bear a new name such as 'training' or 'preparation.'

Would a non-violent fascism, one that found a gentle approach to the termination of class and ethnic opposition, and the prevention of any new formation of thought, bring nothing but an advance in the logic of social relationships?[8] This is the philosophical question that we cannot leave to philosophy. The great Western philosophical tradition that reaches its highest point in the writings of Heidegger is doubly incapacitated when it comes to knowing fascism, first by its dependence on the Greek concept of *polis* for its understanding of politics. The model for politics, which derives ultimately from the self-constitution of a people in a city-state, can have nothing to do with current political formations. Second, philosophy is condemned to failure here by its own brilliance. Because it must look at all sides of a question, it can never provide an accurate account of fascism because there isn't a second side to it. Fascism establishes itself as 'one-sided' and derives its power from being one-sided. What is needed is a field or method which can still remember positivism.

So I am suggesting a sociological way in: what would everyday life be like, how would people and groups relate, family members interact, what kinds of persons would be privileged and honored, and what sort of morality and popular style would characterize a society in which, increasingly, the social articulations are soft paths to fascism? I have found the current widespread speculation on the 'postmodern' to be extremely helpful in beginning to address these questions. The success of postmodernist writing as an explication of soft fascism can be traced to the fact that it specifically denies that this is its project. The time has come for us to be open about this. There are too many points of correspondence to ignore: the death drive, the attack on the notion of truth as so much metaphysical baggage, the sense of living in an infinite instant at the end of history, nostalgia for the folk-primitive-peasant, schizophrenia at the level of culture, and general ennui periodically interrupted by euphoric release from all constraint. All these are named characteristics of both classic fascism and postmodern aesthetics. In what follows, I provisionally affirm that the correspondence between Euro-fascism and postmodernity, including the double declaration of the end of history itself, are but early and late expressions of the same epoch and the same consciousness.[9] I do this knowing that it is a misuse of the theory of the postmodern, convinced that it is, nevertheless, the best use to which this theory can be put. My aim here is to re-cast postmodern theory to find an opening in this epoch through which we might re-enter history.

POSTMODERN STYLE

The postmodern valorization of surfaces makes a double indirect reference to fascism. First, it is a clear enunciation of the *fetishism of the ordinary*, a hiding of everyday reality behind an overstated version of the Real, an inflation of the value of the signifier, a splitting of the norm into what *is* and what is *ideal*, which is allegedly only a technicolor version of what is. Again, this seems perfectly innocent. But it is too perfectly innocent – I will eventually argue that there cannot be any possible motive for it except to cover up violence. Second, leaving nothing to chance, postmodernism has welcomed and internalized the dialectic so that its valorization of the surface, and the superficial, ultimately advances conservative, individualistic ideology with its promotion of the Center and the Interior. As soon as anyone announces that now everything is superficial and banal, that we have lost touch with authentic, original things, with real reality, there is not a person alive who will not react against such a pronouncement and mount at least an individual rebellion, proclaiming, 'I, at least, have a soul.' In California, in precisely those regions that are most markedly postmodern, where overdevelopment of the surface is most advanced, we also hear almost constant chatter about 'getting in touch with' one's own 'true,' 'inner' feelings, 'centering,' and so on. There is no ethos of getting in touch with someone else's inner feelings. The predictable result is an aggressive promotion of the ego and individualism. Popular bumper stickers read, 'Welcome to California – Now go home,' and 'The more I get to know people, the more I love my dog.'[10] A 15-year-old female rock star proclaims that she would rather die than engage in 'deep conversation.'

Attention to the surface does not, as Jameson suggests, 'replace depth.' It claims to replace depth and thereby conjures its opposite. But the 'center' that appears by this sleight-of-hand is always and inevitably only an inflated nothingness, no matter what claims are made for it – a kind of mechanistic, fascist authenticity. These arrangements are perhaps most obvious in design practice. A characteristic feature of contemporary architecture, its mirror stage, celebrates the surface, but it does not, as it might at first appear, replace depth or de-center the subject. The mirror glass wall provides a singular viewpoint from both the inside and the outside. What is seen through the glass from the inside is the same as what is seen in the glass from the outside: namely, the viewing subject.[11] The postmodern surface, which is both transparent and reflective, simultaneously undermines subjectivity *and* re-centers the subject (now completely lacking in confidence), rigidly enforcing a unified perspective, a kind of anxious self-important nothingness. In pop-psychological terms, the emergent postmodern subject is an insecure ego-maniac, the 'California Personality Type,' if we could still speak of such things.

The built environment is the focus of much postmodern criticism,[12] but it is the automobile, curiously neglected after Barthes' classic essay on the Citroen DS 21, that is a better index of the ideology that seals the gap between personal and corporate bodies.[13] Although generic cars are now 'issued' simply to serve transportation needs, Californians still purchase cars with an eye to their potential symbolic opposition to mere transportation. And although there is an increasing tendency for automobiles to perform flawlessly, they still break down, or jam up, reminding us that we have not yet achieved the perfect integration of time, space, and human action that is both a fascist and a corporate ideal. Toward this end, a telephone can be installed in your car, but the computer map on which you become a cursor moving down the streets of a dash display (and presumably also on a display in corporate headquarters) is available to drivers only in Tokyo. Elsewhere, we must depend on hard copy or our own cognitive maps, and our use of the car is proof that these maps are real, that we traverse a space held in common, not just imaginary space. We get to work even with our minds on something else entirely, unable to recall having made the necessary stops and turns. We have stayed within the lines, while controlling a device we know is capable of violating boundaries, racing down sidewalks, crashing through the glass front of any office, shop, or restaurant.

As a constant reminder of the control we ordinarily exercise, fictional cars and drivers in popular entertainments are always driven beyond hope and beyond real physical exigency. The car can exceed all limits and weave across the line to the side of the unbounded, in literal opposition to the aesthetic representation of corporate control in the postmodern built environment. Just as teens once desired shiny cars, rebellious teens today want cars with a patina of dents, signs of survived encounters with the hard stuff beyond lines demarcating prescribed routes and parking places. With all the resistance that the car, by virtue of its form, potentially offers to any spatial-aesthetic totalization, it is perfectly predictable and symptomatic of the deepest sublimation that among the most popular forms of cars today is the 'off-road' vehicle with high-gloss paint, automatic transmission, cruise control, and concert hall-quality stereo. And it should not come as any surprise to learn from market reports that these 'off-road' vehicles are no more likely to be driven off the pavement than are their conventional, two-wheel-drive counterparts. As any sadist can attest, it is not enough to exercise full control over your subject by physical restraint and threatened or actual violence; it is necessary for the subject to obey, voluntarily, even lovingly. It is not enough that our movements are fully contained by a social order that violently opposes itself to history and to nature; it is necessary that we manifest our full submission to this order by owning and driving vehicles purportedly designed to go beyond the bounds of civilization, to enter nature, but which we voluntarily keep on the road.

The most popular automobiles in the USA and California today are Japanese (Nissan, Honda), and the most desired are German (Porsche, BMW, Mercedes, and the Audi before people started believing it to be 'possessed'). Immediately after World War II, there were only two *types* of automobiles in California: American sedans and British sports cars. By the mid 1950s an ideal American sedan (a fully equipped Buick, for instance) floated over the road absolutely disconnected from surface variation, in total silence, every function automated requiring only feather-light finger and toe-tip touches on minimal controls. The entire ensemble of elements was as far removed from the natural or the organic as was industrially possible. And it was also remote from the driver. Its tendency was to maintain a constant speed in a straight line, plowing and wallowing in response to any human command to accelerate, stop, or turn. The mid–1950s British sports car (an AC Bristol, for example, or especially a Morgan) transmitted even the smallest road imperfection directly to the seat of the pants, steering and brakes were heavy, gear selection was done by hand through a notchy gate, often without the benefits of synchromesh, the wind and rain entered the car even when the top was in place. Body parts were often made of wood or leather, the exhaust note was loud, and the car was utterly, uncannily responsive to the driver: it would do exactly what you wanted it to do, no matter how aggressively driven or difficult the road. The American sedan and the British sports roadster of the 1950s offered to consciousness an authentic opposition, a requirement to make conscious choices, coupled to an implicit demand for accountability, or at least a justification or excuse for the choices made.

Compare this to the existential situation of the contemporary German automobile, a Mercedes, for example, which by its own account dominates the libido: 'Haven't you always wanted a Mercedes? You do not have to wait.' Its design consciously synthesizes the extremes represented by the post-war American sedan and British sports car. It is perfectly silent *and* perfectly responsive; fully automated and fully under the control of the driver. The Mercedes is the post-industrial object *par excellence*, with 'tasteful' appointments that are natural, but it is necessary to be a connoisseur to know this, because *Mercedes* wood and leather have actually achieved the perfection of *plastic copies* of wood and leather. In order to accomplish its goals, it is first necessary to design, as much as possible, all sensation *out* of the interior of the automobile and the controls, then to engineer back in, in a controlled way, certain natural sensations of road surface variation and engine 'sound,' a certain 'feel of the road' is 'fed back' into the steering, brakes, and even into the seat cushions. Contemporary Mercedes design centralizes and totalizes values that had come to be associated with extremes of automobiles, now all contained in a single unified technological-libidinal-aesthetic-commodity-object. The rhetoric used by auto journalists to describe Mercedes automobiles goes beyond hyperbole:

> The car rides tautly, is quick steering, and feels bull powerful – a meaty delight in the hands. The engine is like a good bluecheese dressing: creamy-cool with lots of satisfying little chunks of V–8 pulse in it. The neo-Hammer simply storms down the road, gathering way like a steam locomotive that's snapped loose from its train.... It felt as solid and comfy as hurtling along inside a rocket-assisted, leather-lined gun safe.
>
> (From *Car and Driver* magazine as quoted in the *San Francisco Chronicle*, November 28, 1990: A8)

It is no longer a matter of having to make a choice, or of refusing to choose; it is a matter of an authoritative elimination of the need for choice now marked as an ultimate good. It is a unity that beckons with a sense of inevitable finality. An advertisement claims that it is 'simply instinctual' to want a Mercedes. The ultimate meaning of the conflation of metaphoric and mechanical unity may come to consciousness for an instant when you enter a Mercedes (or 'leather-lined gun safe') and close the door; it is difficult not to feel that you have been shut into a coffin. If there is such a thing as an 'instinctual desire' to own a Mercedes, it can only be a sub-species of the death instinct.

Recently, the principle of the 'inflation of the center' has become palpably manifest in automotive design practice. The Porsche 928, the new 'rounded' Mercedes and Audis, designs which are now widely emulated as, for example, by the Mercury Sable, the Ford Taurus, and the Mazda RX7, tend toward a spherical ideal. Their steel skins appear to be stretched tight around an inflated interior, inhibited in their taught sphericality only by a residuum of practical requirements to have wheels and windows. The 'center' remains the norm, or ideal. Aesthetic depthlessness places an inflated value on the nothingness and silence within, a nothingness which desires, and sometimes claims to have a form of its own, but can never be anything other than a totalization of dead values raised to the level of an ideal: something that must be contained in industrial-strength exo-skeleton, steel spheres, and other ego-mimetic devices.

It follows, I hesitate to say 'logically,' that in addition to depthlessness in postmodern culture we also find a quite well-developed Hippie ontology which could almost be read as a healthy burlesque of Heidegger, except that it is not sufficiently conscious of its own origins to be burlesque: a popular bumper sticker reads, 'Be Here Now, It's All There Is,' and another, 'This is Being.' On a wall in Berkeley, someone has sprayed, 'I feel therefore I am.' When these two elements are found together – namely, an aesthetics of surfaces and ontological speculation, a 'romanticism of steel and blood,' as they said in Germany – what we have increasingly resembles the other time and place where industrial culture thought it arrived at its final moment. We find our way by turning the signposts around and following the arrows backwards so we can tell ourselves we are leaving fascism and going someplace else, to the 'postmodern.'

The 'post-scarcity' society

In the Introduction to his edited volume on 'the politics of post-modernism,' Andrew Ross specifically rejects any parallel, such as the one being drawn here, between postmodernism and fascism. He claims that the separation between the two is given by history:

> Although a postmodernist politics might share some of the formal aspects of, say, Adorno's 'negative dialectics,' it has not been obliged, as Adorno and others were, to declare and affirm its distance from the politics of authoritarian centralism, other-wise known as totalitarianism. Somewhat remote from the experience of fascism and Stalinism, its relation to a 'center' has been historically different, and articulated, primarily, within the context of Western liberal capitalism. As a result, postmodernist politics has been posed as a politics of difference, wherein many of the voices of color, gender, and sexual orientation, newly liberated from the margins, have found representation under conditions that are not exclusively tailored to the hitherto heroicized needs and interests of white, male intellectuals and/or white male workers. In this respect we can only see social gains.
>
> (Ross, 1988: xvi)

This postmodernist wants to view social class as only one difference among the many that are embraced or subsumed by postmodern-ity. Rosi Braidotti has helpfully remarked to me in conversation on the 'feminization' (and to this I would add the 'colorization') of the philosophical concept of *difference*. Her point was that the woman is admitted into theoretical discourse not as another sub-ject or subjectivity, a worthy interlocutor for the old Western male cogito. The woman's place in postmodernity is secured alongside of class, ethnicity, and the other 'differences' which no longer make a difference. The concept of *difference* is supposed to be critical theory's 'affirmative action' program. But so far, it has only in-creased the distance between the controlling cogito and new class, ethnic and gendered thinking, even as it admits the latter to its club. If the result is human difference without essentialism we can perhaps believe that some gains have been made. But if it is difference without class, gender, or ethnic *specificity*, the gains have been taken back. The result is a kind of 'United Colors of Benetton' philosophy.

In their drive to incorporate every form of thinking, current philosophy and theory eventually arrive at the need to claim that the hypermodern areas of the West, at least, have secured for everyone, or are about to secure, the same freedoms that the arrogant old Western philosophical cogito has always enjoyed: freedom from material and other wants and desires. Postmodern theorists do not suggest that the Marxist's dream of a classless society has been achieved: what they seem to claim is that in the West the lowest classes now have, or are about to have, adequate food, shelter, medical care, and clothing. John Fekete (1987: i ff.) claims that postmodernity is the culture of a post-scarcity society. He calls for a 'more-than-ethical perspective on value, fit for a postmodern and a post scarcity prospect' (at the end of the Acknowledgements, not paginated).

If you work as a social scientist in California, especially as a social scientist in the great Central Valley of California, as I do, you will soon discover that the old modes of production are very much in operation in 'post-modern' civilization. California is not merely an industrial state, it is pre-eminently an agricultural state. Agriculture is still the number one economic activity. With all the miracles of mechanization, all the chemical use and water transfers, California's number one 'industry' still depends on stoop labor, illegal labor, labor that works at sub-minimum wage under sub-human conditions to put more food on the tables of others than they can put on their own tables.

The removal of *work* from the present; the romanticization and fetishization of work and of the worker; its naturalization; taking work out of history by consigning it to the 'Historical'; these are all postmodern or soft-path fascist articulations that effectively suppress from consciousness the exploitation and suffering still associated with production processes.[14] Jameson (1984) has written that the paradigm case of the transition from the merely modern to the postmodern is in the comparison of Van Gogh's painting of 'Peasant Shoes' to Andy Warhol's painting of 'Diamond Dust Shoes.' It would seem that diamond-dust, high-heeled pumps are quintessentially Californian, Hollywood. But California is still the place of the work shoe that might reveal to us that the food we eat was gathered at the cost of exploitation and human suffering. Heidegger prepared the intellectual ground for the postmodernist lie about agricultural work in his comments on Van Gogh's painting:

In them, there vibrates the silent call of the earth, its quiet gift of ripening corn and its enigmatic self-refusal in the fallow desolation of the wintry field. This equipment belongs to the earth and it is protected in the world of the peasant woman.... Van Gogh's painting is the disclosure of what the equipment, the pair of peasant shoes, *is* in truth.... This entity emerges into the unconcealment of its being.

(Quoted in Jameson)

Here, the 'peasant woman,' now fully inscribed into the *folk*, appears as a de-proletarianized worker. 'The folk' is the subject position of the worker mythified positively: they have joy in their work. Andy Warhol's diamond dust shoes cannot in and of themselves complete this lie which calls itself the truth unless they are impressed into the service of the concealment (which calls itself 'unconcealment') of the grinding work, privation, and class and ethnic oppositions on which 'postmodern' civilization depends.

The commentary on these shoes of Van Gogh's is paradigmatically postmodern. Everyone must say something about these shoes, and it seems that everything that might be said has been said. *Except*: again there is a repression; no one has observed the obvious, or asked the clear and simple questions that Marx or Rousseau might have asked. Van Gogh painted these shoes in such a way as to suggest that they had been broken down by hard work. Heidegger noticed this much and immediately wanted to consign the shoes to the realm of the 'proper product,' to the work of some kind of generic *peasant* woman. But, in all the commentary, no one asks who gained from the work that broke these shoes. Did Van Gogh present them in such a way as to cause us to repress this question? If we turn for clarification to Derrida's (1987) essay, we are in for some serious embarrassment. Derrida, according to his usual practice, insists on legalistic uncertainty. Heidegger could not have known beyond a shadow of a doubt if these were peasant shoes or Van Gogh's shoes, women's shoes or men's shoes, whether their laces were tightened or loosened, if they were a pair of shoes or two left shoes. If Heidegger attributes everything he attributed to these shoes, it can only mean that he is working through his own Oedipal problems: his incest and castration fantasies. The 'truth' of the matter, according to Derrida, is that Van Gogh's shoes are absolutely ambiguous and can only 'refer' to the ultimate ambiguity; that is, the shoes fetishistically 'stand for'

Heidegger's mother's missing penis. Derrida is too polite to say it outright, but this is his reading. How else are we to explain why Heidegger, without any cause that can be discovered in the painting itself, used the painting as an occasion to imagine himself at the foot of a peasant woman, gazing upward through a veil into the mystery of Being? Having provided us with this virtuoso reading of Heidegger's Van Gogh, arrived at, as he puts it, 'very carefully,' 'very cautiously' in the course of 225 pages, Derrida comments on the 'poverty' of the previous 'quarrel' over the Van Gogh painting. At no point does he comment on the poverty of the shoes.

Intentionally and unintentionally, the skilled moves of post-modernist criticism suppress the real class, ethnic, and gender differences that still exist, that we are trying to pretend don't exist, or trying to re-inscribe as mere difference, drained of all specificity. Jameson's extended comment on the absence of marking around the entrances to the Bonaventure hotel in Los Angeles is another case in point. Jameson comments:

> I want to suggest about these curiously unmarked ways-in is that they seem to have been imposed by some new category of closure governing the inner space of the hotel itself.... [T]his new total space corresponds to a new collective practice, a new mode in which individuals move and congregate, something like the practice of a new and historically original kind of hyper-crowd.
>
> (1984: 81)

Perhaps. There is also the issue of where the Bonaventure was built, on the site of a former barrio. The unmarked ways-in are symptomatic of a desire to exclude the displaced barrio residents from the 'new collective practice.'

Values that are still operative in the formation of human relationships are concealed absolutes. The best way to keep a cultural form alive is to pretend to be revealing its secrets while keeping its secrets. The postmodern thesis, lacking ethnographic and historical specificity, appears less as a critique, more as a perpetuation of the form, as the super-structure of postmodernity: in this case, the critique of ideology is ideology of the same type, only more advanced.

MOURNING THE DEAD SUBJECT

Under his heading 'Euphoria and Self-Annihilation,' Jameson quips: 'Such terms inevitably recall one of the more fashionable themes in contemporary theory – that of the "death" of the subject itself.' (1984: 59). In the way in which Jameson has enunciated it, this particular 'death' of the subject stands as a perpetuation of concern for the individual within a framework that labels itself as a critique of individualism. Specifically, he characterizes his 'death' of the subject in the following terms: '[it is] the end of the autonomous, bourgeois monad or ego or individual.'

My concern here is with the motive for the somewhat arbitrary move to individualize and psychologize *the subject*. There are other, non-individualistic, non-psychological ways of conceiving the 'death of the subject': for example, the death of the anthropological subject, or the subject of anthropology; that is, the death of a particular kind of subjectivity. Even on quasi-psychological grounds, there are still more radical ways of approaching the question of the death of the subject than the one suggested by Jameson. We must consider the possibility, for example, that the subject cannot die because it never existed in the first place. What we are really witnessing in the postmodern epoch is the death of an ideology which was based on false confidence in the constitutive powers of subjectivity. Of course, Jameson knows the relevant intellectual history, so he has specifically rejected these alternative conceptions before retreating to psychological and individualistic grounds.

Even before current scholars informed themselves on these matters via deconstruction, the *transcendental* subject was sentenced to death by existentialism, by Sartre and Goffman. Sartre commented:

> The transcendental *I* has no *raison d'être*.... If it existed it would tear consciousness from itself; it would divide consciousness; it would slide into every consciousness like an opaque blade. The transcendental *I* is the death of consciousness.
>
> (Sartre, 1957: 40)

The transcendental subject has been sacrificed in order to make a place for everyday, worldly, engaged subjectivity. The psychological individual remains, still somewhat self-centered, perhaps, but no longer corrupted by the pretense of absolute superiority that comes from identification with the transcendent.[15] Finally, there are the 'decentered' subjects of semiotics who have recently found themselves to be no longer alone in the universe, who are compelled, for the first time in history, consciously to create relationships with other subjects by means of an exchange of signs.

Any and all of these versions of the fate of the subject are superior to the one that Jameson and others have proposed for the subject in postmodernity. It is not just that we should be mentally predisposed to keep death in its place: a simple result of old age, serious illness, violent accident, suicide, poisoning, or murder; nothing more. My concern here is that the dramatic staging of the 'death of the subject' by postmodernists is a way of restoring the privilege and centrality of the subject by mourning its loss. Jameson describes subjectivity after the death of the subject as a kind of free-fall upward into Being:

> This is not to say that the cultural products of the postmodern era are utterly devoid of feeling, but rather that such feelings – which it may be better and more accurate to call 'intensities' – are now free floating and impersonal, and tend to be dominated by a peculiar kind of euphoria.
>
> (1984: 64)

If we ask what or who is being liberated here, what or who is experiencing this giddy 'intensity,' the answer can only be a new self, or a new subject, born again in postmodernity. The postmodern 'critique of individualism' is fully integral with revised individualist ideology.

THE ROUTINIZATION OF VIOLENCE

So, too, is the routinization of violence, which also hides out in the open in postmodern culture. The metaphor of death in current theoretical writing represents it as a frozen feature of the landscape of postmodernity, always avoiding the question of its articulation to violence and the death drive of fascism. Jameson remarks:

> The great Warhol figures – Marilyn herself, or Edie Sedgewick – the notorious burn-out and self-destruction cases of the ending 1960s, and the great dominant experiences of drugs and schizophrenia – these would seem to have little enough in common anymore, either with the hysterics and neurotics of

Freud's own day, or with those canonical experiences of radical isolation and solitude, anomie, private revolt, Van Gogh-type madness, which dominated the period of high modernism. This shift in the dynamics of cultural pathology can be characterized as one in which the alienation of the subject is displaced by fragmentation of the subject. Such terms inevitably recall one of the more fashionable themes in contemporary theory – that of the 'death' of the subject itself.

(Jameson, 1984: 63)

Let me urge against this assessment that the dominant cultural pathology of modernism was not typified by Van Gogh or Freud's neurotic patients. It was Nazi-type madness, the orders that compelled the 19th Brigade to charge against machine guns at Paardeberg, the *Endlosung*, and the decision to use nuclear weapons on Japan.[16] Jameson inexplicably undercuts his own stated aspirations for his work on postmodernity. In an interview, Jameson says he wants to 'reconquer some genuine historical sense' (in Ross, 1988: 17). Yet his thoughts on death do not lead him to pause for even a moment before the trenches at Verdun, before Auschwitz, or Hiroshima. He does not even pause before Freud's 'Thoughts for Our Time on War and Death.' Once again, this phrasing of the 'death of the subject' has an overlay of historical referentiality but it is radically de-historicized. The historical ground on which the 'fragmentation of the subject' was real before it became metaphor has been repressed. The real ground of deaths today has been avoided – Jonestown, My Lai, Jimmy Dean who died in a Porsche, a Porsche similar to the one nostalgically represented in a recent advertisement under the text, 'It is human nature. The Desire to live forever.' Or, even 'Marilyn herself,' so long as Jameson brought it up, hers having been an absolutely ambiguous, postmodern type of death, a murder-accident-suicide.[17]

We must not continue to erase, or otherwise forget, these deaths that give postmodern life its meaning. It is only by confronting these deaths in their specificity that we might begin the process of refounding our humanity on the discovery that every private who was torn to bits by machine-gun fire, every soul vaporized at Nagasaki, was a human being, someone who in life feared death and experienced their own deaths as real, not as statistics, not by the tens or hundreds of thousands, as we the living experienced their deaths, but as their own, one-and-only death. To suggest 'the death of the subject' as a slogan (or 'one of the more fashionable themes') for postmodernity, drained of its specificity and historical referent, is to accept without comment the processes that led to the policy decisions to counter machine-gun fire with human bodies, to 'test' nuclear weapons on Japanese civilians and Solomon Islanders, to the *Endlosung*. The energy that post-modernists expend discussing 'the death of the subject' should be redirected to critical study of the institutional framework for decisions to kill as a matter of public policy, in the name of the state or of 'democracy.'

It is time to move the sociological question yet to be asked by postmodernists: why fascism?

WHY FASCISM?

Historically, there have been numerous efforts to impose fascist thought from the top down, including nineteenth-century Bona-partism, Boulangism, Action Française, the Patriotic Union of Primo de Rivera, Renovacion Española, Dollfuss's Vaterlandische Front, the Deutschnationale Volkspartei, OZON in Poland, the Imperial Rule Assistance Association in Japan, and so on.[18] But none of these was as successful as the fascist movements that empowered groups with little political base other than what they won through their own initiative: the Italian *Fasces* Party and German Nazis. The paradox of successful fascist movements is that they combine anti-democratic and grassroots elements. What could possibly be the appeal of politicians who run for office on the promise that, if elected, they will abolish free elections and the principle of impartial justice? Fascism openly opposes democratic processes, justice, and every other arrangement that results in a distribution of power. According to fascist doctrine, democratic forms betray weakness of leadership and irresolution on the part of the group.[19] Understanding of fascism necessarily awaits a combination of sociological and psychoanalytic methods of analysis.

In his essay, 'Everyone Wants to be a Fascist,' Felix Guattari (1977) claims that fascism draws on resources deep in the human psyche; on a potential that exists there for a confusion of death and love. Specifically, fascism gives erotic free play to the death instinct at the level of mass action, leading inexorably to a slurry of cyclonite, blood, and semen. In Guattari's words:

> All fascist meanings stem from a composite representation of love and death, of Eros and Thanatos now made into one. Hitler and the Nazis were fighting for death, right up to and including the death of Germany; the German masses agreed to follow along and meet their own destruction.
>
> (Guattari, 1977: 96)

On a parallel path, Roland Barthes has searched for the basis of absolute authority in the structures of language:

> I am obliged to posit myself first as subject before starting the action which will henceforth be no more than my attribute.... In the same way, I must always choose between masculine and feminine, for the neuter and the dual are forbidden to me. Further, I must indicate my relation to the other person by resorting to either *tu* or *vous*; social or affective suspension is denied me. Thus, by its very structure my language implies an inevitable relation of alienation. To speak, and, with even greater reason, to utter a discourse is not, as is too often repeated, to communicate; it is to subjugate.... Language... is quite simply fascist.
>
> (1977; 1979: 31–4)

Guy Debord suggests that fascist violence is a more or less automatic response to economic crisis:

> [F]ascism is not itself fundamentally ideological. It presents itself as it is: a violent resurrection of *myth* which demands participation in a community defined by archaic pseudo-values: race, blood, the leader.... Fascism is a *state of siege* in capitalist society, by means of which this society saves itself and gives itself stop-gap rationalization by making the State intervene massively in its management.
>
> (Debord, 1970: thesis 109; not paginated)

Umberto Eco suggests that fascism is a kind of disorder of historical consciousness that comes from historical impotence:

> [I]t is hard to apply punishing irony to these pathetic ventures [he has been describing the 'castle' built by the American publisher William Randolph Hearst], because other power

people have thought to assert their place in history through the Nuremberg Stadium or the Foro Mussolini, and there is something disarming about this search for glory via an unrequited love for the European past. We are tempted to feel sorry for the poor history-less millionaire who, to recreate Europe in desolate savannahs, destroys the genuine savannah.

(Eco, 1986: 28)

And, much like Barthes, who finds the fascist substrate in language, Derrida has added his voice to tell us of an essential link between violence and the proper name:

There was in fact a first violence[:] to be named. To name, to give names that it will on occasion be forbidden to pronounce, such is the originary violence of language which consists in inscribing within a difference, in classifying.

(Derrida, 1974: 112)

The origin of the desire to be postmodern is in these master texts of post-structuralism, which seem to give us no way out of fascism or vice versa, suggesting that the only escape is to draw an arbitrary line and leap across, imprisoning fascism forever in 'history' or in the unconscious.

It can be added, from the perspective of sociology, that proto-fascism is found not just in the structure of language, in the psyche, and in our philosophies; it is also implied in the formation of any human group. No group is entirely free of hatred for some racial or cultural other. There is as much residential and social segregation of racial and cultural groups in American or Soviet society today as there was in pre-war Germany. Every society gives its soldiers and its surgeons the license to kill. Every group suppresses open discussion of some kinds of knowledge. And every group demands, at least from its high-status members, loyalty to the leader and silence on any of its practices that, if generally known, might discredit its officially positive view of itself.

By universalizing fascist values Derrida, Debord, Eco, Guattari, and Barthes do not help us to understand Why fascism? as a recognizable, self-conscious, historically bounded form. According to their treatment of it, fascism is simply an aspect of the human condition, no more noteworthy than upright posture or the prohibition against incestuous marriage. They make it more difficult to answer the historical question. An odd, unstated liberalism comes through their writings. If proto-fascist tendencies can be found in every group, every psyche, every language, every carefully developed system of thought, human history must reappear before us as a magnificent story of self-restraint, and *resistance* to outbreaks of virulent, brutal fascism.

One need not look far to find evidence for resistance to fascism. It has been said, for example, that Adolf Eichmann was not an anti-Semite, that he maintained close and friendly ties with some Jews, visiting them even after he sent them to the death camps, and that in the first days of the Final Solution, his impulse was to try to find safe shelter for his charges rather than sending them to their deaths.[20] It would be comforting to believe that anti-fascist sentiments enjoy some sort of 'natural superiority' over fascism. It is tempting to turn away from the teaching of Barthes, Guattari, *et al.* and join with Andrew Ross, Fredric Jameson, Jonathan Culler, and others who reassure us that the case is closed, that there was nothing to fascism except ugly beliefs and brutal behaviors, that these beliefs and behaviors were unnatural, or perhaps distinctively German, and they could not manage to take over any important party or state apparatus after World War II.[21] But, Eichmann's example unfortunately makes all too clear, it is also the case that 'anti-fascist' values are found in conjunction with fascism, as one of its main supports. Anti-Semitism, anti-Bolshevism, genocidal policies, and brutality survived the battlefield defeat of National Socialism. They persist as official policy only on the margins of modernity – for example, in South Africa, Guatemala, Indonesia, El Salvador, and Thailand, certainly not in California. These are the grounds for hope that the case is closed. But if Barthes and Guattari are even partially correct, we could empower by our very hope the quiet building of soft-fascist articulations, allowing them to develop to the point of affecting every subjectivity and every moment without ever having been called into account.

THE SOCIAL CONTRACT OF FASCISM IN CALIFORNIA

California is sociologically complex and interesting because of the experiments that are performed daily to test the adaptive significance of couples, groups, cooperatives, families, and communities. Californians know better than anyone else in the world how much individualism is humanly possible. The Fall of Public Man in California has not produced just some alienated *flâneur* wandering down urban boulevards, a few lonely existentialists listening to blues in their private quarters or mingling together in a new 'hypercrowd' at the Bonaventure. It has produced millions of single-parent families; socio-economic conditions that have placed over 50 per cent of 6-year-olds in California's capital city below the federal poverty standard; thousands of homeless people; kids who are punks and also actually in pain. These new human types, real *individuals*, now for the first time actually in that they have no social ties, are absolutely dependent on strangers, and on the state, for their tokens of humanity. They constitute a living critique of individualism. They are also potential soldiers in a fascist army, and some have already volunteered. We recently celebrated White Workers' Day in San Francisco, for example, and there is an all-volunteer Mexican border patrol that calls itself 'The Iron Guard.'

What is being suppressed in California, and in the postmodern, generally, is any distinction we might once have been able to make between intersubjective violence and physical violence. This suppression assumes many forms. It can be found embedded in banal speech acts ('How are you doin'?' 'I'm surviving.') *and* in advanced theoretical discourse: for example, on the 'death of the subject.' Beneath its slick surfaces California is an increasingly violent place. This is not just traditional class-based violence, but new and almost unimaginable postmodern forms. University of California physicists are the nuclear weapons masters of the Western world. Santa Cruz is (or was) the serial murder capital. Charlie Manson. Drive-by shootings. School yard massacres. Pesticide poisoning. (In a recent and valuable manuscript on the Chicano experience in California, University of California at Irvine Professor Maria Herrera-Sobek recounts for us that when someone dies of pesticide poisoning it is said of them simply that they were 'bitten by the breeze.') Immigration and Naturalization Service drownings. Choke-hold killings. Juan Corona. Symbionese Liberation Army. The reverend Jim Jones. Zodiac killer. Hillside strangler. Or we could begin to list the victims: Bobby Kennedy, Harvey Milk, Sharon Tate.... What is more impressive than this violence is its everyday denial. New York City is the violent place, not California. Whenever there is a racial incident in a middle-class high school in California, we can be certain that the principal and the mayor will come forward and deny that there is a race problem in their school or community. Every such act of violence is an 'isolated incident.' When a serial murderer is caught, we can be certain that his or her neighbors will say that s/he was a 'kind of normal, ordinary person.' 'Nothing unusual, really.'

REPORT FROM GERMANY, 1933–45

If we are ever to expose the soft paths to fascism it will be necessary first to answer the question: *What kind of average, everyday social relations do not resist fascism?* One way to go about answering this question would be to attend to the background, seemingly incidental, features of eyewitness accounts of life in Germany in the pre-war years, the recollections of ordinary German citizens, and immediate post-war descriptions provided by military observers. In focusing on the disattended detail, I do not join with those who claim the fanaticism and brutality, which properly occupy a central place in most eyewitness accounts, have been exaggerated. Some things are not susceptible to exaggeration, and what the Nazis did is first among them. The fanaticism of the average German was impressive even to Nazi Party officials. Dr Goebbels' private diaries are filled with bemused remarks on the popularity of National Socialism in the final stages of the war, even after the entry of the USA, even after Stalingrad when eventual defeat became inevitable. For example, Goebbels writes:

> *November 29, 1943* Naturally the destruction is enormous, but insofar as the people themselves are involved, they take it with the best of humor.... There were deeply touching scenes. One woman had given birth to a child during an air raid two or three days ago; nevertheless she insisted on getting up when she heard I had come, dressed and hurried to the Platz. We can never lose this war because of defective morale.

> *December 8, 1943* Even as I stepped on the stage a veritable hurricane of applause greeted me, such as I experienced only in the time of our struggle for power.
>
> (Goebbels, 1948: 537–8, 546)[22]

Earlier, Gregor Ziemer (1941), headmaster of the American Embassy School in Berlin until diplomatic relations were broken, described his visits to the *Helfswerk Mutter und Kind* Nazi homes for unwed mothers. He was disconcerted by the pregnant women who told him to his face that he was a mental and physical weakling simply because he was an American, from a country that takes in 'all the dregs of Europe' (p. 38). When he asked one of them, pregnant for the first time, if she was afraid to have the baby, he reports that she answered, 'Afraid?... Do you know what I am hoping? I am hoping that I will have pain, much pain when my child is born. I want to feel that I am going through a real ordeal for the Fuehrer!' (pp. 32–3).

It is easy to classify such expressions as on the political right, as clear examples of right-wing fanaticism. But this is an outsider's viewpoint, one that entirely misses the average Nazi's self-image. Adherents to National Socialism specifically chose not to understand it in political terms. They saw it as an essential, not quite but almost inevitable, realization of the enormous potential locked up in the heart of the People or the State if they could only get beyond the wastefulness of class and ethnic division and the tensions of partisan politics: that is, viewed from within, National Socialism was neither left nor right but a powerful new ordering of the *center*.[23] It was conceived in the first place as a 'middle ground' between American capitalism and Soviet communism.

The spread of fascism appears to depend on a specific set of everyday social practices. Provisionally, these practices can be grouped under the heading *the fetishism of the ordinary*, or the over-valorization of the social norm. My aim here is not to suggest that California today is like Germany of the 1930s. Rather, it is to show the extent to which Germany of the 1930s resembled California of today. What is striking about everyday life under fascism is its understanding of itself as ordinary, an understanding that runs so deep that it is communicated to others and accepted by them as an accurate reflection of the actual state of affairs. This comes across very clearly in eyewitness accounts. One of the first US military observers sent into Germany reported back to Eisenhower's headquarters:

> The crossing of the German frontier is something of a shock. Even in Nazi Germany the cows have four legs, the grass is green, and children in pigtails stand around the tanks. Self-indoctrination by years of propaganda makes it a shock to rediscover these trivialities. All the officers with whom we spoke reinforced this. The people left behind in this area are human beings with a will to survive. Just because we are conquerors

and they knew it, they are in certain ways easier to handle than the liberated Belgians or French.[24]

Another GI observer wrote:

> The average soldier of our army... cannot understand the nice and clean looking people with their well-kept homes and their sense of law and order could be dangerous or guilty of any crime. As for the adults, they strike most Americans in Germany as decent, pleasant, rather kindly people, who respect their parents, love children, and lavish affection on pets; they are admirably clean and orderly, and have all the solid qualities.[25]

These accounts suggests that what we have here is not merely the ordinary, but the Ordinary raised to a principle; regulative social norms raised to ideals. The defeated Germans appeared a little too clean, too orderly, too correct. This also caught the sociological eye of Everett C. Hughes, himself an immediate post-war observer:

> How could these millions of ordinary people live in the midst of such cruelty and murder without a general uprising against it and against the people who did it? How, once freed from the regime that did it, could they apparently be so little concerned about it, so toughly silent about it, not only in talking with outsiders – which is easy to understand – but among themselves? How and where could there be found in a modern civilized country the several hundred thousand men and women capable of such work? How were these people so far released from the inhibitions of civilized life as to be able to imagine, let alone perform, the ferocious, obscene and perverse actions which they did imagine and perform? How could they be kept at such a height of fury through the years of having to see daily at close range the human wrecks they made and being often literally spattered with the filth produced and accumulated by their own actions?.... How could such dirty work be done among and, in a sense, *by* the millions of ordinary, civilized German people?

> (1979: 89)

Hughes, among the greatest teachers of sociology, gives us the key to the answer in the way he put the question. The dirty work occurred *in the name of* the ordinary. Hughes's student, Erving

Goffman, would eventually discover that candor and honesty are harmful to the 'smooth working of society,' and that any social 'order' depends on the maintenance of a 'surface of agreement,' a 'veneer of consensus' in which each individual conceals 'his own wants behind statements which assert values to which everyone present feels obliged to give lip service' (Goffman, 1959: 8). In short, a smoothly functioning society is already one that is tending toward fascism and postmodern aesthetics, by definition. Elsewhere, without naming it as such, Goffman provides the best description yet of fascist self-delusion, the repression that has its origins intra-psychically:

> a performer may be taken in by his own act, convinced at the moment that the impression of reality which he fosters is the one and only reality. In such cases the performer comes to be his own audience; he comes to be performer and observer of the same show. Presumably he intracepts or incorporates the standards he attempts to maintain in the presence of others so that his conscience requires him to act in a socially proper way. It will have been necessary for the individual in his performing capacity to conceal from himself in his audience capacity the discreditable facts he has had to learn about the performance; in everyday terms, there will be things he knows, or has known, that he will not be able to tell himself.
>
> (Goffman, 1959: 80–1)

There is no apparent limit on the capacity for self-delusion along these lines. In virtually every account of daily life under fascism, someone suppresses or glosses over the obvious in order to smooth out and normalize a terrible event, coolly reinscribing the most gruesome facts into the realm of the ordinary. Milton Mayer, a Chicago journalist and immediate post-war observer, describes the case of an unemployed tailor's apprentice who proudly confessed to having helped set fire to the Kronenberg synagogue on November 9, 1938, but who steadfastly refused to admit, even in the face of eyewitness testimony, that he had stolen the four cans of floor wax he used to fuel the fire (Mayer, 1955: 19–20). As an aspiring Nazi, he wanted recognition for having torched the synagogue, but, as an upstanding citizen, he was resolutely determined not to be stigmatized as a petty thief. This could be called the 'fascist double bind.' It is the condition in which fascists find themselves at all times and that the most effective fascists manage to pass along

to their interlocutors. A psychiatrist who examined Adolf Eichmann for the Jerusalem District Court prior to his trial for the
murder of 40,000 Jews certified him to be 'normal – More normal,
at any rate, than I am after having examined him' (reported in
Arendt, 1965: 25).

Toward the end of the war, when the children were made
anti-aircraft gunners, after the 'All Clear' sounded, some parents
would make their way to the gun emplacements to check on the
kids. A 15-year-old *Flakhelfer* describes how he handled a potentially embarrassing situation:

> Herbert's parents stood at the entrance looking for their son. I
> happened to be right there. I thought, Oh, my, how can I, a
> young boy who's still alive and healthy, be the one to tell them
> that their son is dead? All I could say was, 'Poor Herbert, he's
> not feeling so well'.
>
> (Lang, 1979: 16–17)

Even when confronted with absolute unreason, fascist thought
effortlessly finds reasonable expression, representing itself, even
to itself, as deliberate and cautious, normalizing, efficient, the end
of partisan politics, the end of merely ideological concerns, most
of all as 'responsible.' On their return from the camps after
the war, the forty-two surviving Jewish citizens of Essen were
presented with a bill for the previous twelve years' unpaid ground
rent on the Jewish section of the city cemetery (Dinnerstein, 1980:
242). Fascist excess could never be justified in merely political
terms, or even in terms of race hatred. The justification for this
much viciousness could only be in terms that everyone might
accept; no one should steal, so-and-so can't meet you now because
he is not feeling very well, *everyone* should pay their bills. Et cetera.
The excess derives from an overdeveloped sense of the importance
of seeming to be morally correct, normal, or right, to the point
where a slick surface of correctness develops as a cover for absolute
moral rot. There is no question that the average fascist can enjoy
getting away with doing something terribly wrong so long as it is
inscribed in the normal, ordinary, correct. Eichmann, at his trial,
told stories, most apparently true, of his efforts to shield individual
Jews, friends of his, from extermination. He even went to visit one
of them in the camp:

Eichmann had received a telegram from Rudolf Hoss, Commandant of Auschwitz, telling him that Storfer had arrived and had urgently requested to see Eichmann. 'I said to myself: OK, this man has always behaved well, that is worth my while.... I went to Auschwitz and asked Hoss to see Storfer. 'Yes, yes [Hoss said], he is in one of the labor gangs.' With Storfer afterward, well it was normal and human, we had a normal, human encounter. He told me all his grief and sorrow: I said: 'Well, my dear old friend [*Ja, mein lieber guter Storfer*], we certainly got it! What rotten luck!'

(Arendt, 1963)

Apparently Eichmann was able to arrange for a light work assignment for Storfer, and he gives his reaction as follows: '[Storfer] was very pleased, and we shook hands, and then he was given the broom and sat down on his bench. It was a great inner joy to me to see that I could at least see the man... and that we could speak with each other' (Arendt, 1963: 51). Hannah Arendt reports the records show that six weeks later Storfer was shot to death at Auschwitz.

The fetishism of the ordinary implies a substantial 'value added' to stability, civility in face-to-face interaction even under conditions of strained relations, the smooth functioning of organizations, apparent domestic peace, rational conduct, 'product orientation,' orderliness, and so on. We can know when we have set foot on a domain governed by the fascist social contract when the system that produces this added value is never questioned as a system – when it is taken for granted as the proper state of affairs. Where hypostatic normality collides with a localized requirement for some kind of artful expression, as in home décor, one always finds an anti-aesthetic, heaps of gimcracks, each one individually proclaiming itself to be 'decorative' while collectively, they uglify. William Shirer, CBS Berlin correspondent from 1934 to 1941, on his arrival in Germany wrote in his private diary of his relief that he had been able to rent a flat from a fleeing Jewish sculptor: 'We were lucky to get this place which is furnished modernly and with good taste. Most of the middle-class homes we've seen in Berlin are furnished in atrocious style, littered with junk and knick-knacks' (Shirer, 1942). But we must not imagine that this litter, and other evidence of the fascist fetishism of the ordinary, is ever promoted in the name of the ordinary. Far from it.

THE SOCIOLOGY OF FASCIST AESTHETICS

There are two main ways of conceiving 'everyday life,' and the manner of conceiving it becomes heavily implicated in fascist arrangements. According to Freud, Goffman, and Garfinkel everyday life is the site of the only truly significant drama; it is on the basis of everyday life performances that one's competency, character, and dignity are determined, as well as whether or not one is classified as sane, decent, or someone less nice than a human being need be. The view of everyday life that emerges from German existentialism, Husserl and Heidegger, and the French 'situationists,' Blanchot, *et al.*, is that everyday life is the realm of contingency and accident; it is average, ordinary, and boring. The deal between fascism and aesthetics is based on a radicalization of this second view of the 'everyday.' Fascist social engineers draw a line between that which is classified as the realm of the everyday and ordinary, and on the other side, the realm of the ecstatic and sublime. It is precisely the falseness of this opposition that Freud opposed himself to in every word, mining from the quotidian, unanticipatable variations on our most complex dramas. The mutual hatred of Freud and the Nazis had a real basis in theory.[26] The crime against fascism committed by Freud was in his theoretical insistence that the everyday is the ground for the circulation of desire; that control over desire should not be monopolized by political and/or corporate leaders.

The fascist maintenance of a line between the ordinary everyday and the sublime cannot be based on a degradation of the ordinary; rather, it must be based on raising the Ordinary to the level of a positive principle. No group fits the model of 'ordinary folk' supplied by this line of theory unless it is attempting to commercialize itself as 'folk.' There is naive folk art and street-wise folk art. Fascist folk art always represents itself as being of the first type. An over-valuation of the ordinary-as-such always requires a sacrifice, a suppression, or a deferral. The Ordinary, raised to the level of a principle, prepares the ground for a sudden desublimation of suppressed desire, which rips through the ordinary and splits it open. German workers under National Socialism were rewarded for excellence with tourist trips to the coast of Spain, often their first visits outside the borders of Germany. This was the 'Strength Through Joy' program. The aim of the suppression of excitement and drama from everyday existence is the over-valuation and over-dramatization of events that are classed as non-ordinary: political rallies, a trip to Spain, the birth of a future soldier, and so on. Within Freudian, Goffmanian, ethnomethodological, or eth-nosemiotic perspectives these events are no more (perhaps less) dramatic than everyday life, but within a fascist frame they are endowed with uncommon significance by their opposition to the enforced ordinariness of everyday life.

In other words, the fascist genius is not merely the aesthetiza-tion of politics, as has often been remarked. It is more complex. It is an aggressive splitting-off of drama and aesthetics from the quotidian. Accordingly, one would express fascist 'love' for 'the wife' or 'wifey' or 'the husband' or 'hubby' in a careful and decent way that emphasizes domestic duty and responsibility. The whole manner of expression would promote duty to the point that the question of whether or not it is actually 'love' that is expressed becomes moot: one expresses one's love by doing one's duty, or perhaps the performance of duty is not an expression of love. What difference does it make? The key point is that one loves one's husband or wife decently in order to love one's Fuehrer with crotch-drenching intensity.[27]

If ordinariness is no longer just one way among several of arranging human lives, if it is now raised to the level of a positive principle (that is), we ought to be ordinary, certain pleasures will have to wait, perhaps forever. Any effort to draw a line between Art, Politics, and Life; any effort to separate analytically, institu-tionally, ethically or ethnically, Culture from Society, or aesthetics from everyday 'ordinary' social relations, cannot be innocent when it comes to questions of repressive power and control. All such lines are drawn arbitrarily; simultaneously effected and enforced by a raised stage, a silk cord, or a gold frame, a fig leaf placed over the 'aesthetic' object. Andreas Huyssen (1986: 178–9) describes the response to his 5-year-old son's failure to toe the line at a 1982 exhibit of postmodern art in Germany:

> As Daniel tried to feel the surfaces and crevices of Merz's work, as he ran his fingers alongside the stone plates and over the glass, a guard rushed over shouting: *'Nicht beruhren! Das ist Kunst!'* And a while later, tired from so much art, he sat down on Carl André's solid cedar blocks only to be chased away with the admonition that art was not for sitting on.... The guards, of course, only performed what Rudi Fuchs, organizer of this

Documenta and in touch with current trends, had in mind all along: 'To disentangle art from the diverse pressures and social perversions it has to bear' (the internal quote is from the exhibit catalogue).

The point Huyssen is trying to make with his example is that a life lived entirely on the other side of this line – that is, a life drained of art, or vice versa – is abject and susceptible to the crudest manipulations.

It is only under these conditions that political rallies can be promoted to the status of some kind of 'political aesthetic.' All that is actually happening is that dramatic, cheap tricks are being used to work a crowd that is susceptible to such tricks because they have been incapacitated when it comes to the recognition of drama in their lives. Accordingly, the political rally is then experienced as some kind of deeply meaningful ritual, as collective drama that transcended everyday hierarchies, an occasion for the joyous overthrow of status distinctions; as a thrilling intimacy between the leaders and the led.

Within the framework of the fascist social agreement to separate the ordinary from the realm of ultimate subjective experience, marriage exists in the first place as the basis for extra-marital affairs. Ultra-normal, or hyper-normal, middle-class families are made for father–daughter incest. Highly self-conscious heterosexuality is made for an occasional exciting homosexual encounter. 'Ordinary' reality is made to be split open by drug-induced hallucination. Framed in this way, these acts are no longer major and minor failings or the strong and weak adaptations of individuals caught in structural binds or driven by uncontrollable passions. Within a fascist framework, they are socio-symbolic acts, necessary to preserve the structural integrity of fascist society, and they can be engaged in without any passion whatever, because it is cool to be extra-ordinary, to have an affair, merely super-masculine to be homosexual, simply godlike to commit incest, and so on. It has been well documented that assignment to the task of concentration camp executioner was a punishment for serious criminal offenders, and if anyone showed any sign of enjoying this work they were replaced. These kinds of extraordinary socio-symbolic acts of murder could also be engaged in for the thrills if one stayed cool about it.

THE DEATH DRIVE IN WARTIME GERMANY AND TODAY

At its extreme, the routinization of death – making death an ordinary, everyday experience – can transform all of life into an exciting rupture, an escape from the ordinary, from death. Dr Goebbels describes his feelings in the last days of the war on witnessing the saturation bombing of his city:

> The sky above Berlin is bloody, deep red, and of awesome beauty. I just can't stand looking at it.... It seems as though all the element of fate and nature have conspired against us.... I had only a brief restless sleep. What a life we are leading! Who would have prophesied that at our cradle! I don't believe anyone can lead a more dramatic...life.... It has great and impelling impulses. One must throw oneself into this life with abandon both to taste it to the full and to help shape it. Later generations will not only admire us but be jealous.
>
> (1948: 534–5)

There is no reason to continue to focus on the 'dead subject' as a technico-theoretical issue. As Lacan taught us, there is always a second death following the first, the death in hell. Now the first death of the subject is speaking to us in history and also in the present, trying to warn us of our death in hell. In philosophical discourse it talks of a movement of theory away from the Cartesian subject, a movement more or less guaranteed by the enunciation, *cogito ergo sum*, which, in its first inflection, we now know to mean, 'I think therefore you aren't.' Here is an evident aggressivity. The 'death of the subject' is really the murder of the other.[28] With the spread of Saussurian semiotics, the idea of a 'decentered subjectivity' is taking the place of the 'dead subject.' One notes between Jameson's early and late comments on postmodernity a shift from the 'dead' to the 'decentered' subject: 'Still, I always insist on a third possibility beyond the old bourgeois ego... : a *collective* subject, decentered but not schizophrenic' (Jameson interview in Ross, 1988: 21). This is an encouraging move at least at the level of conscious rhetoric, but it has come too late. Even as specific mention of the 'dead subject' disappears from the text, death imagery reappears on almost every page expressed in and through a language that does not even trouble itself to question its own aims. In response to a request that he clarify his concept of the 'hysterical sublime,' Jameson replies:

> Dialectically, in the conscious sublime, it is the self that touches the limit; here it is the body that is touching its limits, 'volatilized,' in this experience of images, to the point of being outside itself, or losing itself. What you get is a reduction of time to an instant in a most intense final punctual experience of all these things, but it is no longer *subjective* in the older sense in which a personality is standing in front of the Alps, knowing the limits of the individual subject and the human ego. On the contrary, it is a kind of nonhumanist experience of limits beyond which you get dissolved.
>
> (Interview in Ross, 1988: 5)

Can it be said that we are now in a position to recognize the death drive when it appears among us in everyday life? It does not follow simplistic psychological principles and announce itself, as Kristeva imagines, fiercely. It appears, rather, as a kind of misplaced casualness or nonchalance. American correspondent William Shirer found himself in the strange position of being able to observe behavior of German soldiers on what they knew to be a literal 'death drive.' Invited to accompany the German army on its *Blitzkrieg* attack on Belgium in late May, 1940, Shirer writes in his diary:

> What magnificent targets these endless columns would make if the Allies had any planes! And what a magnificent machine that keeps them running so smoothly. In fact, that is the chief impression you get from watching the German army at work. It is a gigantic, impersonal war machine, run as coolly and efficiently, say, as our automobile industry in Detroit. Directly behind the front, with the guns pounding daylight out of your ears and the airplanes roaring overhead, and thousands of motorized vehicles thundering by on the dusty roads, officers and men alike remain cool and business-like. Absolutely no excitement, no tension. An officer directing artillery fire stops for half an hour to explain to you what he is up to. General von Reichenau, directing a huge army in a crucial battle, halts for an hour to explain to amateurs his particular job.... I remember a company of engineers which was about to go down the Scheldt River to lay a pontoon bridge under enemy fire. The men were

> reclining on the edge of the wood reading the day's edition of
> the army daily paper, the *Western Front*. I've never seen men
> going into a battle from which some were sure never to come
> out alive so – well, so nonchalantly.
>
> (Shirer, 1942: 379–80.)

How do we know when we are caught in the death drive? It is when
we want more than anything else in this world to be 'laid back' and
'cool.'

The drive of fascism is to compress mind and body, ego and the
collective, truth and non-truth, life and death, into a singularity.
Ideas are grasped fully by identification with absolutes: for
example, 'Pure Science seeks to establish eternal patterns and
universal laws.'[29] 'Great artists intuitively conform to universal
principles without necessarily consciously knowing them.' 'When
the universal principles that apply to nature, art, politics, and
economic relations are fully understood, human kind will be able
to establish an irrevocably stable social order.' Implicit here is the
'leader principle.' In every domain, above and beyond – always
encompassing – embracing – individual subjectivity is the subjectivity of the rightful Leader. *The law* transcends mere local
regulation.[30] Above and beyond the leader and the law is the
transcendental self, being-in-general, and eventually absolute
Being.[31]

This putting into practice of the 'death of the subject' is supposed to be experienced as a joyful release. The ideal trajectory of
subjectivity is supposed to be always upward, ever freer from
material and moral constraint, ever simpler and happier, and in
ever greater control of the subject-position in general. Hitler's
Education Minister, Rust, told an American visitor, 'Germany
always has been and by rights ought to be the focal point of culture
in the world' (Ziemer, 1941: 13–14). In California, bumper stickers
proclaim 'Another day in paradise.' California does not need a
Minister of Education, or even of tourism, to promote itself as the
end of the death drive and focal point of world culture today. Nazi
subjectivity never quite managed to achieve this level of un-self-
conscious realization. It was probably over-designed. The jargon
of 'purity,' 'perfection,' 'singularity,' 'authenticity,' were too obviously consciously promoted, leading automatically to suspicion
that something quite different was being covered up. One suspects
that early Euro-fascism had planned obsolescence built in, that it

was designed to fail. It effectively caused 'civilization' to collapse into nationalism, and nationalism in its turn to collapse into racism. Perhaps this is all the foundation that is necessary for the deployment of soft-core fascism, which will always look good by comparison. Far from being a merely philosophical category, 'Transcendence' became the route, arranged in advance, for escape from punishment for crimes against humanity.

CONCLUSION: IN THE LIVING ROOM OF THE POSTMODERN

Postmodernism is driven by a desire to forget the horrors of modernity, specifically the brutality of National Socialism and the emergence of the Nuclear State.[32] This forgetting cannot be real, not in a context that is avowedly political, as much postmodernist discourse claims itself to be. Still, one does not find in the substantial postmodernist writing on the Modern any sustained analysis of fascism, the Holocaust, or Hiroshima and its aftermath.[33] We are given accounts of modern art, architecture, and literature written in language that is nervously aware of itself as language; language that is symptomatic of repression.

The postmodern desire to forget fascism in the name of memory – that is, by providing a pseudo-totalization of the past, which arbitrarily puts fascism out of the picture – is not a minor matter. It seems to me an incredible distortion of real historical events that empower a new fascism, softer and therefore more virulent than the first, backed by an intelligentsia of humanist scholars who are perfectly unconscious of their role. I am suggesting that we treat the postmodern as a double suspension: at the level of discourse in historical and critical writing, and in society where a new fascist mentality is taking root with postmodern cultural forms.[34] It is not easy to write about such things. But they must be written, even if inelegantly. We have arrived at a 'moment of truth' in our theorizing and in history; a moment of pure potential in which history can turn toward fascism and theory decisively away from it. The direction of these turns is now being decided in California and in the other overdeveloped regions of the modern world.

Jameson wants to call it a 'cultural dominant,' but it is less awkward to conceive *Postmodernity* as a Weberian 'ideal type.' This means that it cannot be fully realized at the level of history. Still, it is impossible not to notice the 'postmodern' in accumulating historical evidence. This noticing itself becomes the decisive horizon in the further development of the type. At this point in time, what can we say we already 'know' with virtual certainty about the postmodern? We know that its commentators promote a theory of the simulacrum and the movement itself assumes the form of a simulacrum of the avant garde: that is, it is self-consciously avant gardish.[35] In the place of the *new* is a nostalgic recycling of stylistic and intellectual conventions from the past; a whimsical privileging of the historical in such a way as to demonstrate an absence of real concern for history. In the place of history is a valorization of the contemporary, physical surfaces, 'looks' and 'gloss,' superficiality in human relationships, and a trivialization of any distinction that might once have been important to specific forms of consciousness. For example, the postmodern subject is positioned beyond the distinction between the political left and right, which are seen as equally coercive and corrupt. Social class structure is mainly unchanged; perhaps it regresses to an earlier arrangement, but it, too, is ideologically conflated. It has been widely reported in the popular press that Malcolm Forbes rode a Harley Davidson motorcycle with the Hell's Angels.

The aggressive reinscription of structural difference into merely ideological difference – that is, into a difference that should not make a difference – extends to the traditional Western privileging of originals over copies and truths over lies.[36] Again, according to the postmodern theory, copies and lies have been proved to be the equals of originals and truths in terms of their 'truth effects.' Energy spent on maintaining traditional distinctions between truth and non-truth only serves artificially to propel classes of scientific and artistic elites forward into a history no longer of their making.

The power of the postmodern thesis to organize and make sense of ethnographic materials is greater than any claims that have been made for it. If it no longer includes the case around which it was first elaborated, the punks, it continues to model the 'style' of other social types, especially those that are not intuitively classifiable as 'postmodern.' One might go so far as to suggest that the dialectical inversion of the postmodern type had actually taken place before anyone ever noticed or wrote about 'postmodernity.' Excepting some that are decorated as 'Modern,' virtually every living room in America is silently but nonetheless heavily marked by the modalities of the postmodern: the 'random cannibalization of styles of the past,' the simulacrum, pastiche, attention to shining surfaces, folkish or 'folksiness,' flattening and trivialization of difference, an occasional euphoric punctum. This is especially true of those settings and objects which are emphatically not attempting to be 'postmodern,' which would want to be thought of as normal, even hypernormal. Here one finds such things as 'French Country Style' coffee tables with smoked glass inserts; machine-made 'area' rugs not quite identifiable as Mediterranean or Latin American style, but suggestive of some generic 'peasant' handicraft always already under colonial influence; a lamp in the form of a vase that has been 'antiqued' so it seems to have come from Antiquity; an 'Oriental' screen with plastic mother-of-pearl inlay which, ironically, may in fact have come from Asia; a 'Napoleon' mantle clock with quartz movement; and so on. If there is an actual antique in the arrangement, a great deal of care will have been taken to build the totality around it in such a way that it blends in, so it does not announce itself as different from the copies. Prints of famous etchings are framed with the same care that is given an original. There are highlighted (literally) gewgaws such as African tourist art or European souvenirs that have an obvious origin, but never local. The functional pieces, chairs and couches, often defy classification according to any historical or regional system of reference. They are velvet, tufted, and ruffled, but otherwise without identity. They have arrived *ex nihilo* from the realm of 'Tradition.' Everywhere in this environment the surfaces are polished, not to a high gloss, but in a way that makes a double reference to their surfacity; that is, a high gloss that has been broken down to a smooth, buttery patina. At the interior of the postmodern one finds a morbid decadence of the Ordinary.

This inverted 'postmodernism' is the original, strongest, and the most repressed variant of the 'postmodern' type in America. It crosses class lines from the rich to the poor (who can assemble a credible simulacrum of the same hodgepodge at garage sales). It has lost all ethnic, class, regional, gender, or other denotation, and provides the formula for passing from the humanly specific to the realm of generic humanity. It is the approved code of domestic appearances for everyone from well-to-do farmers to black urban professionals – for example, Bill Cosby's television living room. It is a sufficiently powerful type so that it need never be intentional. It will compose itself as if by accident. It spans the 'tasteful' and the 'tasteless' with an unbroken continuum from the polished living rooms of the upper-middle class to black velvet paintings. When the values that are operative here are raised to the level of a norm, or a principle, when they become coercive in their singularity, we have a kind of kitsch totalitarianism, or the evil of banality.

The postmodern belongs to persons who are immune to incoherence, who can accept, even enjoy, discontinuity and schizophrenia at the level of culture. Psychologically this might include someone with a fragmented consciousness on a plane parallel to that of postmodern culture itself. More likely, it would be one who is at once absolutely calm and absolutely anxious, one who can suck all difference into a vacuous singularity of perspective. The characteristic social-psychological manifestation of postmodernity would be a kind of intense, strained casualness that sometimes fails to hold and is overturned by euphoric frenzy and ecstatic violence.[37]

Desire is largely absent from postmodern life. If it is felt, it cannot be acknowledged or expressed. One can desire to *be* postmodern, but there are few subsidiary specific desires. The only permissible postmodern desire is for *attention* or *fame*, and not fame for any specific accomplishment. It is a new, pure kind of fame without subject or predicate, like the kind of sensation that might be derived from being admired while riding in someone else's Mercedes Benz. The anonymous noticing of a murderer is the same as that of a scientist who makes a 'breakthrough.' The only thing that is eventually important is they both get equal time framed in a flat media image not even for fifteen minutes.

Repetition, a constant striving for a reduction of tension, a final moment of fame, all mark a *death drive*, which finds expression in historical practice and in constant loose theoretical reference to the 'death of the subject.' The postmodern ethos conceives itself to be 'standing by' for an infinite instant at the end of history.

The postmodern 'type' has been derived mainly from criticism of architecture, fiction, film, and music. Beyond casual references to street-level sources of punk aesthetics, and so on, too little work has gone into questioning how the postmodern relates to actual social practices and relationships.[38] Postmodernism would seem to appeal to those among us whose communities, careers, households, work, and recreational spaces have been fragmented by war, by corporate decisions now made on a global, not local, level, and by technologies of cultural and biological reproduction that do something other than transfer information and replace work. Postmodernism would seem, then, to appeal especially to punk sensibilities, but there is some evidence that the punks, first to be conscripted into the postmodern, may be the first to escape it. According to the principle of antithesis, punk style has apparently become the only locally accessible code for kids who hate violence and do not want to take drugs.

The postmodern ethos continues to proffer certain comforts of identification to those whose lives would be 'normal' but are unexpectedly disrupted; who live in one community but must work in another; who might be married but do not often see their husband, wife, or children; who are emotionally prepared to do one thing but are employed to do something else. The human being that emerges from the postmodern type is fragmented, but, unlike the punks, their alienation does not constitute a positive statement. The true postmodern type is a mirror image of the punk (or vice versa): a disconnected functionary in a global corporation. One imagines a junior executive in a chain of aerobics salons owned by a multi-national food and cosmetics company. She is married but has not seen her husband for months. She drives a sport truck that has been painted to match her fingernails, she has spent her credit cards to the limit and is broke. She was transferred and has been sleeping temporarily on her mother's couch for over a year. She is both tired and ambitious, and the envy of her women employees because she is 'with it,' and perhaps 'gorgeous.'[39]

A conscious or unconscious understanding of the postmodern ethos permits its adherents to flip off the new left and the yuppie right. She does not need class-based criticism of the conditions of her existence or her relationship to the means of production. She does not need health food, feminism, a home, or even a room of her own. She does not need a human relationship or an alternative to her current situation. And she especially does not need desire. The intrusion of any sense of *need* would disrupt the exquisite balance of postmodern negativity and produce certain horror. All she needs is an ideology of fulfillment that unifies the negativity of her existence into a singular totality, a totalization that increases its power to attract and hold as energy is drained from it: a transfixing negativity. Postmodernites need not seize control of the means of production in order to transform culture. They need only catch their own reflection in the mirror of production. Messing around, playing around, going between jobs, between mates, between homes, is not a sign of social breakdown in the postmodern epoch. These are occasions for celebratory release – a kind of 'camping out' in the homosexual sense. Resistance and displeasure become pleasure. If you are broke and you want something, put it on a credit card and don't pay the bill. Declare yourself to be a part of the Third World. What difference does it make? The postmodern ethos is primary narcissism at the cultural level and the blueprint for a hitherto unthinkable exploitation of the human spirit.

NOTES

1 This chapter was written in the winter of 1988–9 in response to a Routledge reader's request that I expand on some earlier remarks I made on 'postmodernity' (MacCannell, 1989). It has not been previously published.

2 Perhaps by the time this is in print, the term 'postmodern' will no longer be in use. Beginning in 1984 and continuing through 1989, its use was taken up by almost everyone, including philosophers, architects, critics, journalists, and advertisers. Obviously it is not possible to provide a single definition as used by others. In art and architecture, postmodernism seemed first to refer to works that consciously rebelled against modernist aesthetics, valorizing the styles which modernism belittles. In criticism, two usages can be discerned. Lyotard (1984), Huyssen (1986), and Soja (1989) treat postmodernity as the final epoch of modernism. According to this view, postmodern culture is the coming to consciousness of modernity, it is modernity's reflexive reaction to itself. Huyssen, in particular, argues that postmodernism is a weak rebellion by groups and individuals who lack the intellectual power to create new cultural forms. Jameson (1984) and Baudrillard (1975), to the contrary, have influentially argued that postmodernity *is* a new form of consciousness and it opens an epoch that makes an absolute break with the immediate modern past: that the postmodern challenges the political left with yet a new transformation of global capital. In this chapter, I am concerned with the ethnographic evidence for this last position: namely, that something like a postmodern culture is beginning to establish itself as radically different from other cultural forms. Journalists and entertainers now use the term to refer to anything that is current that strikes them as being slightly ridiculous or bizarre, especially over-involvement with images.

Here at the beginning, I want to comment that while virtually everyone who has written on the 'postmodern' traces the term back to Lyotard's respected *The Postmodern Condition: A Report on Knowledge*, first published in French in 1979 and in English in 1984, it was the sociologist C. Wright Mills who coined the term in something like its current usage twenty years earlier. In his *Sociological Imagination*, Mills was concerned that Western societies had reached the point where the continued parallel development of rationality and individual freedom was no longer possible; that freedom and rationality are now opposed:

> We are at the ending of what is called The Modern Age. Just as antiquity was followed by several centuries of Oriental ascendancy, which Westerners provisionally call the Dark Ages, so now the Modern age is being succeeded by a postmodern period. Perhaps we may call it: The Fourth Epoch.... The ideological mark of the Fourth Epoch – that which sets it off from the Modern Age – is that the ideas of freedom and of reason have become moot; that increased rationality may not be assumed to make for increased freedom.
>
> (1959: 165–7)

My sociological handling of the relationship of fascism and postmodernity in the following pages was cued partly by this passage in Mills, and also by several articles critical of the postmodern thesis. See especially Benhabib (1984), Fraser (1984), and several others cited more specifically below.

3 Here and elsewhere in this chapter I have pushed the concepts of postmodernity beyond the point of their application by their inventors. Jameson means for his comments on the valorization of 'surface' and 'depthlessness' to be applied to photo-realism in painting. My point is that if there are other cultural objects to which the conception refers with equal, and sometimes even greater precision, it must be extended to cover these objects: for example, photo-realist *and* black velvet paintings. Any less energetic application both undercuts the seriousness of the conception of postmodern culture and skews our understanding of it.

4 I have given a great deal of thought to the propriety of this term. Obviously it borrows shamelessly from Amory Lovins's 'soft path energy development.' What I am attempting to describe here is virtually the opposite kind of social formation to the one Lovins envisioned in his 'soft' (that is, low technology, decentralized, solar) path to energy development. The association between 'soft path fascism' and 'soft path energy development' is merely metaphorical. I suspect there is a real connection between 'hard path energy development' and 'soft path fascism,' however. So I will go ahead and maintain this usage, even though it could lead to confusion, to memorialize Lovins's chilling insight even as he put forward his brilliant analysis: that the soft path to energy development was 'the road not taken.' Today, after only fifteen years further down the hard path to development, virtually every one of Lovins's dire predictions have come true, and we are also on the 'soft path to fascism': the road taken.

5 This is the term Tom Bower (1988) uses to describe the immediate post-war process by which Pentagon and State Department officials arranged for high ranking Nazis to be brought to the United States, where they were given respectable new identities and a say not merely in academic and scientific matters, but also in US foreign policy, especially toward the Soviet Union.

6 This was also apparently the reason for the 1948 to 1959 blacklisting of CBS Berlin correspondent William L. Shirer, on his return to the United States after the war. For his own account, which is remarkably free of bitterness, see his *A Native's Return* (1990).

7 There is also much evidence in recent advanced critical writing that 'fascism' *is* the proper name, the only name, for what I am describing here. One finds the word used in a free, consensual mode, imbued with emergency, but without any sense of need to demonstrate or justify its use as a descriptor for the current cultural arrangement in California, the United States, and elsewhere in the West. See, for example, Avital Ronell's admirable *Telephone Book* (1989) in which she comments:

> Heidegger nonetheless accepted the call. It was a call from the SA Storm Trooper Bureau. Why did Heidegger, the long-distance thinker par excellence, accept this particular call, or say he did? Why did he turn his thought from its structure or provenance? Averting his gaze, he darkens the face of a felt humanity: 'man is that animal that confronts face to face.'... Today on the return of fascism (we did not say a return *to* fascism), we take the call or rather, we field it, listening in, taking note. Like an aberrant detective agency that maps out empirical and ontological regions of inquiry, we trace its almost imperceptible place of origin.
>
> (p. 6)

For a helpful analytic account that describes the mechanisms that subvert democracy in democratic states, see Gross (1980).

8 Phillipe Lacoue-Labarthe faults Heidegger for misapplying his philosophy to sociological questions along these lines. See the helpful discussion by Fraser (1989: 69–92).

9 As noted in Chapter 1, the most recent strong advocate of the 'end of history' idea is Francis Fukuyama, deputy director of the US State Department's Policy Planning staff, his article on the subject appearing in the Summer 1989 issue of *The National Interest* magazine. He is careful to comment that 'the opinions expressed in this article do not reflect those of the RAND Corporation or of any agency of the US government.'

10 Long before it appeared on bumper stickers, this sentiment was expressed in writing by Dr Joseph Goebbels (1948: p. 8) in his melancholic diary entry of August 9, 1926: 'The only real friend one has in the end is the dog. The more I get to know the human species, the more I care for my Benno.'

11 For a discussion of the mirror glass wall in postmodern architecture that makes a similar point; see Dorst (1989: 107).

12 See, e.g., the previously cited study by Soja on (1989) or Preziosi (1988).

13 Barthes applied close reading techniques ordinarily reserved for canonical texts to the analysis of the interior and exterior appearance of the 1953 Citroen in his *Mythologies* (1972: 88–91). The automobile continues to try to insinuate itself into the unconscious, now trading as much on the machinery that is hiding beneath the skin, as on its

surface features. Today, any reprise of Barthes's critique of the automobile will necessarily have to deal with its technological heart as well
as with its metal, glass, and plastic exterior.

14 Here, I am again taking up a matter that I began to examine in *The
Tourist*. See the sections on 'The Work Experience,' pp. 34–7, and on
'work displays' and the 'origins of alienated leisure,' pp. 53 ff. in
MacCannell (1976).

15 I have addressed this matter at greater length in sociological terms in
my 1990 paper, 'The Descent of the Ego.'

16 For an alternate account of modernity which does not fail to consider
these matters, see Wilden (1987).

17 Graham McCann has provided an excellent study of the cultural
significance of Marilyn's life and death. See his *Marilyn Monroe* (1988)
and MacCannell (1987).

18 For a helpful account of these and similar efforts to produce a political
outcome that would consolidate and legitimize power already held by
corporate, monarchical, and other oligarchies, see Linz (1976).

19 In its early stages, the fascist attack on democracy was launched in the
name of democracy – that is, from the perspective of a 'superior'
understanding of 'democracy.' I do not personally subscribe to the
currently fashionable belief that everything is ultimately undetermin-
able. But there are certain textual issues that can never be decided. It
is eventually impossible to decide whether these attacks on democracy
in the name of democracy are the work of evil genius or of the seriously
deluded. Consider the following example. Hendrik de Man attempts
here to write on the difficulty of mobilizing the masses, how 'the aims
of a small minority can be brought into effect by transforming the
customary motives of the masses':

> This may sound extremely undemocratic – for those democrats who
> have not yet learned that we are talking romanticist fiction when
> we regard the masses as consisting of absolutely free and equal
> persons endowed with the power of self-determination. In the
> opening phases of the struggle for democracy, the phase of agitation
> and propaganda, this fiction might certainly provide an aim; but it
> no longer has the value of even a working hypothesis when the time
> has come for the realization of democracy. In our days, the
> establishment of a sound democratic system is dependent on the
> understanding of the complicated psychological laws controlling
> the interactions between leaders and led.
>
> (de Man, 1927: 65–6)

It is interesting in this regard that de Man taught briefly at the
Frankfurt School. It is evident that Walter Benjamin's Eleventh Thesis
on the philosophy of history (1969: 258 ff.) was written in direct
response to such theses.

In its mature form, fascism will not bother with false alignments with
popular forms and it attacks democracy openly. The Nazi Secretary of
Education, Dr Bernhard Rust, directed school teachers to explain
democracy as a 'form of government in which there is no real leader-

ship,' one that 'wastes time' and other resources. (See Ziemer, 1941: 69.)

20 See Arendt's fine study (1965) for an account of Eichmann's 'Zionism', which does not attempt to reveal it as a lie, nor is she persuaded by it as potentially mitigating his crimes.

21 Ross has already been quoted on this matter. In the last chapter of his *Fables of Aggression: Wyndham Lewis, the Modernist as Fascist*, titled 'Hitler as Victim,' Fredric Jameson remarks on the 'defeat of institutional fascism,' clearly implying that he thinks fascism is a dead issue. For example, he speaks of Lewis's post-war interest in fascism as a 'libidinal involvement in chronic negativity,' and as mere 'oppositionalism.'

> Coming in the midst of the Cold War, and after the utter annihilation of Nazism as a presence on the world political scene, this retrospective evaluation of World War II may seem anachronistic, and the reader may see it as a tired survival of thoughts that were alive for Lewis in the 20's and 30's.
>
> (p. 184)

In his defense of Paul de Man's wartime writing, one writer suggests that we should regard fascist policy as a strictly limited phenomenon, perhaps even still-born, even in its own historical context:

> Some articles do take an optimistic view of the new European order established by what seemed at the time the German victory, but de Man insists on the value of the national traditions of Belgium and France in 'moderating excesses' that might be produced by the German mentality. They take it as given that the future of Europe now depends on Germany, but when they praise things German it is aspects of German culture, but not Hitler, not the Nazi party, not the German government or its policies.
>
> (Culler 1989: 777–8)

22 Apparently, late in the war, not all Germans were enthusiastic about attending these political events. Several German respondents of mine who were there have told me that even if they supported National Socialism before Stalingrad, they hated it afterward and the leadership had in fact lost general credibility before Goebbels wrote this entry.

23 The ultra-right French group surrounding the journal *Combat* openly states their position in these terms:

> We do not say that the words right and left no longer have a meaning. We say that they still have one, and it should be taken away from them, for they signify routine and utopia, death through paralysis and death by decomposition.
>
> (During, 1989: 682)

24 From SHAEF, PsyWar Div, Mr R-H. S. Crossman, 'Impressions of a Brief Tour of Occupied Germany,' Nov. 4, 1944: file no. SHAEF SGS 091.4/1. Quoted in Trefousse 1980: 236.

25 Union O. S. E. *Report on the Situation of the Jews in Germany* (Oct./Dec., 1945). Geneva, 1946: 18. (Quoted in Trefousse, 1980: 243.)

26 In the March 4, 1941 edition of the Belgian newspaper *Le Soir*, published under Nazi occupation and censorship, face-to-face with Paul de Man's now infamous review of 'The Jews in Literature' appears an even more interesting article entitled 'Une doctrine juive: Le Freudisme.' The two pieces are separated by a cartoon of Jews being cast into hell. See Hamacher, *et al.* (1988: 286–93) for photo-reproductions of this page. For a passionate defense of de Man's collaborationist writings, see Derrida, 1988: 590–652, and for an even more passionate defense of his defense, see Derrida, 1989: 812–73.

27 One of the great successes of the Nazi regime, in its own terms, was its attractiveness to women. Hitler was able to produce in women the same kind of highly personal and intense love for the Fuehrer that he would expect, even demand, from a soldier, from a man, but not necessarily a woman. Goebbels conveys some sense of these gender-non-specific feelings in his diaries:

> *November 6, 1925: Brunswick.* We drive to see Hitler. He was just eating his dinner. Immediately he jumped up and stood facing us. He squeezed my hand.... And those large blue eyes! Like stars. He is happy to see me. I am supremely happy....
>
> *November 23, 1925: Plauen.* I arrive. Hitler is there. My joy is great. He greets me like an old friend. And lavishes attention on me. I have him all to myself. What a guy! [*So ein Kerl!*] And then he speaks. How small I am! He gives me his picture. With a greeting.... His picture is standing on my table....
>
> (pp. 6–7)

28 There are two reasons for desiring the death of the so-called Cartesian subject which are eventually opposed. One is as an occasion for mourning. This would be the Oedipal stance of those who identify with the Cartesian subject, who would want to occupy its place. The second would be as an occasion for celebration on the part of those who have been excluded from the position of the Cartesian subject – women, ethnic minorities, children, the handicapped. I caution women and minorities against entertaining thoughts of a Realpolitik accommodation with those who are nostalgic for the Cartesian subject. Any concern for 'subjectivity' that is expressed in these terms will eventually support the economic or sexual positions that are threatened by withdrawal of interest from the Cartesian subject.

29 These 'principles' have been paraphrased from the arts and leisure and op ed sections of European newspapers published under Nazi occupation and subject to Nazi censorship. I have tried to select ideas which seemed especially important to the Nazi cause, that were subject to prominant and repeated publication.

30 Quoting from new statutes, Frieda Wunderlich explains the principles behind the changes in labor law under the Nazis:

> 'Law is what is useful to the German people.' 'The vital root of the

law reaches down into the secret depths of the national conscience and thence furnishes its inner validity and affirmation.' Thus law is transmitted by blood, given application by statute. Since National Socialist philosophy is the purest expression of the Germanic spirit, all that is not in conformity with it is illegal. Right is whatever promotes the interests of the regime.

(1946: 151–2)

31 It was precisely on the point of the absence of any logical justification within phenomenology for the category of 'transcendental subjectivity' that Sartre reproached Husserl. (See Sartre, 1957: especially 50–1.)

32 Critical examination of the effects of nuclear technologies on culture and the unconscious has been initiated and should be continued in the face of the enormous repression of the nuclear which operates not merely on the psyche but on public policy. See the special issue of *Diacritics*, Summer, 1984, on 'Nuclear Criticism,' Dean MacCannell's 'Baltimore in the Morning After,' (pp. 33–46) in the *Diacritics* special issue, and Juliet Flower MacCannell's discussion in her *Regime of the Brother* (1991).

33 The exception is Lyotard's original statement. On the face of it, Jameson's study of Wyndham Lewis (1979) would seem to be an exception. It is subtitled, 'The Modernist as Fascist.' But the book does not examine fascism. Jameson lets stand Lewis's claim to have been sympathetic to fascism, then goes about the business of explicating the texts. Everything that might have been pertinent to the question of the relationship between Lewis's writings and the theory and practice of fascism was left unsaid.

34 I do not wish to be read as suggesting that Jameson, Baudrillard, Hebdige, and the other proponents of the postmodern 'rupture' are intentionally complicitous in the production of a new fascism. There can be no doubt that the theoreticians of postmodernity want to think of themselves as anti-fascists. Jameson (1979: 281 ff.) has declared himself as such. I only want to challenge the postmodernists to confront the seriousness of their distortion of history and their failure to attend to socio-political forms.

35 This is Huyssen's criticism (see especially *After the Great Divide* 179: ff.). Huyssen's position on these matters has been nicely explicated by Anne Friedberg in her forthcoming review essay, 'The Mercator of the Postmodern: Mapping the Great Divide.'

36 The theory of *difference*, as it is absorbed into postmodern discourse, is producing bizarre political effects. It would seem to be progressive in that it recognizes and welcomes difference, formerly excluded classes, groups, and orientations: ethnic minorities, women, homosexuals. But entry of these groups and classes into the postmodern is contingent on their willingness to agree that identity differences are only dramatic effects, that there are no essential differences in the postmodern state. This can produce an ultimate kind of mystification. For even if social differences are not technically *essential* when viewed from a philosophical perspective, under circumstances where material

conditions have not changed, these non-essential differences remain real enough in their social consequences. Thus the kind of postmodernist liberalism which ideologizes difference as 'mere difference', without changing anything, hides power out in the open by getting everyone to pretend that it is 'unreal.'

37 As described by Jameson in his 'Postmodernism, or the Cultural Logic of Late Capitalism,' 146 (1984): 53–92.

38 An important exception is Hebdige (1979).

39 This is a reprise of Edward Sapir's (1961: 92) discussion of the 'telephone girl' as the embodied representative of 'the great cultural fallacy of industrialism'; the negative consequences of 'harnessing the majority of mankind to machines.' I used Sapir's example in *The Tourist* (1976: 35) without modifying it. Here, I propose to substitute the 'junior executive' example as the embodied representative of the great cultural fallacy of post-industrialism, or postmodernity.

Chapter 10

Spectacles[1]

Two crucial gaps or divisions operate as generative principles in treatments of festival and spectacle which have come to be regarded as influential. First, the Collège de Sociologie, based loosely on Durkheim's school, posits a gap between everyday life which is lived in dispersed, mainly individualistic pursuits, and the periodic excitement of coming together for ritual purposes. The aspect of festival which interests Bataille *et al.* is the release from ordinary constraint and excessive indulgence of sexual and other appetites during festival. In his lecture on 'Festival,' May 2, 1939, Roger Caillois remarks:

> In contrast with life that is regular, busy with everyday work, peaceful, caught inside a system of prohibitions, taken up by precautions, where the maxim *quieta non movere* keeps order in the world, is the ferment of the festival.... It implies a noisy and excited throng of people. These huge gatherings are eminently favorable to the birth and contagion of an intense excitement spent in cries and gestures, inciting an unchecked abandonment to the most reckless impulses. Even today,... even the carousing at the end of the Nüremburg Congress in national-socialist Germany, [is] evidence of the same social necessity and its continuation. There is no festival... that does not consist of at least the beginnings of excess and revelry.
>
> (In Denis Hollier, ed. 1988: 281)

According to this perspective, only a rigorous separation of the festival from everyday life licenses the kind of ordinarily prohibited abandon which is essential to festival as they define it. The focus here is not on the events that are celebrated in festival, nor is it on the content of ritual performances or other aspects of staging. It is on the intensity of the emotions produced.

Some caution might be exercised in applying this idea of festival. It implicitly suggests that mob violence is a simple trans-formation of ritual celebration. But it does not give any transformational rules that might help to guard against this exigency.[2] Even though it claims to be based on Durkheim, it leads to decidedly anti-Durkheimian conclusions, specifically in the suggestion that the most social moment, the moment of coming together for ritual celebration, is also the moment of greatest release from social constraint. Freud, or any infantryman who has survived a firefight, would be quick to seize upon the Nazi example in the passage quoted above as symptomatic: the moment of complete abandonment of self-control is also necessarily the mo-ment of complete accession to state control.

Bakhtin's (1984: 1–58) treatment of festival is more complex, suggesting a wider range of potential functions and transforma-tions of festival. Alongside the division between everyday life and the festival, noted by the Collège de Sociologie, Bakhtin finds a second division between festivals that are officially sanctioned by church and state versus their unofficial reprise in entertainments put on by the people for their own enjoyment. Established hierar-chies are inverted and institutional form is purposefully violated in the 'undestroyably nonofficial nature' of the Rabelaisian form of folk entertainments. Here, according to Bakhtin, is the origin of carnival: the solemnity of official Christian drama is re-fash-ioned outside the confines of the church and the polis, returning the celebration to the people. Bakhtin searched for structural differences between official festivals in which existing socio-cultural arrangements are celebrated and sanctified opposed to unofficial, quasi-official, and semi-official carnivals, rowdy in form and lightly subversive in intent.

The first characteristic of carnival is that it plays upon, or parodies, official pageantry, as occurs, for example, in the medie-val European *festa stultorum*, the feast of the fools, and the feast of the ass. Carnival parody in its original form was not, according to Bakhtin, negative as parody often is today. It denied only in order to renew, and was inclusive of the parodist as well as the butt. It functioned to make the community whole at the same time that official rituals were establishing hierarchies and distinctions as between the sacred and the profane spheres of life. Carnival can be distinguished from festival in that it is free of dogmatism and piety. It is embodied to the point of being almost biological, making humorous references to eating, drinking, urination, defecation, copulation, deformation, and so on. Bakhtinian carnival deploys itself against and literally 'fills in' the first gap like Lacan's *objet a*, that between everyday life and high drama, by breaking down the distinction between actors and audiences. For the duration of carnival it encircles every aspect of life; it invades every inch of space and every moment of time. In short, carnival denies the distinction between everyday life and festival on which the Collège de Sociologie idea of celebratory release depends. Finally, carnival is the form in which the fundamental social values of *freedom* and *equality* appear to be preserved and renewed against the forces deployed against such *jouissance* in the name of restraint, order, leadership, and so forth as celebrated at official festivals.

Unfortunately, none of this has much to say about contemporary festivals such as the Los Angeles or the Edinburgh Festival. This is not because modern peoples have lost their ability to stage meaningful festivals. The problem may be that moderns are too able in this regard. Official festival has taken over the form of carnival, filling in the second division between official and non-official celebration just as carnival filled in the first, leaving no space of liberation or even resistance. Walter Benjamin describes the proletarianization of epic theater in such a way as to warn the reader of the potential for repression when democracy becomes a mere form, or a dead form:

> Epic theater allows for a circumstance which has been too little noticed. It may be called the filling in of the orchestra pit. The abyss which separates the players from the audience as it does the dead from the living; the abyss whose silence in a play heightens the sublimity, whose resonance in an opera heightens the intoxication – this abyss, of all elements of the theater the one that bears the most indelible traces of its ritual origin, has steadily decreased in significance. The stage is still raised, but it no longer rises from an unfathomable depth; it has become a dais.
>
> (Benjamin 1969: 154)

This dais, or high table, whose sole function is to impress upon an audience the distance and status difference between itself and the august personages represented on stage, becomes the only residual of the collapse of the staging apparatus which was once the primary basis for the difference between official and unofficial drama. In the guise of getting rid of distinction, only the most arbitrary and groundless distinction remains. Bakhtin was aware that this would be the outcome of any official re-appropriation of the carnival form. He made carnival bear too much historical responsibility for humanity, for what he called 'the second life of the people' in opposition to their abject position in official structures. It was the carnival that made real the 'utopian realm of community, freedom, equality, and abundance' (p. 9). More than once he asserts that the true life of the people as manifest in the carnival is 'indestructible.' It is to be hoped that he is correct on th:s matter, but even if indestructible, the true spirit of the people can be swallowed whole. This is what seems to occur in totalitarian democracies.

I propose that we should try to re-find the free space of Bakhtinian laughter now perhaps entirely hidden inside the Official. How can we liberate carnival that has been absorbed by official festival, by Nazi political rallies, for example? The only method for this search is the one that humanists and structuralists no longer use. It is biological and surgical. Its proper name is *reductionism*. In the following I will argue that at the interior of both carnival and festival is the *spectacle*, and at the interior of the spectacle is the *iconic sign*. If it is possible, eventually, to describe the mechanisms of iconic representation as they operate in spectacular performances and events, it may also be possible to arrive at that which is irreducibly resistive to totalitarian manipulation, even in democracies.

Tourists are absolutely promiscuous when it comes to festival versus carnival, official versus unofficial drama. They seem to have a natural capacity to seize the spectacle that is essential to both forms as the aspect of both that was made especially for them. Thus it is possible for a tourist to enjoy a Watusi ceremony for the singing and dancing that occurs without any knowledge of, or interest in, its ritual significance.

The form of tourist attraction that is called a 'spectacle' includes such famous shows as the Bolshoi, Ballet Folklórico Méxicano, Parisian burlesque, Easter Mass in Vatican Square, the Olympic Games, and the Passion Play at Oberammergau. Lesser relatives of these major attractions include fire eaters, other circus and carnival acts, the playing of liturgical music from speakers hidden in a grove of redwood trees, sleazy stripper routines, wrestling matches, and the like.[3]

If we turn for a definition to Guy Debord, who theorized the spectacle with admirable energy and insight, we shall find ourselves disappointed.[4] Debord confines himself to a discussion of the effects of spectacles, rigorously avoiding any discussion of what is common to them as a class. He suggests that spectacles are derived from religious observances but are now fully in the service of preserving existing class relations; like myth, the spectacle tries to exercise power over history. In his fourth thesis, Debord comes as close as he ever does to providing a definition: 'The spectacle is not a collection of images but a social relation among people mediated by images.' His reticence in providing even a minimal definition is understandable. He presupposes a Cartesian subject. How else could he imagine a social relation *not* mediated by images? Debord is not quite ready to take up the question of a self held captive by its identification with the image of the other: 'I think of you therefore I am.' If he did, his treatment of the spectacle would be re-visited by the dialectic; that is, he would have to deal with the impossible (for him) prospect of a liberating spectacle, one in which the presentation of the image, as a gift, releases the self into the custody of the self.

Is it possible to accept Debord's definition without entering into complicity with his residual Cartesianism? At least it is worth a try. Let me propose that spectacles are performances-*for-others*. They are not 'performances-with-others' such as occur in routine face-to-face interaction; they are *for others*. The determination that the performance has been devised 'for others' can be made by either performer or audience and verified by the presence of certain enhancements. In minimal spectacle these enhancements would include such small shifts of demeanor as an intense or fixed stare, or its opposite, that is, dramatically 'freezing out' the other; a raised tone of voice, or its opposite, a whisper intended for a specific other. Ideally the determination of spectacle is made by both performer and audience. Some consensus in this regard is assured by the presence of staging apparatus, but just as the orchestra pit is no longer required for epic theater, the raised dais is no longer required for spectacle. It was often noted by her friends and acquaintances that Marilyn Monroe had the ability effectively to turn herself on and off as spectacle seemingly effortlessly and without any perceptible clues as to what was making the difference.

Actor Kevin McCarthy remembers sitting next to her at the Actor's Workshop in New York:

> This tousled piece of humanity was sitting on my right looking like nothing. Then fifteen minutes later, after I'd interrupted the scene with some fairly rude comments, I looked again. I realized that a breathing, palpitating Marilyn Monroe had developed out of that nothing.... I remember looking and thinking, 'My God it's her' – she'd just come to life.
>
> (Quoted in Summers, 1985: 130)

Eli Wallach was similarly shocked to discover that he could walk with her on a crowded New York street without anyone noticing and then, suddenly, without any evident change in her manner, everyone would begin to turn to ogle and stare. 'I just felt like being Marilyn for a moment,' she explained (ibid.).

Spectacles, great and small, are productions of moral-aesthetic equations and ratios which provide evaluative frameworks for the full range of human qualities and accomplishments: an Olympic victor is crowned in laurels; a nude dancer is surrounded by pink ostrich feathers and accented with rhinestones; and so forth. The force of the spectacle derives from its *direct* representation of good and evil, daring, endurance, coordination, cunning, sensuality, luck, pulchritude, and other qualities. Spectacular enactments, when they occur in 'real life,' necessarily involve a great deal of actual good and evil, daring, and so forth in their accomplishment. Also, the achievement of verisimilitude in staged spectacular performance, especially those of a physical variety, often requires that the performers actually possess some of the qualities, and experience some of the feelings, being represented: for example, athletic achievements, the performances of motion picture stuntmen, and those of Greek actor-slaves whose play parts called for them actually to have their tongues cut out on stage.[5] Mimetic images are fully dependent on iconic signs.

ICONIC SIGNIFICATION

Charles Peirce (1955: 98 ff.) defined the sign as a relationship between (1) a representation and (2) its object which determines (3) its interpretant. He suggests three basic types of signs corresponding to differences in the form of the interpretative relationship between the representation and its object, or signifier and signified. The three types of signs are icons, indices, and symbols. Symbols represent their object by conventional association, as, for example, reckless daring can be represented by wearing a necklace made from the teeth and claws of vicious beasts. Indices are produced by the direct action of that which they represent: an index of reckless daring would be facial scars received in dueling. Iconic representation is based on similitude or likeness: a human cannon-ball act or jumping a jet motorcycle across a deep river gorge are iconic representations of reckless daring. They are also spectacles. A spectacle is a semion (cluster of associated signs) ultimately based on iconic representation. In spectacles, beauty is represented by spectacularly beautiful actresses, transcendence is represented by flight (sometimes made possible by an invisible wire), strength is represented by bulging muscles and the act of pulling down the Temple, and so on.

Some problems with Peirce's conception of the icon

If we had to devise a single term to cover Peirce's taxonomies it would be balance. He laid out 'interpretation, representation and object,' 'rhetoric, grammar and meaning,' 'Qualisign, Sinsign and Legisign,' 'images, diagrams and metaphors,' even 'firstness, secondness and thirdness' with unmatched impartiality. Peirce gives us no indication of any tendency (rife in subsequent semiotic speculation) to privilege one term over another (signifier over signified, for example) in such a way as to set in motion a theoretical drift which would eventually establish criticism over mathematics, science over art, or some similar intellectual hierarchy. But in an entirely uncharacteristic move, at the core of his taxonomy of signs (icon, index and symbol – always given by Peirce in that order) he privileges icon over the other two. This is clearly evident in the qualifier at the end of one of his most famous passages, a line usually not quoted with the rest: 'Omne symbolum de symbolo... Symbols grow. They come into being by development from other signs, *particularly from icons*' (Peirce, 1955: 115, my emphasis). He posits a similarly dependent relationship between indices and icons. For example, he suggests (ibid.: 109) that a yardstick is an indicator or index of a unit of measure but, in order for it to function as an index it must also be an iconic representation of (that is, resemble) the mental bar yard standard that is kept in London. He generalizes this claim saying that 'any index' must have 'an icon as a constitutive part of it' (108).

The central problem for subsequent semiotic analysis of Peirce's definition of icon is that, while Peirce specifically claims the icon is the most important type of sign, he also suggests that it might not even be a sign. The 'Pure Icon' is the mental grasping of a similarity between an object and its referent, a similarity which is not itself represented but simply fills consciousness. 'A possibility alone is an icon,' says Peirce, but a sign may be iconic (p. 105). This grasping of an unreflected sense or feeling of a connection or relationship (which I am suggesting is equally constitutive of the spectacle) can overpower subjectivity. Interestingly, Peirce's example is a spectacle, the performance of a Shakespeare play. The play's representation of tragedy can engulf an audience with an 'immediate characteristic flavor,' 'a total tragic feeling.'[6] Peirce has found the limits of an epistemological approach to the sign in his characterization of the icon. He attempted to go alone to the heart of the icon. Had he pressed his speculative effort further, he would have discovered that an icon cannot be suspended in a single consciousness but can only exist in a group setting. Of course, Peirce recognized the social principle in semiosis which he expressed as 'the community without definite limits.'[7] But Peirce's concept of a community without limits is an abstract idea, a revised subjectivity. Icons cannot exist in relationship to a generalized subjectivity, even one that has been socialized. Icons exist in particular relationships to particular groups (such as a cult, a group of fanatics, spectators at a spectacle); they are not found outside of communities which have definite limits. If the Shakespeare play imparted to Peirce an 'immediate characteristic flavor,' 'a total tragic feeling,' it is only because he is a member of the cult of Shakespeare.[8]

SIGHTS VS. SPECTACLES AND THEIR AUDIENCES

The comportment of tourists at sights fits notions about the atomized nature of modern culture and the absence of interpersonal solidarity.[9] Some of my college-educated respondents told me of purposefully avoiding popular *sights* like the Eiffel Tower presumably because they did not want to be identified with all those other 'tourists' who had visited such places. I suspect many went incognito, if it is possible to go incognito to a place where no one would know you anyway. This kind of touristic attitude is the opposite of that at a spectacle – a major league baseball game, for example, or an opera – which derive excitement as much from the audience's univocal response as from the action up front that evoked it.

The difference between sights and spectacles is determined by differences in the manner of staging them. Spectacles are bounded in time as human lives are, and their structure and pace conforms to and reproduces the contours of the emotions. The link between spectacular action and emotional response is direct. Through conventional codes (bursts of applause and laughter, coughing, foot stamping, cat-calls, hisses, coming forward to be saved, tearing down goal posts – this list can be extended) an audience transmits an attitude toward a performance. And for their part, the actors in a spectacle, at least those who have a live audience, can alter their output in response to the audience, again by conventional means: open displays of contempt, walking off-stage, or, on the happy side, curtain calls, encores, removal of G-strings, throwing kisses, bowing, and so on. When in response to an appreciative audience, timing becomes more precise and actors put more expression into their voices, more speed in their kick-off returns, more 'life' into their acts, the audience can rightly feel drawn up close to the action, an important part of what is happening.[10] At spectacles, then, some of the felt forms of alienation may wither away, or be cured, leaving the individuals in the audience feeling satisfied or, like Charles Peirce at the Shakespeare play, filled all the way up with a single intense emotion.

Whereas sights such as the Eiffel Tower are experienced mainly visually, and are apprehended as solidity and temporal tran-scendence, the experience of spectacles is both differentiated and temporally bounded. Spectacles send the same messages to their audiences by more than one channel. When attention is deflected from one mode of perception to another, the audience can still continuously pick up the meaning. Also, when all attention is focused on the unfolding action, information processed by vision can reinforce that meaning arriving by way of the other sense, and the several interacting codes can build on one another, driving up the level of excited awareness. Décio Pignatari (1978: 96) has characterized iconic representation as 'simultaneous,' 'synthetic,' and 'synchronous.' The best description of this that I have been able to find is 1,500 years old, written by St Augustine who was evidently a close student of a type of spectacle that is no longer staged:

He [Augustine's friend, Alypius], not relinquishing that worldly way which his parents had bewitched him to pursue, had gone before me to Rome, to study law, and there he was carried away in an extraordinary manner with an incredible eagerness after the gladiatorial shows. For, being utterly opposed to and detesting such spectacles, he was one day met by chance by divers of his acquaintance and fellow-students returning from dinner, and they with a friendly violence drew him, vehemently objecting and resisting, into the amphitheater, on a day of these cruel and deadly shows, he thus protesting: 'Though you drag my body into that place, and there place me, can you force me to give my mind and lend my eyes to these shows? Thus shall I be absent while present, and so shall overcome both you and them.' They hearing this, dragged him on nevertheless, desirous, perchance, to see whether he could do as he said. When they had arrived thither, and had taken their places as they could, the whole place became excited with the inhuman sports. But he, shutting up the doors of his eyes, forbade his mind to roam abroad after such naughtiness; and would that he had shut his ears also! For, upon the fall of one in the fight, a mighty cry from the whole audience stirring him strongly, he, overcome by curiosity, and prepared as it were to despise and rise superior to it, no matter what it were, opened his eyes, and was struck with a deeper wound in his soul than the other, whom he desired to see, was in his body;... directly he saw that blood, he therewith imbibed a sort of savageness; nor did he turn away, but fixed his eye, drinking in madness unconsciously, and was delighted with the guilty contest, and drunken with the bloody pastime. Nor was he now the same as when he came in, but was one of the throng he came unto, and a true companion of those who had brought him thither. Why need I say more? He looked, shouted, was excited, carried away with the madness which would stimulate him to return, not only with those who first enticed him, but also before them, yea, and to draw in other.[11]

THE DIALOGIC STRUCTURE OF THE ICONIC IMAGE

No single writer did more than Peirce to establish the importance of iconic signs for modern semiotic study. But we must turn to Saussure for a dialogic model of the sign, one that includes an addresser–addressee relationship, if we are to go further into the nature of icons and spectacles. In pursuing this line of inquiry it is helpful to refer again to the work of the great Soviet semiotician, Mikhail Bakhtin, who considerably refined the Saussurian model for sociological and literary analysis.[12] Bakhtin's lesson is that signs, whether they are found in works of art or everyday discourse, mediate historically real social relations, and these relations are typically not between social equals.[13] Signs communicate and they also make the point that the 'speaker–hearer relation' is often not 'ideal' from the standpoint of social equality. When an executive intones, 'What's your problem?' to a subordinate, he may do so in such a way as to convey no concern whatever for the other's 'problem.' Quite the opposite: the question can be a demand that the other delete from discourse any open references to 'problems,' or perhaps it is an invitation for the subordinate to confess to precisely the kind of weaknesses and failings that are useful in justifying his or her placement in a subordinate position in an organization. And signs can be used to make exactly the opposite point; namely, that the addresser is inferior. Presumably the response to 'What is your problem?' in any smoothly functioning bureaucracy could serve as illustration.

But the case of the icon and the spectacle are different in an interesting way. Instead of the iconic sign mediating hierarchial relations between addresser and addressee, either

$$\text{addresser} \rightarrow \text{sign} \rightarrow \text{addressee}$$

or

$$\text{addresser} \leftarrow \text{sign} \leftarrow \text{addressee},$$

the iconic sign permits humankind to subordinate itself to its own semiotic production by existing in a position of superiority to both addresser and addressee:

$$\begin{array}{ccc} & \text{icon} & \\ & \uparrow \quad \uparrow & \\ \text{addresser} & & \text{addressee} \end{array}$$

The addresser and addressee are not communicating so much as they are co-participating in a semiotic production in which they are mutually complicitous in the exaltation of an iconic image. Of course, priests, starlets, and quarterbacks, by virtue of their direct involvement in the production of particular sensations, may enjoy some socio-semiotic superiority over their fellows. But they maintain this superiority only by absolute subservience to iconic sign production.

The icon unites the addresser and addressee in a cult, and the cult–icon articulation is antecedent to any interpretation that might subsequently be performed. 'Interpretation' in the cult–icon articulation is bent upon improving the quality of the production of the spectacle or iconic image and rendering more total and secure the subordination of actors and audiences to the production. Another way of saying this is that, in the case of the iconic sign, the actor- (or artist-) audience relation stands for, or replaces, the interpretant. But the interpretative procedures that are followed in the production of spectacles are precisely the opposite of those followed by modern semioticians and semiotically inclined critics. In this regard, Peirce's 'failure' to complete his analysis of the icon can be read as a successful reproduction of the consciousness of the cult of an icon or actors and spectators at the spectacle. Umberto Eco (1976: 195 ff.) faults Peirce for making icon an umbrella term and in his definition for using the word 'similitude' in a 'merely metaphorical' way to stand for both physical resemblance and mental analogies. What Eco says about Peirce is entirely true, but Peirce's grasp on the sense of the icon remains stronger than Eco's. When Peirce (1955: 114) claims that the 'icon has no dynamical relation to what it represents, it simply happens that its qualities resemble those of that object,' he is, in effect, exalting the form of belief that is typical of a cult member. The relation does not 'simply happen.' It requires that some specific someone is in there with the icon saying, 'Yes, this is the face of the holy mother,' or 'Yes, this ninth inning come-from-behind homer is an orgasmic thrill of a lifetime.' It is precisely the moment when the feelings evoked by the iconic representation are replaced by an interpretative understanding of the difference between metonymic and metaphoric associations (that is, Peirce's description of the icon is replaced by Eco's) that the icon ceases to be an icon and becomes a text. Eco fills the gap in Peirce's icon with a sort of activity (criticism) that is antithetical to cult membership, and thereby transforms the icon into another type of sign, one that is more amenable to traditional forms of semiotic analysis.

Peirce's handling of the icon proves that he recognized the

limits of his cultureless, emotionless 'interpretant.' I am arguing that we neither let stand Peirce's incomplete conception of the icon, nor follow Eco's lead and transform the icon into a text. Rather, I am suggesting, once again, that we take our cues from Bahktin and closely attend the participation of real people in real situations as essential to the constitution of iconic representation.[14] The association of icons and spectacles with human feelings suggests the participation of beings not as external interpreters but as internal to the sign itself. The gap in the iconic sign can never be filled in the abstract but must be occupied by a particular group of spectators and actors or cult members. When an icon loses its cult it can exist only as an object of mystery or irony, or perhaps a sign of spectacular failure. Percy Bysshe Shelley has given poetic expression to the effect on an icon of the loss of its cult:

> I met a traveller from an antique land
> Who said: Two vast and trunkless legs of stone
> Stand in the desert... Near them, on the sand,
> Half sunk, a shattered visage lies, whose frown,
> And wrinkled lip, and sneer of cold command,
> Tell that its sculptor well those passions read
> Which yet survive, stamped on these lifeless things,
> The hand that mocked them, and the heart that fed:
> And on the pedestal these words appear:
> 'My name is Ozymandias, king of kings:
> Look on my works, ye Mighty, and despair!'
> Nothing beside remains. Round the decay
> Of that colossal wreck, boundless and bare
> The lone and level sands stretch far away.[15]

In sum, the gap in the icon cannot be filled in the abstract or by memory. It must be occupied in the living present by a particular unification of audience and performance (or artistic rendering). By extending common usage somewhat, the audience-performance component of the iconic representation can be called its 'cult.' The involvement of its cult is essential to the constitution of the iconic image, as icon, and to any concrete understanding of the principle of similitude in the relationship of signifier to signified. For example, to a non-cult member, any similarity between bread and the body of Christ is difficult to grasp. The relationship of the cult to its icon is one of inborn complicity, a never explicit articulation of feelings, attitudes, and objects.

THE SOCIAL VULNERABILITY OF ICONIC REPRESENTATIONS

Icons, and spectacles that are composed of iconic imagery, are totally dependent upon (1) their actualization by a particular performer–audience relation, or cult, (2) a rigorous ritual relation of the iconic sign to the cult in which (3) the cult is subordinated absolutely to the sign. Any purposeful or accidental activity which effaces the sign, decreases the verisimilitude of the representation, reduces the ritual distance between the representation and its audience, or increases the critical power of the audience (that is, training in semiotic analysis) and destroys the icon. The following sections describe some of the social contingencies which destabilize iconic representation.

The routinization of spectacles and over-involvement with the mechanics of production

In the production of spectacles, the very vulnerability of iconic imagery can lead to great efforts to overcome contingencies, to routinize the production to the point where nothing can go wrong. It is not possible to achieve absolute perfection, of course; in a technological society, a power failure can ruin almost any production. But here I am concerned with a kind of failure that can occur even, or especially, when everything comes off as planned. An over-organized spectacle can produce an interpretative consciousness within a technical frame or too much involvement with the mechanics of production. A hi-fi buff, for example, may spend more time listening for perturbations in the bass section of his amplifiers than to music. An example of a device that is trying too hard to be a spectacle is the Grand Haven, Michigan, Music Fountain:

> A 250-foot-long fountain which blends water, colored lighting and music here, is described by the city fathers as 'The world's largest electronically controlled musical fountain.' No one seems to have disputed the claim ... the fountain's evening performances on the shores of Lake Michigan ... are the pride of this port city 30 miles west of Grand Rapids. The apparatus includes 1,300 nozzles for the water, colored lights totalling 100,000 watts and 400 watts of amplification for tape-recorded music. The water, lights and music are synchronized to produce

a delightful melange, water jets jump and sway and patterns of light change color and intensity, all in time to the music.

The show begins with a recorded announcement: 'I am the Music Fountain! Welcome!' The report continues:

At dusk on the night of our visit, the fountain began its show suddenly with the crashing horn chorus from Wagner's 'Tannhäuser', which fairly shook our seats, even across the river. The water jets, glistening in a brilliant blue light, leaped up to a height of 100 feet. The fountain gyrated through a spectrum of colors mostly purples and blues, and through an ever-changing sequence of water. Then the music shifted to a medley from 'My Fair Lady', a theme from 'Swan Lake', several other popular numbers and then a stirring rendition of the 'Battle Hymn of the Republic', which ended the performance.... What is especially striking about the performance is the precision displayed in coordinating all the elements. The water under pressure of 110 pounds a square inch, shoots into the air with no perceptible lag behind musical passages. The programs are varied during the season; they are produced by programmed magnetic tapes.[16]

I am not trying to suggest, in the way I have framed these examples, that the guts have gone out of modern spectacles as we have progressed from gladiatorial blood sports to the Music Fountain. The Music Fountain is a kind of gimmick that has long existed in Western culture. Its relatives include the clockwork orchestra made for Beethoven to play his terrible unnumbered symphony, 'Wellington's Victory at Vittoria.' The mechanized spectacle is especially well suited to illustrate a particular way that any spectacle can fail; that is, by calling attention to the technical side of production, as occurred in the unmasking of the Wizard of Oz. The writer of the report on the Music Fountain says that the device produced a 'stirring rendition,' but at the same time she makes clear that she was not so much 'stirred' as interested in how the thing works. It is important to note, in this regard, that no matter how mechanized a spectacle is, it need not fail in this way, at least not in the eyes of true believers.

The report cited above was written for the *New York Times*, which may explain its objective tone. There was no such distance displayed by most of the thousands of visitors to the Disneyland Hotel

Music Fountain I observed in the course of my study of tourism. Their attitude was clearly one of reverential awe. In fact, two boys, about ten years old, who thought the dancing water and sentimental music was hilariously stupid, and so indicated by their quiet but ironical comments between the acts, were asked to leave.

Absence of faith or belief in the represented associations

A second way that an iconic representation can falter is when it is played before non-cult members:

> Amsterdam, Nov. 2 (Reuters). – Conductor Bernard Haitink of the Concertgebouw Orchestra walked off the stage during a concert here today, complaining that the audience was noisy and not listening. The 80-man orchestra followed him. The orchestra was giving the concert for the 40th World Travel Congress of the American Society of Travel Agents.... Witnesses said the conductor had just started on the 'Benvenuto Cellini' overture by Berlioz when he suddenly flung down his baton and walked off stage.[17]

It is interesting, in this regard, that spectacles are far more vulnerable than sights to expressions of disbelief. The graffiti that disfigure a sight do not destroy it completely and are usually read more as a negative reflection on the vandal than on the sight that is vandalized. But a disfigured spectacle can be a total loss. In a few moments, the travel agents in the audience did to the 'Benvenuto Cellini' overture what would take several generations of pigeons and seagulls to do to the Statue of Liberty.

In the last example, the disbelievers were in the audience. A structurally similar problem can occur when a performer manifests disbelief in the part she/he is playing. I once asked a graduate student in Divinity School whether it was necessary to believe in God to get an advanced degree from his institution? He answered, 'It used to be required, but no more.' It is well recognized in most areas of social life that belief on a performer's part is not so crucial to the integrity of the cult, and iconic representation, as is belief on the part of the audience:

> Brokers and clerks in the financial canyons of lower Manhattan had been noticing Francine Gottfried, 21, for a couple of weeks, Clad in tight sweater and skirt, she would emerge from a

particular subway exit around 1:30 p.m. and head for her job as an IBM machine operator. The word got around and the crowds began to increase. Thursdays, as though someone pulled a switch, the 'bulls' and the 'bears' turned into 'wolves.' Miss Gottfried emerged from the subway, about 5,000 brokers, bankers and clerks were waiting along the young lady's line of march to the Chemical Bank of New York Trust Co. The crowds were thick along the sidewalks and in the narrow streets. Those males unable to make it down to street level peered from windows. One man was on a roof. Photographers were out in force. Miss Gottfried, a 5-foot-4 brunette, had chosen to wear a yellow sweater and red skirt. Suddenly a cheer went up from the massed males, and the mob crowded around her, many asking for autographs.... Miss Gottfried, who lives in Brooklyn and measures 43–25–37, was bewildered by it all, 'I think they're all crazy', she said. 'What are they doing this for? I'm just an ordinary girl.'[18]

Francine Gottfried makes it clear that some disbelief, or feigned disbelief, on the performer's part does not necessarily ruin a spectacle. But her attitude carries risks for the integrity of iconic representation. Had she only flaunted her 'ordinariness' and not her measurements, she might have failed as a spectacle, and as an iconic representation of an admired form of feminine pulchritude. Certainly no spectacle, or icon, can survive double disbelief, that is, on the part of both performer and audience. In some settings (the strippers', or 'exotic' dancers' acts in small suburban nightclubs that cater for traveling salesmen provide examples) Gottfried's kind of failure to appreciate appreciation is quickly met by a failure of appreciation, and no emotion of any kind builds up on either side of the footlights.

Diverse technical contingencies

Spectacles are often complex shows requiring a great deal of preparation as well as on-the-spot attention to detail. Even under conditions where performers and audience believe in the parts they are playing and the associations that are being represented, there remain infinite possibilities for slip-ups, miscues, forgotten props and lines, and so on. Some spectacles fail to come off because of problems that arise in the preparation phase before any audience shows up:

Steve Smith has made his first and last flight as a human cannonball. He was too big for the cannon. Showman Joe Weston had hired the 210-pound, 22-year-old stuntman to be shot from a new 16-foot cannon at Leicester, England. Wearing goggles and helmet, Smith climbed into the gun for a tryout. A one-pound charge of gelignite was set off. Smith took off and so did half of the cannon barrel. Both landed 10 feet away in a pool of water. The other half of the gun backfired, wrecking the truck that was its launching pad. 'Never again', said Smith.[19]

A spectacle, then, can fail because the main character backs out, and also because he (or in this case, she) does not show:

New York (AP) – Francine Gottfried, the most popular IBM machine operator on Wall Street, disappointed an estimated 15,000 men Friday. She did not show up for work. The crowd, up from a mere traffic-jamming 5,000 who turned out Thursday, began gathering as early as 9 a. m. spurred by news reports of the sensation caused by the super shapely brunette's daily stroll to work. But Miss Gottfried, 21, who's 5-feet-4 and measures 43–25–37, was home in Brooklyn. 'We gave her the day off and she'll be off Monday and Tuesday, too,' said a spokesman for the bank where she works. Reports of the spectacular appearance of Miss Gottfried, who usually emerges from the Broad Street subway exit at 1:28 p.m. on her way to report for the afternoon shift, had circulated through the district for two weeks. Clerks and bankers, brokers and errand boys had been arranging their lunch hours so they would be free to see Miss Gottfried, who favors tight-fitting sweaters and blouses and walks briskly to her job. 'It's all crazy,' she commented again Friday. 'These people have all the responsibility of handling millions of dollars and they act like they're out of their minds.' By not going to work she missed the sight of a building-to-building crowd of girl watchers and a banner which someone hung out saying 'We Love You.' Police said four car roofs crumpled from the weight of excited spectators who climbed atop for a better view.[20]

Even when all the ingredients of a spectacle are assembled, failures and breakdowns can occur in the course of the performance:

Kiteman looked up at the flags on the rim of Veterans Stadium. The flags were dancing in the wind. Kiteman looked down into the stadium, where 38,000 people were waiting. Kiteman tried to light a Salem but the wind blew out the match.... The Phils – showing a rich sense of humor – had built a 100-foot plywood ramp down the center field, upper level seats. It was only eight feet wide. Kiteman had a stubby pair of water skis. In theory, Kiteman would slide down the ramp until he hit 40 or 50 mph, take off with his big nylon kite, and sail to home plate with the game ball. That was the theory.... So Richard Johnson – a wiry, sunburned, supercool man from Cypress Gardens, Fla. – found himself atop the stadium last night, adjusting his 16-by-23-foot kite while fireworks bombed past his ear.... 'Two minutes, Kiteman!' shouted the walkie-talkie guy.... 'Go, Kiteman,' yelped the walkie-talkie man as the organ and the PA system blared far below. Guys sloshed buckets of water down the ramp. Kiteman crouched, watching the wind-whipped flags, then peering down the ramp, as the people chanted, 'Jump! Jump!'

Then Kiteman went.

He rumbled down the ramp, 50, 60, 70 feet, the red and blue chute filling with air. Suddenly a crosswind struck from the right, and Kiteman fought it. Then in a bad split-second he was tumbling off the ramp, swishing through seats and railings, tearing steel out of concrete....

'Damn wind', growled Kiteman, angry and embarrassed but unhurt. Then he showed real Kiteman class. He leaped up and threw the game ball about 200 feet toward second base. 'Let's have a cheer for Kiteman!' said the PA man. And Philadelphia fans, in their great tradition, booed.[21]

Upstaging the representation

We are supposed to think that our girlfriends look like movie stars, Julia Roberts, Joanne Whalley, and so on, not that Whalley or Roberts look like the girlfriend. The potential reversibility of the iconic representation (object for referent – referent for object) that is rarely actualized was one of the mysteries of iconic signs first described by Thomas A. Sebeok (1975: 242 ff.):

Peirce's definition speaks of 'a mere community in some quality', and ours of a 'topological similarity', which would both apply backwards just as well as forwards. Is it merely an unmotivated convention to assign a progressive temporal sequence to the relation between signifier and signified?

(p. 243)

Sebeok has discovered that the most basic principle in iconic representation is arbitrary hierarchy: the signified is always set above the signifier, and the sign is set above the addresser–addressee relationship, but for no apparent reason that can be derived from the logical structure of the sign itself. What I am suggesting here is that Sebeok's 'unmotivated convention' is precisely the socially based elevation of the icon over its cult: that is, the product of specific social organization. The ritual elevation of the sign, especially the signified, seems to be a requirement of organized group life, the basis for a collective agreement not merely on meanings but on the importance of certain meanings.

We can maintain a sense of the social superiority of the iconic signified only by means of an absolute double standard, for performances in the 'spectacle' class vs. everyday routines. Junior high-school students in California, who are quite as pretty as Madonna, are trained to believe they are not so attractive as the model, and are effectively encouraged to cut their hair and make themselves up as copies. Madonna is thought to be prettier or prior because she is the model for the copy, not because of any superior physical attributes. This double standard is preserved by staging devices, elevating the performance over the audience, lowering the houselights, maintenance of audience decorum, and so on. However, this ritual work can, and does, break down, potentially opening the question of the superiority of the signified. Two sociologists who study a vulgar form of spectacle describe one such ritual breakdown and a last-ditch effort to preserve a double standard:

The 'degenerates' continue to be a source of sarcasm, if not dismay, to many strippers regardless of their number of years in the occupation. Eleven of our subjects claimed that 'degenerates' were highest on the list of things they disliked about the occupation. Such claims often seemed paradoxical, however. For example, one stripper, upon leaving the stage after an act of prolonged sexual spasms which included spreading her vagina, complained that someone in the first row had been exposing himself.

(McCaghy and Skipper, 1972)

Any claim that can be made against the sign to the effect that it is not elevated, superior, prior, undercuts its potential power as an iconic representation. My favorite example of destabilizing representational hierarchies is provided by the playwright Anton Chekhov who, in *The Seagull*, tells the story of a famous baritone who is upstaged by someone in the audience singing out 'BRAVO SILVA' three octaves lower than Silva himself could sing.

CONCLUSION

The social complexities of iconic representation are great and far from being exhausted in this short treatment. Here at the end, I want to make explicit the central dialectical point of the argument: namely, that out of the type of a sign based on equality of signifier and signified, the icon, comes the social principle of inequality. Specifically, a powerful form of semiosis is required in human communities, composed originally of equal human beings, to maintain the collective agreement that in every arrangement of persons, deeds, gestures, and objects, there is hierarchy. Any form of inequality which had an objective basis could not serve as the ultimate justification for the kind of unchecked, runaway inequality that exists in every area of modern social life. Only a basis for agreement that unequal things are equal and equals are unequal is adequate to the preservation of modern social relations. It is this fit with the exigencies of social life that privileges the icon over the other signs. In a spectacle, a plain actress can be made to represent beauty, and a beautiful girl can be made to think of herself as plain, all under the aegis of a single iconic representation.

Bakhtin was impressed by the people's appropriation of the power of iconic representation in carnival, by their transformation of institutionalized inequality back into original equality of all humans in their simple bodily form:

Rank was especially evident during official feasts; everyone was expected to appear in the full regalia of his calling, rank, and merits and to take the place corresponding to his position. It was a consecration of inequality. On the contrary, all were considered equal during carnival. Here, in the town square, a special form of free and familiar contact reigned among people who were usually divided by barriers of caste, property, profession and age. The hierarchical background and the extreme corporative and caste divisions of the medieval social order were exceptionally strong. Therefore such free, familiar contacts were deeply felt and formed an essential element of the carnival spirit. People were, so to speak, reborn for new, purely human relations.

(p. 10)

But carnival only goes so far as to counter the power of the icon with the power of the icon, leaving intact and unexamined the semiotic apparatus of institutional power. And, in the modern world, this is not far enough to secure the grounds for authentic human relationships that Bakhtin claimed was the province of carnival in the medieval world. If freedom and equality are to continue their movement toward zones of oppression, if we are to clear free territories in which, once again, Bakhtinian laughter can be heard, it is necessary to enter the icon itself.

In this chapter, I have tried to map some of the openings in the icon, and describe the social mechanisms protecting iconic representation. One thing that is clear from the foregoing is that there is a kind of urgent intimacy, a mutual fragility and co-dependence between icons and social life. One way to end this would be to recommend Baudrillardian quietude – standing at the ready to provide careful descriptions of the debris of smashed icons or 'simulacra'. According to this perspective, change happens. Iconic representation is autoclastic or self-destructive. Icons are made to be destroyed, and only a specific kind of social sentiment, called fervor, protects them. But the people are growing weary of living in iconic garbage. It is not as if the power relations originally hidden behind the spectacle disappear when the icon breaks. Indeed, just as Peirce said, what remains in the aftermath of the spectacle are symbols and indices. 'Omne symbolum de symbolo....' For example, from the spectacle of the Crucifixion there remains the Christian symbol of the cross, not just one, but billions of crosses in battlefield cemeteries throughout the world. From out of the spectacle of the Russian Revolution came the symbol of the hammer and sickle. And arrows from the bloody spectacle of ancient battles are now used to point to departmental offices. Symbols are not bio-degradable.

Following Roland Barthes's (1972: 9) comment on *semioclasm*, an interesting alternative might be to try to keep the icon intact while raising the audience to its level. Rather than *subordination to an image* of power, morality, courage, beauty, and so on, why shouldn't everyone be allowed *to live* moral, aesthetic, courageous lives? This would not necessarily require the creation of new kinds of festivals and spectacles, although such a creation is not precluded. It would require movement beyond the division of celebration from everyday life and beyond the division of the official from the unofficial. This is hardly a move in a Utopian direction since it involves no more than ridding the world of *arbitrary* authority and the corruption that protects it. Some change would be required. Some officials would have to become subversives working for the general good, for example, and it would be necessary to start teaching the tricks of television and other media in the schools. There would have to be generalized competency in explicating how spectacles operate on the mind.

It is crucially important that no one should make a 'big deal' out of entry into the interior of the icon: that is, it should not become the special province of 'deconstruction,' 'postmodernists,' 'critical theorists,' and other virtuosi initiates into arcane languages and methods. The best models for this kind of critical activity are still found in traditional festival, carnival, and ritual, and popular entertainments. One notes, for example, that while Javanese puppets are designed to appear as shadows on a screen, they are nevertheless exquisitely painted, suggesting that they have an audience inside the spectacle as well as out front; that is, their audience is also in the place where the spectacle is made by and for the people.

Often it is no more than knowing the history of performance that invites the audience inside the icon to witness the 'indestructible spirit of the people.' Nothing would seem more 'official' than Cambodian Court Theater, and, indeed, nothing is, except that during the Khmer Rouge terror there was an official policy of genocide of artists and performers in the name of a return to an 'authentic' peasant society. So in 1979, when dissident Khmer Communists invaded and established the new People's Republic of Kampuchea, the Court Theater survived only in the minds of some old women who had once attended the murdered artists. In spite of its royal origin and its destruction at the hands of Pol Pot, the memory of the Court Theater was revered by the people. Every musical instrument, song, and dance step was reconstructed from memory. Now, the more official seeming the spectacle of the Cambodian 'Court' Theater is, the more it stands as a monument to the self-determination of the people.

NOTES

1 This chapter was written in 1971, originally as a chapter for my 1976 study of *The Tourist*. I left it out of *The Tourist* because I did not think it was ready when the time came to send the final manuscript to press. Eventually, it was published as a part of a Festschrift for Thomas A. Sebeok under the title 'Sights and Spectacles' (MacCannell, 1986a). I am indebted to the Festschrift editors, Michael Herzfeld and Paul Bouissac, for suggesting re-interpretation of my examples of spectacles in terms of iconicity.
2 René Girard (1977) has extended this line.
3 Paul Bouissac (1976) pioneered the semiotic study of spectacles with his research on the circus. Bouissac suggests that the spectacle of the circus transforms 'nonsense' into meta-sense.
4 The version of Debord's important treatise which I have is the unauthorized (1970) translation by the Black and Red commune in Detroit. It is not paginated, but the theses are numbered and each one is fairly short. I have given the thesis number rather than a page number in all specific citations here.
5 For contributions to the semiotics of tourism, see Culler (1981) and van den Abbeele (1980).
6 Quoted in Damisch (1975: 35), who also makes the point that I am repeating here: namely, that Peirce's icon lacks an interpretant.
7 For a discussion of Peirce's concept of a community without definite limits, see Fisch (1978), MacCannell (1980), and MacCannell and MacCannell (1982: 146 ff.)
8 The idea of a cult, or of a culture, as necessary to the constitution of iconic images is implicit in Eco's (1976: 191 ff.) important critique of Peirce's conception of the icon. An excellent demonstration is found in Bohannan's (1966) 'Shakespeare in the Bush,' which makes the point that for the Tiv there is nothing especially tragic about *Hamlet*.
9 Daniel Boorstin (1961) based his theory of tourism on the alienation of tourists. For the discussion of the limits of this approach, see: MacCannell (1973); Brian Dickenson in the *New York Times* (1970).
10 The electronic media take great pains to build this 'audience participation' dimension into their spectacular productions by filming before live audiences, filling in with taped laughter and applause, and by actually involving members of the audience as featured guests.
11 Augustine is translated and quoted by Erich Auerbach (1957: 59).
12 See especially Bakhtin's 'Discourse in Life, Discourse in Art,' published

in 1976 under the name V. N. Volosinov (see 'Appendix I: Discourse on Life, Discourse on Art').

13 See Juliet MacCannell's (1985) helpful review of Bakhtin's concept of the contemporary and his semiotics.

14 This is also M. Herzfeld's point in his paper (1986) on the rhetoric of iconicity. See also MacCannell (1979) and MacCannell and MacCannell (1982: 68 ff.).

15 Shelley's 'Ozymandias,' written in 1818, is reprinted in Allison *et al.* (1975).

16 Brian Dickenson in the *New York Times* (1970).

17 The *International Herald Tribune*, November 3, 1970: 14.

18 Associated Press story in the *Warren Tribune Chronicle*, Warren, Ohio, September 20, 1968: 1.

19 Reported in the *Philadelphia Evening Bulletin*, April I, 1972: 2.

20 Reported in the *Warren Tribune Chronicle*, Warren, Ohio, September 21, 1968: 1.

21 In Sandy Grady's column in the *Philadelphia Evening Bulletin*, April 18, 1972: 3.

Chapter 11
The future of ritual[1]

In the social science literature, there is substantial agreement that ritual serves the double function of linking individuals to the community or society, and bridging the gaps separating social differences as between social classes, families, men and women, and so on. It is through the agency of a ritual that individual behavior and accomplishment are ratified as socially appropriate or inappropriate, exemplary, worthy of advancement, demotion, respect, disgust, or as typifying a particular social position, class, or category. After van Gennep's *Rites of Passage* (1960), and Victor Turner's (1967; 1977) generalization of van Gennep's insight to all of ritual, it is a widely acceptable that the 'interstices of social structure' are filled with ritual.

> Ritual codes are often utilized to regulate social behavior at times and places of transition between existing forms of social organization. They are customarily used for marriages, births, deaths, changes in the season, changes in authority, initiations, the beginnings and endings of meetings, the day, or the week.
> (Bird, 1980:23)

According to this formulation, ritual simultaneously shapes individual identity and the macrostructures of society and culture. But what does this tell us of postmodern social arrangements? It would seem to make ritual a crucially important category for post-touristic communities that are characterized by extremes of human difference. At at the same time, it radically undermines ritual's unique powers to bestow individual identity and simultaneously to unify the community.

The greatest difficulty in understanding the future of ritual and its continued serviceability in the current touristic community derives from its long-term association with religion. Are ritually mediated relations possible across lines of difference as great as already occur in communities made up of tourists, ex-primitives, peasants, and postmodernites, peoples who can have no religious common ground? The analytic models we now have suggest not. '[R]ituals may be defined as culturally transmitted symbolic codes which are stylized, regularly repeated, dramatically structured, authoritatively designated and intrinsically valued' (Bird, ibid.). Continued efforts to conceive the future of the community and ritual within a quasi-religious framework will produce coercive conversion and proselytizing activities, bizarre religious fantasies (namely, 'New Age religions'), and despair. How can anything be 'intrinsically valued' or 'authoritatively designated' in a differentiated, polyglot community, unless there is an application of coercive power or the demand for the wholesale embrace of a new religion or religion substitute?

In this chapter, I argue that the religious emphasis and conservative bias in functional analysis of ritual do not account for its most essential features, and are, in fact, a particular ideology of ritual, an ideology that maintains the fiction that religious unity and economic hierarchy in human communities are necessary.

THE DIALECTICS OF RITUAL

One of the striking features of academic definitions and accounts of ritual (such as the one quoted above) is its emphatically anti-dialectical character. It seems that ritual, positioned as it is in exactly a place where something more than merely dramatic might happen, can call forth language that is even flatter and more bureaucratic than ordinary social science language. Standard definitions of ritual are written with the kind of cautious deliberation of someone attempting to defuse a time bomb. They appear to be a kind of 'counter-magic' deployed against the dialectical potential of ritual. There is no reason for this beyond an unfortunate tendency for students of ritual to get caught up in doing some ritual work. There are perhaps no better examples of a living dialectic than those provided by a close examination of ritual performances. Consider some of the key phrases found in every academic definition of ritual; for example, that ritual is a 'regularly repeated, culturally transmitted symbolic code.'

'*Culturally transmitted symbolic codes*': It is perhaps arguable that ritual forms are culturally transmitted. Priests officiate; oaths are sworn. But there are always exceptions. If no priest can be found, a ship's captain can substitute. It is as if the ritual form was put in place only so that it could be revealed as mere form. Similarly, it cannot be rigorously argued that symbolic codes are 'culturally transmitted.' It is true that ritual performances are framed as pre-set, as culturally transmitted. But they are also always famously occasions for failure to uphold standards, distance from cultural codes, detachment, and opposition to code. It would be better to approach ritual occasions as the privileged place where symbols are modified for the entire community just because they are supposed to be the place where the symbol is affirmed. Brides are invited to re-write even (or especially) traditional vows; all hosts give toasts that are either more or less eloquent than a toast might be; graduate students flunk exams – or once they did; teenagers mumble apologies, or fail to apologize. Even if these were statistically marginal exceptions they would be worthy of note. But they are generic to ritual occasions even in traditional communities and highly ritualized societies. Japanese tea ceremonies, which to an untrained eye might appear to have been performed at an unimaginable level of perfection, are often determined to have been riddled with errors and faults. Apparently some tea ceremonies, as when a young woman is invited to serve her prospective mother-in-law, are scheduled with the purpose in mind of finding fault with the performance.[2] The dialectics of ritual assure that it cannot be otherwise: the more rigorous the ritual form, the more inevitable the deviation from it. This was precisely Alexander Goldenweiser's central point in his classic (1936) study of creativity among primitives: the more ritually constrained they were in their art work, the more creative they actually felt in their artistic expression; every minuscule variation, which usually went unnoticed by the untrained eye, was experienced by the primitive artist as a kind of creative breakthrough and a high individual achievement. Any careful empirical or ethnographic study of a specific ritual performance will always contain as much evidence for deviation from or variations on codes as for the ideal form of the ritual. The primary function of the idea of a 'culturally transmitted code' is to produce a linkage of deviation from and failure to uphold ritual codes and feelings of both guilt and elation when it comes to our ritual responsibilities as upholders of the social order.

'*Regularly Repeated*': No ritual has ever actually been repeated.

This is the precise dialectical point to ritual; that through the repetition of form, radically different events can be made to seem repetitions of the same event, to produce a fiction of a social order. There is a different president at each inauguration, and even in the case of a second term, with the same wife's hand to hold, the same Supreme Court justice to do the swearing, and the same Bible to swear on, it is a continuation – not an 'inauguration.' The deviation and variations already discussed work against repetition. We need greet our co-workers with a ritual 'hello' only the first time we meet them in the morning, not on subsequent encounters in the course of the same day. And in the same time slot in the following mornings, we need not repeat the ritual 'hello' to accomplish the ritual performance: we can smile, wave, nod, burlesque a cheerful face, or a disgusted face, almost anything will do. Catholic weddings must not be repeated by the same performers. Funerals cannot be. One could argue that, contrary to definition, in principle, rituals should not be repeated, that it is essentially degrading to be caught in a ritual performance that is just a repeat of an earlier performance, as anyone who has heard the same speech at ten different graduation ceremonies can attest. The bride is ritually required to wear something old and something *new*. But the form of our knowledge of ritual suggests a fixation on the old, a metaphysical need to think of ritual performances as repeat performances.

If we turn away from sociological definitions to common sense, we find the same frozen dialectic. For example, rituals, along with job and placement interviews, serious business and marital proposals, and tests, trials and examinations, are among the few areas of social life that are actually rehearsed prior to their enactment. Even more than these other prepared social events, rituals are highly formulated in advance, learned and taught in their smallest detail. Yet, rituals are also the prepared events that are supposed to contain an element of mystery and to produce unspecified emotions.

This element of 'emotional mystery in the context of full knowledge' may be a part of an age-old sham necessary to the smooth functioning of patriarchal communities. The evident structuredness of old rituals is, itself, an interesting social fact, distinguishing them from dialogic forms such as *argument* which can be entered without necessarily having been learned, and that have outcomes that are somewhat open. The obviousness of old ritual forms renders them ambiguous in terms of the importance of their social functioning. On the one hand, it can be argued that old rituals are crucially important to the maintenance of existing social orders, and that is the reason they are carefully preserved and performed. According to this view, some sort of 'science' of ritual is a constitutive part of ritual itself. On the other hand, it can with equal conviction be argued that anything of ultimate social importance, such as the grammar of a language, or the capacity to sort objects and beliefs into the categories 'sacred' and 'profane,' must be do-able without ever having been subject to conscious learning processes. In other words, a science of religion, or a science of language is, strictly speaking, a surplus activity from the standpoint of already existing social orders, the relevant categories, relationships, and logics having been 'hard-wired' into culture and consciousness. It is in the interests of any existing social order to neutralize even a positivistic social science. A social science that can routinely deal with paradox, ambiguity, and rhetorical forms would be dangerous, as would a science that seeks to discover the dialectic as it exists in life.

TOWARD A REVISIONIST READING OF RITUAL

One finds in the social science literature some definitions which, by virtue of their frustration with its immanent dialectic potential, or perhaps it is just willful overstatement, begin to describe the oscillation of idea and event in ritual. In his cross-cultural studies of male initiation ceremonies, Frank Young (1965) concluded that the function of the rituals he studies was to 'dramatize status.' The linguist, Charles Hockett, said that 'ritual is a relatively lengthy and complex episode within which uncertainty is reduced to zero' (Hockett, no date). Victor Turner (see, for example, 1967) suggests that rituals mark 'liminal' moments when individuals are not firmly anchored in social structural positions. Rather than decrying the disorganized quality of these definitions, taken together, I suggest that they be approached as a basis for a revision of ritual analysis that would be serviceable in the (post-)touristic community.

The disarray of definitions can be traced back to the two main (and quite different) conceptions of ritual underlying most contemporary sociological thought on the subject. First, following Durkheim, ritual is seen as a conventionalized expression of obeisance to a sacred being or object, which operates as a symbolic substitute or stand-in for a system of socially approved relationships. Durkheim even went so far as to suggest that the formula could be reversed; that it is the ritual which makes the object sacred. But Durkheim may not have arrived at the point that Goffman would eventually reach along this line; that there need be no agreement in advance for the formula to work; that ritual is constitutive of social conscience as well as vice versa. Second, following Darwin and the ethologists, ritual is seen as an exaggerated, stylized communication act which effectively signals some state of the organism (openness to sexual advance, preparedness to fight) and reduces error in the inter- and intra-specific interactions of speechless beings, among whom we must sometimes count ourselves, especially when we find ourselves in a polyglot, composite community.

Erving Goffman advanced understanding of ritual in face-to-face interaction most broadly conceived so as not to preclude the possibility of the beginning of interaction on the empty meeting ground of the post-tourist community. His methodological procedure was to synthesize the Durkheimian and the Darwinian perspectives on ritual. This line must be extended if we are ever to have a social understanding in and of what I have been provisionally calling the new post-tourist, polyglot, or composite community. But there are at least two problems that remain to be solved which stand in the way of the future development of this line.

The first problem is methodological and has largely been taken care of by Goffman, but it still requires notice. The very visibility and obviously bounded quality of what is taken to be ritual has blocked the development of real definitions. What is 'ritual' is taken to be obvious, and most definitions are little more than generalized description of something that everyone agrees is an example of a ritual. The methodological issue here goes beyond ritual. All functionally important social forms, among which ritual is certainly to be included, hide their operations and effects by only *seeming* to be obvious. That this is the secret of their success as social forms, and also the source of the aura of 'mystery' which surrounds them. The only way to advance on social forms methodologically is to destabilize what are taken to be the 'natural' boundaries around them, and otherwise to 're-frame' them – that is, analytically. Following Goffman, I will eventually suggest a definition and approach that opposed the idea that there are 'obvious,' naturalistic boundaries around rituals. I will suggest, rather, that ritual can overlay all social behavior, potentially providing a basis for common regard and common action even on the empty meeting ground of the post-touristic community.

Second, there is a residuum of religious belief, and of sciences of religion, in sociological studies of ritual which both localize ritual effects and predisposes sociological theory to fall into alignment with a very old metaphysics of unity, in this case social unity based on religious unity. In Goffman's earliest writings on the subject, the religious analogy is patent:

> [T]his secular world is not so irreligious as we might think. Many gods have been done away with, but the individual himself stubbornly remains as a deity of considerable importance. He walks with some dignity and is the recipient of many little offerings. He is jealous of the worship due him, yet, approached in the right spirit, he is ready to forgive those who have offended him. Because of their status relative to his, some persons will find him contaminating while others will find they contaminate him, in either case finding that they must treat him with ritual care. Perhaps the individual is so viable a god because he can actually understand the ceremonial significance of the way he is treated, and quite on his own can respond dramatically to what is proffered him. In contacts between such deities there is not need for middlemen; each of these gods is able to serve as his own priest.[3]

Even Goffman's later descriptions of everyday, secular rituals, such as saying 'Excuse me' when you have stepped on another's toes, while drained of specific religious analogies, still invoke the 'sacredness' of the person. Goffman's last published definition of ritual is purged of direct religious reference, but it has not been separated from its religious roots: interpersonal ritual, Goffman (1971: 1) wrote, 'can be defined as perfunctory, conventionalized acts through which one individual portrays his regard for another to that other.' On first reading, this sounds formal and mechanical, as though the entire religious sense has gone out of it. But perhaps this loss can be accompanied by a gain. If these little gods can constrain their temptations toward narcissism, perhaps there are grounds here for intercourse across absolute human difference.

POLITICAL GROUND RULES FOR SMALL GODS

We have only to turn away from ostensible theory to the actual language of ritual studies to discover an almost purely political vocabulary. One finds in the literature on ritual highly developed concerns for power, status, control, domination, the containment of potential disruption, the social order, stability, and so on. The political vocabulary in ritual studies is far more developed than its ostensibly religious conceptual framework. I do not bring this up to reprise Foucauldian despair that we are all trapped on the powerless side of a power relation. My aim is quite different. One might go so far as to say that almost everything we know about the politics of everyday social relations, about empowerment at the level of real human relations, is found in studies of ritual in face-to-face interaction. Goffman's study of *Gender Advertisements*, written with an open concern for ritual relations between the sexes, can be read as a virtual phenomenology of the political organization of interaction, even, or especially, the first stage of interaction which is always and of necessity between strangers. Here is a characteristic passage:

> [Ritual] displays thus provide evidence of the actor's *alignment* in a gathering, the *position* he seems prepared to take up in what is about to happen in the social situation. *Alignments* tentatively or indicatively *establish* the *terms* of the contact, the mode or style or formula for the *dealings* that are to ensue among the individuals in the situation.... [Ritual] displays don't communicate in the narrow sense of the term.... They provide evidence of the actors' *alignment* in the situation. And displays are important insofar as *alignments* are.
>
> (Goffman, 1979: 1; my emphasis)

What is most interesting and intriguing about Goffman's, and others', writings on the structure of face-to-face interaction is that, as they displace political concerns from the macro-realm of government and political economy, to the intimate details of our mutual day-to-day dealings, *the term 'politics' is never used*. One cannot help but wonder why so many fine scholars and ethnographers apparently feel they cannot openly discuss what is possibly their greatest contribution? Perhaps they have already laid the ground work destabilizing existing relations, for re-alignments, and new dealings.

One need not be a post-structuralist to know that a certain blindness to potential, especially one's own, can help us to get through the day. Existentialists and Freudians figured that out. Jean-Paul Sartre (1969: 55 ff.) labeled our unwillingness to face up to the politics of our own behavior as 'bad faith.' I strongly recommend, as a matter of methodological urgency, that we adopt the use of such ethically loaded terms in confronting the organization of everyday life. Otherwise we will miss most of what is happening. As Goffman (1971: 208) has commented, what Sartre has called 'bad faith' is merely good social engineering. We cannot go much further into the ritual process, especially as it occurs on the vastly expanded horizon of possible interactions in the post-touristic community, until such time that we make 'bad faith' and the political dimensions of face-to-face behavior the explicit focus of analysis rather than residual categories.

Continued suppression of the category of interaction ritual-as-politics is what enables only some of us, but not the others, to be 'little gods' of interaction and little officials of the invisible college and the government of the new community. There has been no effort to hide the motivation behind this suppression. It is made clearly explicit in the writings of the 'little gods' of social theory. Citing Emile Durkheim as his authority, Talcott Parsons (1937: 436) wrote:

> [I]t is through the agency of ritual that the ultimate value attitudes, the sentiments on which the social structure and solidarity depend, are kept 'tuned up' to a state of energy which makes the effective control of action and ordering of social relationships possible.

The passage seems to have the mark of theoretical sophistication, a dialectical quality, or at least, a two-way causal arrow: social structure effectively controls action; ritual, in turn, keeps the structure and solidarity 'tuned up.' But it is a frozen dialectic. Parsons is clearly intrigued only by the 'law and order' potential of ritual at the service of a social order that can be called 'existing' or 'established.' There is no real risk in Parsons' account, as there would be in a true dialectic of ritual and structure, for ritual to subsume and reform social structure. His comment on ritual has stood for over forty years as unquestioned general policy in American sociological theory. Goffman, not a dedicated Parsonian, was nevertheless attracted to this definition. He said of the passage just quoted: 'The best discussion of these issues is still, I think, the very fine section on ritual in Talcott Parsons, *Structure of Social Action*' (1971: 118).

Parsons discovered for mid-twentieth-century social theory that ritual is *the* way to harness the religious authority of ritual to the doing of politics. 'Rediscovered' would be a better term, since this is a trivial insight when viewed from the elevated standpoint of European royalty before the Reformation. Of course, in Parsons' treatment of it, as in Goffman's, the proper name 'politics' has been suppressed in favor not of *dealings* and *alignments* this time, but *effective control of action* and the *ordering of social relationships*. This intellectual formulation evaded challenge by threading its way unnoticed through an irresponsible theoretical language (theory in bad faith – since theory is nothing when it becomes unaware, or pretends to be unaware, of its own language) which gives authoritative voice to the forces of repression but does not comment directly upon them. In the United States today, the same linkage of religious ritual and politics is being re-made out in the open where moral ideas about human relationships – for example, on abortion – originally developed for use in Fundamentalist pulpits, are being put forth as possible bases for social policy formation at the national level.

The relationship of ritual and religion to a desire for social order that can be called 'established' – that is, for an old base for control of the grounds of interaction – is so deeply inscribed that it haunts even those structuralist accounts that are methodologically secure and equipped to handle the structuredness of 'structure.' This desire is at the heart of René Girard's otherwise superior account of sacrifice, for example. Girard (1977: 92–3) states:

> I contend that the objective of ritual is the proper reenactment of the surrogate-victim mechanism; that is, to keep violence *outside* the community.... If the surrogate victim can interrupt the destructuring process, it must be at the origin of structure.

The logic here is both dialectical and perverse: ritual, by staging and situating violence, by containing it in a social form within the community, also rules it out of the community, thereby incorporating the most potentially disruptive acts not merely within the framework of order, but by transforming them into the very mechanism which insures order: for example, corporate and state violence, capital punishment, and the like. Girard may be correct for the old community which based its social solidarity on religious unity, or on pathological variants of the old community such as the postmodern community which makes the homeless its surrogate victim. But he cannot be correct for the new composite community where social order can only result from a successful negotiation between all the gods.[4]

RITUAL AND 'POLITICS' PROPERLY SO-CALLED

From this point on, I want to argue that precisely because of their reputation as guarantor of social orders that can be called 'established,' there could hardly be a more effective blind than ritual for political action leading to social change. Political programs as conventionally defined and understood exist in quite specific ritual conditions which may be their only quality. It is in the interests of powerless groups – adolescents in the United States, for example – to eliminate or omit rituals of the dominating society. Fascists are in a double bind relative to ritual. They are sympathetic to its authoritarian dimensions but hostile to any change it might mask. Thus, after fascists seize power, they engage in a massive transfer of ritual from one social sector to another, as from military to civil affairs, destabilizing real traditional authority, harnessing a hypostatic, imaginary 'Tradition' to their own political goals. When revolutionaries seize control they attempt to make up new rituals to celebrate the triumph of reason, the breakdown of old religious, gender, ethnic, and economic hierarchies, and the broader base of power. After the French Revolution, the political right has justly been terrified of revolutionary ritual celebration. Following is a conservative nightmare of a revolutionary celebration gratuitously inserted into a Baedeker guide (1900 ed.: 225) description of Notre-Dame Cathedral in Paris:

> On 10th November ... the church was converted into a 'Temple of Reason,' and the statue of the Virgin was replaced by one of Liberty, while the patriotic hymns of the National Guard were heard instead of the usual sacred music. On a mound thrown up in the choir burned the 'torch of truth,' over which rose a Greek 'temple of Philosophy,' adorned with busts of Voltaire, Rousseau, and others. The temple contained the enthroned figure of Reason (represented by Maillard, the ballet dancer), who received in state the worship of her votaries. White-robed

damsels, holding torches, surrounded the temple, while the side-chapels were devoted to orgies of various kinds.

RITUAL AND CREATIVE SOCIAL EXPRESSION

Any ritual can be approached as a combination of codes and signs, an occasion for a close reading aimed at decoding the meaning of the component gestures, incantations, and apparatus. Umberto Eco (1976: 49 ff.) has provided us with detailed concepts and methods for this type of work which is the current main mode of proceeding in ritual studies. My aim here is not to decode a particular ritual but to continue a lateral movement across rituals and ritual analysis in search of their peculiar quality as species of social expression and for the potential for creative social change and new social combinations that may be locked up in their peculiar quality.

We can learn from this traverse that rituals are a form of what Derrida has called 'arche-writing,' which I will discuss in a moment. Empirically, rituals are political tracts on practical lines of action that can be written with the body and other ready-to-hand materials. They are an applied behavioral science of the concrete. Here are two examples:

A A sixtyish working-class woman trapped in talk with two friends repeatedly attempts to leave only to be drawn back into the conversation. She finally says, 'I really gotta go now,' and starts off. But instead of walking away, she does a cute little jogging imitation for about eight steps before breaking into her normal gait. (Adopted from Goffman, 1971.)

B A young married couple are at home chatting with an unmarried male friend who is their house guest. The husband leaves to run an errand, leaving wife and friend alone together. The conversation continues, but the male friend places a magazine across his lap and methodically turns the pages even though he rarely looks down at the pictures. (From my field notes.)

The ritual in these examples is the mock run of the old lady and the page turning of the young man. The woman is saying with her body, in effect, that she is really late to get someplace – that she is not just bored with her friends' conversation. She is attempting, consciously or not, to take over control of their interpretations of her untimely departure in a way that can be called 'politic.' She wants both to accomplish her own agenda and to maintain good relations with her friends, and she creates a ritual solution to her political problem. Similarly, the young man is blocking, in advance, any potential interpretation of a silent interruption in the conversation as an opportunity for him to 'put the make' on his friend's wife. He suggests, in effect, that he is meaningfully engaged elsewhere, that the conversation is really the interruption and, therefore, cannot itself be interrupted. Perhaps also turning the pages in the lap is an expression of a suppressed desire via an action analogous to unzipping. His use of the magazine permits the young man ritually to negotiate the double bind of showing proper regard for both the young woman and her marriage.

I want to be the first to point out that these 'rituals' are only recognizable as ritual from the standpoint of the theory being proposed here. They are not pre-labeled 'ritual' by common sense, as, for example, waving goodbye or reciting Hail Marys in contrition for having yielded to a temptation of the flesh is labeled 'ritual.' But once the expressive function of ritual is described, it is discernible as an idiom like any other, formulated for specific occasions, but also open to creative invention and new applications, specifically in contexts where there can be no presumption of agreement on cultural values. That the ritual in my examples represents creative and perhaps one-shot solutions to the kind of behavioral/political problems only a ritual can solve does not make them any less rituals than Hail Marys. They are only less ritualistic. But the existence of creative expression within the ritual idiom does call into question definitions of ritual which focus on the apparent predictable and formulated aspects of rituals that are labeled as such by common sense.

In what sense can we call ritual expressions writing? And what, if any, are the analytical gains from so doing? Here it is helpful to recall Derrida's criticism of Lévi-Strauss's chapter on the writing lesson in *Tristes Tropiques*. Before it was possible to discern the mutual complicity of the ex-primitive and the postmodern, Lévi-Strauss wanted to make some methodological (and by now it should go without saying, political) points about the way the ability to write separated moderns from primitives and empowered the former over the latter. Derrida took exception to the way Lévi-Strauss identified writing with systems of linear phonetic notation. This, he said, was the ethnocentrism at the heart of our most anti-ethnocentric discipline. Derrida noticed that in Lévi-Strauss's account of them, these same Nambikwara, who were alleged not to write, nevertheless prohibited the use of 'proper names.' Derrida found their capacity to suppress a name 'constitutes the originary legibility of the very thing it erases' (Derrida, 1974: 109). In other words, the Nambikwara did possess a form of archewriting, a play of difference between the symbolic and the real. Derrida summarizes:

> If writing is no longer understood in the narrow sense of linear and phonetic notation, it should be possible to say that all societies capable of producing, that is to say of obliterating, their proper names, and of bringing classificatory difference into play, practice writing in general.
>
> (1974:109)

I want to position ritual on new grounds relative to the debate between Lévi-Strauss and Derrida, but in an odd way. I am not repeating Derrida's point that savages write as we do, and that it is merely an advanced form of ethnocentrism, one that is unconscious of its own motives, which claims they don't.[5] Rather, I want to suggest that through our rituals we continue to write like savages, that ritual expression is the common ground for all of humanity, even its allegedly extreme forms.

Ritual is deployed against practical behavior as a tattoo against the skin, often giving the same result. When her boyfriend or husband is jailed, a Chicana in California may have the image of a tear-drop tattooed beneath her eye. The practice seems almost a direct response to Homer's question in the *Odyssey*, 'How else can innocence and beauty be born except in ritual?' Only, as often happens in the study of modern society, and always in the study of modern politics, we might need to place quotation marks around 'innocence' if not around 'beauty,' thereby sending out a third stream of ritual demarcation of a ritual demarcation of behavior.

Ritual as I am now using the term is related to what Eco has called 'rhetorical overcoding' (1976: 14; and 1979: 19). But Eco seems to suggest that when an author takes the trouble to insert reader competency into a text, this is usually to signal the tropic nature of textual language in order to block, in advance, any naive readings. Overcoding is thus taken to be a collaborative act between author and reader, or, again, a ritual celebration of a complex solidarity. In social life similar moves often have other purposes. The aim of ritual overcoding can be to clarify intentions, *or* it can be a deceptive effort to insert interpretive incompetence into the proceedings, to block feasible but undesired understanding while substituting other concerns. This second utilization of ritual overcoding is always a high-risk gamble, of course, because it can be discovered, and when it is discovered it undermines the character of anyone caught trying it.

The model of ritual I am attempting to develop here is mainly for use in the composite community, to facilitate initial interactions as the first step in the formation of new relationships, and as protection of fragile relations when there can be no presumption of common backgrounds. But it can also be retro-fitted to the analysis of older ritual forms, those surviving ritual mastodons called religious pilgrimages: the Haj, the crawl across Mexico to the shrine of the Virgin of Guadalupe, and so on. These great ritual treks are undertaken, for the most part, by persons who are illiterate but who nevertheless live under historical conditions of literacy. They can be conceived by social scientists as they are already conceived by the individuals who make the trip, as a form of writing with the entire body, a barely legible scrawl across the face of the Earth made in the hope that the pilgrimage will empower the pilgrim to live within the unknown of history under some pretense, as phonetic writing empowered Lévi-Strauss to live in history.

This analysis of ritual today assumes a division. It is not between language and the self, or behavior and the psyche, or even within the psyche or consciousness, where Freud and Durkheim found divisions. It is a division within expression between ritual and practical action. I am suggesting that on the absolute meeting ground of primitive and modern, practical action is a *tabula rasa* for ritual which is a kind of applied metaphysics or mini-superstructure to which we all make a contribution.

POSITIVE AND NEGATIVE RITUAL GLOSS

The treatment of ritual as arche-writing suggests the direct applicability of another early Derridian idea; namely, the theory of the supplement, that of writing as a supplement to speech on which speech depends. By analogy, ritual is a supplement to practical, everyday behavior on which behavior depends. But in order to extend or apply Derrida's conception in this way it is necessary to modify it to accommodate social practices. Ritual work is often accomplished by deletion of existing rituals which have come to occupy more or less stable positions relative to specific behaviors. When you step on someone's toes, you excuse yourself. But if you make a point of not excusing yourself, you still express yourself on the social order ritually, by ritual deletion. The early Protestants made a political point of eliminating Catholic ritual. But this did not prevent them from ending up in a bizarre ritual condition that Weber called 'worldly asceticism,' coating every detail of their daily lives and still inhibiting the expression of most 'true' Americans. In a way that strangely mirrors the early Protestants, modern-day surfers on the beaches of southern California are ethically opposed to any exuberant display especially of joy or delight. They have a saying, 'stamp out amp out.' ('Amp out' refers to the explosion of sound made by an overloaded stereophonic amplifier blowing up and, by extension, to any expression of intense emotion.) These surfers (who are now almost exclusively male and tending more toward the subproletarian Nazi image than that of the vacationing fraternity boy) want to transform their own alienated existence into an ideological critique of the surrounding society. They accomplish this by ritual suppression of any lapses which might suggest they are excited by riding waves, watching half-naked girls, or otherwise having fun, having fun. If we are to accommodate these and similar materials into studies of new ritual forms via Derrida's theory of the supplement it will be necessary to devise some concept such as negative supplement to account for ritual props for behavior that are created by eliminating expression that might be there.

In addition to positive and negative, in everyday life, the opposition between the material conditions of practical action and the ritual gloss takes two other main forms; that is, operating either in series or parallel. Durkheim (1915 and 1965: 250–1) nicely describes the series form as it occurs in Australian aboriginal society:

> The religious life of the Australian passes through successive phases of complete lull and superexcitation, and social life oscillates in the same rhythm. This puts clearly into evidence the bond uniting them to one another.... By concentrating itself almost entirely in certain determined moments [rituals], the collective life has been able to attain its greatest intensity and efficacy.

While I want to preserve Durkheim's notion of an essential opposition of ritual and the practical aspects of everyday routines, I want to point out that the strength of the opposition is not so great as to enforce the rigid segregation claimed by Durkheim. At least not in the post-tourist community. There are, of course, many survivals of serial opposition of ritual to everyday routines: Friday night, Sunday morning, Fasching, Christmas, Eid, Tet, birthdays, and so on. But the main form of creative ritual is simultaneous with and parallel to practical behavior. It is usually inscribed directly upon the behavior to which it is referring. Any social occasion or strip of everyday behavior has the capacity to become a vehicle for a ritual performance. This is precisely what empowers ritual to give preliminary form to relations among strangers and the barely acquainted, to put strangers in or out of the way of future relations. One can say 'Pass the salt,' or 'Would you be so kind as to pass the salt,' or one can slap the table and say 'Pass the fucking salt.' Even when a near acquaintance says, 'Pass the fucking salt,' a ritual opportunity opens to pass the salt silently, to acquiesce to whatever arrangement is being re-enforced by the gloss on the request. Or, one might pass the salt and remark, 'You have no just cause for anger.'

The point here is that every and any utterance, every slight bit of behavior, even in the post-touristic community, may be ritually glossed, and it is in this sense that we can say that our everyday existence is fully politicized. Every contact of speaker/hearer, tourist/local, every service encounter, every meeting can and does become an occasion for transgressions of others' subjectivity. In this new context for ritual, it is an act of signification which does not so dependably establish a particular interpretation as it establishes a difference between itself and practical behavior. And only a new social-logic is capable of jumping the gap between ritual and behavior. Even under conditions where the purpose of ritual is to prop up and protect a practical line of action, which seems usually to be the case, ritual undermines the practical. The mere existence of ritual suggests a basic failure of everyday, practical behavior, an inability for it to stand on its own. Every ritual act can be read as a thinly veiled plea, an invitation to join in a new solidarity. From this view, disciplines, political programs, and personal styles which make a metaphysics of the 'practical' and the 'real,' which attempt to purify and elevate some Marxist or bourgeois version of 'material conditions,' are those most blind to their own ritual desires.

But there is even ritual for those who would seek to re-establish traditional authority in the simple meeting of two free and independent subjects, or subjectivities. The teleotype of this un-necessary kind of ritual is the prefatory statement, always launched against efforts to tamper with materialist ideology, 'I am a simple man,' or 'I'm from a working class background,' or Kenneth Burke's (1962: 522) favorite, 'I was a farm boy myself.'

It is necessary to note that increasingly, not merely theory, but life itself is post-structural. Life is not structurally unified. Rather, it is lived across differences: tourist, local, ex-primitive, post-modern, homeboys, heterosexuals, rednecks, intellectuals, peasants, revolutionaries, and so on. The traverse of difference is an ineluctable feature of contemporary existence and the primary ground of ritual performances, politics, and creativity. Of course, difference need not engender creative ritual. The indeterminacy of the field of difference can become the occasion for the genera-tion of enormous ritual evasions: 'middle age,' 'the middle class,' 'suburbia,' and other wholesale conversions of differences into fantasies of unity. But this evasion is not strictly speaking necess-ary. There is no need to deny difference. The millions of creative ritual performances made daily can strengthen and affirm human difference and interdependence. It is right here on the meeting ground of real human difference, where the consequences of the ritual work in which we are habitually engaged are directly experi-enced, that the link between ritual and politics takes on its most important meaning. Each time you gloss your behavior with a ritual overlay, you are re-enforcing a particular structural relation-ship or suspending or undermining it: that is, somehow re-writing it. I leave aside questions of whether these ritual performances are witting or unwitting and whether they operate for or against the interest of the performer. These must be determined in the first place by each person. A science will follow.

When re-examined from this perspective, status rituals (deference and demeanor) are precisely those best suited to under-mine the symbolic ratification and affirmations of oppression and domination of one class by another. To be sure, ritual deference re-affirms status differences and they lend considerable credibility to a Marxist version of social relations and the role of the super-structure. But they also facilitate interactions across structural barriers which might not otherwise be surmounted. Goffman provides a finely wrought illustrative example of an interaction across class, age, sex, and probably (he was too much of a liberal to mention it) racial lines:

> In an airline waiting room, I once saw a young, Southern, upper middle-class man engage in a twenty-minute conversation with a drunken, working-class, middle-aged woman, which she initiated with him after having failed to embroil three prior targets. He maintained a considerate show of interest in her stories but all the while [here is the ritual] held a slight twinkle in his eye and a focus of attention that included more of her than might be accorded someone not in the performer role. Without these gentle means of establishing his distance from her for others, his gallantry might not have been possible.

Rather than looking at deference and demeanor only for signs of oppression, we should look into these forms for creative opportunities to undo oppressive interaction. This process could well begin with deletion of non-ironical use by stigmatized minorities of pejorative rituals originally used against them, as when a woman cut off by another in traffic ritually splutters 'woman driver.' Here is an indication of an oppression so deep that the oppressed join in the ritual work of maintaining it. Along these same lines, I was once walking with a homosexual in Greenwich Village who, when embarrassed and annoyed by unwanted advances from another homosexual, turned to me and said, 'Did you see that guy? Tried to pick me up. Lousy faggot!'

CREATIVE RITUAL AND THE OTHER KIND

My aim here has been to suggest a model of ritual that is adequate to the post-touristic community that does not require any major overhaul of previous careful sociological or anthropological conceptions of ritual. There are, of course, some glaring apparent differences, including especially my insistence that ritual should be regarded as a primarily creative realm rather than the locus of absolute determinism. But I would want to counter that this only restores to contemporary ritual performances an original and authentic sense of what ritual has always been. *Somebody* invented the old rituals, and I strongly suspect that when they were first performed they were then perceived as wildly innovative yet effectively responsive to some new community problem. There are other aspects of the model I am proposing here which only seem to contradict earlier studies of ritual.

First is the idea put forward by virtually every student of ritual that the details of concrete ritual performances are specifically non-utilitarian or merely symbolic. Certainly when the Pope washes the feet and kisses the big toes of twelve Africans, as a previous Pope is reported to have done, we are not supposed to read his act as having any practical significance. And my examples would seem to fit this model as well. If you need salt, you can just ask for it without ritual overlays. It is not strictly speaking necessary for a little old lady to 'funny up a run' on her departure. She could just walk away. And the guy in the other example might have celebrated the sanctity of his friends' marriage without the help of a magazine. However, when ritual is transferred from a religious to a political framework, it becomes evident that it can and does exert a powerful influence on practical affairs, on the building up and tearing down of the social order. But the power of the ritual depends entirely on its seeming to be disconnected from its referent; that is, on its appearing not to have a *direct* bearing upon practical matters. In other words, I am suggesting that creative rituals are not 'merely symbolic,' as both Goffman and Parsons have claimed for the other kind. Rather, I want to advance the more complex claim that ritual (of all types) effectively shapes social life only when it is seemingly merely symbolic, when it guides interpretation and understanding of social life without overtly appearing to do so. And this, of course, is the point at which the student of society must make a fundamental choice: to be complicitous with ritual in blinding us to its actions, or to expose it.

In most previous studies of ritual, the referent of any ritual act is always found in theory. That is, the subject, of which ritual is the object, is not a person or a group, but the 'subject matter' of psychoanalysis, structural sociology, and the like. Thus an adept reading of a ritual performance can transport us to the heart of psychoanalytic theory where we might attach our observations to ideas about pollution, decontamination, sublimation, and so on. Or we might read rituals as affirmations of 'ultimate symbolic values' and the ascendancy of the group over the individual. Several times Goffman has remarked in an uncharacteristically flat-footed way: 'Whatever else it might do, ritual signals the presence of a social relation' (see Goffman, 1971: 199). This tendency within ritual studies is a repetition of the temptation toward idealism that is endemic in the still too Cartesian social sciences. As a counter we need only ask the most basic semiotic question: What is the sign character of ritual?

Interestingly, ritual can be instantly remade in the image of a Peircian sign. Peirce (1955: 99) wrote: 'A sign, or representamen is something which stands to somebody for something in some respect or capacity. It addresses somebody, that is creates in the mind of that person an equivalent sign, or perhaps a more [or less? DMacC] developed sign.' As a corollary, *a ritual is something which stands to somebody for something in some respect or capacity. It addresses somebody.*

The program of any politically conservative ritual is to assure that the response to a particular line of action is not a response at all except insofar as it is predetermined by the ritual performance. This is exactly what is meant by 'intersubjective violence.' (Don't bother to make up your mind about this. I'll do it for you.) Here is the specific way a semiotic definition shifts the direction of analysis of ritual. Consider the phrase, 'It addresses somebody.' Now ask Lacan's question, 'Who is speaking, and to whom?' When we take these questions seriously our first impulse is not to anchor our observations in existing theory but to stay in the empirical context where we discover soon enough that the signified of ritual is only indirectly the individual or social structure. The 'something' ritual is about, the 'something' it is quite literally taking its stand upon, is a bit of actual behavior. The old lady's mock trot ritual is a comment on her departure. And the work the ritual does is politics in perhaps its most elementary form: in other words, the aim of the ritual is, if not to control thinking, at least to influence another's mind, to guide understanding of behavior. The little old lady does not want her friends to read her early departure as an insult. Her run says this, and, as with any political act, it is all the more meaningful when it is also a lie. Recall that for Derrida, writing equals the possibility of intersubjective violence. But we must be on guard at this point not to over-react to this term 'violence' even in the context of examination of politically conservative, or right-wing ritual performances. It can have nothing to do with physical violence. It only goes so far as to name certain procedures (such as lying, withholding information, pretending to agree) used to mystify others. But it also names (and this is where Derrida might have given us more precise conception) every procedure used to enlighten and to educate. Ritual as a form of political arche-writing is only this: performance aimed at directing and producing, in the mind of another person or persons, particular interpretations of behavior. It is our responsibility to notice and determine the validity of the actual procedures that are used.

It is worthwhile to point out in this regard that there was a strong political overtone in Peirce's original definition of the sign even before it is modified for the analysis of ritual, and writing. This is explicit in his wording, 'a sign stands for something.' A willingness to stand for something (with or without understanding) is the basis of all political action. And if it is argued that all Peirce intended was a logical relation of substitutability, I will respond that even or especially here in the acceptance of a substitute is the acid test of political support for the program or paradigm in which the substitutions occur. Now consider some simple sociological properties of ritual semiotically defined.

First, ritual can, and often does, refer to the behavior of its author. This seems to have been the case in most of the examples I have supplied so far.

Second, ritual can refer to the behavior of another. Goffman (1971: 160) provides an example and some interpretation: 'a wife can hold a smile of amused patience on her face over the entire period during which her husband nearby flirts with another woman, the smile proclaiming that his actions are not to be taken seriously.' A point to be made here is that this wife, as Goffman has described her, appears to be ritually frozen, unable to build up a line of practical action underneath her ritual comment on her husband's behavior. This seems to happen often in ritual references to the behavior of others.

Third, certain virtuosi at ritual expression can, with a single gesture, set up positions on their own behavior and that of others, saying something quite different about each. Professor Harold Bloom, of Yale University, when he lectures brilliantly and at great length, often appears to wipe his brow. Only if you look closely, you see that he does not actually make hand-to-forehead contact. The gesture very eloquently expresses that this is very hard work, but not for Harold Bloom. Similarly, Jacques Derrida, when lecturing at the Ecole Normale in Paris in the late 1960s, was in the habit of lighting his cigarette while informing his students that smoking was not permitted in his classroom. And Paul de Man would often sit just behind and out of sight of a hapless colleague whose task it was to introduce him before a lecture or colloquium.

So positioned, de Man would shake his head in disagreement with everything being said about him, especially the inevitable comments of a highly complimentary nature. This shaking of the head established de Man as an exceedingly humble man, but also one superior in intellect, judgment, and taste to the unwitting straightman who had to do the introductions.

CONCLUSION

Now I want to return to a problem raised at the beginning: the unutterability of the proper name 'politics' in the context of ritual studies as these were originally conceived and executed. Why was this a professional taboo? The clue is in our conception of practical, everyday behavior. Interestingly, as Goffman noted, no one really did do a better job of helping us to make up our minds about this than Talcott Parsons in his (1937) *Structure of Social Action*. If the book is no longer read, it is not because the ideas it contains are *passé*. Rather, it is because the analysis of social action Parsons gave us became so general and accepted that the reading can only re-enforce ideas so entrenched they do not now need the heavy-duty scholarly maintenance that was evidently required in the 1930s when Parsons wrote it.

Parsons sub-titled his book 'A Study in Social Theory with Special Reference to a Group of Recent European Writers.' The readings Parsons gave us of Alfred Marshall, Pareto, Durkheim, and Weber are intended to show that their contributions to our understanding of society and behavior derive in a straightforward way from the classical economic tradition of Smith, Hobbes, and Malthus. Parsons fitted the great nineteenth-century explosion of knowledge about social institutions into an individual-level 'ends means' schema as if nothing had occurred except a peaceful progression of increasingly precise socio-economic theory as it applies to individual behavior.

It is evident that the exclusion of Marx from his 'Group of Recent European Writers' was not an oversight. It is exactly Marx's criticism of classical economic thought, and any critique that might easily be deduced from Durkheim, Weber, and the others, that Parsons is laboring to suppress. His was a form of ritual scholarship. Now we have a (it is actually the only official) framework for answering the question, what is practical everyday behavior?

On the one hand, according to Parsons, there is an infinite

aggregate of individual acts. On the other there is an ideal, a view of the acts from the perspective of a human faculty or disposition: the profit motive, the desire to avoid pain or seek pleasure. Every social structural arrangement emerged from this division of human action from desire or disposition, and every arrangement is a response to the division. For example, if everyone is seeking pleasure, institutional regulations come into existence and intervene to prevent one man from getting his at another's expense. This, still according to Parsons, explains the prohibition of monopoly in the economy, the institution of marriage, and all the other quasi-effective means by which random desires are rationally organized so that everyone gets as much as he can without nevertheless cornering some market. The progress of history is the progress of rationality in the relating of desire to activity. Rationality implies structure, but a structure that is entirely subordinated to wants, ends, means, and action. Except for some archaic institutions which are slow to pass out of existence after they are no longer functional, structural arrangements always automatically develop and modernize. This is because, according to his view, institutions have no autonomous capacity to specify practical action, they merely reflect the level of its efficiency. In Parsons' own words:

> This is on the whole the orthodox Anglo-Saxon view of economic history: the barriers must be removed, but once they are removed, modern capitalism – or free enterprise – becomes established of itself. It needs no specific propelling force – and if it consists merely in rational conduct, why should it.[6]
>
> (Parsons, 1937: 157)

By now the reasons the proper name of politics could not be uttered in ritual studies should be quite clear. The version of practical behavior, against which any analysis of ritual is necessarily set, is already fully politicized or aligned with one economic system, not any other. Our current understanding of ritual has not emerged in opposition to practical behavior as such, but to a capitalist myth of 'merely rational conduct' for which the Western social sciences are fully responsible. Our social system does need a specific propelling force: millions of concerted ritual expressions, performed everyday, beginning with going to work with a smile on your face. Of course studies of ritual have been in bad faith. But the discovery of the politics in ritual might be a first step in exposing the myth that there is such a thing as 'purely practical' behavior and a further declaration of independence for current socio-theoretical thought.

NOTES

1 This chapter was originally prepared and delivered as the James A. Becker Lecture at Cornell University, October, 1983. It is published here for the first time.
2 I want to thank Manar Hammad for having taken the trouble to explain the Japanese tea ceremony to me based on his exhaustive study of it.
3 Erving Goffman, 'On the Nature of Deference and Demeanor' (1956; and 1967: 95). See also Michel de Certeau's fine study of *The Practice of Everyday Life* (1984). There is a nice echo of the Goffman remark in de Certeau's comment on Freud: 'As the representative of an abstract universal, the ordinary man in Freudian theory still plays the role of a god who is recognizable in his effects, even as he has humbled himself and merged with the superstitious common people' (p. 3).
4 I do not wish to be understood as suggesting that every analysis of ritual as a conservatizing force has conscious conservative political origins. For the most part, it appears as just another one of those intellectual accidents that is scheduled to happen in our kind of civilization, the result of assigning 'busy work' to professors who may not be up to the task.
5 It is interesting in this regard that in Hebdige's (1979) study of punks, the metaphor he uses at the beginning of the book is, 'they are like the graffiti on the subways.' He sees the whole movement as a forbidden form of writing.
6 Unfortunately, it is no longer necessary to argue the point that the ultimate means by which the 'orthodox Anglo-Saxon view of economic history' establishes itself world-wide, the way it breaks down the 'barriers' that 'must be removed' is warfare.

Chapter 12

The Vietnam Memorial in Washington, DC[1]

November 11, 1984. Davis, California. Maya Ying Lin is on the television. She is the young Chinese-American architect who designed the Vietnam Memorial in Washington, DC. She is sitting with State Department officials at a dedication ceremony for the Frederick Hart statue of three bronze combat soldiers that has been set near the monument she designed. There has been quite a bit of controversy and protest over the memorial, and some individuals and groups have expressed the sentiment that the Hart soldiers should become the 'real' memorial. Lin does not speak. I wonder what she thinks?

November 7, 1984. On the plane from Washington, DC to California. I have been in Washington for one day to work for the Congress' Office of Technology Assessment. Late afternoon, I have an hour to visit the memorial before my plane leaves. Workmen are preparing bleachers and temporary landscaping for the unveiling of the Hart addition, or is it the Hart 'correction'? I hurry past to the memorial. [First visit.]

What I see is nothing more than a unity of five enormous Vs, dug out of the earth, out of the side of a grassy knoll, faced in polished black granite engraved with the names of 58,022 Americans who died in Vietnam. It appears to be proudly embarrassed to have barely achieved three-dimensionality, like origami. One deep V fallen over to the left, another fallen over to the right, joined at the legs to make upside-down and right-side-up shallow Vs, then bent slightly at the join to make a three-dimensional fifth V if viewed from above. You can reproduce its shape by putting your hands naturally in front of your chest, palms facing you, making a narrow V with the index and second fingers of both hands, joining the fingers together at the tips, then bending the palms together slightly.

The design seems simple and direct. A multiplication of Vs for a victory that proved to be illusory, in black, the official color of mourning in America. It is impossible for me not to harbor deep suspicion of memorials. They must lie about the events they memorialize. Widows who murder their husbands wear black and moan the loudest. It must be the same for this memorial. But there is still the controversy to be accounted for. If this was standard war-memorial hypocrisy, there would be no controversy. Is it possible that this particular all-too-obvious color choice might serve as a thin veil covering a truth? Isn't it true that most of the American men who died in Vietnam, whose names are on this black memorial, were black? Miss Lin's choice of the official color of mourning serves as the best possible excuse for expressing a suppressed truth.

In the back streets of the universe where the literal and the figurative converge, in the unconscious, black is also the color which permits reflection. When you approach the Vietnam Memorial, you see yourself clearly reflected in the polished surface. It involves you, as the war involved all young Americans, those who fought in it and those who fought against it. You enter the memorial following a path that begins at the point of the V that has fallen over to the right, and descends the shallow, right-side-up V. First you see your feet only. It is not really you. It is just your feet. Then you descend the gentle slope, and the monument ascends above you, and the names of the dead, written not alphabetically, but in the order they died, mount, piling up in ever higher columns. You are drawn into the monument, into the war, into a rare, personalized, temporal accounting of death. Suddenly, at about the moment you no longer notice the reflection of your own feet, you see your own face in the monument with the name of a dead soldier written across it, one across your forehead, another across your eyes, cheeks, mouth. This is the moment, often remarked, where many of the visitors to the Vietnam Memorial, even those who are not there to search out the name of someone they loved or knew, break down and cry.

But you must go on, deep and deeper still (the path is one-way and does not permit backing out) until the names of the dead are piled up above your head and written against the reflected sky.

Here close to the bottom, your feet, face, and entire figure are only a small part of the Vietnam Memorial.

Then you arrive at the bottom, anxious to climb out, to see the names of the last to die. Here the polished surface breaks slightly to the right, producing several simultaneous effects, a convergence of experience that could only occur in that place at that moment. Just when you are the smallest, or the listing of the dead is the longest, the Washington monument appears reflected in the surface, bracketed perfectly from top to bottom by the two longest lists. And at the same instant, the entire memorial reflects upon itself: the right side of the memorial reflects on the left. As you pass the center, the image of the Washington Monument doubles, your own image doubles – you are beside yourself and coming to meet yourself at the same time. It is dis-Orienting.

Questions on leaving the memorial. How did it happen that an Asian-American woman was permitted to make a memorial for American men who died fighting in Asia? And how did it happen that this monument to the manly art of war assumes a multi-cuneiform shape, technically an overdetermined female sign, five Vs? And how was it permitted to be situated in such a way as repeatedly to capture the phallic image of the Washington Monument at its exact center? Is it possible, once again, to say, 'Only in America'?

There is no way on God's Earth that the Frederick Hart figures could 'correct' the Lin Memorial. It is semiotically too precise to admit correction, and it memorializes too much: genuine compassion for those who died, but also the official madness of United States policy, and finally the impossibility of war under conditions of gender equality. It is to Hart's great credit that he arranged for his traditional bronze combat soldiers to be set up in a way that acknowledges all of this. I go over to the Hart figures, which had just been set in place, but were not yet veiled so they could be unveiled at the ceremony on Sunday. They appear to be coming out of some bushes, looking upon the memorial. They appeared to me as if they have just paused to gather enough strength and courage to go over to the memorial to find their own names.

NOTE

1   These are fieldnotes, reproduced as written.

Afterword
Misplaced traditions and the new 'folk–urban continuum'

The failings of Frazerian anthropology are well-enough known that one might wonder, why bother to bring it up again? We know that the way Sir James collected and compared traits and practices from no matter what epoch or people was not as disciplined as it might have been. His standards for what constituted a carefully obtained field observation varied widely. He seemed to be over-much concerned with the inexplicable and fantastic, and too little concerned for the original cultural context of the practices he compared. James Boon (1983) has said he was not even a very thoroughgoing evolutionist in the way he handled his data. And in her 1986 Frazer lecture, Marilyn Strathern (1990) repeated the reproach, among others, that he was 'too literary,' that he wrote too well to qualify as a modern scientific anthropologist. And to all of this we could add that he was more hung up on the legend of Aricia than any student of the human condition need be.

But the very need to bury Frazer for a second time seems symptomatic. Wasn't the definitive discrediting of Frazer the central accomplishment of Malinowski and functionalist ethnography? Now we know better than to compare cultural traditions out of context. Even if they are superficially similar, they might have totally different meanings in their original cultural setting. But if contemporary anthropologists as talented as Strathern and Boon feel the need to repeat the charges against Frazer, this may signal a new sense of currency for his approach.

In this 'Afterword,' I argue that by virtue of his global, unruly, 'cabinet of curiosities' approach, his search for a mythic common-ground, Frazer speaks directly to important aspects of contemporary cultural experience, at least more directly than functionalist ethnography can speak to it. Frazer's misplaced traditions stand in a strong allegorical relation to the situation of the modern migrant, the displaced person, the refugee, the tourist, either condemned to, or volunteering for, a life out of context. I will not eventually argue that we should adopt Frazer's methods, however, because there are specific clear and present dangers.

NEITHER FRAZER NOR MALINOWSKI

Even more problematical would be continuing efforts to adapt functionalist ethnography to the understanding of cultural forms that are emerging between the classic analytic division between mechanical and organic societies; Gemeinschaft and Gesellschaft social relations; folk and urban communities; cold and hot cultures. Emile Durkheim, following Rousseau, discovered the basis for communal relations in common sentiments, a kind of absolute solidarity founded on a normative order that is so uniformly thought to be just that no one would think to violate it. Ferdinand Tönnies described the benefits of generalized and unbreakable human attachments, he called them 'irrational,' as opposed to voluntary and conscious, instrumental, specialized, temporary relations. Robert Redfield and Milton Singer sought to put this model to a test by organizing a series of four ethnographic studies of Yucatan communities arrayed along the 'folk–urban continuum' from Merida (the city) to Tusik (the primitive or tribal group). Max Weber, and later Jürgen Habermas, interpreted the same opposition in terms of traditional power and coercion versus the bureaucratic form – the breakup of unified culture into discrete institutional sectors (science, art, morality) each governed by its own instrumental rationality. Claude Lévi-Strauss and Jacques Derrida debated the relationship of writing and literacy to historical self-understanding, alienation, and the destruction of 'community.' Their debate brought the 'structuredness' of structure into question, preparing a new and not always happy ground for the human sciences that would eventually be named 'poststructuralism.'

In all these accounts, with the possible exception of Derrida's, the marked term of the 'primitive/modern' opposition has been the 'primitive,' thought to be temporally prior, the first form of the human community, original and authentic. In the various pairings of 'primitive' and 'modern,' the primitive is so marked that in most accounts, the word 'community,' which has a positive value connotation in this context, is used to describe only the 'primitive,' 'traditional,' 'simple,' 'folk' member of the pair. Gemeinschaft and Gesellschaft are translated into English as 'community' and 'society.' The idea that 'progression' from 'primitive' to 'modern' is ineluctable is built into the model, as is the idea that all such 'progression' is necessarily accompanied by a 'loss of community.' This was very eloquently stated by Tönnies:

> Trade and commerce, urban life, the growth of big cities, the power of money, capitalism, class differentiation, and the striving for middle class status and education – all these are facets of the same development of civilization, which... is injurious to custom. Even the country folk soon find their own customs peculiar and absurd. Cheap glittering wares impress them more than the old-fashioned household wares with the beautiful if quaint designs. And so it is in everything. The pattern of the metropolis is imitated. Goods quickly manufactured with mechanized techniques are often ugly and not durable, like the fashion from which they spring. All *gesellschaftliche* civilization has a quality utterly opposed to the artistic spirit which is rooted in tradition and integrity. It is superficial and external. The items of mass production are flimsy, uniform, monotonous; they lack genuineness.
>
> (*Custom* 134–5)

The assumption of 'the primitive,' the 'custom,' 'the folk,' as the 'proper' locus for the ethnographic act, at or near the center of a unified culture, of a privileged position for the ethnographic point of view, simply cannot be sustained in the field between the ex-primitive and the postmodern. Our models of cultural isolates exhibiting unified traditions, and the associated concepts of mechanically organized, Gemeinschaft, non-literate, 'cold' folk societies, were framed precisely coincident with the disappearance of cultural isolates from the face of the earth.

No contemporary 'primitive' can be unaware of the existence of technologically advanced societies, of the capacity of other human groups to build and fly airplanes, record and play back the human voice, accumulate and use money, read and write and make photographic images, communicate by wireless radio, and build and deploy orbiting earth satellites. Some modern primitives have become professional actors and models in production companies formed to make documentaries and feature films about primitive existence. Others earn their living by selling their handi-crafts to tourists, or by performing versions of their rituals. In my chapter on tourism at edges of capitalism, 'Cannibalism Today,' I used the terms *ex-primitive* and *performative primitive* to designate formerly primitive peoples whose special adaptation to the contin-gencies of modern existence is to act-primitive-for-others. A special ethnological class or category is needed here because these ex-primitives could not possibly continue to possess the consciousness of 'authentic primitives,' i.e., of the beings they are supposed to represent on film or in ethnography. Nor would they necessarily think in exactly the same ways as the merely modern crews that are filming them, even if they come to acquire full technological competency with the medium, as apparently some quickly do. Access to the life of performative primitives, among whom I occasionally count ourselves, requires an as yet not fully developed theory of the split subject, and the composite community, and a method for their study.

THE 'WRITING CULTURE' SCHOOL

I have also argued that the jury is still out on the question of the degree to which postmodern theory and the Writing Culture school of cultural anthropology enlighten us about these new cultural subjects. Certainly further conceptual and methodological work needs to be done. It seems to me that the followers of these various new movements of thought have been mainly overwhelmed and disabled by their understanding of Heidegger-de Man-Derrida's post-structuralism or deconstruction. If there is no center, no being-present of culture as the ethnographic subject or object, no possibility of ethnographic truth as a transcendental signified; if the classic ethnographic project has been invaded and fully taken over by language to the point where it reveals no longer cultures, but only a one-sided discourse, shouldn't we abandon ethnography as a method? I don't think so.

There is a field of study that lies between the ex-primitive and the postmodern which I have reason to suspect will continue to yield insight to serious students using conventional ethnographic methods: e.g., substantial time commitment in the field setting, careful collection of observations and material artifacts, close at-tention even to seemingly trivial detail, and testing of models and hypotheses derived from the anthropological tradition. I entered this field twenty-five years ago, beginning with my studies of tourism, the re-arrangement between the sexes, myth in advertising, etc. I have not been unmindful of the methodological questions that have been raised by the 'Writing Culture' School against the prospect of ethnographic research in this and other domains. But for me, the fascinating quest remains the discovery of the theoretical principle in the ethnographic materials. For example, the radical undecideability of ordinary language, as advanced especially by de Man, can be discovered in commercial advertising: 'It's not a car, its a Volkswagen'; or 'Be all you can be. Join the Army.' Deconstruction helpfully alerts us to the ways these utterances are doomed to ultimate undecideability; the ways they are equally well-suited to convey utterly opposed meanings. But deconstruction do not tell us much about the practical mechanisms of repression or suppression of meaning in the utterance in use: why do Volkswagen and the United States Army assume that only the meaning they desire, the one that is in their interest, will circulate? And why are they mainly correct in their assumption? These are not theoretical questions. The answers require ethnographic, and perhaps psychoanalytic study of authority.

In short, I am arguing that postmodern cultural forms are real and susceptible to ethnographic description, but such study does not necessarily yield a postmodern cultural subject as currently theoretically given. This is clearly evident in John Dorst's recent ethnographic report on Chadds Ford, Pennsylvania, *The Written Suburb* (1989). It is the best descriptive community study I have read documenting the implosion of an opposition that was once fundamental to Marxist theory: that between *means* and *production*. Human labor, the everyday existence of the people, the natural resources of the region, the barns, the shops, of Chadds Ford, all formerly endowed with proletarian dignity as the 'economic base' are now alienated *product*. Operating this effacement is the artist Andrew Wyeth, patriarchal head of the family of artists who have made Chadds Ford what it is today, a represented subject in two-dimensional art, a human community condemned to struggle endlessly to be just like its image, pure surface. When the tourist enters Chadds Ford, it should precisely conform to the postcard and other widely circulated Wyeth images of the region. Dorst is sensitive and alert to the many details of everyday life which signal that this subjection penetrates the mind of the people of Chadds Ford in the form of a collective unconscious understanding that failure to be like a painting would result in serious economic loss. One could argue that this is a generic feature of the postmodern condition: life imitates art as a matter of economic necessity. But in Chadds Ford this formula has a characteristically hard edge: this is not just art; these are Wyeths. The meeting point of nature in Chadds Ford is cold. Summer is out of place here, it is in a state of perpetual fallow, and on closer examination the figures which seemed to be alive might actually be exemplars of the embalmer's art.

Fuzzy theoretical writing on postmodern cultural subjects should not be allowed to stand in for or supersede carefully obtained ethnographic observation. Umberto Eco explains that the cultural complex he calls 'hyperreality' is the result of a simple combination of high consumerism and a nostalgic longing for 'tradition' on the part of a historyless people. (He did not visit Chadds Ford, but Chadds Ford would certainly qualify.) As theory, this is pretty vapid, little more than the kind of snide comment any European bourgeois intellectual might make on American foibles. However, the observations he makes in the same essay on tourist attractions in the American sunbelt, are precise, reproduced in brilliant detail, and worthy of re-analysis. Postmodern ethnography potentially gives results that are different from postmodern theory, even opposed to it. For example, Dorst's account puts into question the putative 'depthlessness' and 'centerlessness' of the postmodern cultural form. In Chadds Ford, the literal depthlessness of the two-dimensional representation of the community encrypts a cult of personality. The claim of 'depthlessness' on a theoretical level appears as an alibi for some older cultural forms: the honoring of fathers and families and the ancient power arrangements between them, and a mythic sense of a deep convergence of biological and cultural reproduction. Not mere phallogocentrism, but a kind of meta-phallogocentrism, hiding behind the cover of postmodernity. And why not. After the feminist critique of it, the paternal order can no longer travel overground undisguised.[1]

In this book, I have been interested in the simultaneous arrival of the ex-primitive and the postmodern and the parallels between the two: the current official promotion of the almost paleolithic doctrine of historylessness; neo-totemism, the possibility of the discovery of a non-trivial sense in which Mickey Mouse is the totemic animal spirit of the lonely crowd; a pervasive aesthetic of violence that qualifies as 'savage'; tourism as the answer to cargo cult prayers. Here at the end, I hypothesize that ethnographically informed theory of ex-primitives will continue to yield the post-modern and vice versa. It will potentially give us, for example, fine-grained descriptions of actual instances of 'historical rupture,' the real conditions of existence of 'fragmented subjects,' actual expressions of the 'valorization of surfaces,' and concrete examples of the 'simulacrum' or simulations of authenticity. But it will not necessarily yield the absence of a center, or subject, or subjectivity, but rather the emergence of new forms of authority and the movement of traditional forms of authority to a still higher ground, above the clouds.

THE COLONIAL IMPASSE

I want to make it clear that I intended something more than the commonplace critique of anthropology as having had too cozy a relationship with empire. Anthropology's complicity in engineering colonialism may have been overstated. There are many examples of heroic resistance in the literature as well as the other kind of example. And in any event, this is an easy criticism of all Western social science, psychology, sociology, history included, disproportionately heaped on anthropology. What interests me here are the conceptual precipitates of anthropological work undertaken during the period of colonialism and empire. We cannot re-write history. But we can avoid continuing falsely to affirm dead historical forms if we are careful to review and revise our concepts so we no longer view the world from the perspective of a colonist. This revision is a huge task and we should all be thankful to Jim Boon, George Stocking and the others who have shown both the ability and some willingness to undertake it. Here, I would comment briefly on one obvious point bearing on the methodological question of positioning ethnography between the ex-primitive and postmodern.

Underlying the classic theoretical model of 'primitive' versus 'modern' as operationalized in ethnographic writing after Boas and Malinowski was an assumption of little or no interaction between representatives of the two polar types. Ideally, the two types could persevere in their uniqueness without significant internal reference to the other. The record shows that these conditions of relative isolation occasionally seemed to hold for peasants and primitives even after first contact with Western explorers, and sometimes extended into the early colonial and ethnographic phase. But the day has long passed where missionaries, anthropologists, and colonial administrators occupied a privileged position as the only arbiters of 'primitive' versus 'modern' modes of existence. Today, the double movement of tourists to the remote periphery (e.g., 'Cannibal Tours'), and of recent ex-primitives and peasants to centers of wealth and power, is undoing the dignity once enjoyed both by 'culture' and by 'anthropologists.'

In short, one way classic theoretical understanding is flawed stems from the fact that 'primitive' and 'modern' types of culture were conceived to be in mutual isolation when they actually exist in a determinate historical relation, empirically manifested at the community level in ways that are not specified by theory. This is no mere structural linkage in which representatives of primitive and modern cultures meet in the community, each playing a part in determining the future. It would have been interesting indeed if folk and urban were related dialogically or even dialectically. But we are about to leave a period of history in which the 'primitive,' 'traditional.' 'rural,' 'folk' end of the continuum was frozen, not in the Lévi-Straussian sense, more in the mechanical sense, as in 'jammed.' Even as they were put on a pedestal as 'original' and 'authentic,' traditional communities were specifically denied all known paths to development, exploited for cheap labor and raw products, their local industries were destroyed and they were forced to consume Western things from pop culture to Fast Food. They were driven into a kind of existence that no savages, left to their own devices, would have tolerated. I suspect that in the final accounting the so-called 'primitives' will have some measure of revenge, a Pyrrhic victory in that none will be around to enjoy it. Before the final accounting, any continued promotion of the myth of mutual isolation of 'primitive' and 'modern' must be designated for what it is: a component of the conquering ideology of the modern world, preparing the ground for the continued free-play of exploitation.

Even if there had been no deconstructive critique of ethnography, the institutional and much of the conceptual framework of the social sciences would still be obsolete except as ideology. The communities anthropologists study can no longer be made to fit neatly on either side of the 'primitive/modern' pair, not without fudging, nor is it possible any longer to classify the communities studied by rural and urban sociologists as either 'rural' or 'urban.' Much has been said about the penetration of techno-forms into traditional societies, but the corresponding adoption of 'primitive' practices by moderns is perhaps more of an embarrassment to current theoretical models. Still, even as the breakdown of the macro-theoretical tradition in the Western social sciences becomes fully evident, there is some resistance to re-drawing analytical boundaries, as existing university departments and scholarly reputations have been built on old ones. The result could be that, with each passing year, everyone in the cultural sciences will themselves be working at a further remove from their disciplines, eventually jeopardizing the institutional footing of the disciplines themselves.

Anthropology's current methodological predicament does not stem from the undecideability of ethnographic truths because they must be expressed in language, the deconstructive insight which, if taken too seriously would wither the development of any field. A version of this insight was commonplace in anthropology before it found philosophical justification in deconstruction, as Derrida decently noted in his critique of Lévi-Strauss. Anthropology's predicament is more the result of the specific relationship of its conceptual traditions to colonial history. The correction can only come from a revision of the conceptual traditions.

CULTURAL TRADITION I

This kind of work will continue to call into question the notion of 'tradition' itself, which is the main conceptual precipitate of functionalist ethnography and the polar typologies of classical macro-theory in the social sciences. The entire functionalist episode can be re-read as legitimizing our interest in savagery by representing them as The Good, as a footnote to Rousseau that Rousseau would not necessarily have desired. Let me reproduce the cumulative result of inductivist ethnography as a specific kind of projection; the dream of a 'primitive isolate' as a necessary self-deception of a people who live between ex-primitive and postmodern modes of existence. (The most reflexive part is, or should be, the most embarrassing. Here is anthropology as data.) Our scientifically supported fantasy goes something like this.

In its original, natural and most perfect form, the human

community is small and intimate. Each member knows every other member based on a lifetime of face-to-face interaction on a daily basis. There is intense internal communication and very little external communication with anyone from outside the community. There is a simple age and sex based division of labor, few or no complex tools, and little or no use of natural (wind and water) power. Nevertheless, the original community manages to enjoy a very high degree of economic independence from other communities. There is no writing, or at least no books or learning based on books. The transmission of knowledge from the past is effectively accomplished in oral arts: story telling, singing, aphoristic speech. The community's sense of its own history is either fuzzy or highly formulaic, there being no institutionalized grounds for periodic revision of historical self-understanding. All problems are defined and solved within an integrated system of knowledge in which both the goals and the means for achieving these goals are not subject to questioning. Under these conditions, wisdom on matters from technical to moral is a simple function of age: as the members of the original community grow older, they grow wiser. A feeling of genuine intimacy extends in an unbroken line from the human to the realm of nature, to relations with animals, plants, wind, rain, snow, the soil and the heavens. The community understands itself to be an arrangement not of individuals but of families and clans. There is no motive for strongly marked creativity or economic gain. The individual consciousness does not desire to separate itself from the social consciousness and, as a result, all behavior seen from the perspective of an outsider appears conformist, but is experienced internally as uncalculated, spontaneous. Reason need never be given for words and deeds that are fully embedded in the framework of tradition. Total constraint is felt as total freedom. A strong set of rituals frames the totality, imbuing even small everyday details with sacred significance, assuring that the meaning of life is never lost. Finally, everyone really does believe in the effectiveness of magic.

This is not an innocent view of primitive innocence. We are supposed to feel solidarity with traditional peoples represented in this way because we, too, are Good. But we have been expelled from the garden. As the 'opposite' of 'traditional,' 'modern' peoples can represent themselves to themselves as condemned to live in a highly complex division of labor, believing in science more than religion, overwhelmed by thousands of meaningless, imper-

sonal associations, disconnected from family, etc.[2] I am not concerned here to argue the empirical basis of this system of beliefs
which I think is less substantial than it is mythically thought to be,
more a cover for the stinginess of global capitalism when it comes
to the distribution of the minimal requisites for a decent way of
living. Here I am concerned with the way in which the image we
have created of 'tradition' enables modernized peoples to think of
themselves as 'victims' of their own heterogeneity while patting
themselves on the back for their technological creativity. This
enabling fantasy is a quasi-necessary correlate of the petty viciousness and actual violence that are the other marked features of
modern existence. How does the suburban community undertake
to make itself a better place to live? By ridding itself of peoples who
are different. By transforming itself into a highly self-interested,
motivated simulacrum of the 'primitive isolate'; a fantasy based on
a fantasy. How does the suburban husband justify dumping his
wife? By saying, 'All the magic has gone out of our marriage.'

The ideological use to which this version of 'cultural tradition'
has been put has been to allow modernized peoples to think of
themselves as sad primitives living overly complicated, meaningless lives, lacking spontaneity. When this belief is combined with a
linear view of history, and it seems to have been designed with this
in mind, 'traditional' cultures, and all the positive values that have
been projected upon them, come to be defined as the barrier to
'historical progress.' So, according to this complex formulation,
there is no possibility of a decent historical progression, or socio-
economic development that is humanly valid or interesting. The
destruction of human intimacy comes to be viewed consensually
as the regrettable price of progress.[3] A foundational phrase in
modern solidarities is: 'do you think I like this any more than you
do?' 'Get real.' Or, 'grow up.' 'That's just the way life is.' This
construct is, like all cultural constructs, perfectly arbitrary *and*
perfectly motivated. It empowers the principal operatives in the
destruction of primitives, peasants and nature to claim that they
are suffering the most, that we should pity *them*, not the primitives
and peasants they are destroying, because *they* are martyrs, sacri-
ficing *their* souls to history.

This construct is also, incidentally, the basis for the rampant
promotion of 'folkishness,' 'traditional values' pushed by right-
wing politicians, and the other forms of nostalgic pseudo-intimacy
that are so characteristic of the modern and postmodern

community. Modern society, while enormously complex, is nevertheless simplifiable and rendered fully susceptible to manipulation by the narrowest of interests, so long as it is widely thought to be opposed to social forms that are held in ultimate esteem ('traditional' cultures) that are now unfortunately dead. Commercial reconstructions of 'tradition,' as occur most characteristically in tourism and post-partisan politics, are immediately seized with hope that they will proffer more than economic costs and benefits. The constant repetition of the fantasy of Gemeinschaft effectively promotes economic and other forms of individualism and blocks the formation of concerted group action. It plays shamelessly on the right-wing notion that the basis for interhuman relations is ultimately unknowable, and is in any event a thing of the past. This can only be the work of ideologues who want to keep people apart, especially apart from those groups that have managed to hold on to their basic humanity. The current official 'groupings' (i.e., men, women, Blacks, Whites, Chicanos, etc.) are precisely engineered in such a way as to produce a sense of double detachment, first, internal to the 'groupings' and second, between them. An aggregate of individuals, even 'demographically similar' individuals, is the opposite of a community; it is more like a suburb.

Certainly the great thinkers and field researchers who gave us the classic conception of cultural types did not intend that it end up in its current historical predicament. The classic conception foundered on its own genius, on its drive for conceptual clarity and methodological precision. These laudable goals would eventually tempt the most brilliant theoreticians and field workers to establish pure types in theory and holism and boundedness in ethnography. Thus we were given Gemeinschaft *versus* Gesellschaft, and 'primitive' *versus* 'civilized,' and the methodological assumption of the 'cultural isolate.' Yet the main historical drama occurring during the period of creation of the classic concepts of community was the violent disturbance of the mutual isolation of the primitive and the civilized parts of the world. The conceptually indeterminate space between folk and urban, theoretically barren ground, was the site of intense exploration, experimentation, exploitation and resistance. The original social formation, the traditional community, was invaded and disrupted precisely coincident with its appearance in theory, rendering its theoretical conception obsolete at the exact moment of its enunciation.

It is not difficult to discover what sustains the modern fantasy of 'tradition' beyond its scientific utility in this disturbed historical moment. There are social facts which modern peoples understandably would not want to face. There is the matter of the enormous division of labor in modern society. Every division of labor implies interdependence and cooperation, just as Durkheim tried to teach us. But apparently there comes a moment in increasing complexity and interdependence when further social differentiation no longer produces understanding of one's dependence upon and responsibility toward others. Rather it leads to a repression of any sense of mutual dependence and social responsibility. The answers to the most basic social questions cannot be faced except in the mode of denial. As moderns become increasingly dependent on commercial agriculture for their food, the construction industry for their homes, the garment industry for their clothing, on the police and fire departments for protection, on the entertainment industry for amusement, they forget that these departments and industries are nothing more than the organized efforts of human beings. Who was involved in getting the food we eat to the table? One would have to construct a model of awesome complexity. And we would have to acknowledge our dependence on farm workers, mothers, and others who do not merely labor, but who must labor in stigmatized status positions that we may eat. Thus modernity is experienced as a general condition of abject helplessness which can only be broken by individualistic violence. It is deeply ironic and, at the same time, perfectly predictable that as people become increasingly dependent on one another for everything from food production and preparation to psychological support, they develop an ideology of extreme individualism and struggle to consign the concept of 'community' to the pre-historic past or the utopian future.

We need a new analytic model of human relations, one that does not fictionalize situations of culture contact in such a way as to continue to suggest the inevitability of the ascendency of the West over the rest and to justify, at least implicitly, the violence that occurs when the natural superiority of the West as 'the Modern' is questioned. I have attempted to position the papers in this book so that they problematize the beliefs and behaviors of Western bourgeois peoples, in their role as theorists and tourists, for example, no less than the non-Western peoples they visit.

But more than re-positioned ethnography is needed. I would join with Alex Callinicos (1989) in the suggestion that we 'abandon the problematic of modernization.' He comments, 'drawing the contrast between traditional and modern society leads only too easily to an ahistoric parody of the range, diversity and complexity of social formations prior to the industrial revolution.' (pp. 34–5.) It is important not to gloss over the implications of this comment. Any effective critique of the theory or practice of Western international 'development' and 'modernization' programs requires abandoning not merely the 'problematic of modernization' but also the concept of the unified, 'homogeneous,' 'traditional' community, which is used to justify 'modernization' initiatives. It would be an inspiration to all thinking and feeling peoples if a branch of the human science refused to essentialize unity, simplicity, decency, and honesty under historical circumstances where the only true unity has been of the forces opposed to decency and common humanity.

CULTURAL TRADITION II

Thus, there are ideological grounds for deep suspicion of the concept of 'cultural tradition' and even better technical grounds having to do with the internal consistency of the concept and its fit with the data which allegedly gave rise to it. Perhaps I am too easily impressed, but I really admire the creative spirit of the person who invented god, or phonological opposition as a vehicle for conveying abstract meaning, a system of classification of kin and the incest prohibition, meter and harmony in music, selective breeding of grasses that eventually resulted in the creation of corn. I do not admire the person who invented trade, a good idea perhaps, but not a very hard one. But I cannot fit these radically creative acts into the so-called 'traditional' groups that produced them for all of humanity. It is time that we re-examine the concept of 'tradition.'

If we take the simplest definition of cultural tradition, that it is a model for human conduct given to the living by the dead that is usually preserved in the form of a narrative, it is clear that all human groups equally have traditions. The important question, or issue, is not whether some groups are more traditional than others, it is the attitude or the stance the group takes on its traditions, how traditions are marked and fitted into everyday living arrangements. Some communities and individuals practice a veritable cult of the dead, moving through the day certain that the ancestors are watching and may even come back and yell at anyone who swerves from tradition. Even, or *especially*, in its most extreme manifestation among disciplined traditionalists one finds anti-tradition. A tradition that is guarded as such, as in 'this is our sacred way,' always marks another way that is not sacred. 'Eat with your fork dear, only barbarians eat with their fingers.' A tradition owes its very existence to its protective sense of its own superiority over other traditions. It exists because it is thought to supersede earlier forms, or the cruder practices of neighboring peoples: 'one must not bleed the cattle twice, that is the Dinka way, not the Nuer way.' In short, every tradition presupposes a symbolic order that it, the tradition, is overthrowing: whatever else they might be, traditions are also revolutions in bad faith.

In the range of possible group attitudes toward tradition, *modernity* would like to position itself at an extreme position. Self-consciously modern peoples place high value on conduct which is judged to be non-traditional, or anti-traditional. If anything, the 'modern' attitude is more fixated on cultural tradition than is the 'traditional.' The most radically self-conscious movements of art, science, and behavior which call themselves 'modern' are committed to advancing a claim of self-sufficiency when it comes to the past. The anthropological form of this alienation, syncretic holism, somehow achieved by total immersion in a tradition and total detachment from it, reflects the subjective positioning of ethnography during what Marilyn Strathern has called its 'modernist phase.' In her Frazer lecture in 1986, referring to the break between *The Golden Bough* and the kind of ethnographic report written after Malinowski, Strathern (1990: 103) remarks:

> The audience had to accept the naturalness of Trobriand ideas in their context – once that context had been created in the separation of the culture of those to whom he was speaking from the culture about whom he was speaking. The audience was required to connive its distance from the anthropologist's subject matter. Meanwhile the anthropologist moved between the two. His proximity to the culture he was studying became his distance from the one he was addressing, and vice versa. This, *tout court*, is how the modern(ist) fieldworker has imagined him- or herself ever since.

According to Strathern (1990: 88), the bounded ethnographic

report evolved as a highly controlled account which claims privilege and authenticity because it abjures the use of literary conventions, clichés and affectations. *The Golden Bough* was consigned to history's trash heap because 'it was too well written, too literary.' Of course, it did not take the critics long to discover that modernist ethnography's claim not to be literature is its most characteristically literary aspect, something it shared with all other modernist literatures; that there is a heavily fictionalized aspect to modern ethnography even as takes hold of cultural reality; that it often produces culture and ethnicity in the mode of staged authenticity and hyperreality even as it traffics in carefully obtained field observations.

Modernites may think themselves to be self-constituting. But the first thing one learns from close examination of any symbolic system is that it is organized around a problem that it cannot solve and cannot acknowledge – e.g., childhood sexuality. The modern strategy for containing tradition is to erase it. In so doing, modernites also suppress the anti-traditional core of tradition, something they might want to identify with on an ideological level. So modernity characteristically deploys itself as smooth and shining surfaces, self-contained aesthetic and practical objects, seamlessness, functionality. But the repression of tradition is signified in every modern gesture, and the stage is set for the return of the repressed.

This return is already quite a bit advanced on the plane of global cultural arrangements. What are the well-formed cultural choices before the ex-primitive? Between the ex-primitive and the postmodern are at least two forms of the return of tradition which have already been described. The first, which I have called 'staged authenticity' is a kind of repressive de-sublimation of tradition. This refers to the many distinctive re-constructions of traditional objects, thoughts, and behavior which are such evident features of contemporary communities: restorations of old buildings, cars, handicrafts, etc., nostalgic re-constructions of previous eras in attire, social relations, the search for ethnic roots. While the gesture behind staged authenticity seems to be a valorization of tradition, its deepest effect is the opposite. Every instance of staged authenticity delivers the message that tradition does not constrain us, but rather we control it. When the re-constructed traditional object is fetishized to the point that the representative of tradition is intended to be better than the original (e.g., Hearst Castle), the end result is 'hyperreality.' In hyperreality, acceptance of tradition is in the mode of total and perfect control, i.e., re-incorporation of the traditional on the condition that it assumes the form of a perfected version of itself. Of course, this much control has its costs. In the case of hyperreal re-constructions of ethnic identity, the demand for conformity to a range of putative 'traditions' can be rigorous. It is not enough simply to be Black, or Chicano, now it is necessary to be a perfect model of Blackness, etc. Not only is the re-constructed tradition subject to minute control, so too is the behavior of those who assume the responsibility for producing it. What has been gotten rid of is not *tradition*. That has been preserved. What we are losing is any chance we might have to make contact with the creative, or anti-traditional base of tradition.

The hypostasis of tradition reaches something like its final flowering in the various movements of art and behavior that are called postmodern.

Marilyn Strathern and James Boon stop just short of the claim that Sir James George Frazer was a postmodernist *avant la lettre*. Still, we cannot escape the thought. Frazer's misplacement of traditions, his false evolutionary sequences, pseudo-totalizations, random juxtaposition of traits and elements represented as meaningful, all anticipate the playful recycling and random re-combination of traditions that mark both postmodernist aesthetic practice and tourist itineraries. This, of course, is the final choice before the ex-primitive, to play a part in the wild and zany drama of postmodernity. It would seem to be the choice which proffers the greatest freedom, there being a complete absence of any criterion of authenticity. And it might even work out this way at the level of a certain kind of individual consciousness. But it should not go unremarked that the postmodern ethos is also the first to re-inscribe the traditional into the contemporary without any concern whatever for the original integrity of the traditional subject or object. The modernist impulse is fully determined by its opposition to tradition. The transitional forms (staged authenticity and hyperreality) contain and control tradition more effectively than does high modernism, but not without concern for the authenticity and reality of tradition as the grounding of its repro-duction. Postmodernism is the first effective attack on the past operating on the pretense that the world can be made over without serious concern for ancestral thought, but entirely according to infantile wishes. It accomplishes this not by rejecting the past, or selectively controlling its careful reproduction, but by a kind of cold teasing of the past aimed at reducing it to insignificance.

Again, this may be experienced at the individual level as a kind of freedom, but this can only be the feeling of freedom that the seriously deluded might derive from identification with oppressive authority, and not any actual freedom. This is the dark side of our modern version of democracy. There is a pretentious taken-for-granted quality to it, a veneer of agreement that authorizes the free-play of oppression. This is mainly left unsaid in current postmodernist writing, and even in most criticisms of it. But it is clearly enunciated in Frazer's anticipatory postmodernism. The result and the motive for his 'cabinet of curiosities,' pseudo-total-ization of human customs, is never very far from the surface, and occasionally breaks the surface as in the following:

> If the history of the custom [he has just been writing of exoga-mous marriages] could be followed in the many different parts of the world where it has prevailed, it might be possible every-where to trace it back to this simple origin; for under the surface alike of savagery and of civilization the economic forces are as constant and uniform in their operation as the forces of nature, of which indeed, they are merely a peculiarly complex manifes-tation.... [T]he practice of exchanging daughters or sisters in marriage was everywhere at first a simple case of barter, and that it originated in a low state of savagery where women had attained high economic value as labourers, but where private property was as yet at so rudimentary a stage that it had practically no equivalent to give for a wife but another woman.
> (Strathern, 1990: 104–5; Frazer, 1918: 220)

This is a first draft of the blueprint for the New World Order, an economic system that apparently awaits the establishment of post-modern culture for its full implementation without 'traditional' constraints. With all its seeming openness and friendliness to tradition, postmodernism is the most serious threat so far devised. It articulates a pretense that there is no symbolic order, there are just fragments of things that might have once been symbolic. It would like to come off as a kind of twisted fantasy, nihilism or despair. Since we now know that no tradition is universally valid, they must all be equally invalid. I am concerned that the record will eventually show that the primary effect of undermining tradi-tion in this way is to unleash a new kind of centralized authority which is not marked as such and, as a consequence, is set up in such a way that it need not answer to anyone.

CONCLUSION

The theory and methods of the first phase of the development of the human sciences (statistical accounting, sympathetic understanding and cultural relativism) did not secure a place for all of humanity. We have just witnessed the disappearance of the original human type, primitive hunters and gatherers, peoples who, during the two million years of their existence, remained relatively unchanged until the moment of their extinction. I am arguing on moral, historical, and scientific grounds that we drop the use of the 'folk' versus 'urban' or 'primitive' versus 'civilized' opposition from our theoretical vocabularies. But this is decidedly *not* the same as dropping concern for the peoples who were formerly classified as 'folk.' The fate of the ex-primitive and the ex-peasant continues to bear heavily upon the constitution of the new cultural subject, however this may be conceived. Redfield (1941) noted that the construction of cemeteries somewhat removed from the town is one of the changes that occurs along the 'folk–urban' continuum; the tribal people of Tusik buried their dead next to the homes of the living, outlining the bodies with white stones. I am proposing a similar 'primitive' practice here at the level of theory.

One of the main ideological accomplishments of the modern fiction of a 'folk' is the same as that of the detached cemetery. It detaches the living from the dead and helps the living to repress the fact that they are still fully dependent for their humanity on things invented by their forebears. These things are so basic, so complex and so brilliant of conception that the modern mind refuses to think of them as having been created by people, much less 'simple' or 'primitive' people. We would rather think of music, language, ritual, kinship systems, and agriculture as 'given' or even 'God given,' especially now that the kind of people who invented these things have been forced out of existence. There is an implicit challenge in the disappearance of the primitive that, even though we are completely on our own now, we should be able to come up with new community arrangements sufficiently well-adapted to human needs, and to the limitations of nature, that they might last another two million years. It is not surprising that the period during which the so-called 'primitive' was driven to extinction has been marked by collective anxiety on the part of those responsible for the destruction of the original mode of human existence. One effect of dropping the conception of 'primitive' or 'folk' society, as it is currently theorized, would be to allow moderns to look 'primitive' inventions in the face and to reflect on their own responsibility for comparable social accomplishment.

An historic solution that permitted us to hear directly from 'primitive' peoples would have been preferable. Several of the chapters in this book are based on an attempt to reverse the procedures of comparative ethnology, or to reclaim from anthropology a kind of 'primitive' viewpoint concerning 'modern' social relations. Some groups of hunters and gatherers would make the transition from a propertyless nomadic existence to the life of peasant agriculturalists in geographically fixed settlements. Others would not. Any of them might have something interesting to say about the terms and conditions for human relationships when community is not a *place*. For tourists, hunter–gatherers, refugees and other nomads 'the community' is not a locus of the human life cycle. It is more a dramatic effect, a symbolic representation of collective desire. The question of living in a determinate place versus maintaining a nomadic or at least a semi-nomadic existence must have occupied much of the thought of hunters and gatherers during the last seven thousand years: not a small number of them based a life decision on it.

Let me suggest, in the place of the 'primitive to modern' continuum, an alternative conceptual model as follows:

EX-PRIMITIVE——MODERN——POSTMODERN

This schematic model of what I take to be the three dominant modes of culture today is the organizational framework for most of the papers in this book. I have tried to keep opening the questions of 'What is the *Ex-primitive, modern*, and *postmodern*?' I have assumed these three cultural modes are *alternatives* having no determinate diachronic relations one to another. For example, I have not suggested that groups 'evolve' from ex-primitive to modern to postmodern. There is evidence that the opposite kind of 'evolution' occurs, as well as no change at all. Some of the kinds of socio-cultural experiences and collective action, arrayed across the spectrum from ex-primitive to postmodern, that I have touched upon here, include:

- Struggles for cultural and economic self-determination on the part of primitives and peasants who, like the Quintana Roo Maya, are unwilling to give up their lands and way of life and have adopted modern methods of handling conflict ranging from the mobilization of world public opinion to guerrilla warfare.
- Efforts on the part of ex-primitives and ex-peasants to adopt 'modern' ways, to assimilate and acculturate themselves into the modern world.
- The re-construction of ethnicity and development of other touristic forms: i.e., ex-primitives and ex-peasants 'being-them-selves-for-others' or maintaining the appearance of traditional lifestyles in order to attract tourists and hard currency exchange, or to back their claims for special political status.
- Efforts on the part of governments and other agencies to implement economic and social change and a way of life that is alien to, or not desired by, the people who are the target of the programs. This is often done in the name of 'progress' and modernization, but it can also be done in the name of a 'return' to traditional values as recently occurred in the Sudan.[4]
- Collective action based on a sense of guilt for not having done enough to prevent or ameliorate the negative consequences of the 'modernization' process: e.g., the search for 'roots,' Peace Corps volunteerism, Greenpeace type activism, and so forth.
- Embedding of 'traditional' and 'natural' referents in design and behavior: staged authenticity, hyperreality, reconstructed pseudo-gemeinschaft, the destruction of nature and simultaneous Production of simulated natural environments, and so forth.
- Postmodern declaration of the 'end of history' and collective denial of the genocides and other horrors necessary to the establishment of a "New World Order."[5]

These are not mutually exclusive stances or positions. They can be regarded as stratagems in the current war that is being waged over the definition of 'community'; the bases for new moral and ethical positions with which people can identify, fight against, and otherwise base collective action. And there is certainly more work to be done here, of both a theoretical and a practical nature.

In the simplest form that I can put it, the theory of *Empty Meeting Grounds* is that the community is always and inevitably the site of human *difference* which is suppressed on both theoretical and practical levels. This is even so for the paradigm case of Tusik, deep in the Yucatan bush, the case selected by Redfield as exemplary of the 'folk' end of the 'folk–urban continuum.' On first examination, Tusik appears to exhibit the requisite isolation, ethnic and linguistic homogeneity, absence of literacy, etc. But we also learn that the 107 inhabitants of Tusik along with the other Quintana Roo Maya have been in a war of resistance with the Mexican government for almost a hundred years. They resettled deeper in the bush during the War of the Castes in 1847, and at the time of Redfield's study in the 1930s deliberately concealed the paths leading to their village. Their continued 'isolation' is thus partly strategic, based on the form of their interaction with the national government. Their linguistic distinctiveness and homogeneity had a similarly wilful and strategic aspect: 'Except for one man who speaks broken Spanish, no one in the subtribe has any command of that language. As the speech of the enemy and the oppressor, Spanish is depreciated' (Redfield, 1941: 54). Ethnically, the people were mainly pure Mayan with an overlay of Spanish culture and religion, except, Redfield notes, that a few Chinese had crossed the border from British Honduras in the 1880s and settled among them. The existence of possible Sino-Ibero-Mayan cultural forms is a scandal only in the context of the theory of Gemeinschaft isolation, homogeneity and simplicity. The theory notwithstanding, one cannot but be impressed by the integrity of Redfield's ethnographic practice, which allows us to see the arbitrariness of the theory vis-à-vis the ethnographic materials on the same pages where both appear.

The community is not 'of men' or 'of women,' 'of Chinese' or 'Mayan,' 'of guerillas' and 'government soldiers,' etc. It is the ground of the problematical encounter between them, and between classes, religious and ethnic groups, totemic clans, etc. I have argued that this is a dialectical, if not always dialogic, view of the community: it is only when we come to view the community as the site of not mere difference, but essential difference, that sub-communities can flourish in their distinctiveness. And, of course, I would argue the opposite: namely, that the primary result of the valorization of gemeinschaft is to kill off close, warm, intimate human relationships. *Empty Meeting Grounds* was written in opposition to phenomenological and cultural nationalist solutions to the 'community problem' because these seemed to me to be based on a desire to retreat into simpler, ego-centered social forms, a retreat into a kind of primitive fiction.

There is some affinity here with the implicit theory of community found in the writings of postmodernists and critical theorists, but there are also substantial grounds for disagreement. For example, Baudrillard's idea of living in the space of absolute simulation, where there is no distinction between 'models of' and 'models for' behavior, seems to me to be ethnographically accurate for some territories of contemporary existence. But it does not articulate the empirical conditions of the electronic mass media back to the form of social relations which they pre-suppose, engender and support. I have argued that the rhetoric of total simulation, the pretense that everything 'important' has been swallowed by the *simulacrum* always serves as a diversionary move from *real* not simulated forms of oppression. My argument departs from postmodernist and critical theory at exactly the point where they suggest that the break-up of the 'grand narratives' and/or fragmentation of existence inaugurates a new era of equality and freedom. Far from providing a new direction for social thought and community development, the idea of the 'freeplay of the signifier' may be a guilty suppression of social class and other older forms of oppression: i.e., it lays the groundwork for a kind of 'lived superstructure' which permits arbitrary authority to operate without being opposed as such.

The characteristic feature of this 'lived superstructure' at the community level can be called *positive involution*: the community turns in on itself, transforming its qualities and characteristics into symbolic resources for its own future development. Examples would include restoration projects, rediscovery of the contribution of ethnic minorities to the history of the community, a celebration of human diversity by marking ethnic neighborhoods, cuisine, festivals, etc., as things that can be appreciated by everyone, the museumization of historical periods, nineteenth-century factories, fisherman's wharves, traditional farms, reconstructed and turned into shopping malls, etc. It is noteworthy that a shameful past is not necessarily a barrier to positive involution. In the 'Locke Case,' a 'living monument' was proposed as a way of acknowledging a painful history of exploitation of Chinese farm laborers. It also incidentally continues to exploit the descendants of the laborers, who now must serve as tourist attractions. Positive involution can lead to a radical opening of community potential and it can also lead in the direction of a negative dialectics wherein a celebration of difference, even class difference, can be made to serve the interests of a single class. Something like the former occurred at the Los Angeles Festival in September, 1990, and something like the latter occurred in the 'Statue of Liberty Restoration Project.' When a single class or group gains control of the symbolic resources of an entire community, a political rhetoric of preserving the integrity of ethnic neighborhoods, the natural environment, etc., can mask the class dynamics in the process of 'gentrification.' Rather than making the community a better place to live for all of its actual and potential residents, the effect of the restoration of poor neighborhoods is to drive out the people whose homes have been improved, forcing them to the margins, eventually into homelessness. In a society that needs to think of itself as 'humane' this sort of thing cannot be explicit or avowed. It could only be accomplished by policy makers who claim to be doing the opposite, who have mastered the art of disguising narrow class interests in a rhetoric of 'diversity,' 'preservation' and the like. The relevant cases here are the homeless in Orange County (see especially Chapter 2), and the urbanization of Yosemite National Park reported in 'Nature Incorporated' (Chapter 4).

One of the strongest tendencies in current community set-ups and in theory is nostalgia for the putative universality of social forms which are thought to flourish in communities caught between the primitive and the modern state: ethnic solidarity, an attachment to the soil, belief in a 'high' or 'universal' God, in the superiority of 'traditional' social relationships, etc. Thus, some anthropologists continue to ask what life was like before the white man came, and some sociologists continue to study the community as a local isolate shaped by its relationship to its resource base, internal class conflict, fertility and migration. This nostalgia is not restricted to the backward-looking social sciences, social and cultural criticism. It is also a prominent feature of the motive for international tourism, and the rhetoric of cultural nationalism (see, for example, 'Reconstructed Ethnicity.') This nostalgia, and other characteristically liberal responses to life in complex communities, especially cultural relativism as it is practiced, can be bad-faith celebrations of 'folk society.' They are in bad faith if they ultimately serve to promote artificial simplicity in order to contain and control human relationships. This move parallels the promotion of pseudo-complexity in 'modernity' also in the interests of control: e.g., the widespread notion that modern problems, for example, drugs, AIDS, and gang warfare, are insoluble.

My main motive for writing these chapters is that I have not been able wholeheartedly to embrace the doctrine of cultural relativism as the ultimate formula for understanding human difference. In my undergraduate years at Berkeley in anthropology, I was trained as well as anyone in the doctrine of cultural relativism, and it still occupies the highest moral ground in my way of thinking, along with the labor theory of value, and freedom of expression. But the message that came through the anthropological teaching is that its version of relativism is founded on a still more basic principle, that of cultural isolation. If the anthropological doctrine of relativism is taken as a model of inter-group relations in the contemporary community, we would have a kind of relativism that requires cessation of all relations between groups. Under these conditions, a kind of 'peace' seems to prevail because no group has any known dealings with any other group except mechanistic trade or ritual warfare, etc. as described in the ethnography. The flaw here is that the requirement of zero relationship, or purely mechanistic group-level relationships, is never met. The intellectual scenario has become a scandal: by suggesting that the proper form of inter-group relations is 'relativity' while specifically refusing to describe actual inter-group relations, anthropology has positioned itself silently to express the formidable authority of Western politics, philosophy and science as mere ethnographic description of remote cultures. If every human group is asked to think of itself as equal to every other group in a kind of equivalence based on mutual isolation and triviality, and especially under conditions where every group has bought the notion that it should be trying to return to its authentic traditions, one can be certain that the entire system is being controlled from above.

In the place of the 'White Peace Solution,' which is what the doctrine of cultural relativism may eventually come down to, it is necessary to create a comparative perspective as it is actually lived by real people in real communities. Within the framework of this kind of research, we might be especially attuned to the kinds of confrontations between groups that lead to warfare versus those that do not. There are clues in the interactions between tourists and modern 'primitives' about the language of lived comparison and naturally occurring evaluation of group differences (see 'Cannibalism Today.') One also finds evidence that the entire interaction ritual process (the one Goffman studied) is being rebuilt globally. Rather than just affirming inter-group solidarity, ritual is being creatively transformed to bridge the unknown between groups (see 'The Future of Ritual.')

Empty meeting grounds is liberational in spirit, committed to clarifying actual social and cultural arrangements in the community as it currently exists, and to building a broader base of control over the future evolution of the community. Continuation of this line of research will require a shift in the direction of graduate training. We need a social science that is simultaneously empirically tough and speculative; a kind of science that might be credible to the peoples who have been discriminated against under the doctrine of relativism. Clarity of vision, political grittiness, and freedom to think about the future of the human community are exactly the qualities that graduate training in the social sciences seems to have been designed to eliminate. We must turn this situation around and begin to honor the combination of strong *critical* and *observational* talents. If a science that is proper to the contemporary community can be created, we have reason for hope. The emerging structure, namely the composite community in which culturally different peoples are obliged to work together, is not essentially flawed. Quite the opposite: the composite community, in which there is a place for every human being, even those among us who are bi- and tri-cultural, sexual and lingual, may be our invention and gift to the future, eventually regarded with the same respect that we give to language, kinship, music, and the other earlier inventions.

NOTES

1 Similar shocks and surprises can be found in, for example, Deirdre Evans-Pritchard's forthcoming study *Tradition on Trial*, Dan Rose's (1989) ethnography of the American upper class, Meaghan Morris's (1988) critical study of motels and malls, and others.

2 There is a substantial 'loss of community' literature. See, for example, Maurice Stein (1960), Robert Nisbet (1962), or Jane Jacobs (1961). For a nice summary and antidote, see Charles Perry (1986).

3 Jacquelyn Rose has re-examined childhood in a parallel way in her 1984 study of *Peter Pan*.

4 There are some political leaders who have made a quasi-theoretical version of gemeinschaft a basis for their authority. Cambodia and the July 1989 military coup in the Sudan provide ugly examples. Omar Hassan Ahmed al-Bashir, the leader of the Sudan junta, has an-

nounced to the somewhat surprised Sudanese that they are a 'traditional folk' people who do not want to be governed by such complex Western inventions as multi-party political systems, etc. A benign example, in that it has an apparently real basis in the chosen way of life of the people, would be the Pennsylvania Amish as studied by John Hostetler (1963). They have made a self-conscious re-construction of Gemeinschaft the ground for their resistance to incorporation by 'secular' society. In this case, what was once dead theory is transformed into living rhetoric. Political action involves a highly reflexive ethnographic reprise of the theoretical concept of 'folk.' Some American Indian groups have organized their resistance to United States society along similar lines.

5 As a matter of scholarly and political precision, double quotes must be used whenever this phrase appears in print. The phrase "New World Order" was first used by Nazi propagandists to describe their vision of international relations after the German victory in the Second World War. The first set of quotation marks refers to that use. Today, "New World Order" is used by the United States President and State Department to refer to their vision of international relations after the United States victory in the Cold War.

Bibliography

Adorno, Rolena (1981) 'On Pictorial Language and the Typology of Culture in a New World Chronicle', *Semiotica* 36 (1/2): 51–106.

Allison, Alexander W. *et al.* (1975) *The Norton Anthology of Poetry*, New York: W. W. Norton.

Almirol, Edwin (1979) 'Economic strategies and ethnic alternatives', *Human Relations*, 31 (4): 363–74.

Arendt, Hannah (1965) *Eichmann in Jerusalem: A Report on the Banality of Evil*, New York: The Viking Press.

Auerbach, Erich (1957) *Mimesis: The Representation of Reality in Western Literature*, Garden City, NY: Doubleday.

Baedeker, Karl (1900) *Paris and its Environs*, Leipsic: Karl Baedeker Publisher.

Bakhtin, Mikhail (1984) *Rabelais and His World*, trans. Helene Iswolsky, Bloomington: Indiana University Press.

Barash, David P. (1979) *The Whisperings Within*, New York: Harper & Row.

Barth, Frederik (1969) *Ethnic Groups and Boundaries*, Boston: Little Brown.

Barthes, Roland (1972) *Mythologies*, trans. Annette Lavers, New York: Hill & Wang.

—— (1979) 'Lecture: In Inauguration of the Chair of Literary Semiology, Collège de France, January 7, 1977', trans. Richard Howard, *Oxford Literary Review* (Autumn): 31–44.

Bateson, Gregory (1958) *Naven*, 2nd edn, Stanford: Stanford University Press.

Bateson, Gregory, D. Jackson, J. Haley and J. Weakland (1956) 'Toward a Theory of Schizophrenia', pp. 3–32, in Carlos Sluzki and Donald Ransom (eds) (1976), *Double Bind: The Foundations of the Communicational Approach to the Family*, New York: Grune & Stratten.

Bateson, Mary Catherine (1984) *With a Daughter's Eye: A Memoir of Margaret Mead and Gregory Bateson*, New York: Washington Square Press.

Baudrillard, Jean (1975) *The Mirror of Production*, trans. Mark Poster, St Louis: Telos.

—— (1988) *America*, trans. Chris Turner, London: Verso.

Benhabib, Seyla (1984) 'Epistemologies of Postmodernism: A Rejoinder to Jean-François Lyotard', *New German Critique*, 33 (Fall): 103–26.

Benjamin, Walter (1969) *Illuminations*, trans. Harry Zohn, New York: Schocken.

Benveniste, Emile (1971) *Problems in General Linguistics*, trans. Mary E. Meek, Coral Gables, Florida: University of Miami Press.

Bersani, Leo (1990) *The Culture of Redemption*, Cambridge, MA: Harvard University Press.

Bird, Frederick (1980) 'The Contemporary Ritual Milieu', pp. 19–35 in Ray B. Brown (ed.), *Rituals and Ceremonies in Popular Culture*, Bowling Green: Bowling Green University Popular Press.

Blacking, John (1977) *The Anthropology of the Body*, London: Academic Press.

Bloom, Allan (1969) *Introduction to A. Kojeve, Introduction to the Reading of Hegel*, Allan Bloom and Raymond Queneau (eds), trans. James Nichols, New York: Basic Books.

Bohannan, Laura (1966) 'Shakespeare in the Bush', *Natural History*, 75 (Aug.–Sept.): 28–33.

Boon, James (1977) *The Anthropological Romance of Bali, 1597–1972*, Cambridge: Cambridge University Press.

—— (1979) 'An endogamy of poets and vice versa: exotic ideals in Romanticism/Structuralism', *Studies in Romanticism*, 18 (Fall): 333–61.

—— (1983) 'Functionalists Write, Too: Frazer/Malinowski and the Semiotics of the Monograph', *Semiotica* 46–2, 4: 131–49.

—— (1984) 'Folly, Bali and Anthropology, or Satire Across Cultures', pp. 156–77 in E. Bruner (ed.) (1984) *Text, Play and Story: Proceedings of the American Ethnological Society*.

—— (1985) 'Mead's Mediations: Some Semiotics from the Sepic, by way of Bateson, on to Bali', In B. Mertz and R. Parmentier (eds) *Semiotic Mediations*, New York: Academic Press.

—— (1990) *Affinities and Extremes: Crisscrossing the Bittersweet Ethnology of East Indies History, Hindu-Balinese Culture and Indo-European Allure*, Chicago: University of Chicago Press.

Boorstin, Daniel J. (1961) *The Image: A Guide to Pseudo-Events in America*, New York: Harper & Row.

Bouissac, Paul (1976) *Circus and Culture: A Semiotic Approach*, Bloomington: Indiana University Press.

Bower, Tom (1988) *The Paperclip Conspiracy: The Battle for the Spoils and Secrets of Nazi Germany*, London: Paladin Grafton Books.

Boyd, William (1960) 'Genetics and the Races of Man', pp. 17–27 in Stanley M. Garn (ed.), *Readings on Race*, Springfield. IL: Charles Thomas.

Brennan, Teresa (1990) Review of Leo Bersani's *Narcissism and the Novel*, unpublished.

Buckley, William (1986) 'The Crisis at Dartmouth', *Sacramento Bee* (2 March): 136.

Bundeson, Lynne (ed.) (1986) *Dear Miss Liberty: Letters to the Statue of Liberty*, Salt Lake City: Peregrine Smith Books.

Burke, Kenneth (1957) *The Philosophy of Literary Form*, New York: Vintage (originally published in 1941).

—— (1962) *A Grammar of Motives and Rhetoric of Motives*, Cleveland, OH: Meridian.

Caillois, Roger (1988) 'Festival', pp. 279–303 in Denis Hollier (ed.), *The College of Sociology 1937–39*, trans. Betsy Wing, Minneapolis: University of Minnesota Press.

Callinicos, Alex (1989) *Against Postmodernism: A Marxist Critique*, Cambridge: Polity Press.

Campbell, Don G. (1981) 'Palm Springs is an Exemplar of Land Lease System', *Los Angeles Times* (22 March, Section VIII): 1 ff.

Campbell, Mark B. (1989) 'Fishing Lore: The Construction of "Sportsman"', *Annals of Tourism Research*, 16 (1): 76–87.

Carmichael, Stokely (1966) 'Power and racism', pamphlet distributed by the Student Nonviolent Coordinating Committee: no pagination.

Chodorow, Nancy (1989) *Feminism and Psychoanalytic Theory*, New Haven and London: Yale University Press.

Chu, George (1970) 'Chinatown in the Delta', *California Historical Society Quarterly*, 49 (March): pp. 21–38.

Clifford, James and George E. Marcus (eds) (1986) *Writing Culture: The Poetics and Politics of Ethnography*, Berkeley: University of California Press.

Cohen, Alain J.-J. (1978) 'Rêves d'ordinateur', *Traverses*, 10: 126–36.

Cohen, Erik (1979) 'A Phenomenology of Tourist Experiences', *Cahiers Canadiens de Sociologie* (13): 179–201.

—— (1982) 'Marginal Paradises. Bungalow tourism on the islands of Southern Thailand', *Annals of Tourism Research*, 9: 189–228.

—— (1989) '"Primitive and Remote": Hill Tribe Trekking in Thailand', *Annals of Tourism Research*, 16 (1): 30–61.

Cowan, Michael (1986) 'Competing for Liberty: The Political Culture of "National" Celebrations', unpub. paper given at West Coast meetings of the American Studies Association.

Crick, Malcolm (1985) '"Tracing" the Anthropological Self: Quizzical Reflections on Fieldwork, Tourism and the Ludic', *Sociological Analysis*, 17: 71–92.

—— (1989) 'Representations of International Tourism in the Social Sciences', *Annual Review of Anthropology, 18: 307–44.*

Culler, Jonathan (1981) 'Semiotics of Tourism', *American Journal of Semiotics*, 1 (1/2): 127–40.

—— (1989) '"Paul de Man's War" and the Aesthetic Ideology', *Critical Inquiry*, 15 (4) (Summer): 777–83.

Damisch, Hubert (1975) 'Semiotics and Iconography', pp. 27–36 in Thomas A. Sebeok (ed.), *The Tell-Tale Sign*, Lisse: de Ridder.

Darwin, Charles (1956 [1874]) *The Expression of Emotions in Man and Animals*, Chicago: University of Chicago Press.

Debord, Guy (1970) *Society of the Spectacle*, Detroit: Black & Red.

de Certeau, Michel (1984) *The Practice of Everyday Life*, Berkeley: The University of California Press.

de Janvry, Alain (1975) 'The Political Economy of Rural Development in Latin America', *American Journal of Agricultural Economics*, 57 (3): 490–9.

Deleuze, Gilles and Felix Guattari (1987) *A Thousand Plateaus: Capitalism and Schizophrenia*, trans. Brian Massumi, Minneapolis: University of Minnesota Press.

de Man, Henri (1927) *Der Kampf um die Arbeitsfreude*, translated as *Joy in Work* (no date), New York: Henry Holt & Co.

de Man, Paul (1974) 'Nietzsche's theory of rhetoric', *Symposium* (Spring): 33–51.

—— (1988) *Wartime Journalism, 1939–1943*, Werner Hamacher *et al.* (eds) Lincoln, NB, and London: The University of Nebraska Press.

Derrida, Jacques (1974) *Of Grammatology*, trans. Gayatri Spivak, Baltimore, MD: Johns Hopkins University Press.

—— (1978) *Origin of Geometry*, trans. John Leavey, Jr, Brighton: Harvester Press.

—— (1987) *The Truth in Painting*, trans. Geoff Bennington and Ian McLeod, Chicago: University of Chicago Press.

—— (1988) 'Like the Sound of the Sea Deep within a Shell: Paul de Man's War', *Critical Inquiry*, 14 (Spring): 590–652.

—— (1989) 'Biodegradables: Seven Diary Fragments', *Critical Inquiry*, 15 (4) (Summer): 812–73.

Dickenson, Brian (1970) 'I am the Music Fountain! Welcome!', *New York Times* (24 May/Sunday 'Travel' Section): 32.

Dinnerstein, Leonard (1980) 'German Attitudes Toward the Jewish Displaced Persons (1945–50)', pp. 241–7, in Hans L. Trefousse (ed.) *Germany and America: Essays on Problems of International Relations and Immigration*, New York: Brooklyn College Press.

Dorst, John D. (1989) *The Written Suburb: An American Site, An Ethnographic Dilemma*, Philadelphia: University of Pennsylvania Press.

Drummond, Lee (1977) 'On being Carib', pp. 76–88 in Ellen Basso (ed.) *Carib-speaking Indians: Anthropological Papers of the University of Arizona*, Tucson: University of Arizona Press.

During, Simon (1989) 'Raymond Williams in the Modern Era', *Critical Inquiry* (Summer): 681–703.

Durkheim, Emile (1965) *The Elementary Forms of the Religious Life*, trans. Joseph Ward Swain, New York: The Free Press (originally published in 1915).

—— (1984) *The Division of Labor in Society*, trans. W. D. Halls, New York: The Free Press (originally published in French in 1893).

Eco, Umberto (1976) *A Theory of Semiotics*, Bloomington: Indiana University Press.

—— (1979) *The Role of the Reader*, Bloomington: Indiana University Press.

—— (1986) *Travels in Hyperreality*, trans. William Weaver, New York: Harcourt Brace Jovanovich.

Evans-Pritchard, Deirdre (1989) 'How "They" See "Us": Native American Images of Tourists', *Annals of Tourism Research* (16): 89–105.

—— (forthcoming) *Tradition on Trial*, Philadephia: University of Pennsylvania Press.

Feil, D. K. (1987) *The Evolution of Highland Papua New Guinea Societies*, Cambridge: Cambridge University Press.

Fekete, John (ed.) (1987) *Life After Postmodernism: Essays on Value and Culture*, New York: St. Martin's Press.

Ferry, Luc and A. Renaut (1990) *Heidegger and Modernity*, trans. Franklin Philip, Chicago: University of Chicago Press.

Fisch, Max H. (1978) 'Peirce's General Theory of Signs', pp. 31–70 in Thomas A. Sebeok (ed.) *Sight, Sound and Sense*, Bloomington: Indiana University Press.

Forbes, Jack D. (1979) *A World Ruled by Cannibals*, Davis, CA: D-Q University Press.

Fraser, Nancy (1984) 'The French Derridians: Politicizing Deconstruction or Deconstructing Politics', *New German Critique*, 33 (Fall): 127–54.

—— (1989) *Unruly Practices: Power, Discourse and Gender in Contemporary Social Theory*, Minneapolis: University of Minnesota Press.

Frazer, Sir James George (1918) *Folklore and the Old Testament: Studies in Comparative Religion, Legend and Law*, London: Macmillan.

Freud, Sigmund (1950) *Totem and Taboo: Some Points of Agreement Between the Mental Lives of Savages and Neurotics*, trans. James Strachey, New York: W. W. Norton.

—— (1966) *Introductory Lectures on Psychoanalysis*, trans. James Strachey, New York and London: W. W. Norton.

Fukuyama, Francis (1989) 'The End of History?', *The National Interest* (Summer): 1–18.

Fussell, Paul (1980) *Abroad: British Literary Travelling Between the Wars*, New York: Oxford University Press.

Gabriel, Teshome (1990) 'Thoughts on Nomadic, Aesthetics and the Black Independent Cinema: Traces of a Journey', pp. 395–410 in Russell Ferguson *et al.* (eds) *Out There: Marginalization and Contemporary Cultures*, Cambridge, MA: The M. I. T. Press.

Galpin, Charles Josiah (1924) *Rural Social Problems*, New York: The Century Company.

Giddens, Anthony (1979) *Central Problems in Social Theory: Action, Structure, and Contradiction in Social Analysis*, Berkeley: University of California Press.

Gillenkirk, Jeff and James Motlow (1987) *Locke*, excerpts in pp. 6–19 of *The Sacramento Bee Magazine*, 15 Nov. 1987.

Girard, René (1977) *Violence and the Sacred*, trans. Patrick Gregory, Baltimore, MD: Johns Hopkins University Press.

Goebbels, Joseph (1948) *The Goebbels Diaries*, ed. and trans. Louis P. Lochner, New York: Doubleday & Co.

Goffman, Erving (1956) 'On the Nature of Deference and Demeanor', *American Anthropologist* 58 (June): 473–502.

—— (1959) *The Presentation of Self in Everyday Life*, Garden City, NY: Anchor Doubleday.

—— (1967) *Interaction Ritual*, Chicago: Aldine.

—— (1971) *Relations in Public*, New York: Basic Books.

—— (1974) *Frame Analysis: An Essay on the Organization of Experience*, New York: Harper & Row.

—— (1979) *Gender Advertisements*, New York: Harper & Row.

Goldenweiser, Alexander (1936) 'Loose Ends of a Theory on the Individual, Pattern, and Involution in Primitive Society', pp. 99–104 in R. Lowie (ed.) *Essays in Anthropology*, Berkeley: University of California Press.

Gottdiener, M. (1982) 'Disneyland: A Utopian Urban Space', *Urban Life and Culture*, 11 (2): 139–62.

Graburn, Nelson H. H. (ed.) (1976) *Ethnic and Tourist Arts: Cultural Expressions from the Fourth World*, Berkeley: University of California Press.

—— (1982) *To Pray, Pay and Play: The Cultural Structure of Japanese Domestic Tourism*, Aix-en-Provence: Centre des Hautes Etudes Touristiques.

—— (ed.) (1983) 'The Anthropology of Tourism', *Annals of Tourism Research*, 10 (1): Special issue.

Greimas, A. J. and J. Courtès (1979) *Sémiotique*, Paris: Librairie Hachette (trans. as *Semiotics and Language: An Analytic Dictionary*, Bloomington: Indiana University Press, 1982).

Gross, Bertram (1980) *Friendly Fascism: The New Face of Power in America*, Boston, MA: South End Press.

Guattari, Felix (1977) 'Everyone Wants to be a Fascist,' *Semiotext(e)*, 2 (3): 86–98.

Gusfield, Joseph R. (1975) *Community: A Critical Response*, New York: Harper & Row.

Hamacher, Werner, Neil Hertz and Thomas Keenan (eds) (1988) *Responses: On Paul de Man's Wartime Journalism*, Lincoln, NB: University of Nebraska Press.

Harris, Marvin (1978) *Cannibals and Kings: The Origins of Cultures*, New York: Vintage.

Hayden, Richard S. and Thierry W. Despont (1986) *Restoring the Statue of Liberty*, New York: McGraw Hill.

Hebdige, Dick (1979) *Subculture: The Meaning of Style*, London: Methuen.

Hechter, Michael (1975) *Internal Colonialism*, Berkeley: University of California Press.

Heisenberg, Werner (1958) *Physics and Philosophy: The Revolution in Modern Science*, New York: Harper & Row.

Herdt, Gilbert (1981) *Guardians of the Flute*, New York: McGraw Hill.

Herzfeld, Michael (1986) 'On Some Rhetorical Uses of Iconicity in Cultural Ideologies', pp. 401–19 in Paul Bouissac *et al.* (eds) *Iconicity: Essays on the Nature of Culture* (Festschrift for Thomas A. Sebeok), Berlin: Stauffenburg Verlag.

Hockett, Charles (no date) 'Ethnolinguistic Implications of Studies in Linguistics and Psychiatry', *Proceedings of the Linguistics Roundtable*, Washington, DC: Georgetown University Press.

Hostetler, John A. (1963) *Amish Society*, Baltimore, MD: The Johns Hopkins Press.

Hughes, Everett C. (1979) *The Sociological Eye*, Chicago: Aldine.

Hutchinson, H. N., J. W. Gregory and R. Lydekker (no date) *The Living Races of Mankind* (vol. 1), London: Hutchinson & Co.

Huyssen, Andreas (1986) *After the Great Divide: Modernism, Mass Culture, Postmodernism*, Bloomington: Indiana University Press.

Jacobs, Jane (1961) *The Death and Life of Great American Cities*, New York: Vintage.

Jafari, Jafar (1979) 'Tourism and the Social Sciences, A Bibliography 1970–78', *Annals of Tourism Research* (6): 149–78.

Jameson, Fredric (1979) *Fables of Aggression: Wyndham Lewis, the Modernist as Fascist*, Berkeley: University of California Press.

—— (1984) 'Postmodernism, or the Cultural Logic of Late Capitalism', *New Left Review*, 146: 53–92.

Jorgenson, Joseph G. (1971) 'Indians and the Metropolis', pp. 66–113 in Jack O. Waddell and O. M. Watson (eds) *The American Indian in Urban Society*, Boston, MA: Little Brown.

Jules-Rosette, Benetta (1984) *The Messages of Tourist Art, An African Semiotic System in Comparative Perspective*, New York and London: Plenum.

—— (1986) 'You Must Be Joking: A Socio-semiotic Study of Ethiopian Jokes', *American Journal of Semiotics*, 4 (1/2): 17–42.

—— (1989) 'Images of Women in African Tourist Art: A Case Study in Continuity and Change', pp. 143–60 in Juliet Flower MacCannell (ed.) *The Other Perspective in Gender and Culture: Rewriting Women and the Symbolic*, New York: Columbia University Press.

Jung, C. G. (1959) *Four Archetypes: Mother, Rebirth, Spirit, Trickster*, trans. R. F. C. Hull, Princeton, NJ: Princeton University Press.

Kagiwada, George (1982) 'Report on Locke: A Historical Overview and Call for Action', *Amerasia*, 9 (2): 57–78.

Keller, Evelyn Fox (1985) *Reflections on Gender and Science*, New Haven, CT: Yale University Press.

Kochman, Thomas (1981) *Black and White Styles in Conflict*, Chicago: University of Chicago Press.

—— (1984) 'The Politics of Politeness: Social Warrants in Mainstream American Public Etiquette', in Deborah Schiffmin (ed.) *Georgetown University Roundtable on Languages and Linguistics*, Washington, DC: Georgetown University Press.

Kojève, Alexandre (1969) *Introduction to the Reading of Hegel*, Allan Bloom and Raymond Queneau (eds), trans. James Nichols, New York: Basic Books.

Koonz, Claudia (1987) *Mothers in the Fatherland: Women, the Family and Nazi Politics*, London: Methuen.

Lacan, Jacques (1977) 'The Agency of the Letter in the Unconscious or Reason Since Freud', in *Ecrits*, New York: W.W. Norton and Company.

Lamphere, Louise (1976) 'The Internal Colonization of the Navajo People', *Southwest Economy and Society*, 1 (1): 6–14.

Lang, Daniel (1979) *Germans Remember: A Backward Look*, New York: McGraw Hill.

Lee, Richard B. and Irven DeVore (eds) (1968) *Man the Hunter*, Chicago: Aldine.

Lefebvre, Henri (1976) *The Survival of Capitalism: Reproduction of the Relations of Production*, trans. Frank Bryant, London: Allison & Busby.

Leung, Peter (1984) *One Day, One Dollar: Locke California and the Chinese Farming Experience in the Sacramento Delta*, L. Eve Armentrout (ed.) El Cerrito, CA: Chinese/Chinese-American History Project.

Lévi-Strauss, Claude (1967) *The Scope of Anthropology*, trans. S. O. Paul and R. A. Paul, London: Jonathan Cape.

Lewis, Oscar (1951) *Life in a Mexican Village: Tepoztlan Restudied*, Urbana, IL: University of Illinois Press.

Linz, Juan (1976) 'Some Notes Toward a Comparative Study of Fascism in Sociological Historical Perspective', pp. 3–124 in Walter Laqueur (ed.) *Fascism, A Reader's Guide*, Berkeley: University of California Press.

Lochner, Louis P. (ed. and trans.) (1948) *The Goebbels Diaries: 1942–1943*, Garden City, NY: Doubleday & Co.

Lortie, Frank (1979) 'Historical Sketch of the Town of Locke', in the Department of Parks and Recreation's Locke Feasibility Study, Sacramento: Parks and Recreation Dept.

Lyotard, Jean-François (1984) *The Postmodern Condition: A Report on Knowledge*, trans. Geoff Bennington and Brian Massumi, Minneapolis: University of Minnesota Press.

McCaghy, Charles H. and J. K. Skipper, Jr (1972) 'Stripping: Anatomy of a Deviant Life Style', in Saul D. Feldman and G. W. Thiebar (eds) *Life Styles: Diversity in American Society*, Boston, MA: Little Brown.

McCann, Graham (1988) *Marilyn Monroe: The Body in the Library*, London: Polity Press.

MacCannell, Dean (1973) 'Staged Authenticity: On Arrangements of Social Space in Tourist Settings', *American Journal of Sociology*, 79 (3): 589–603.

—— (1976) *The Tourist: A New Theory of the Leisure Class*, New York: Schocken.

—— (1977a) 'Negative Solidarity', *Human Organization*, 36 (3): 301–4.

—— (1977b) 'The Tourist and the New Community', *Annals of Tourism Research*, 4 (4): 208–15.

—— (1979) 'Ethnosemiotics', *Semiotica* 27 (1): 149–71.

—— (1980) 'A Community Without Definite Limits', *Semiotica*, 31 (1/2): 87–98.

—— (1982) 'The Case of Locke, California', in T. Carroll (ed.) *American Chinatown*, California Arts Council.

—— (1984a) '"Baltimore in the Morning... After": On the Forms of Post-Nuclear Leadership', *Diacritics* (Summer): 33–46.

—— (1984b) 'Reconstructed Ethnicity: Tourism and Cultural Identity in Third World Communities', *Annals of Tourism Research* (11): 361–77.

—— (1986a) 'Sights and Spectacles', pp. 421–35 in Paul Bouissac *et al.* (eds) *Iconicity: Essays on the Nature of Culture* (Festschrift for Thomas A. Sebeok), Berlin: Stauffenburg Verlag.

—— (1986b) 'Tourisme et identite culturelle', *Communications*, 43: 169–86.

—— (1987) 'Marilyn Monroe Was Not a Man', *Diacritics* (Summer): 114–27.

—— (1988) 'Industrial Agriculture and Rural Community Degradation', pp. 15–75 in Louis E. Swanson (ed.) *Agriculture and Rural Community Change in the US: The Congressional Research Reports*, Boulder, CO, and London: Westview Press.

—— (1989) *The Tourist*, reprinted with a new introduction by the author, New York: Random House.

—— (1990a) 'Cannibal Tours', *Society for Visual Anthropology Review* (Fall): 14–23.

—— (1990b) 'Nature, Inc.', *Places: A Quarterly Journal of Environmental Design* (Spring): 24–6.

—— (1990c) 'The Descent of the Ego', pp. 19–40 in Stephen Riggins (ed.) *Beyond Goffman: Studies on Communication, Institution and Social Interaction*, Berlin: Mouton de Gruyter.

MacCannell, Dean and Juliet Flower MacCannell (1982) *The Time of the Sign: A Semiotic Approach to Modern Culture*, Bloomington: Indiana University Press.

MacCannell, Juliet Flower (1985) 'The Temporality of Textuality', *Modern Language Notes* (Dec.): 968–87.

—— (1986) *Figuring Lacan: Criticism and the Cultural Unconscious*, Kent: Croom Helm Ltd/Routledge 1989.

—— (1989) 'Resistance to Sexual Education', *Strategies* 2: 92–112.

—— (1991) *The Regime of the Brother: After the Patriarchy*, London: Routledge.

Mandel, Ernest (1978) *Late Capitalism*, trans. Joris De Bres, London: Verso.

Manz, Beatriz (1988) *Refugees of a Hidden War: The Aftermath of Counterinsurgency in Guatemala*, Albany: State University of New York Press.

Marcus, George (1980) 'The Ethnographic Subject as Ethnographer', Rice University Studies (Winter): 55–68.

Marin, Louis (1984) *Utopics: Spatial Play*, trans. Robert A. Vollrath, Atlantic Highlands, NJ: Humanities Press.

Mauss, Marcel (1967) *The Gift: Forms and Functions of Exchange in Archaic Societies*, trans. Ian Cunnison, New York: W. W. Norton (originally published in 1925).

Mayer, Milton (1955) *They Thought They Were Free: The Germans 1933–1945*, Chicago: University of Chicago Press.

Mead, Margaret (1972) *Blackberry Winter: My Earlier Years*, New York: William Morrow & Co.

—— (1977) *Letters from the Field: 1925–1975*, New York: Harper & Row.

Means, Russell (1980) 'For the World to Live, "Europe" Must Die', *Mother Jones* (Dec.): 25 ff.

Mills, C. Wright (1959) *The Sociological Imagination*, New York: Oxford University Press.

Mitchell, William E. (1978) *The Bamboo Fire: An Anthropologist in New Guinea*, New York: W. W. Norton.

Montaigne, Michel de (1943) *Selected Essays*, trans. Donald Frame, New York: Walter J. Black.

Morris, Meaghan (1988) 'At Henry Parks Motel', *Cultural Studies* (Jan.): 1–47.

Murray, Timothy (1987) 'Subliminal Libraries: Showing Lady Liberty and Documenting Death', *Discourse* 9 (Spring-Summer): 117–24.

Nash, Hugh (ed.) (1979) *Amory Lovins and Others, the Energy Controversy: Soft Path Questions and Answers*, San Francisco: Friends of the Earth Press.

Nisbet, Robert (1962) *Community and Power*, New York: Oxford University Press.

O'Rourke, Dennis (1987) *Cannibal Tours*, film and programme notes by the producer, Canberra: O'Rourke & Associates.

Parenti, Michael (1980) *Democracy for the Few*, New York: St Martin's Press.

Parsons, Talcott (1937) *The Structure of Social Action*, New York: McGraw Hill (rev. edn, New York: The Free Press, 1949).

—— (1975) 'Social Structures and the Symbolic Media of Interchange', pp. 94–120 in Peter M. Blau (ed.) *Approaches to the Study of Social Structures*, New York: The Free Press.

Peirce, Charles S. (1955) *Philosophical Writings*, ed. Justus Buchler, New York: Dover.

Perry, Charles (1986) 'A Proposal to Recycle Mechanical and Organic Solidarity in Community Sociology', *Rural Sociology* 51 (3): 263–77.

Pignatari, Decio (1978) 'The Contiguity Illusion', in Thomas A. Sebeok (ed.) *Sight, Sound and Sense*, Bloomington: Indiana University Press.

Pines, Jim and Willemen, Paul, (eds) (1989) *Questions of Third Cinema*, London: British Film Institute Publications.

Poplin, Dennis E. (1979) *Communities: A Survey of Theories and Methods of Research*, New York: Macmillan.

Portes, Alejandro (1981) *Labor, Class, and the International System*, New York: Academic Press.

Preziosi, Donald (1988) 'La Vi(ll)e en Rose: Reading Jameson Mapping Space', *Strategies*, 1 (Fall): 82–99.

Porzecanski, Teresa (1989) *Curanderos y Canibales*, Montevideo: Luis A. Retta Libros.

Quiggin, A. Hingston (1949) *A Survey of Primitive Money: The Beginnings of Currency*, London: Methuen.

Redfield, Robert (1941) *The Folk Culture of Yucatan*, Chicago: University of Chicago Press.

Rojek, Chris (1985) *Capitalism and Leisure Theory*, London: Tavistock.

—— (ed.) (1989) *Leisure for Leisure*, London: Macmillan.

Ronell, Avital (1989) *The Telephone Book: Technology, Schizophrenia, Electric Speech*, Lincoln, NB: University of Nebraska Press.

Rosaldo, Renato I., Jr (1978) 'The Rhetoric of Control: Ilongots Viewed as Natural Bandits and Wild Indians', pp. 240–57 in Barbara Babcock (ed.) *The Reversible World: Symbolic Inversion in Art and Society*, Ithaca, NY: Cornell University Press.

Rose, Dan (1977) 'A Public Argument in an Afro-American Urban Locale', *Journal of the Steward Anthropological Society* (Spring): 137–53.

—— (1989) *Patterns of American Culture: Ethnography and Estrangement*, Philadelphia: University of Pennsylvania Press.

Rose, Jacqueline (1984) *The Case of Peter Pan or the Impossibility of Children's Fiction*, London: Macmillan.

Ross, Andrew (1988) *Universal Abandon? : The Politics of Postmodernism*, Minneapolis: University of Minnesota Press.

Sahlins, Marshall (1976) *Culture and Practical Reason*, Chicago: University of Chicago Press.

Salecl, Renata (1990) '"Society Doesn't Exist"', *American Journal of Semiotics*, 7 (1/2): 45–52.

Sapir, Edward (1961) *Culture, Language and Personality*, David G. Mandelbaum, (ed.), Berkeley: University of California Press.

Sartre, Jean-Paul (1957) *The Transcendence of the Ego: An Existentialist Theory of Consciousness*, trans. Forrest Williams and Robert Kirkpatrick, New York: Farrar, Straus & Giroux.

—— (1969) *Being and Nothingness*, trans. Hazel E. Barnes, London: Methuen.

Sassen-Koob, Saskia (1983) 'Recomposition and Peripheralization at the Core', pp. 88–100 in Marlene Dixon and Susanne Jonas (eds) *From Immigrant Labor to Transnational Working Class*, San Fransisco: Synthesis Publications.

Schieffelin, Edward L. (1976) *The Sorrow of the Lonely and the Burning of the Dancers*, New York: St Martin's Press.

Sebeok, Thomas A. (1975) 'Six Species of Signs: Some Propositions and Strictures', *Semiotica* 13 (3): 233–60.

—— (1980) 'The Domain of the Sacred', *Journal of Biological Structure*, 3: 227–9.

Shirer, William L. (1942) *Berlin Diary: The Journal of a Foreign Correspondent, 1934–1941*, New York: Alfred A. Knopf.

—— (1984) *The Nightmare Years: 1930–1940*, Boston: Little Brown.

—— (1990) *A Native's Return: 1945–1988*, Boston: Little Brown.

Simmel, Georg (1950) *The Sociology of Georg Simmel*, trans. and ed. by Kurt H. Wolff, Glencoe: The Free Press.

Soja, Edward W. (1989) *Postmodern Geographies: The Reassertion of Space in Critical Social Theory*, London: Verso.

Stein, Maurice R. (1960) *The Eclipse of Community: An Interpretation of American Studies*, Princeton, NJ: Princeton University Press.

Strathern, Marilyn (1990) 'Out of Context: The Persuasive Fictions of Anthropology', pp. 80–122 in Marc Manganaro (ed.) *Modernist Anthropology: From Fieldwork to Text*, Princeton: Princeton University Press.

Summers, Anthony (1985) *Goddess: The Secret Lives of Marilyn Monroe*, New York: Macmillan.

Sweet, Jill (1989) 'Burlesquing "The Other" in Pueblo Performance', *Annals of Tourism Research*, 16: 62–5.

Theweleit, Klaus (1987) *Male Fantasies*, trans. Stephen Conway, Minneapolis: University of Minnesota Press.

Thompson, John (1957) 'The Settlement Geography of the Sacramento–San Joaquin Delta', PhD Dissertation, Stanford University.

Timberlake, Michael (ed.) (1985) *Urbanization in the World Economy*, Orlando: Academic Press.

Todorov, Tzvetan (1984) *The Conquest of America: The Question of the Other*, trans. Richard Howard, New York: Harper & Row.

Tönnies, Ferdinand (1957) *Community and Society*, East Lansing, MI: Michigan State University Press.

—— (1961) *Custom: An Essay on Social Codes*, Chicago: The Free Press.

Trefousse, Hans L. (ed.) (1980) *Germany and America: Essays on Problems of International Relations and Immigration*, New York: Brooklyn College Press.

Turner, Victor (1967) *The Forest of Symbols: Aspects of Ndembu Ritual*, Ithaca, NY: Cornell University Press.

—— (1977) *The Ritual Process: Structure and Anti-Structure*, Ithaca, NY: Cornell University Press.

Urry, John (1981) *The Anatomy of Capitalist Societies: The Economy, Civil Society and the State*, London: Macmillan.

van den Abbeele, Georges (1980) 'Sightseers: The Tourist as Theorist', *Diacritics* (Winter): 2–14.

—— (1984) 'Utopian Sexuality and its Discontents: Exoticism and Colonialism in the "Supplement au Voyage de Bougainville"', *L'Esprit Createur* (Spring): 43–52.

van den Berghe, Pierre (1970) *Race and Ethnicity*, New York: Basic Books.

—— (1979) *Human Family Systems: An Evolutionary View*, New York: Elsevier.

—— (1980) 'Tourism as Ethnic Relations: A Case Study of Cuzco, Peru', *Ethnic and Racial Studies*, 3: 375–92.

van Gennep, Arnold (1960) *The Rites of Passage*, trans. M. B. Vizedom and G. L. Caffee, Chicago: University of Chicago Press.

Volosinov, V. N. (1976) *Freudianism: A Marxist Critique*, trans. I. R. Titunik, New York: Academic Press.

Wallerstein, Immanuel (1974) *The Modern World System: Capitalist Agriculture and the Origins of the European World Economy in the Sixteenth Century*, New York: Academic Press.

Wilden, Anthony (1987) *The Rules Are No Game: The Strategy of Communication*, London: Routledge and Kegan Paul.

Will, George F. (1991) 'War May Push Arabs into Modernizing', *Contra Costa Times*, (20 Jan., 1991): 10B.

Wilson, Edward (1975) *Sociobiology: The New Synthesis*, Cambridge MA: Harvard University Press.

Wright, T. and Vermund, Anita (1990) 'Small Dignities: Local Resistances, Dominant Strategies of Authority, and Suburban Homeless', unpublished paper presented at the 1900 meetings of the American Sociological Association, Washington, DC.

Wunderlich, Frieda (1946) *German Labor Courts*, Chapel Hill: University of North Carolina Press.

Young, Frank (1965) *Initiation Ceremonies: A Cross-cultural Study of Status Dramatization*, Indianapolis: Bobbs-Merrill.

—— (1971) 'Reactive Subsystems', *American Sociological Review*, 35: 297–307.

Ziemer, Gregor (1941) *Education for Death: The Making of a Nazi*, London: Oxford University Press.

Zizek, Slavoj (1988) *Tout ce que vous avez toujours voulu savoir sur Lacan sans jamais oser le demander à Hitchcock*, Paris: Navarin.

—— (1990) 'The Limits of the Semiotic Approach to Psychoanalysis', pp. 89–110 in *Psychoanalysis And...*, Richard Feldstein and Henry Sussman (eds), New York and London: Routledge.

Name index

Subject index

statistic and symbolic: similarities
89, 90
statistical significance 91
stereotypes, negative ethnic 138,
179; as commercially enforced
178; undoing 136
striptease 234, 249
structural arrangements and
structuralism 12, 131, 165, 218
student-worker rebellions in
US/Western Europe in 1968 63
sub-communities 179; as tourist
attractions 178
sub-community 179
subject, the 7, 63, 129, 193, 197,
214; as absent 3; as decentered
89, 214; in postmodernity 198;
see also death of the subject
subject, the Cartesian 234
subjectivity 189, 197; of the
author 10
subordination (*see* domination)
suburbs 77, 294; hypersuburbia
79; as a simulacrum of
idealized primitive
communities 293
surfaces, valorization and
thematization of 111, 188,
189, 219, 288
surfers 270
symbol 24, 29, 60, 89, 92, 154,
168, 236
symbolic analysis 52, 91, 93

table top fusion 29
teens 190
telephone girl 229n
theory 6, 20, 197, 218, 228, 269,
305; as ground of freedom 6, 7
Third World 12, 124, 158
'Thousand Year Reich' 185
total social fact 11, 67
totem and totemic 49, 56, 67,
95; residual forms in
modernity 127; *see also*

neo-totemism
tourist and tourism (general
references throughout the text
not indexed)
tourism as ground for production
of new cultural forms 1
tourism as occupying gap
between primitive and
modern 17, 35, 307
tourism: the outerboundary of
capitalism 1, 286
tourism: way of life of
ex-primitives 18–20, 101
tourists as dead ancestors of
primitives 46
tourist language 43, 44, 46
tourist as real hero of alterity 29
tourist trips for workers in Nazi
Germany 211
toxic waste 105
trade, invention of 296
tradition 94–7, 99–101, 112, 283,
285, 291, 299; anti-tradition as
mark of tradition 297;
tradition manufactured as
'natural' resource 102, 294
tradition vs. modern 295
traditional elements in
postmodern style 219
'triumph of the West' 62
trousers 70n, 71n
truth, the 128, 130, 132, 187

uncertainty principle 6, 21
unconscious 25, 41, 45, 67, 68,
92, 139, 202
understanding 7, 121
unity, white ethos of 169
universal values, 'universality' 66,
100, 101, 171, 306

vagina, its disavowal 40
vaginal intercourse as failed
investment 71n
valorization of vagueness 79
value 9, 116